Studies in the Shoah Editorial Board

Editor-in-Chief
Zev Garber
Los Angeles Valley College
University of California Riverside

Alan Berger	Florida Atlantic University
Rachel Brenner	University of Wisconsin, Madison
Seymour Cain	University of California, San Diego
Harry James Cargas	Webster University
Yaffa Eliach	Brooklyn College, City University of New York
Irving (Yitz) Greenberg	The National Jewish Center for Learning and Leadership
Steven Katz	Boston University
Steven L. Jacobs	Temple B'nai Shalom, Huntsville, Alabama
Richard Libowitz	St. Joseph's University
Franklin H. Littell	The Richard Stockton College of New Jersey
Hubert G. Locke	University of Washington
James F. Moore	Valparaiso University
John K. Roth	Claremont McKenna College
Richard L. Rubenstein	University of Bridgeport

CONFRONTING THE HOLOCAUST

A Mandate for the 21st Century

Part Two

Edited by

**Stephen C. Feinstein
Karen Schierman
Marcia Sachs Littell**

Studies in the Shoah

Volume XX

University Press of America,® Inc.
Lanham • New York • Oxford

Copyright © 1998 by
The Annual Scholars' Conference on the Holocaust and the
Churches
University Press of America,® Inc.
4720 Boston Way
Lanham, Maryland 20706

12 Hid's Copse Rd.
Cummor Hill, Oxford OX2 9JJ

All rights reserved
Printed in the United States of America
British Library Cataloguing in Publication Information Available

ISBN 0-7618-1081-1 (cloth: alk. ppr.)

The paper used in this publication meets the minimum
requirements of American National Standard for information
Sciences—Permanence of Paper for Printed Library Materials,
ANSI Z39.48—1984

~ Dedicated to ~

Rabbi Max A. Shapiro

In Honor of his retirement as
Founder and Director of
the Center for Jewish-Christian Learning
at the University of Saint Thomas

A TRIBUTE TO THE WORK OF
RABBI MAX SHAPIRO

Rabbi Max A. Shapiro is rabbi emeritus of Temple Israel in Minneapolis where he served for 30 years prior to becoming the founder and director the Center for Jewish-Christian Learning at the University of St. Thomas. The Center is now known as the Jay Phillips Center for Jewish-Christian Learning, of St. John's University and the University of St. Thomas.

Rabbi Shapiro has been on the faculty of Hamline University, an adjunct professor at the United Theological Seminary, and a lecturer at the University of Minnesota, Carleton College and Macalester College. He holds seven degrees, including a doctorate in education from the University of Cincinnati, an honorary doctorate from the Hebrew Union College-Jewish Institute of Religion, and another from the University of St. Thomas.

Rabbi Shapiro has had a prominent career in local and national activities, and an extensive history of community commitment. He has been the recipient of many prestigious awards, compiled and edited a number of liturgical volumes, and contributed articles to various publications. He is the author of *Here Am I, Send Me,* a personal history of 30 years at Temple Israel, which also includes a collection of sermons and brief essays.

A firm, unwavering commitment to strengthening Jewish-Christian relations has built the foundation of Rabbi Shapiro's life and work. Thus, serving as the Chairman and Host of the 26th Annual Scholars' Conference on the Holocaust and the Churches was an appropriate symbolic milestone to mark the culmination of his tenure at the Center for Jewish-Christian Learning.

The convening of the Annual Scholars' Conference would not have been possible without the initiative and perseverance of Max Shapiro. Three years prior to the convening of the Annual Scholars' Conference on a very cold March day, Rabbi Shapiro, whose work in establishing and developing the Jewish-Christian Learning Center at the University of St. Thomas has been recognized both regionally and nationally as a major step in fostering interfaith dialogue, asked Franklin H. Littell, his friend and colleague for half a century, whether it would be possible to bring the Scholars' Conference to the Twin Cities. When Professor Littell agreed and the Board of Directors of the Center gave conditional acceptance, Rabbi Shapiro provided not only the services of the Center and Staff, but undertook an energetic process of raising sufficient funds to make the conference work. The result was not only an event for the international academic community, but also a series of events that involved the community of Holocaust Survivors in the Twin Cities and the general public.

The Center for Jewish-Christian Learning has attracted leading figures of all faiths to the campus and the surrounding community. Exploring the problems and questions of the traditional concerns of both Judaism and Christianity, the Center has promoted and fostered an awareness of a common heritage.

The Center has touched the lives of thousands of people from all over Minnesota and beyond, helping to build interfaith understanding and an appreciation of the bonds that bind Jews and Christians together.

Activities at the Center take many forms. In the Center's academic component, formal academic courses in Judaism at St. Thomas are augmented by guest lecturers in sociology, history and theology classes. Another aspect of the center brings interfaith exchange and dialogue to organizations beyond the Twin Cities.

The Center also helps send students of the Graduate School of Divinity of the University of St. Thomas to study in Israel, where they take at least one course at Hebrew Union College-Jewish Institute of Religion in Jerusalem and meet with Israeli families. Another project has been the development of an interfaith library within the Archbishop Ireland Memorial Library adjacent to the School of Divinity campus.

The most visible of the Center's activities are the public programs it sponsors every year. Each fall and spring the center reaches out to the Twin Cities metropolitan area with major programs that focus on Jewish-Christian relations. Featuring renowned Jewish and Christian speakers and panelists, the programs address issues such as religious liberty, education, theology, social justice, and biblical interpretation among others. A compilation of its scholarly lectures and discussions is published by the center in the annual Proceedings, which is sent to a mailing list of Jews and Christians throughout the world. A volume, *Jews and Christians Speak of Jesus,* published by Fortress Press, includes presentations of eight of the most renowned scholars in this field in the United States.

The Annual Scholars' Conference marks the culminating event of Rabbi Shapiro's tenure at the Christian-Jewish Learning Center. Since 1970, The Annual Scholars' Conference has, as a primary mission, the study of what humanity can learn from the horror of the Shoah and how and why institutions dedicated to faith and human betterment failed. The problems that emanate from this subject indicate the need for Jews and Christians, and other individuals interested in *Tikkun Olam*, the "repair of the world," to come together in the spirit of scholarship and solidarity to carry out this mission. This has been the goal of Max Shapiro's life and work.

Stephen C. Feinstein
Professor of History
University of Wisconsin, River Falls
Acting Director, Center for Holocaust and Genocide Studies
University of Minnesota, Minneapolis

Karen Schierman
Program Coordinator for The Jay Phillips Center for
Jewish-Christian Learning
University of St. Thomas
St. Paul, Minnesota

Marcia Sachs Littell
Director, National Academy for Holocaust and Genocide
Teacher Training at The Richard Stockton College of New
Jersey and Executive Director, Annual Scholars' Conference
on the Holocaust and the Churches
Merion Station, Pennsylvania

ACKNOWLEDGEMENTS

This volume was made possible by a grant from

THE SHARON GUTMAN - CHARLES LIGHTNER PUBLICATION FUND

with the cooperation of

THE PHILADELPHIA CENTER ON THE HOLOCAUST, GENOCIDE AND HUMAN RIGHTS

and the

CENTER FOR JEWISH-CHRISTIAN LEARNING OF THE UNIVERSITY OF ST. THOMAS

CONTENTS

Introduction   xvii

SECTION ONE:
THEOLOGICAL QUESTIONS

Chapter 1	Dialogue at the Mountain: Thoughts on Exodus 24 and Matthew 17:1-13 Zev Garber	1
Chapter 2	Post-Holocaust Theology: The Event as Normative Donald J. Dietrich	13
Chapter 3	Bearing Witness to the Murder of God: The Testimony of Holocaust Diaries David Patterson	25
Chapter 4	The American Protestant Press and the German Church Struggle: 1938-1945 Robert Ross	41
Chapter 5	Our Dangerous Moral Selves: On Nazism's Spiritual-Erotic Seduction and the Emergence of the Holocaust Bystander James Bernauer	55
Chapter 6	Selective Resistance: The German Catholic Church's Response to National Socialism Kevin Spicer	71
Chapter 7	Contract v. Covenant in Post-Holocaust Theology and Society W. Royce Clark	89

| Chapter 8 | The Auschwitz Convent Controversy: The Challenge of Repentance and Reconstruction
Susan E. Nowak | 109 |

SECTION TWO:
HISTORICAL QUESTIONS AND ISSUES OF MEMORY

Chapter 9	Julius Streicher and Nazi Medievalism Frederick M. Schweitzer	123
Chapter 10	Chosen Children: The Jewish Identity of Jewish Children During the Holocaust Leora Saposnik	137
Chapter 11	Dissenting Voices: U.S. Gentile Rescuers in Service Organizations During the Holocaust Barry Trachtenberg	169
Chapter 12	Why Did Hitler Permit a Jewish Hospital to Function Throughout the War? A Personal and Historical Perspective Gerda Haas	183
Chapter 13	The Politicalization of Holocaust Survivors in Canada, 1945-1985 Franklin Bialystok	193
Chapter 14	Andre Stein: The Category of Dialogue Harry James Cargas	211
Chapter 15	Lawrence Langer and the Holocaust Experience Gary Weissman	223
Chapter 16	They Forced on Me Another Woman's Life: The Impact of the Holocaust on Hebrew Wormen's Fiction Nurit Govrin	247

SECTION THREE:
CONFRONTING THE PRESENT AND FUTURE

Chapter 17   Right-Wing Extremism and the Christian Democrats: The Adenauer and Kohl Eras   269
David A. Meier

Chapter 18   Protection Against Genocide: Towards a Global Human Rights Regime   297
Neal Riemer

Contributors   309

Introduction

The second Volume of Proceedings from the 26th Annual Scholars' Conference continues the theme of the first volume edited by G. Jan Colijn and Marcia Sachs Littell of "Confronting the Holocaust: A Mandate for the 21st Century." At the same time, the papers from the conference reach back to some of the founding concepts of the conference in dealing with theological responses, and end up with questions about contemporary events in a united and democratic Germany, as well as alarming questions about creating an international system that can warn and protect against genocide.

The role of theology and the Shoah has been questioned lately by some scholars. From a purely historical portrayal of the Holocaust, theology may have nothing to do with the event. However, it has been well established that theology perhaps had almost everything to do with defining the initial victims, the Jews, and with giving substance to non-theological variants of anti-Semitism that became genocidal. Despite the theological concepts of the free will of humanity, questions of God's presence and absence, the response of various churches and church leaders, and how one reads Biblical texts in the post-Holocaust world have become compelling.

Section One, therefore, deals with theological issues, many which have the potentiality of not providing answers, but more questions. Zev Garber raises the issue of a radical re-reading of Exodus regarding the giving and taking of the Sinai covenant, questions of sin, punishment and justice of the Jewish people, and the test of Jewish faith in the aftermath of Shoah. Garber juxtaposes the Exodus passages with

Matthew on questions of idolatry, Transfiguration, Jesus's resurrection, and its meaning in light of Jewish rejection of Jesus as Christ and the meaning of such rejection in light of the Shoah.

Donald J. Dietrich examines the Holocaust in a wider ethical context, related to the growth of situational morality and moral relativism since the Enlightenment. Dietrich's main focus is in the area of post-Holocaust Roman Catholic responses, especially the writings of Karl Rahner and John Pawlikowski. He examines concepts of the presence of Jesus in Christian history, and the relationship of God to the material world through the Son. But Dietrich also notes that total reliance on the Jesus-event without reliance on traditions from other faiths can produce a path that not only perpetuates Christian supersessionism, but the theological evil that was one of the underpinnings of Nazism, the independence of God and humanity. Dietrich concludes by suggesting that "incarnational theology can help post-Holocaust dialogue by awakening Christians to the obscenity of the Holocaust." The ultimate provocation is assessing whether or not Christian theology needs total rehabilitation in the aftermath of Auschwitz.

David Patterson's essay examines the testimony of Holocaust diaries, with an emphasis upon theological aspects of these writings. Such diaries reflect, during the course of the event itself, that there was a theological as well as racial aim, as indicated by the war against not only the physical body of the Jewish people, but also the Torah, the synagogue, Jewish rituals, and "prayer that joins humanity with divinity." Diarists also asked the big question during the event: David Kahane's 1942 diary asked God the "Why?" question.

Robert Ross's examination of "The American Protestant Press and the German Church Struggle: 1938-1945," recalls the author's earlier research but with new insights, and especially a new typology which identifies not so much with Jewish persecution, but with the German Church Struggle. Ross documents events which academicians will find especially useful in the classroom for examining the response of the Confessing and Protestant territorial churches. At the end of the war, Ross points out there was a mixture of resentment by some German church leaders about being liberated by the Americans, and also some genuine admission of failure, if not repentance, regarding the churches' unwillingness to intercede to aid the Jews. That German churches, like the former Nazis after the war were also rehabilitated and welcomed

Introduction

into the World Council of Churches, which raises provocative questions about later nostalgia for Nazism.

James Bernauer focuses on the tantalizing question of the "spiritual-erotic seduction of Nazism" and how all parties reacted to that evil. The seduction of the Germans by Nazi evil is linked by Bernauer to "our dangerous moral selves," which encompassed a total surrender of philosophers and professionals to what Hitler promised. Bernauer focuses on the redemptive language of National Socialism, which had a cult-like appeal. So, even philosophers like Heidegger could find Nazism as a replacement for a decaying Christianity. All of this suggests to Bernauer that a vast spiritual crisis was lurking in Germany, which had an erotic appeal of its own and stood against other, especially deviant forms of sexuality. The theological aspect of this interesting depiction of the Hitler State is found in the failure of the churches to confront it.

The entire issue of the failure of the German Churches to effectively respond to Nazism is indeed one of the questions that begets theological responses to the Shoah. Kevin Spicer uses a 1978 analysis of the *Kirchenkampf* by Donald Nicholl as a basis for understanding Nazism. However, Spicer, while citing significant elements of Nicholl's argument which argued for the necessity by historians to place themselves into the world view of the dictatorship, also criticizes Nicholl for ignoring the intellectual atmosphere of the Roman Catholic church. The essay reflects and enhances Donald Dietrich's examination of the soteriological (theology of salvation through Christ) mission of the Roman Catholic church and also the issue of submission by clerics to the will of the state. Spicer concludes that the Church's silence on the Holocaust was related to a misdirected dogma on soteriology which limited the religious activity of the church to salvation, recalling to some degree, the compromise which Martin Luther also made with the German states during the Reformation.

W. Royce Clark's "Contract v. Covenant in Post-Holocaust Theology and Society" is essentially an analysis of the implications of Richard Rubenstein's seminal work, *After Auschwitz*. Clark's appreciation of Rubenstein's contribution to our understanding of the theological implications of the Shoah must be underscored by the fact that Rubenstein's work was the subject of a plenary session at the 27th Annual Scholars' Conference in Tampa in 1997. Clark examines some of the major concepts of Rubenstein's theology, especially those which have been influenced by the writer's extensive contact with Japanese society. Clark examines the concept of "cognitive monopoly," which reflects a Rousseau-like model of the "general will," and how it can lead to radical solutions to social problems, even genocide. Critical to Clark's argument is the implication of social contract in a world without God, and the need for a "transcendent, binding covenant between disparate peoples in order to avoid genocide...."

The controversy about the Carmelite Convent at Auschwitz was resolved in 1995, when the convent was moved from near the entrance gate at Auschwitz to a site down the road. Nevertheless, the issue was significant because it raised the question of who owned the memory of Auschwitz in a Poland now almost absent of Jews. In addition, the continued issues of bad taste with the potential construction of shopping malls across from the camp, and more than residual anti-Semitism flaring in Poland, raises theological concerns. Susan E. Nowak approaches this issue in her article, "The Auschwitz Convent Controversy: The Challenge of Repentance and Reconstruction." She analyzes the dynamics of theology that underpin the controversy and concludes that the Church must change its theological base for understanding itself as well as Judaism. The principal elements which Nowak addresses are Christology, Ecclesiology, and Covenant.

Section Two:

Section two contains articles less focused on theological concerns, and more in the realm of selected historical, contemporary and literary issues connected with the memory of the Holocaust.

Frederick M. Schweitzer's article is about "Julius Streicher and Nazi Medievalism." Streicher, of course, was notorious for his anti-Semitic ravings. At the Nuremberg Trial, Streicher asked for an anti-Semitic lawyer, a request that may have played a role is his being given the death sentence. Nevertheless, as Schweizer points out, Streicher's anti-Semitism harkened back to medieval judeophobia, and suggests the lethal quality of contemporary anti-Semitism in any form, but especially that variant which creates the victim based on old images. Schweitzer thus reveals one of the paradoxes of Nazi victimization of the Jews: the persecution of the Jews after September 15, 1935 was based on "race." But the imagery in the case of Streicher remained medieval, with his insistence of the "fact" of ritual murder even during his 1946 trial.

Introduction

Leora Saposnik examines the Jewish identity of Jewish children during the Holocaust in her article, "Chosen Children." This essay deals with the complex problem of Jewish identity during the Shoah, but in particular, with how children saw themselves as Jews as the events of the Holocaust unfolded. Saposnik documents the legal aspects of Nazi policy toward the Jews that cut younger people off from schools and peers in Germany. One response was the draw closer to Judaism and Jewish life, and even some optimism that there might be a way out of desperation through emigration. In the ghettoes of the East, the situation was more critical from the outset, which led to both positive and negative views of Jewish identities. A partial rejection of Judaism was useful for some children who had to pass to the Aryan side in order to survive. Hidden children, on the other had, are noted by the author to have undergone tremendous strain, as they were alone.

Barry Trachtenberg's article on "Dissenting Voices: U.S. Gentile Rescuers in Service Organizations During the Holocaust," is an examination of a specific group within a society that had a complex, and disappointing response toward rescue. The paper focuses on the Women's International League for Peace and Freedom, which fought immigration restrictions for refugees seeking to enter the United States. An interesting focus of the author's research are letters between the WILPF's Ellen Starr Brinton and the Kulka family, who tried to gain refuge for their family members from Slovakia. Here, we see an example of a non-governmental organization trying to become involved in rescue, when overall American policy toward this end was hostile.

Gerda Haas, herself a survivor of Terezin, examines an interesting part of the historical past, which is also her past, the existence of a Jewish hospital in Berlin until March, 1943. Drawing from her own experiences as a nurse in the hospital, Haas concludes that this medical facility served as a facility to hold and house *Mischlinge,* who, because of being half-Jews or involved in mixed marriages with Germans, fell into a clouded category. This paper may be related to other research on "half-Jews," some of which has recently revealed that up to 10,000 such individuals served in the Wehrmacht with the consent of the Nazi leadership.

Canada was notorious for its failure to take Jewish refugees before the outbreak of World War II. Franklin Bialystok examines the question of "The Politicization of Holocaust Survivors in Canada, 1945-1985." Canada received 35,000 Holocaust survivors after 1946.

The internal problems of Canadian Jewish identity, against the backdrop of the English/French identity issues in Canada itself, created a complex backdrop for the absorption of Holocaust survivors. Refugees who came to Canada had some of the same memory and storytelling problems as Jewish refugees who came to the United States. However, the multiple variants of Jewish communities in Canada reacted differently to the complex national issues which emerged in the 1960s. Factors which influences this identity included Quebec nationalism, neo-Nazism, pursuit of war criminals in Canada, and the impact of the Middle East crisis in Canadian affairs. Bialystok concludes that the impact of Holocaust survivors in the national debates on these and other issues was substantial by the mid-1980s.

Harry James Cargas's focus is the issue of dialogue in relationship to the Shoah, particularly the work of Andre Stein. Stein's important written works about the Holocaust are *Broken Silence, Quiet Heroes,* and *Hidden Children.* Cargas reproduces the text of a dialogue recorded with Stein as a means to show how he reached out to three Christian and one Jewish scholar/survivors in order to gain some greater understanding of the Shoah, especially the roles of victims and perpetrators. Cargas's discussion with Stein is a testimony to the pain of memory, the legacy of silence, and the emergence of the need to tell the story, and to help others tell their stories. Stein felt particularly remote from rescuers as a group, for he could not understand their motivations. But his analysis of them helped remold his view of the human community.

There is no doubt that Lawrence Langer's commentaries on Holocaust literature and testimonies have helped formulate many of our own views of how we perceive the Shoah. Gary Weissman approaches Langer's work with a critical eye, especially on how one can understand "The Holocaust Experience." Weissman is critical of what he identifies as Langer's failures on several levels: why not the search for a redeeming message from the Shoah?; why the "tedious regularity" with which "we refer to memory?;" why if history is inadequate to tell the story, can literature get one closer to Auschwitz? In essence, Weissman is testing the very important issue of historical facts in telling the story versus the power of literary imagination. Weissman asks the critical and important questions: can a "shared experience" be created between survivor and scholar, and can we, as outsiders, know "the way it was?"

Introduction

Nurit Govrin approaches the rise of women writers in Hebrew fiction about the Shoah. Govrin indicates that prior to the 1980s, the number of women working in this area were very small. Part of this is related to marginalization in Israeli society for a long time, especially against the life and death backdrop of foreign wars. Since the 1980s, women from the second and third generation of survivors have entered the literary world. Her study focuses on four women writers: Ruth Almog, Savyon Liebrecht, Nava Semel, and Michal Govrin, all of whom have a family connection with the Shoah. Their stories have a Holocaust focus, with women as main characters, with individualized themes of memory, children's relations with parents, remembrance, reincarnation, and the imposition of the memory of victims on the second generation daughter through multiple names and burdens. Govrin also deals with some of the symbols found in this new Israeli literature, which bears a remarkable similarity to the symbols found in contemporary works of the visual arts.

Section Three:

The conclusion of this volume alludes to some contemporary problems in Germany, as well as the underlying issue for studying the Holocaust -- the need to avoid future acts of genocide.

David A. Meier's article on "Right-Wing Extremism and the Christian Democrats: The Adenauer and Kohl Eras," brings together diverse aspects of German policies after 1945 as a means to examine the difficulty of dealing with the German past juxtaposed to the miraculous economy recovery, and the wide variety of right-wing extremism which emerged in Germany by the 1950s. In his detailed examination of these aspects of contemporary German history, Meier raises an important issue: that a legacy of the Holocaust is just as important as memory and remembrance of German history and politics. Most important, Meier clearly sees linkages between "traditional Nazism and contemporary right-wing extremism." The only difference, of course, is that Jews are no longer the principal victims.

Neal Riemer ends with the important question of whether or not it is possible to install a global regime to stop genocide? The question is asked because of recent failures to halt mass murder in places like Bosnia or Rwanda. Urging a creative breakthrough, Riemer advocates strengthened institutions, especially the United Nations Security Council, prudent prevention through creating a better global climate so as to deter or stop genocide through preemptive action.

The challenge here is immense, but is suggestive of the role for academia in creating a vision for domestic politicians and international organizations to help avert genocide. For if the Holocaust/Shoah becomes just one, even if unique or singular, example of genocide in a long list of genocides, will it be remembered?

Stephen C. Feinstein
University of Wisconsin, River Falls

SECTION ONE:

THEOLOGICAL QUESTIONS

Chapter 1

DIALOGUE AT THE MOUNTAIN: THOUGHTS ON EXODUS 24 AND MATTHEW 17:1-13

Zev Garber

I. Dialogue, A Learning Experience

Dialogue gives insight to the temper of our age and to the temper of our own religion. It means to go beyond acquiring bits of information to a critical exchange of ideas and experience. It means to take seriously the four sequential steps of a learning experience:

Confrontation, where the participant experiences the idea superficially; *Analysis*, where the participant seriously probes the occasion or text in light of previous experience and knowledge; *Interaction*, where the participant's mutual or reciprocal communication with others helps him/her benefit from their feelings, ideas, and experiences with the reality under discussion; and *Internalization*, where by turning the new experience and sharing of ideas upon oneself, the participant reacts meaningfully to the new reality as it relates to him/her as an individual and as a member of society.

Dialogical exchange has all the possibilities and dangers inherent in any real communication. On the one hand, dialogue can extend one's experience at the most profound level of his/her religious sensitivities. On the other hand, it can devaluate one's past attitude and ideas and develop a new orientation of what it means to be humane. Comparisons are inevitable, and this may lead to a spiritual death and rebirth. That is to say, the old meaning/orientation may have to disintegrate while a new one emerges. Clearly, an imagery of deconstruction before creation.

II. Torah: When I Say "Torah" What Do You Hear?

Definition: The Pentateuch (the five books of Moses: Genesis, Exodus, Leviticus, Numbers, and Deuteronomy); in a broader sense, the Hebrew Scriptures; in common religious usage, the unity of total revelation, the written Scriptures, and related authoritative rabbinical commentary.

Significance: Torah is a system derived from contact between the human and the divine that instructs by means of narratives, aphorisms, laws, commandments, and statutes, providing rules of life for individuals, nature, and society; the goal provided by Torah is to achieve spiritual and temporal happiness in the full realization of the divine will.

The Term

Torah is a feminine noun formation of the verbal root *yrh* ("to instruct") in its causative conjugational form; the root may be semantically related to the Arabic *rawa(y)* ("to hand down") or to the Akkadian *(w)aru* ("to guide"). The renderings of the biblical Hebrew word *torah* as *nomos* in the Greek Septuagint (first half of the third century B.C.E.) and as *lex* in the early Latin Bible translations have historically and theologically given rise to the misunderstanding that *torah* means legalism and that Torah means "Law." In essence, Torah is not supernatural revelation, religious dogma, or general self-evident propositions. It is the cumulative record of moral truths formed by the divine, and codified by humanity. In addition, modern Hebrew uses the word *torah* to designate the thinking system of a savant (for example, the *torah* of Plato, Maimonides, or Einstein) or a body of knowledge (the *torah* of mechanics).

Dual Torah

Various biblical verses point to the Pentateuch as Torah distinct from the rest of the Scriptures. The verse "Moses charged us with the Teaching (Torah) as the heritage of the congregation of Jacob" (Deut. 33:4) suggests the inalienable importance of Torah to Israel: It is to be transmitted from age to age, and this transmission has become the major factor for the unity of the Jewish people throughout their wanderings.

The rabbis of the Talmud kept the Torah alive and made its message relevant in different regions and times. This has been done by means of the rabbinic hermeneutic of a dual Torah that has been read into verses from the book of Exodus. Regarding God's words to Moses on the covenantal relationship between Himself and Israel, it is said in Exodus, "Write down *(ktav)* these words, for in accordance (*'al pi*; literally, 'by the mouth') with these words I have made a covenant with you and with Israel" (Ex. 34:27), and, "I will give you the stone tablets with the teachings *(torah)* and commandments which I have inscribed *(ktav-ti)* to instruct (by word of mouth) them" (Ex. 24:12). The sages saw the words "write," and "accordance" and "instruct" as the legitimate warrant for the written Torah *(Torah shehbiktav)* and the oral Torah *(Torah shehb'al peh)*. In their view, the written Torah, the teaching of Moses is eternal. The oral Torah is the application of the written Torah to forever changing historic situations, which continues to uncover new levels of depth and meaning and thus makes new facets of Judaism visible and meaningful in each generation.

The Process of Torah: Revelation and Reason

The ninth principle of the Creed of Maimonides (1134-1204) states, "I believe with perfect faith that this (written) Torah will not be changed, and that there never will be any other Torah from the Creator, blessed be His Name." It is clear from Maimonides' philosophical magnum opus *The Guide for the Perplexed* (c. 1200) that the written Torah is not to be taken in a literal fashion. For example, Genesis 1:26a says, "And God said, Let us make man in our image, after our likeness." If Judaism expresses strict monotheism, then what is to be made of the plural cohorative "us" and the notion that humanity and God share a "likeness"? For Maimonides, revelation teaches that God is incorporeal and ineffable, while reason imparts that humanity is finite, thus rending a non-literal reading (that the plural is that of majesty, anthropomorphic language, figurative speech). Not only in narrative but also in legislation are revelation and reason the primary forces in understanding Torah.

The Eternal Torah

The doctrine of the eternity of the Torah is implicit in verses that speak of individual teachings of the Torah in phrases such as the following: "A perpetual statute throughout your generations in all your (lands of) dwellings" (Lev. 3:17) and "throughout the ages as a covenant for all time" (Exod. 3:16). Biblical (Proverbs, in which Torah equals wisdom), Apocryphal (the wisdom of Ben Sira), and Aggadic (Genesis Rabbah) traditions speak of the pre-existence of Torah in Heaven. Though the Talmud acknowledges the pre-revelation existence of Torah in Heaven, which was later revealed to Moses at Sinai, it concentrates more on Torah's eternal values.

Jewish thinkers from the first century to the nineteenth century have proclaimed the Torah eternal, some in terms of metaphysics, others in terms of theology, and most in defense of Judaism against the political polemics of Christianity and Islam, which taught that aspects of Torah are temporal or have been superseded. In the first century, Philo Judaeus spoke metaphysically of the Torah as the word *(logos)* of God, the beginning of creation. In the tenth century, Saadia Gaon proclaimed that the Jews were unique only by virtue of Torah; if the Jewish nation will endure as long as the heaven and earth, then Torah must also be eternal. In the twelfth century, Maimonides extolled the perfection (eternity) of Torah, regarding which there is neither addition or deletion. After Maimonides, the issue of the eternity of the Torah became routine; the Torah's eternity became an undisputed article of belief. The schools of Kabbala, however, declared that the pre-existent form of Torah is eternal but that the words and message of the Torah are recycled every 7,000 years.

In the nineteenth century, the *Wissenschaft des Judentums* (Scientific Study of Judaism) movement, inspired by the scholarship of biblical critics, presented a historical-critical approach to Torah study. As a result, the traditional concept of the eternity of the Torah became a non sequitur and the idea of the Torah as a human book prevailed. By the mid-twentieth century, however, responding to negative trends in higher literary criticism, which are affected by classical Christian bias and "higher" anti-Semitism, objective and critical studies by Jewish loyalists helped to reaffirm the Jewishness of the Bible's origins. No matter how a Jew views the nature of Torah -- as a kind of "mythicizing history" or as a product of the people for the people or as written (inspired) by God -- Torah as ultimate authority is an indisputable article of faith.

Dialogue at the Mountain: Thoughts on Exodus 24 and Matthew 17:1-13

The Way of Torah: Three Paths

Whether the Torah is defined as the result of an exclusive encounter at Sinai or of an evolving journey from Sinai, this national treasure is traditionally understood by the response of *na'aseh venishma'* ("We shall do and we shall hear [reason]"). Accordingly, the way of Torah presents three paths for the contemporary Jew:

1. One should believe that God's Torah given at Sinai is all knowledge. (*Na'aseh* alone.)

2. The Torah-at-Sinai tradition should be abandoned, and Torah should be explained in purely rationalist terms. Torah is made in the image of the Jewish people. (*Nishma'* alone.)

3. One should accept the existential position that God's teaching was shared at Sinai, face to face, with all of Israel, present and future. "Present" implies that God's revelation occurred and that Torah is the memory of this unusual thiophany; "future" hints that Israel's dialogue with God is an ongoing process. This view holds that people know only a part of divine truth and that each generation seeks, makes distinctions, categorizes, and strives to discover more. *(Na'aseh ve-nishma'.)*

Na'aseh alone permits no ultimate questions; *nishma'* alone provides no ultimate answers. *Na'aseh* and *nishma'* together asks questions and attempt answers but leave many uncertainties unanswered. Yet uncertainty is truth in the making and the inevitable price for intellectual freedom.

III. Mattan Torah: The Long Shorter Reading

Moses went and repeated to the people all the commands of the Lord and all the rules; and all the people answered with one voice, saying, "All the things that the Lord has commanded we will do!" Moses then wrote down all the commands of the Lord.

> Early in the morning, he set up an altar at the foot of the mountain, with twelve pillars for the twelve tribes of Israel. He designated the youth of the Children of Israel, and they offered burnt offerings and sacrificed bulls as offerings of well-being to the Lord. Moses took one part of the blood and put it in basins, and the other part of the blood he dashed against the altar. Then he took record of the covenant and read it aloud to the people. And they said, "All that the Lord has spoken we will do

and obey!" Moses took the blood and dashed it on the people and said, "This is the blood of the covenant which the Lord now makes with you concerning all these commands" (Ex. 24:3-8).

Tradition maintains that this giving of the covenant was to the twelve tribes actually present but the receiving of the Torah *(mattan Torah)* was meant for the whole future House of Israel symbolically represented by the "twelve pillars." This may also be learned from the twice repeated "We will do" (vv. 3, 7) and the later Deuteronomic tradition, "I make this covenant, with its sanctions, not with you alone, but with those who are standing here with us this day before the Lord or God and with those who are not with us here this day" (Deut. 29:13-14).

This radical teaching -- the receiving of the Torah takes place at a time different from the giving of the Torah -- permeates Judaism through the ages. Indeed, it may be said that the *Tanach* is a record of attempts, failures, errors and successes in the reconciliation of the Jews and Torah. And the Talmud and the other classics are the commentary. Together they have been one consistent entity to the Nation's natal anthem: *Na'aseh ve-Nishmah.*

> When the Israelites declared their willingness to perform the mitzvot before hearing them, six hundred thousand ministering angels came and bestowed on each Israelite two crowns, one for the promise to perform *(na'aseh)* and for the promise to hear *(nishmah)* (UAHC *Exodus*, p. 595; B.M. 58b.

> The Israelites made their actions precede their hearing, for if one hears, but does not intend to do, it would be better had he not been created. Hence we are taught that he who learns in order to do is given the change to learn, teach and do (UAHC *Exodus*, p. 595).

> The feast of Shavuot celebrates the day of the giving of the Torah, because on that day the Torah was given to Israel. But every person of Israel receives the Torah in his own way and in his own time. (Rabbi of Kotzk).

The receiving of the Torah began in exhilaration ("We will faithfully do"), was ratified by revelation, challenged by reason, and it is continually evolving in the spirit of free will and historic development. Take *lex talionis*, for example.

Three times the Pentateuch mentions the legislation of *lex talionis* (the law of retaliation, of an "eye for an eye"): regarding the penalty for causing a pregnant bystander to miscarry when two individuals fight (Ex. 21:23-25), the case of one who maims another (Lev. 24:19-20), and the punishment meted out to one who gives false testimony (Deut. 19:18-21).

Though the law of "measure for measure" existed in the ancient Near East and persists today in parts of the Muslim Middle East, there is little evidence that the Torah meant that this legislation should be fulfilled literally except in the case of willful murder. "Life for life" is taken literally in cases of homicidal intention, and fair compensation is appropriate when physical injuries are not fatal. Equitable monetary compensation is deemed appropriate by the oral Torah in the case of a pregnant woman whose unborn child's life is lost and when animal life is forfeited. Indeed, the written Torah casts aside all doubts regarding the intent of the biblical *lex talionis* injunction: "And he that kills a beast shall make it good; and he that kills a man shall be put to death" (Lev. 24:21).

Rejecting the literal application of *lex talionis* puts an end to the mean-spirited charge the Judaism is "strict justice." Instead, Judaism advocates remedial justice for the guilty and concern for the injured. The wisdom of *mamon tahat 'ayin*, the "value of an eye," is not arbitrary, but a principle that is central in any democratic system of torts. The modern Jew who carefully probes for the reasons behind the commandments inculcated by the Torah will see their importance not in faith alone but also in association with logic and practicality.

Nevertheless, the severe language of the written Torah's "eye for an eye" sends forth a strong reminder. There is no remuneration in the world that can properly compensate serious injury, death, or any act of serious victimization.

Mattan Torah, like in whose Name it is authorized *(Ehyeh asher Ehyeh)*, is a continuum -- from Sinai to the present day. It is a process of training the Jew to separate "life (from) death, blessing (from) curse and to choose life -- that you and your seed may live -- by loving the Lord your God, heeding His commands, and holding fast to Him" (Deut. 30:19-20a). And from the "Dead of the Wilderness" *(metei midbar)* to the "Murdered in the Camps," we must be reminded that it cannot be a straightforward learning procedure.

Diverse doubts, rejections and theologies from within and *contra-Judaeous* teaching from without are obstacles we can overcome. For many post-Shoah Jews, however, a more somber statement of Israel's predicament has come about: "And God did not give you a heart to know and eyes to see and ears to hear until this very day" (Deut. 29:3). Nonetheless, we must remember that thousands of years of living by "the blood of the covenant" (v. 8) and the complete sacrifice offered by the youth of the Children of Israel (v. 5) assures us of one thing: The Presence and giving of Torah are not merely metaphorical; they continue to be witnessed by Israel despite or in spite of Shoah.

IV. Cry Justice

For some reading Scriptures after the Shoah is grounded in historical inevitability. Certainly our position on *mattan Torah* contains biblical motives set in a teleological framework. Yet we challenge the position of some Jews and Christians who see ordinary and extraordinary issues and circumstances as well as understand the relationship between individuality and group association (race, gender, ethnicity, religion) as product of chance or fated by a predetermined goal. We consider the nature and importance of causal relation and speak out against the attitude that says there is a necessary connection between cause and effect. For us all events are wholly distinct and separable from one another. To be sure, a certain effect follows a certain cause. But what guarantee do we have if we repeat a cause the same effect will always follow? There is absolutely no certain clue in past experience to what will happen in the future. Certain causal sequences may have held in the past, perhaps necessarily, but is there any evidence for assuming that they must hold in the future?

To illustrate, religious orthodoxy, in particular Hasidism, and secular Zionist ideology practice foresight in an attempt to make sense of the Shoah. The former sees the Event foreordained caused by the sins of assimilation and nationalism; the latter depicts Shoah victims as complicit *sôn latebah* ("sheep to slaughter"), who choose not to "liquidate the Diaspora" and ultimately were silenced by the Great Catastrophe. Also, we judiciously condemn the skill of politicians, professors and other pundits who postulate post-Auschwitz signs of genocidal tendencies back into the Shoah. Contra foresight and hindsight, we posit "now-sight" -- an alternative position which asserts a certain power or force residing in every present with the potential of determining separable, multiple futures.

It is essential to recognize here that any discussion on the Children of Israel in Hitler's inferno must reject "the logic of historical inevitability, (which) explicitly suggests that the murdered children were already doomed to perish in the Shoah the instant they were born, hence it would be inconsistent to mourn the adult lives they never experienced or the accomplishments they never attained."[1]

Irretrievable loss elicits anger, outrage, pain and demands cry justice: Forgive them not Father for they know what they do.

V. Transfiguration Spells Transformation

Exodus 24 talks of the revelation and ratification of the Covenant idea that was to turn disparate tribal bands into a faith-people endowed with divine purpose and earthly mission. Matthew 17:1-13 records the transfiguration of Jesus ("his face shone like the sun, and his garments became white as light;" v. 2) before the heavenly visitants, Moses, representative of the Torah and Elijah, representative of the Prophets. On a high mountain top (either Tabor or most probably, Mt. Hermon, near Caesarea Philippi), God's voice called from a bright cloud (an allusion to the Shekinah), "This is my beloved Son, with whom I am well pleased; listen to him" (v. 5). For devout Christians, these quintessential words, similar to the utterance at the Baptism (Matt. 3:17), proclaim the supreme majesty and universal sovereignty of God in Christ.

There are comparative points between Exodus 24 and Matthew 17:1-13 which are important enough to warrant discussion:

• Matthew 17:1 speaks of the ascent of Jesus with Peter and the two sons of Zebedee (Matt. 4:21), James and John. This is reminiscent of Exodus 24:9-18, which gives details of the ascent of Moses, assisted by Joshua, and accompanied by Aaron, his sons Nadab and Abihu, and seventy of the elders. Here we are given details of the climb in accordance with an attested biblical literary method of first making a general statement *(klal)* and thereafter mentioning the particulars *(p'rat)*.[2] Additionally, "three" represents the twelve apostles and is a hint to Christological Trinitarianism; "seventy" symbolize Jacob/Israel's core beginning (Ex. 1:5) and (later) the Nations of the World.

• "Booths" (v. 4) suggest the *mishkan* ("The dwelling place [of God], Tabernacle") where the Wilderness cult was conducted (Acts 7:38, 44). The sight "of the Glory of God was like a consuming fire ... before the eyes of the Children of Israel" (Ex. 24:17) parallels the sound of the voice of God, "When the disciples heard it, they fell on their face, and were sore afraid" (v. 6). Also, "Booths" intimates the Feast of Tabernacles (Sukkot). The Torah reading for the seven day Sukkot festival mentions 70 bullocks offered as sacrifices (13 bullocks on the first day, 12 on the second, and so on, up to seven on the seventh day for a total of seventy) -- symbolic and anticipatory of the messianic time for the Nations of the World. And this is suggested from the haftarah of the first day of Sukkot:

> All who survive of all those nations that come up against Jerusalem shall make a pilgrimage year by year to bow low to the King Lord of Hosts and to observe the Feast of Booths. Any of the earth's communities that does not make the pilgrimage to Jerusalem to bow low to the King Lord of Hosts shall receive no rain. However, if the community of Egypt does not make this pilgrimage, it shall not be visited by the same affliction with which the Lord will strike the other nations that do not come up to observe the Feast of Booths. Such shall be the punishment of Egypt and of all other nations that do not come up to observe the Feast of Booths (Zech. 14:16-19).

Finally, the Lord alone shall be worshipped and shall be invoked by His true name:

> And the Lord shall be king over all the earth; in that day there shall be one Lord with one name[3] (Zech. 14:9).

• "And when they lifted up their eyes, they saw no one but Jesus only" (v. 8). Though present at the Transfiguration, Peter, James and John did not experience directly the corner stone of this theophany, i.e., the *bright cloud* from which God spoke (v. 5). Similarly, Ex. 24: 15-18 portrays Moses alone, in the absence of Joshua, Aaron and Hur, encountering the divine glory -- albeit, not fully -- on the mountain of God. Jewish sages and mystics maintain that no mortal being can truly penetrate the inner essence of ha-Shem (the Lord); ha-Shem as known to ha-Shem is beyond human conception, perception and reasoning. Consider, for example, God's "afterglow" in Ex. 34:6-7, which is interpreted in rabbinic Judaism as ways of understanding His revealed nature.[4] Christian tradition agrees, no man can see God and live. Yet Jesus "suffered death, so that by the grace of God (Jesus) tasted death for everyone" (Heb. 2:9) and has "the words of eternal life" (John 6:68).

• Elijah, John the Baptist and Jesus (vv. 9-13) are a rewrite of Mark 9:9-13. The meshing of John the Baptist and Elijah the Prophet is no doubt rooted in the Jewish belief that Elijah would return as a forerunner of the messianic age (Mal. 4:23; Lk. 1:17).[5] However, the contemptuous suffering of Elijah and the "Son of man" within the Jewish tradition is an enigma; unless, of course, Matt. 17:12 is a reflection of the martyred servant of Is. 53.

• Traditionalist Christianity maintains that in the charge of Jesus, "Tell the vision to no man until the Son of man is risen again from the dead (v. 9)," we have a clue to the people's non-recognition of Elijah/John the Baptist as the messenger of the messianic age. From the beginning, man has wisdom of good and evil (Gen. 2:17) and Israel the ability to choose life (Deut. 30:19) but they have become clouded in disobedience and curse. The people "hear indeed, but perceive not, it (cannot) grasp with its mind and repent and save itself" (Is. 6:9, 10; Acts 28:26, 27). Thus Jesus was sacrificed on the cross for the sake of mankind, and his vicarious atonement becomes clear when Christ is raised from the dead.

VI. Give Not To Caesar

• In Hitler's ideal state the male-child is not born a citizen but a "subject of the state," and only after state prescribed ideological education, physical training and military service can the individual, if healthy and with a blameless record, be solemnly invested with the rights of State citizenship. Also, the German maid-child is a subject of the state, and only after marriage to a German Aryan is she a citizen. Hitler in his rise to power took advantage of the virulent caricature of the Jews nurtured by centuries of teaching of contempt and persecution of the Jews in the central empires of Europe. Willful surrender to "the Führer and the Führerstaat"[6] contributed to major crimes against humanity by the *Drittes Reich*, of which the near total destruction of European Jewry in the lands of Christendom represents the most heinous depravity.

• Understanding monotheism while deploring idolatry are the focus of our discussion on Covenant and Transfiguration. Our thoughts on Ex. 24 and Matt. 17 are an attempt to suggest how Judaism and Christianity differ in their religious core. How so? The Torah's *na'aseh ve-nishma'* represents Israel's faith in God and devotion to His word; that is to say, the Jews' resolve to do and obey whatever God would command and permit -- even the test of the Shoah. On the other hand, that Jesus "should suffer many things"[7] teaches Christianity's fundamental *torah* that God serves man's needs -- contra Judaism's Torah man serves God's demands -- even at moments of excruciating agony as epitomized by the ultimate killing at the cross. Nonetheless, both Traditions at the Mountain are united in their pledge: Restore mankind prior, during and after the Shoah to the glory of the Lord.

- We all must be reminded of this, and because of our proximity to the Shoah and our common belief in the coming of the Messianic Age, Jews and Christians in dialogue, above all, must believe it. In the dialogue, there is no debate, climb the mountain and see the glory. There is no alternative.

Notes

1. M.A. Bernstein, *Foregone Conclusions: Against Apocalyptic History* (Berkeley: University of California Press, 1994), p. 15.

2. *Klal u-frat* (a general proposition followed by a specifying particular) is the fourth of thirteen principles of rabbinic exegesis in the name of R. Ishmael (Sifre 1) recited in the preliminary prayers of the daily morning service by traditional Jews.

3. Judaism's universal plan for the salvation of all of God's children is programmed from these words. This thought is also the final sentiment of the *Aleinu* prayer recited at the conclusion of all services on Sabbath, festivals and weekdays.

4. The Thirteen Attributes of God in terms of ethical categories are one of the key concepts in the entire Yom Kippur service among all groups of religious Jews. Among the Sepharedim and Mizrahim the attributes are arranged in the tradition of Rav Amram Gaon (821-875) and Rav Saadia (882-942). They are especially appropriate for the holiest day on the Jewish calendar because this day is one of reconciliation and "at-one"ment with God. And this may well explain the liturgical editing of Attribute 13 (cf. Exod. 32:7), from *ve-nakkeh lo' yennakeh* ("will by no means clear the guilty") to *ve-nakkeh* ("acquitting" -- the penitent).

5. On this fearless and zealous prophet of God, see Z. Garber, *Shoah: The Paradigmatic Genocide* (Lanham, MD: University Press of America, 1994), pp. 143-146.

6. Phrase lifted from F.H. Littell, "Inventing the Holocaust: A Christian Response," *Holocaust and Genocide Studies* 9.2 (Fall 1995), p. 177.

7. Mk. 9:12; Matt. 17:12.

Chapter 2

POST-HOLOCAUST THEOLOGY: THE EVENT AS NORMATIVE

Donald J. Dietrich

I.

Since the Enlightenment, Western culture has placed an increased emphasis on the freedom of the individual to shape society and humanity as well as to guide events that can lead to the creation of the "New Man." During this period, the belief emerged that humans have the capability, intellectual and physical, to forge the utopia that would ensure the perfection of the species. One result of this movement toward moral and political self-reference has resulted in the decline of the notion of a transcendent, normative morality. As the importance of the individual's role in creating his existential environment has grown, the importance of such traditional, behavior-governing institutions as Christianity, characterized by an objective morality, have begun to ebb.[1] As a device for asserting the creational power of the individual, modern thinkers have increasingly argued that a normative code of ethics no longer need exist as a legitimate standard for governing human behavior. Religion and morality were thus left to the individual and were conceived as the logical outgrowths of each person's essential rationality as embedded within a specific culture. Under such a perspective, the person was becoming his or her own moral self-referent. Such an approach would legitimate the shaping of ethical norms by each individual.

This type of situational morality or moral relativism has impacted society and politics in the twentieth century, and the Holocaust can be viewed as the most awesome fulfillment of this lack of a transcendent norm. In liberal democracies, it has also become difficult to find a balance between the individual's socio-moral freedom and any responsibility to society as a whole. This individualistic morality has made it difficult for men and women to find a meaningful relationship to an omnipotent God, which can transcend the variegated modes of human existence. Additionally, this system of individualistic morality has helped support the pursuit of the "New Man" of Nazism and the perfect society, which ultimately became a process of marginalizing and persecuting Jews and others.[2] Does this mean that the historically contingent is dominant and that no transcendent norms can guide theologians as they reappropriate their religious traditions to confront sanctioned evil? Can theologians base the religious reflections on events that have transcendent meaning? If so, on which events can theology be based?

Trying to avoid the resurrection as a seminal theological event, or at least as an event that may no longer be useful, A. Roy Eckardt has moved somewhat out of mainstream Christian theology.[3] John Pawlikowski has suggested that the incarnation may be the event that would allow Christians to work toward a theology that can engage Holocaust issues.[4] In light of the Holocaust, theologians have had to choose which discrete experience in the extended Jesus-Event may be most fruitful in interreligious dialogue.

In the area of Holocaust theology, such dramatic terminology as "endpoint," "interruption," "crisis," "break," "rupture," "paradigm shift" and "metanoia" have been used to describe the impact that the Holocaust has had on Christian faith. Christian theology is "event driven," and three theologians have been particularly useful in refocusing the views of Catholic theologians: Karl Rahner, John Pawlikowski, and Johannes Metz.

II.

Such Jewish scholars as Emil Fackenheim, Irving Greenberg, and Arthur Cohen[5] are in agreement that some type of restatement of the God-human person relationship through events has to be at the heart of any new faith-meaning after the Holocaust, and their works have sought to address this issue. Christian theologians have moved more cautiously. They have traditionally used the Crucifixion and Resurrection as avenues into the Jesus-Event. In an effort to address the fragmented, atheistic, anthropocentric nature of modern culture typified by the Holocaust, they have increasingly, however, begun looking to the

Incarnation of Christ as the entry point for non-Jews into the ongoing covenant, since the Crucifixion and Resurrection carry too much antisemitic baggage. Through the Incarnation Jesus is seen as embodying the unity of God and humanity, so that the gulf between creation and the Creator could be transcended. Through an understanding of the Incarnation, Christian theologians are also trying to recognize humanity's creative possibilities and the need to be conditioned by an encounter with the living God.

Perhaps the most influential Catholic theologian of this century, Karl Rahner has posited a Christology that incorporates human freedom and creativity into the larger, transcending role of God. Rahner's theology begins with his notion that the world and its history are evolving toward a unity of matter and spirit. These elements are related to each other in such a way that they result from the creative act of God, and they have a single goal "in the fullness of God's Kingdom."[6] Thus, human existence itself has constituted a motion toward unity with God – a dynamic entity. In Rahner's view we have the capacity to move beyond ourselves, to become something "higher and better," to move closer to existence in God. But such an existence is not completely oriented by God's power; humans also have the capacity to better themselves through their own resources.[7]

This evolution, or state of becoming, is a process that Rahner calls "self-transcendence." Humanity is to incarnate the transcendence as the material aspect of God's creation. Human history emerges within the material world and reflects the history of the active transformation of the material world. The conjunctive histories of humanity and the material world are in a state of incompleteness and trial. Rahner maintains that humans can reject God's self-communication and refuse to enter "this historical movement toward God," but our freedom always remains grounded in the reality of God. We can choose not to participate in this worldly evolution and thus turn away from the transcending power of God. Rahner has asserted, however, that this evolutionary perspective must be our basis for understanding God's role. For Christians Jesus is the object as well as the focus of the unity of matter and spirit in the universe. The presence of Jesus in human history is proof of the goal toward which history is evolving. In Rahner's view, the doctrine of the hypostatic union is not just speculation. Jesus is truly human, a part of the earth. He is a moment in this World's biological process of becoming. In Jesus, God has become a part of the material world. Rahner uses the phrase "essential humanity" to describe Jesus' role as a human being. He is autonomous and free because he has been created as God's own self-expression.[8]

Because humanity is inextricably linked to the material aspect of God's creation and because Jesus was fully human and thus part of human history, dogmatic theology, in Rahner's view, must be "theological anthropology." Since the human person is the being most connected with the transcendence of God, any Christian theology must concentrate on humanity in order to disclose the transcendent God. Only in this way can theological teaching avoid becoming mythologized or expressed in terms that are inapplicable to humanity's earthly, material existence. Rahner has recognized that, in the modern world, any meaningful philosophy or theology must be directly applicable to the human existence.[9] Theology that seeks transcendent meaning has to focus on the specific concerns of humanity in the world today:

> If the themes of this philosophy of tomorrow are going to be hope, society, critique of ideology, a new form of freedom in a new social structure, the experience of God in the experience of man planning himself and his own future, then man becomes once again the indispensable subject matter of philosophy. And so, even from the point of view of the philosophy of tomorrow, the application of a transcendental anthropology is demanded of the theology of today and of tomorrow.[10]

In a theology relevant to an era characterized by sanctioned murder, the human person seems to be the proper focal point. Humanity is to become a partner with God in the evolution toward the union of matter and spirit. A theology that places humanity in a co-creator role with God must, he feels, be asserted. In light of the Holocaust, it is obvious that humanity - as Rahner has argued - exerts a strong influence over the course of history. We can no longer picture God as "the strategist of human history" because the Holocaust has destroyed "all simplistic notions of a 'commanding' God." In Rahner's view Christianity has no predictions to make and no utopian program for the future of humanity. Thus, humans as pilgrims go unprotected into a world that they and God produce. Culture and civilization are conditioned by individuals who are finite images of God. They cannot create their own eschaton. A better future, according to Rahner and Pawlikowski, has to be constructed cooperatively by humanity and God. In such a future each individual would have a value as a spiritual person. Rahner has contended that Christianity has already surpassed all secular ideologies that portray the future, since the Incarnation, it is believed, has already ushered in salvation. By fusing God and humanity, the Incarnation has produced the "New Man" as a model for humans to emulate.[11]

The Shoah has proven that the future of earthly affairs is no longer something that God exclusively will guarantee. Even so, humanity must not be left completely on its own. John Pawlikowski puts it well when he argues that the

> post-Holocaust vision must recognize both the new creative possibilities inherent in the human condition and the absolute necessity for this creative potential to come under the sway of a living and judging God through personal encounter.

This transcendent power for such Catholic theologians as Rahner and Pawlikowski can be the unity of God and humanity exemplified by the presence of Jesus in human history. The desire to break with God and supplant Him as Creator can be thwarted by a reliance on a theology more incarnational in nature then past Christian speculation has been. Christians have to realize a responsibility for the shaping of human events, but also have to insist that this freedom to be compelled and conditioned by the healing, strengthening, and affirming power of "a God who remains a direct source of strength and influence in the conduct of human affairs" is necessary as well.[12] Such a theological anthropology can offer healing to the atomistic culture of modernity that has given birth to a self-referent morality.

The presence of Jesus Christ in human history exemplifies the union of God and humanity and their respective roles as co-creators of history. But to properly confront the cultural dissonance that contributes to individuals' feelings of isolation and unchecked, self-referential freedom, the Incarnation in human history cannot become exclusionary. To insist that any part of the Jesus-Event is a completely self-sufficient, self-sustaining root-experience that has no need to be complemented by supportive traditions from other faith experiences would help perpetuate the "traditional Christian supercessionism." A fundamental mistake of past Christologies has been to consider their unique perspective as exclusive and universal; this hubris was a major assertion that made the tragedy of the Holocaust possible.[13] The Incarnation, however, offers a solution to the fragmentation and isolation inherent in modern society as well as to traditional Christian exclusivism, since co-creation, at least conceptually, can be viewed as one thread of the common Judeo-Christian experience. The Incarnation stresses a communal salvation with God engaged with creation just as in Genesis God and creation were in an interactive relationship. The path to a fullness of life from the Christian perspective also echoes the sense of salvation in and through the sense of community that was central to the Jewish covenantal faith.

John Pawlikowski, for example, has pointed out that Judaism was convinced that no single individual could reach salvation without the entire human family. Christianity has often unfortunately insisted on

> an overly individualistic interpretation of the Incarnational revelation, in which people became convinced they could reach full communion with God by sidestepping or even deliberately isolating themselves from communal relationships.[14]

This earlier perspective has now been critically questioned in light of the murderous events of this century. The Incarnation can best be understood in contemporary Christian theology with an eye toward the Jewish tradition of community. In union with God through Jesus, humans can achieve freedom and responsibility for the creation of history; through this freedom they can work toward the elevation of all humanity to a unity of God and creature. Modern humanity exists in the context of a history, in which everyone is absolutely dependent on everyone else. The current studies of the Holocaust and the history of the individualistic modern world view should encourage Christians to look to the Jewish ideal of communal faith that can serve to help overcome a tendency to any false privatization of religion or moral values.[15]

Pawlikowski, for example, has maintained that the sense of the human person as a co-creator with God definitely has its roots in the Jewish covenantal tradition. As the volatile nature of history in this century suggests, the early claim of Christianity that Jesus had completed the salvation of humanity has to be retired. The reappropriation of the Jewish co-creatorship notion within the Christian church is critical for Christians who oppose the triumphalism that has wreaked such havoc on the Jewish people. The salvation of humankind can be seen as a task yet to be accomplished. The Jesus-Event did not complete, but only supported, the process. The premature claims of Christianity that the messianic kingdom had arrived fully in Jesus helped retard Christians from accepting the responsibility for the destiny of the world. Sensitive to the religious meaning of the Holocaust, theologians have discarded simplistic fulfillment and have assiduously searched for a model based on the Jesus-Event, which can provide the basis for dialogue and for the elimination of any myopic notion of self-referential morality. Moral values, many feel, should be rooted in the historical interdependence of God and humanity. For Christians, the Incarnation can provide a theological tool that opposes an atomistic view of humanity and that fosters a communal approach that can be useful in constructing a morality with transcendent roots.[16]

III.

The Incarnation can provide this "faith basis for continued social involvement." By insisting that the transcendent power of God engage historical culture, the union of God and humanity in Jesus can help create a holistic responsibility to create a society supporting persons and their values. By looking to the Incarnation for guidance, some theologians hope that we can work toward a unity of the divine and the human as well as toward the realistic creation of a "New Man" in history, which can be nurtured by God and humans engaging in the common project of co-creation. Catholic theologians have been focusing on the notion that this salvation of humankind is primarily a task that is still to be accomplished and that the Incarnation has only helped advance the process. Assertions about total fulfillment in Christ have to be abandoned in this model. In fact, in some quarters of the post-Vatican II Catholic Church, social involvement in the "world of marching soldiers" has become the litmus test of the Christian dedicated to normative values and public policy. The theory of justice posed by these activists has in part been based on the biblical theme of the co-creational responsibilities shared between God and humanity. This encounter with the living and judging God can help create the notion of the transcendent God to counterbalance the evil created by the Nazis trying to construct such utopias as an Aryan society. In essence, the heightened sense of human responsibility needs a correlate in the sense of divine transcendence.[17] The Nazis were blind to this interdependence between God and humanity, whom prominent Christian theologians would say have responsibility for creation. But Hitler and his followers were only products of a modern culture that had been nurtured by a focus on the individual and on self-creation as *the* primary values.

With a proper understanding of the meaning of the Jesus-Event, some Protestant and Catholic theologians have suggested that men and women can be healed. They can finally overcome the primal sin of pride, the desire to supplant the creator in power and station, which has led to the modern social fragmentation that lay at the heart of the Shoah. Critical to this awareness is the sense of God's self-imposed limitation manifested on the Cross. This is where Jürgen Moltmann's theology can make a significant contribution. The notion of "divine vulnerability" can become a powerful Christological statement to remind us that we need not exercise power, control, and dominance to be like God. His theology also maintains that God is not simply desirous of absorbing humanity totally back into divine being, but rather in supporting its eternal distinctiveness.[18]

Such Christian perspectives do not just theoretically affirm human dignity, but also reflect the Incarnation's proper meaning. From this perspective theology would have to be person-centered and relate actively to the historical victims of our societies and to the victims of the Holocaust. Theological anthropology calls for a concrete manifestation of faith through the identification with and the support of the victims. Such theologians as Rahner and Pawlikowski have developed an incarnational theology of witness that can help stress the intimate connection between God and humanity in society, since Christ's life in history is as meaningful as his death and resurrection.[19] Helping to understand this union of God and humanity in Jesus is his historical life of witness, which can prepare us to realize that really meaningful Christology has to be rooted in a theological anthropology that can lead humanity to a solidarity with the marginalized victims as humans join with God in an unceasing act of co-creation.

Incarnational Theology can help support post-Holocaust Jewish Christian dialogue by rooting Christianity in a Jesus-Event that is not threatening. But the Holocaust itself is an *event* that has the power to drive Christian theologians to re-examine their theology. In essence, if the event is obscene, check the theology that undergirds the culture that supported the perpetration of murder. Johannes Metz has used this approach to help construct a critical theology. He is trying to establish axiomatically the Holocaust's status as a theological criterion. He has asserted that after Auschwitz every theological "truth" that is unrelated to people and their concrete situation has to be re-examined. Thus, Auschwitz does not merely mandate revising Christian theology in its relationship to Judaism, but is really a matter of re-evaluating Christian theology *in toto*. Can Christian theology lead to a solidarity with all victims?[20] Metz advises that any theology is to be avoided, which could have been exactly the same before or after Auschwitz.

IV.

Rahner and Pawlikowski see the Jesus-Event in the Incarnation as the way to reinforce a co-creation model that places responsibility on both God and humanity. Individual historical events can have transcendent significance and impact moral theology. Earlier Catholic moral theologians tended to concentrate on individual guilt and responsibility, and so the church's traditional view of moral culpability had not, until recently, been prepared to deal with the issue of collective or social responsibility. Under the impress of the Holocaust and Liberation Theologies, the earlier individualistic moral tradition has slowly been transformed into a concern also with macromoral challenges that have to respond to systemic or structural evil, which can, of course, have implications for the political issues of our time. Rahner and Pawlikowski see co-creation as necessary for the construction of socio-political initiatives with a moral foundation. Such theologians as Metz have returned to the Christian message of compassion for the marginalized victims in society. For Metz, the Holocaust has to be seen as the event that demands that Christian theologians have to create an authentic theology on the basis of the event. Auschwitz demands that theology be grounded on human experience. Such a theology would engage the culture, but not dominate it. Catholic theologians, therefore, have been attempting to go beyond the shadow of Auschwitz and into a new era of faithfulness and responsibility, which uses history composed of human events to guide theology to the articulation of the normative values that we seek to guide us.

Notes

1. Zygmunt Bauman, *Modernity and the Holocaust* (Ithaca: Cornell University Press, 1989); Peter Haas, *Morality after Auschwitz: The Radical Challenge of the Nazi Ethic* (Philadelphia: Fortress Press, 1988).

2. Michael Ryan, "Hitler's Challenge to the Churches: A Theological-Political Analysis of *Mein Kampf*," in Franklin Littell and Hubert Locke, (eds.), *The German Church Struggle and the Holocaust* (Detroit: Wayne State University Press, 1974): 48-164; Gary Lease, "Odd Fellows" *in The Politics of Religion: Modernism, National Socialism and German Judaism* (Berlin: Mouton de Gruyter, 1995): pp. 135-188.

3. A. Roy Eckardt, "Salient Christian-Jewish Issues of Today: A Christian Exploration," in A. Roy Eckardt, *Jews and Christians: Exploring the Past, Present and Future* (New York: Crossroad, 1990): pp. 151-177.

4. John Pawlikowski, "Toward a Theology for Religious Diversity: Perspectives from the Christian-Jewish Dialogue," *Journal of Ecumenical Studies* 26 (1989): pp. 144-145.

5. Emil Fackenheim, *What is Judaism? An Interpretation for the Present Age* (New York: Summit Books, 1987); Irving Greenberg, "The Voluntary Covenant," *Perspectives*, no. 3 (New York: National Jewish Resource Center, 1982), p. 15; Arthur Cohen, *The Tremendum: A Theological Interpretation of the Holocaust* (New York: Crossroad, 1981).

6. Richard McBrien, *Catholicism* (Minneapolis: Winston Press, 1980), p. 473.

7. Karl Rahner, "Christianity and the 'New Man,'" *Theological Investigations*, vol. 5, *Later Writings* (Baltimore: Helicon Press, 1966), p. 149.

8. McBrien, pp. 475-477; Geffrey B. Kelly, ed, *Karl Rahner: Theologian of the Graced Search for Meaning* (Minneapolis: Fortress Press, 1992), pp. 184-217; Herbert Vorgrimmler, *Understanding Karl Rahner: An Introduction to His Life and Thought* (New York: Crossroad, 1986).

9. Karl Rahner, "Theology and Anthropology," in T. Patrick Burke, ed., *The Word in History*, (New York: Sheed and Ward, 1966), p. 1; Karl Rahner, "The Theology of the Spiritual Life," in *Theological Investigations*, Vol. III (Baltimore: Helicon Press, 1967), p. 43.

10. Rahner, "Theology and Anthropology," p. 16.

11. John Pawlikowski, "Toward a Theology," pp. 144-45; Karl Rahner, "Christianity and the 'New Man,'" pp. 138-146.

12. Pawlikowski, "Toward a Theology," pp. 145-146; Pawlikowski, "Speaking of Christ," p. 29.

13. John Pawlikowski, *Jesus and the Theology of Israel* (Wilmington: Michael Glazier, Inc., 1989), p. 88; Donald J. Dietrich, *God and Humanity in Auschwitz: Jewish-Christian Relations and Sanctioned Murder* (New Brunswick, NJ: Transaction Press, 1995), pp. 159-198.

14. Pawlikowski, *Jesus and the Theology of Israel*, pp. 89-90.

15. *Ibid.,* p. 91.

16. Dietrich, *God and Humanity*, pp. 115-124, 187-198.

17. John Pawlikowski, *Jesus and the Theology of Israel*, pp. 88-99; John Pawlikowski, "Christian Ethics and the Holocaust: A Dialogue with Post-Auschwitz Judaism," *Theological Studies* 49 (1988): pp. 651, 653, 656-57, 661-667.

18. Jürgen Motlmann, *The Crucified God* (New York: Harper and Row, 1974); A. Roy Eckardt, *Long Night's Journey into Day: Life and Faith after the Holocaust* (Detroit: Wayne State Press, 1982).

19. Johannes Metz, *The Emergent Church: The Future of Christianity in a Post-Bourgeois World* (New York: Crossroad, 1981), pp. 18-27; David Tracy, "God of History, God of Psychology," in Hermann Häring and Johannes Metz, eds., *Reincarnation or Resurrection* (London: SCM Press, 1993), pp. 102-111; Elisabeth Schüssler-Fiorenza and David Tracy, eds., *The Holocaust as Interruption* (Edinburgh: T&T Clark, 1984).

20. Matthew Lamb, *Solidarity with Victims: Toward a Theology of Social Transformation* (New York: Crossroad, 1982); Johannes Metz, *The Emergent Church*, p. 22; Johannes Metz, "Facing the Jews: Christian Theology after Auschwitz," in Tracy and Schüssler-Fiorenza, p. 30.

Chapter 3

BEARING WITNESS TO THE MURDER OF GOD: THE TESTIMONY OF THE HOLOCAUST DIARIES

David Patterson

In the Holocaust the assault on God's Chosen is essentially an assault on God Himself. The idea that an assault on the Chosen is an assault on God is at least as old as Rashi, who in his commentary on the Torah asserts, "Whoever attacks Israel is as though he attacks the Holy One, blessed be He."[1] The validity of the claim that Israel's affliction is God's affliction rests not on a belief in God but on a certain understanding and treatment of the human being as a creature who harbors a trace of something holy. A distinctive feature of the Holocaust is that it is characterized not only by an attack on human beings but also by an assault on everything that sanctifies humanity.

This singular feature of the Holocaust is reflected in the Holocaust diary and its chronicle of an assault on the human being that entails an assault on divine being. "Not only the body of Israel is being attacked," writes Moshe Flinker, for instance, "but also its spirit."[2] The assault on the spirit of Israel manifests itself in the calculated destruction not only of Jewish bodies but of Jewish souls and Jewish prayers, of Jewish texts and traditions, of Jewish homes and families -- everything that goes into the fabric not only of the Jewish community but of any human community. If the spirit of Israel is the community of Israel, it is because the community of Israel is grounded in the Covenant with the Holy One. In Hebrew the word for "community" is *e'dah,* which also means "testimony:" the community inheres in its testimony to God, whose presence, in turn, is revealed through that testimony. Therefore, invoking the word of God, the talmudic sage Rabbi Yannai declares, "I the Lord am not greater than Israel, nor is Israel greater than I."[3] Assailing this relation to God that constitutes Israel as a community, the Nazis assail God Himself.

To be sure, in the Jewish tradition the community of Israel is often identified with the Shekhinah, or the Indwelling Presence of God in the world. The Zohar, for example, teaches us that

> wherever the truths of the Torah are expounded, the Holy One and the Community of Israel (the Shekhinah) are present.[4]

As this passage suggests, the "knot" that ties God and Israel together is the Torah, which in turn is often identified with the Name of God, as well as with God Himself. The Midrash Shemuel teaches us that the Torah "is an integral part of God and, thus, all-inclusive and infinite."[5] Similarly, the Koretzer Rebbe, a disciple of the Baal Shem Tov, once said, "God and Prayer are One. God and Torah are one. God, Israel and Torah are one;" and in the *Tanya* Rabbi Schneur Zalman states repeatedly, "The Torah and the Holy One, blessed be He, are one and the same."[6]

One means employed by the Nazis for destroying the Jewish community and with it the soul of Israel was the destruction of Torah scrolls wherever they could find them. Rabbi Shimon Huberband points out, for instance, that whenever Jews were found with Torah scrolls, they were tortured and the scrolls were burned or desecrated.[7] The Nazis knew, on some level, what the Kabbalist Abraham Abulafia teaches us: "God's intention in giving us the Torah is that we reach this purpose, that our souls be alive in His Torah."[8] They knew, on some level, what Rabbi Adin Steinsaltz teaches us:

> *Kenesset Yisrael* is not the passive bearer of a yoke of Torah and law that has been thrust upon it -- it is an active component of the Torah.[9]

One cannot help but recall here the prayer taken from tractate *Avot* of the Talmud, where we ask God that He grant us a portion in His Torah -- not *of* His Torah but *in* His Torah, as though each Jew were himself a letter that goes into the making of the Torah, himself a syllable in God's utterance, which implies once again a definitive association of Israel with the Torah, of the Torah with God, and of God with Israel.

Hence in his diary from the Vilna Ghetto Zelig Kalmanovitch writes,

> A war is being waged against the Jew. But this war is not merely directed against one link in the triad [of Israel, Torah, and God] but against the entire one: against the Torah and God, against the moral law and Creator of the universe.[10]

In this diary written from the depths of the Event, we discover that the Holocaust diarists were all too aware of the profound metaphysical implications that distinguish the Event as a *novum* in the history of humanity and divinity. This awareness reveals itself in direct ways, as one can see from this passage. But it also reveals itself in other ways, particularly in the testimony to the destruction of holy sites and ritual objects, as well as in the argument with God that these diarists courageously pursue.

The Onslaught Against Rite and Ritual

In Exodus Rabbah we read,

> Thus God said to Israel: "I have given you a Torah from which I cannot part, and I also cannot tell you not to take it; but this I would request: wherever you go make for Me a house wherein I may sojourn."[11]

Therefore a primary scene where the assailing of God transpires during the Holocaust is the place where His Name is invoked: in the synagogue. Very often this assault took the form of desecration, whereby synagogues would be made into latrines, stables, or other such facilities: the place is desecrated by inserting into its midst what is out of place. In one of the first diaries to make its way out of the Warsaw Ghetto, published in 1943, Dr. H. Shoshkes writes, "The synagogue has been transformed into a warehouse for scrap iron."[12] More often, however, the Nazis were not content merely to desecrate the houses of prayer but put them to the torch, often with Jews inside the building, and thereby consigned God Himself to the flames. In her memoir of the Holocaust Judith Dribben makes this point by recalling the utterance of a Nazi as he triumphantly gazed upon a synagogue ablaze: "The Jewish God is burnt to ashes!" And, after an *Aktion* in the Vilna Ghetto, Yitskhok Rudashevski laments,

> The old synagogue courtyard is pogromized. Phylacteries, religious books, rags are scattered under one's feet.... Everything is pervaded by the despair of those who have been wrenched away from here.[13]

What has been wrenched away from this place is the Place that is God Himself, the One who constitutes a place of dwelling where the community may dwell. If His presence continues to be felt, it is felt in the form of a despair that is as omnipresent as God Himself.

One realizes why Adam Czerniakow, despite his secularism, labored to save the Great Synagogue in Warsaw. From November 1941 to March 1942 he records his fear that "the Synagogue cannot be saved,"[14] his effort to "save the Synagogue, so far without success,"[15] and his sorrow that "the Synagogue could not be saved."[16] Of course, what is to be saved in the attempt to save a synagogue is not just a wooden structure but a realm of sanctity and prayer, a place through which God may enter the world even as the world is being undone. The assault on the synagogue, then, is not an assault on a building or on a space but on the encounter between the human and the divine that transpires within and thereby consecrates this space; it is an assault on the capacity of this space to consecrate all other spaces in life. If the God who breathes life into the community and thus consecrates it is to be obliterated, then this encounter must be eliminated; if the substance and meaning of Jewish life are to be erased, then the union with God from which that life derives its dearness must be eradicated.

In order to assail God, the Nazis launch an attack on the prayer that joins humanity with divinity; therefore prayer and the place of prayer must be demolished. On the eve of Tisha B'Av 1940, for example, Chaim Kaplan writes,

> Public prayer in these dangerous times is a forbidden act. Anyone caught in this crime is doomed to severe punishment. If you will, it is even sabotage, and anyone engaging in sabotage is subject to execution. But this does not deter us. Jews come to pray in a group in some room facing the courtyard, with drawn blinds on the windows.[17]

Just so, with blinds drawn on the windows, the Holocaust diarist engages his diary. But what descends on him is the cry of a humanity and the silence of a God under a physical and metaphysical assault. And yet, the utterance of the Holocaust diarist is akin to prayer because through it not only does a silence descend upon him but, in a refusal of silence, he himself rises up to stand as a witness to the assault and to the resistance of the assault. Similarly, as the site where this prayer is uttered, the diary takes on a status akin to the status of the synagogue; the space that opens up when we open the Holocaust diary is a realm of the holy.

Assailing God, the Nazis launch their attack not only on the prayers said in a minyan but also on prayers that assume the form of rituals and that inhere in ritual objects. Recall, for example, the Nazis' prohibition against the use of the mikveh. In an entry dated 12 May 1942 Czerniakow notes an occurrence in the ghetto that at first glance might seem relatively innocuous:

> Avril [an SS sergeant] arrived with the filmmakers and announced that they would shoot a scene at the ritual baths on Dzielna Street. They need 20 Orthodox Jews with earlocks and 20 upper-class women.[18]

But on 14 May Kaplan reveals the perverted, blasphemous intention behind Avril's demand:

> Both sexes were forced by means of intimidation and whiplashes to remove their clothes and remain naked; afterward they were made to get into one bath together and were forced into lewd and obscene acts imitating the sexual behavior of animals.... While one Nazi cracked his whip over the heads of the captives, his partner set himself up in a corner with a camera. Henceforward all the world will know how low the Jews have fallen in their morals.[19]

From a Jewish standpoint this incident far exceeds anything like forced pornography. Staging this outrage in the place of ritual purification, the Nazis assail the whole notion of purification as a means of approaching God. Forcing these people into animal-like sexual behavior, they set out not only to rob them of their humanity but to desecrate their relation to divinity. Since the sexual union of husband and wife, for which the mikveh prepares them, is a sacred expression of this sacred relation, the Nazis' desecration of the mikveh, is a violation of the marriage of Israel to God and is an assault on both.

The synagogue and the ritual bath are components of the sacred center upon which the Jewish community is founded. Tied to that sacred center and sanctified by it is the primary component of the community itself: the home. Therefore, in the assault on God, the enemy launches an attack on the symbols that consecrate the home. One of the most significant of these symbols is the mezuzah, which is a sign of the sanctity of the Holy One, who sanctifies home and family.

The destruction of the mezuzah, then, signifies an attempt to destroy the name of God and with it the Guardian of Israel Himself. Emmanuel Ringelblum, for example, carefully notes, "At the beginning of the Ghetto period, men of valor [Nazis] tore down the mezuzot from the doorposts of Jewish apartments,"[20] and Rabbi Huberband observes, "Mezuzahs were torn off doorposts and ripped apart."[21] This destruction of the mezuzah is an assault not only on the particular homes violated but on the very notion of home as a sanctuary for the sacred. For the home is not merely a place where people take their meals and spend their nights; it is the place of *dwelling,* where mothers and fathers and children create a realm in which the God may dwell.

Well aware of these connections, the Nazis take their onslaught against rituals objects from synagogues and homes to the people that breathe life into them. They took Hebrew artifacts and tefillin, says Huberband, and "ripped them and burned them. They confiscated talis kotons in order that they be used by Jews to clean toilets."[22] When a Jew puts on these holy garments or lays tefillin with the appropriate prayers on his lips, his very body is transformed into a symbol of the divine Presence in the world. We are taught that to wrap ourselves in the prayer shawl is to wrap ourselves in the Light of God. Made of eight threads and five knots, the tsitsit or fringes on the taleysim and talis kotons signify the 613 commandments of the Torah: 613 equals the numerical value of the word for "fringes" plus five plus eight. The destruction and desecration of such ritual objects, then, are tied to the assault on the Torah, on Israel, and on God.

If wearing a talis koton can transform the Jew into a symbol, the body of the Jew -- and particularly the face of the Jew -- can itself become a symbol. Among Jewish men, the symbol that distinguishes the face as a face turned toward God is the beard. Thus Michael Zylberberg laments,

> Saddest of all, perhaps, was the position of the Orthodox. They were ordered to shave their head and face completely, to remove every symbol of Jewishness.[23]

Similarly, Rabbi Huberband notes,

> If a bearded Jew was caught, his life was put in danger. They tore out his beard along with pieces of flesh, or cut it off with a knife and a bayonet.[24]

The Talmud tells us that beard is the glory of the face. If it is the glory of the face, then it makes the face into a sign of the Holy One, who sanctifies the life of the human being; when the face takes on this significance, it forbids us to kill. Such a prohibition is precisely what the Nazis must eliminate, if they are to get rid of God. And they do indeed eliminate it by eliminating those whose faces signify the glory of the One who, through the face, speaks the prohibition. Cast out of their synagogues, stripped of their taleysim, and shorn of their beards, the Jews nonetheless continue to be a sign of the giving of signs that make life not only possible but meaningful. Here their refusal to succumb to darkness is itself the symbol that takes the place of the symbols. And the Holocaust diary is the symbol of that symbol.

The diarists' refusal to succumb to the Nazis, however, did not always take the form of a submission to God. While it is lamentably true that some Jews among the kapos and Jewish police resembled the enemy, Hillel Seidman points out that in the Warsaw Ghetto none of the religious Jews wound up among the ranks of the Jewish police force.[25] And yet the piety of Jews who revered God -- a piety that resisted the assault on God -- very often revealed itself not through their acquiescence to God but through an argument that they took up with Him. What we shall now consider, then, is not on the same order as the Nazis' assault on God.

Rather, it is more akin to the condition of the soul that Elie Wiesel describes when he writes,

> God's final victory, my son, lies in man's inability to reject Him. You think you're cursing Him, but your curse is praise; you think you're fighting Him, but all you do is open yourself to Him; you think you're crying out your hatred and rebellion, but all you're doing is telling Him how much you need His support.[26]

When the Holocaust diarist assails God, he does so with the aim not of assaulting the sacred but of insisting upon the sanctity of the human being and upon the divine basis of that sanctity. The diarist's assailing God, therefore, is another means of opposing the Nazis' assault on God.

The Argument with God

The Jewish tradition of argument with God goes back to the first Jew, to Abraham himself, when he argued with God over the fate of

Sodom and Gomorrah. Why did God bother to consult Abraham in this matter? Because, says Wiesel, "God, knowing the fate of the Jews, wished to teach them the need of arguing, even against Himself."[27] Therefore, the Talmud teaches us, "when the Holy One is conquered He rejoices" (*Pesachim* 119a). This ancient tradition continues into Hasidic texts and teachings; Rabbi Levi Yitschak of Berditchev is a good example.

> On the Day of Atonement, [we are told] he once urged the town's humble tailor to speak up in front of the whole congregation; the man publicly made his confession: "I, Yankel, am a poor tailor who, to tell the truth, has not been too honest with his work. I have occasionally kept remnants of cloth that were left over, and I have occasionally missed the afternoon service. But You, O Lord, have taken away infants from their mothers, and mothers from their infants. Let us on this Day of Days, be quiet. If You forgive me, then I will forgive You." At this the rabbi sighed: "Oh, Yankel, Yankel, why did you let God off so lightly?"[28]

What introduces depth to the prayer offered up to God is our love for our fellow humans beings. Part of keeping the Covenant with God lies in insisting that He keep the Covenant with humanity.

In this insistence lies a key to the link between the teachings of our fathers and the outcry of our contemporaries. Which of the biblical figures has been sculpted and placed near an entrance to the museum at Yad Vashem? It is Job, the one who questioned God and His justice and who in his questioning sought out God. Although God reproves Job, saying, "Who is this that darkens counsel by words without knowledge?" (Job 38:2), He nonetheless declares, "My servant Job has spoken rightly" Why? Not because He approves of Job's words, but because He approves of the fact that Job spoke up in the face of what he understood to be an injustice.

The situation confronting the Jews of the Holocaust, however, is more akin to what Emil Fackenheim describes in a story about

> a small group of Jews who were gathered to pray in a little synagogue in Nazi-occupied Europe. As the service went on, suddenly a pious Jew who was slightly mad -- for all pious Jews were by then slightly mad -- burst in through the door. Silently he listened for a moment as the prayers ascended. Slowly he said: "Shh, Jews! Do not pray so loud! God will hear you. Then He will know that there are still some Jews left alive in Europe."[29]

Perhaps the slightly mad, pious Jew would not have cautioned his fellow Jews about praying so loudly, if their prayers had taken the form of anger. Or perhaps, slightly mad, he had determined that the only way for a pious Jew to exhibit his piety was to refrain from all prayers and observances. After all, Leib Langfus, Lewenthal, and Salmen Gradowski -- diary writers from the Sonderkommando of Auschwitz -- "came from a religious background," Nathan Cohen reminds us,

> and all three continued to observe, to some extent, the precepts of Judaism. However, at the time of writing their testimonies, they no longer regarded religious observance as a proof of man's spiritual qualities.[30]

What proof might remain? Religious anger, the anger that is called "blessed." If religious anger can become a form of piety, then, like piety, it must be cultivated; it is not the starting point but a next stage of what begins with a state of despair. Such a state of darkness that may find the light of God only by assailing God can be seen in the pages of Moshe Flinker's diary. On 9 September 1943, for example, he writes,

> Each time I stand to say the Eighteen Benedictions I direct my whole soul to my lovely land.... I see Jerusalem, with the Mount of Olives, and I see the Jordan as it flows from Lebanon to the Dead Sea. And when I pray and do not see my beloved country before my eyes it is as if my prayer had been rejected and as if I had been praying to the wall.[31]

Moshe's visions are not of heavenly hosts but of the Land, which is the symbol of God's presence in this world and of His Covenant with the Jewish people. "The Land of Israel is not something external," Rav Kook explains. "The Land of Israel is an essential unit bound by the bond-of-life to the People."[32] But in the Kingdom of Night such visions of the Land are clouded by darkness and blood that spill into the soul of the diarist and onto the pages of the diary, until all hope is eclipsed and with it all life.

> The moment I stop hoping, [says Moshe] I shall cease to exist. All I have is hope; my entire being depends on it. And at the same time I have nothing.... Formerly, when I took up my Bible and read it, it was as if I had returned to life, as if the Lord had taken pity on me; even in

my darkest moments I found consolation in Him. Now even this is denied me.[33]

The Nazis who assail God assail the connection to Him; severing that connection, they undermine all hope. And where hope is undermined a *why* appears.

This *why* all but dominates many of the Holocaust diaries; it echoes throughout the questions that pervade these diaries. Nevertheless, the diarists do ask, even demand, "Why?:" they are not silent. In David Kahane's diary, for example, we read in the entry for Yom Kippur 5703,

> The Jews of Lvov were animated by a different spirit on the Day of Atonement of 1942 -- the spirit of protest. Prayers were sounded as a reproach. Master of the world, why? For what sins? For what offenses have you singled us out from all people? Are the Ukrainians, the Poles, the Germans better than we are? Are other nations' moral standards higher than ours? This mood did not resemble anything that came down to us in all the chronicles.[34]

The chronicles deal with Jewish suffering that results from Jewish transgression. But in the Shoah, as Fackenheim points out,

> Jews were murdered, not because they had disobeyed the God of history, but rather because their great-grandparents had obeyed Him. They had done so by raising Jewish children.[35]

While the chronicles recount Jewish suffering, they do not contain an account of the enemy's assault on God, which is a *novum* in human history.

The chronicles abide in a relation to the One who is omnipresent, not in the despair over the One who appears to be omniabsent. Therefore this *why* that haunts the Holocaust diary is a *novum,* unlike other *whys* that human beings have raised to the heavens. It addresses the slumber of the One who does not slumber, as when Kalmanovitch cries out, "Awake, why sleepest Thou, O Lord?"[36] The Jews have not abandoned their prayers but have turned them into a question: why? God Himself is gathered into the questions that come down to a *why,* for gathered into this *why* is the *ahavat Yisrael,* through which His presence is revealed to the world. Thus we see Him at work in the compassion that underlies Avraham Tory's tears and outcry:

> I have seen, many times, these pictures of the wandering Jew -- in books, newspapers, and pamphlets. And each time I am seized by terror. My soul weeps. Master of the Word, why? Why?[37]

Even in His absence, or in the mode of absence, God perhaps abides in this question. For this is not a "Why me?" but "Why my brother?"

Yet even if we stretch the language to suggest that God might be present "in the mode of absence," there is nevertheless no one who is with the diarist, no one who answers, "Here I am," to his own utterance of "Here I am." The *why,* then, is transformed into a *where.* Tory, for example, says

> More than once, Jewish history has seen justice being done. Until then we shall extend our hands toward the sky and cry for help. Oh Lord, where are you?[38]

This inversion of the first question put to the first man comes from a member of the Jewish Council of the Kovno Ghetto; it is echoed by a teenage girl in Hungary. Eva Heyman utters her prayer,

> God, it's true, isn't it, that it is only by accident that You weren't paying attention when they killed Marta, but now You are watching over us?![39]

The child's double punctuation of her sentence punctuates her terror over an assertion that she can make only in the form of a question. For the divine absence "by accident" shows itself in human horrors perpetrated by design. If God is somehow to be preserved and life's meaning to be recovered, then the site of that preservation and recovery is precisely the Holocaust diary -- not in its assertion of "Here He is" but in its question of "Where is He?"

One diary in which this question, this lamentation, resounds with overwhelming depth is the *Warsaw Ghetto Diary* of Chaim Kaplan. From the beginning of the Nazis' assault, on the eve of Simchat Torah 1939, he asks,

> Where are we to look for salvation? It seems as though even our Father in Heaven -- the mainstay of our fathers -- has deserted us.[40]

As Kaplan's diary progresses, the question of where God is takes on implications for how Israel might understand its relation to God's word. When God seems to be absent, His word seems to be drained of meaning: God dwells where meaning dwells in the word, and it is this dwelling that makes possible human dwelling. Here too the fear of God's absence expresses itself in the form of a question curled up in Kaplan's soul: "Will impoverished, homeless parents still find the heart to send their children to study Torah? Will the Eternal break His promise?"[41] God's presence is the presence of God's truth; God's eternity lies in the eternal presence of Israel as His Chosen. A lying God is an absent God, and the absence of God means the death of Israel.

In *A Warsaw Diary*, Zylberberg describes one man who sought a way to stir the heavens in the aftermath of an Aktion that took place on Rosh Hashanah 1942:

> The man kept raising his clinched fists to heaven and the poor woman who led him wept uncontrollably and shouted, "My husband has gone mad." "Jews," he called, "give me stones to throw in defiance of heaven!"[42]

Here stones take the place of prayers; when piety fails, the man tries blasphemy, anything to break the silence. To be sure, the dead themselves cannot seem to arouse the heights, a point that Zylberberg makes by way of a midrashic commentary that comes in the wake of the massive deportations from the Warsaw Ghetto to Treblinka during the summer of 1942. Zylberberg writes that

> The synagogues and prayer houses in Warsaw, are now empty, dark and sad. No traditional candles, no chanting, no prayers. The crowds of men, women and children are now assembled in Heaven. Among them are our two religious men, Reb Zalman and Reb Zishe. The crowds neither pray nor move -- they are stunned into horrified silence. Suddenly Reb Zalman starts moving forward, pushing his way through the crowd. He is now less in awe of his old friend Reb Zishe. At the foot of the Throne his cry breaks the silence, *"Zu Torah ve'zu secharah?* We lived by the Torah; is this the reward?" The echo reverberates through the Halls of Heaven. There is no answer.[43]

Of all the horrors recorded in the Holocaust diary, this is perhaps the most horrifying: that God might be deaf not only to the cry raised from below but also to the cry raised from on high.

Beyond anything that a historical document can contain, the Holocaust diary contains the terrible record of this terrible impotence to move the Most High from above or from below. When the just individual can find no help, the dimension of height that confers meaning on being is erased. And yet the Holocaust diarist struggles to recover that dimension by assailing the God on high in a response to the Nazis' assault from below. And so it is despite his own despair and the Nazis' attempt to murder God that Moshe Flinker asserts, "Not from the English nor the Americans nor the Russians but from the Lord Himself will our redemption come."[44] It is despite being faced with "the horrible truth" that Anne Frank declares,

> Surely the time will come when we are people again, and not just Jews. Who has inflicted this upon us? Who has allowed us to suffer so terribly up till now? It is God that has made us as we are, but it will be God, too, who will raise us up again. If we bear all this suffering and if there are still Jews left, when it is over, then Jews, instead of being doomed, will be held up as an example. Who knows, it might even be our religion from which the world and all peoples learn good.[45]

While these words from two very different Jewish children may not have reached the ear of God, they have reached our ears. And they tell us why the diarists assail God. They do so in a response to the Nazis' assault on God, even when God offers them no response. They do so in an effort to sustain the Creation, even when all creation is crumbling around them.

Notes

1. Rashi, *Commentary on the Torah*, Vol. 4, tr. M. Rosenbaum and N. M. Silbermann (Jerusalem: The Silbermann Family, 1972), p. 146.

2. Moshe Flinker, *Young Moshe's Diary*, tr. Shaul Esh and Geoffrey Wigoder (Jerusalem: Yan Vashem, 1971), p. 43.

3. Rab Kahana, *Pesikta de-Rab Kahana*, tr. William G. Braude and Israel J. Kapstein (Philadelphia: Jewish Publication Society, 1975), p. 99.

4. *The Zohar*, Vol. 3, tr. Harry Sperling and Maurice Simon (London: Soncino, 1984), p. 297.

5. Quoted in Abraham Chill, ed., *Abrabanel on Pirke Avot*, tr. Abraham Chill (New York: Sepher-Hermon, 1991), p. 410.

6. Schneur Zalman, *Likutei Amarim Tanya*, tr. Nissan Mindel, et al. (Brooklyn: Kehot, 1981), pp. 15, 233, 579.

7. Shimon Huberband, *Kiddush Hashem: Jewish Religious and Cultural Life in Poland During the Holocaust*, tr. David E. Fishman, ed. Jeffrey S. Gurock and Robert S. Hirt (Hoboken, NJ: Ktav, 1987), p. 44.

8. Quoted in Moshe Idel, *Language, Torah, and Hermeneutics in Abraham Abulafia* (Albany: SUNY Press, 1989), p. 37.

9. Adin Steinsaltz, *On Being Free* (Northvale, NJ: Aronson, 1995), p. 223.

10. Zelig Kalmanovitch, "A Diary of the Nazi Ghetto in Vilna," tr. and ed. Koppel S. Pinson, *YIVO Annual of Jewish Social Sciences*, 8 (1953): 52.

11. *Midrash Rabbah*, Vol. 3, tr. H. Friedman, Maurice Simon, et al. (London: Soncino, 1961), p. 415.

12. H. Shoshkes, *Bleter fon a geto-tog-bukh* (New York: H. H. Glanz, 1943), p. 75. My translation.

13. Yitskhok Rudashevski, *The Diary of the Vilna Ghetto*, tr. Percy Matenko (Tel-Aviv: Hakibbutz Hameuchad, 1973), p. 46.

14. Adam Czerniakow, *The Warsaw Ghetto Diary of Adam Czerniakow*, tr. Stanislaw Staron, et al., ed. Raul Hilberg, Stanislaw Staron, and Joseph Kermisz (New York: Stein and Day, 1979), p. 301.

15. *Ibid.*, p. 335.

16. *Ibid.*, p. 337.

17. Chaim Kaplan, *The Warsaw Diary of Chaim Kaplan*, tr. and ed. Abraham I. Katsh (New York: Collier, 1973), p. 179.

18. Czerniakow, pp. 353-54.

19. Kaplan, pp. 331-32.

20. Emmanuel Ringelblum, *Notes from the Warsaw Ghetto*, tr. and ed. Jacob Sloan (New York: Schocken, 1974), p.152.

21. Huberband, p. 35.

22. *Ibid.*, p. 44.

23. Michael Zylberberg, *A Warsaw Diary* (London: Valentine, Mitchell & Co., 1969), p. 21.

24. Huberband, p. 35.

25. Hillel Seidman, *Tog-bukh fon Warshever geto* (New York: Avraham Mitlberg, 1947), p. 252.

26. Elie Wiesel, *The Gates of the Forest*, tr. Frances Frenaye (New York: Holt, Rinehart and Winston, 1966), p. 33.

27. Wiesel, *Sages and Dreamers*, tr. Marion Wiesel (New York: Summit, 1991), p. 378.

28. Quoted in Harry M. Rabinowicz, *Hasidism: The Movement and Its Masters* (Northvale, NJ: Aronson, 1988), p. 63.

29. Emil Fackenheim, *God's Presence in History: Jewish Affirmations and Philosophical Reflections* (New York: Harper, 1970), p. 67.

30. Nathan Cohen, "Diaries of the Sonderkommando in Auschwitz: Coping with Fate and Reality," *Yad Vashem Studies*, 20 (1990): 311.

31. Flinker, pp. 81-82.

32. Abraham Isaac Kook, *Orot*, tr. Bezalel Naor (Northvale, NJ: Aronson, 1993), p. 89.

33. Flinker, p. 99.

34. David Kahane, *Lvov Ghetto Diary*, tr. Jerzy Michalowicz (Amherst: University of Massachusetts Press, 1990), p. 76.

35. Fackenheim, p. 6.

36. Kalmanovitch, p. 59.

37. Avraham Tory, *Surviving the Holocaust: The Kovno Ghetto Diary*, tr. Jerzy Michalowicz, ed. Martin Gilbert (Cambridge: Harvard University Press, 1990), p. 319.

38. *Ibid.*, p. 285.

39. Eva Heyman, *The Diary of Eva Heyman,* tr. Moshe M. Kohn (Jerusalem: Yad Vashem, 1974), p. 66.

40. Kaplan, p. 46.

41. *Ibid.*, p. 61.

42. Zylberberg, p. 57.

43. *Ibid.*, p. 61.

44. Flinker, p. 73.

45. Anne Frank, *The Diary of a Young Girl,* tr. B. M. Mooyaart-Doubleday (New York: Modern Library, 1952), p. 221.

Chapter 4

THE AMERICAN PROTESTANT PRESS AND THE GERMAN CHURCH STRUGGLE: 1938-1945

Robert W. Ross

At the 25th Annual Conference on the Holocaust and the Church at Brigham Young University, a paper on part of this project was read, the period from 1933 to 1937.[1] What was said then must be repeated. This is not a paper about the German Church Struggle. Rather, it is a paper about the American Protestant Religious Press and its coverage of the German Church Struggle. The initial question is basic. Did this press in its widely distributed papers or periodicals report on what was happening to the Church in Germany under the Hitler regime?

This paper will pick up where the former paper left off with 1938, and will cover through 1945. As with the Jews in Germany, 1938 proved to be a critical and transitional year on the part of the Protestant Church in Germany, now firmly established and known as the Confessing Synod. It must be said at the outset that one major fact stands out, and is reported and repeated for the entire period under examination. The Confessing Synod was the only institution in Germany that successfully resisted the Nazis and Hitler until Germany was defeated in 1945.

Though its leadership was arrested, and most of its pastors were dismissed from their parishes or conscripted into the military as fighting soldiers, the basic resistance group, numbered most often at about 8,000 clergy persons never ceased in their opposition. This resistance by the Confessing Synod carried through to the end of W.W.II in Europe.[2]

Immediately there is a problem: How to cover eight years of reporting to the end of World War II and beyond through 1945. Why? Because the reporting was constant, across a broad spectrum of Protestant religious periodicals, representative of all theological positions through the entire period. Does one cover the details chronologically, year by year? What alternative is there for a paper of this sort? Answer -- To identify and concentrate on major themes and news items that appeared in the reporting being done and being sent to the Protestant periodicals. In working through the data, certain themes and ideas were noted by number. Number 10 is lifted out at this point. This was to note where the sources were for the information being published by location. The list is impressive. Stockholm, Lisbon, Geneva, Germany (by way of the underground), Poland (underground), Central Europe, Religious News Service (RNS), World Council of Churches News Service, Lutheran News Service (LNS), correspondence from individuals, reports from leading figures in the WCC and FCC (Federal Council of Churches of Christ) in the United States, service personnel and Chaplains, and News Services (non-religious). Even in 1944, the "leanest" year, news was forthcoming.[3]

Themes

1. Martin Niemoeller was arrested on July 1, 1937 and placed in a concentration camp.[4] His incarceration and his ordeal were a constant until his liberation in 1945.[5] Rumors, false information, factual information, his health, his family: all were reported in some measure every year from 1937 through 1945.[6]

2. News of the continuing resistance of the Confessing Synod was also reported for the entire period. Leaders were quoted when possible: Theophilus Wurm, Meisser, Lilje, Dibelius, Cardinal Faulhaber (Roman Catholic Bishop and staunch anti-Nazi), Gruber, von Galen, Bodelschwingh, Niemoeller and later Thielicke and Asmussen, and a host of others.[7]

3. From the American side, those who involved themselves in the concerns for Germany and the occupied countries were: McFarland, Leiper, Cavert. Oxnam, key denominational leaders and from the World Council of Churches, Keller, Visser t'Hooft, Schoenfeld, and the powerful voices of Barth in Switzerland and Tillich in the United States.[8]

4. After 1939 when the Nazis began their expansion, concern for the Churches in Norway, Poland, Czechoslovakia, Austria, Belgium,

Denmark, Holland, France, Rumania, Hungary, Greece: i.e. the occupied countries was reported, because Nazi policies for the churches in Germany were applied in these countries as well.[9]

5. Resistance in some (not all) of the occupied countries was also reported, especially in Holland and Norway where resistance was persistent and partially successful. Bishop Berggrav, Primate of the Lutheran Church in Norway became a hero of the Norwegian resistance. Denmark received special notice because so few of the clergy defected to the Nazis. The murder of Kaj Munk, Danish clergyman and playwright shocked the Christian world.[10]

6. The fate of the Confessional pastors became a concern after 1939. Dismissals, concentration camps, imprisonment and conscription were all reported. Conscription was into the military as fighting soldiers, not as Chaplains. (There were relatively few Chaplains permitted by the Nazis, 1 to 10,000 troops.)[11]

7. The closing of religious publishing houses ostensibly "to save paper" resulted in religious literature, Bibles and religious curriculums virtually disappearing for four years, in Germany and the occupied countries. In 1945, the request for such literature and for Bibles was made almost before requests for food and clothing.[12]

8. By 1942, articles were already appearing about what to do for the churches in Germany and the occupied countries when the war was over. This is in contrast to W.W.I, when no such concerns were voiced by American Protestants. By 1943, plans were taking shape both in Europe and in the United States. The role of the World Council of Churches was crucial in these discussions and plans.[13]

9. In 1943, increasing reports of mobilization of clergy from the Confessing Synod began to be regularly reported. The effect of wartime restrictions on publishing, availability of paper, etc., began to appear. Reports continue, however from within Germany, to train laypersons, both men and women, to serve as substitutes for missing clergy, a plan developed by the Confessing Synod leaders. The Watchman-Examiner reported 1/3 of pastors in the military by the end of 1943. At the end of the war, estimates of 4,000 clergy were given, i.e. those who died fighting. Another report states 3/4 of clergy conscripted.[14]

10. Statements from the Roman Catholic Bishops meeting in Fulda protesting Nazi policies, the spread of resistance to all occupied countries, the "joining" of moderate factions in the German Church and the Confessing Synod were also reported in 1943.[15]

11. A major event widely reported and reviewed was Stewart W. Herman, Jr's book, *It's Your Souls We Want*. He also contributed articles to several prominent religious periodicals. A Lutheran clergyman, he was the last pastor of the American Church in Berlin then worked in the American Embassy until the United States entered the war.[16]

12. The *Concordia Theological Monthly*, in January, 1943, published an address by Bishop Theophilus Wurm obtained from European sources. Wurm was among the most outspoken anti-Nazis in Germany, but was never arrested. After the war he emerged as the major leader in the Confessing Synod. Why was he not arrested? Speculation that the Nazis did not want another prominent martyr.[17]

13. While resistance increased in the occupied countries, so did arrests of clergy such as in Bohemia-Moravia and elsewhere.[18]

14. On January 15, 1943 the Archbishop of Canterbury delivered a sermon in the German Lutheran Church in London, honoring Martin Niemoeller's birthday. It was widely distributed in the United States.[19]

15. The successful distribution of anti-Nazi, anti-Quisling literature by the Norwegian underground was reported. Why? Because this literature was being read from pulpits all over Norway in direct defiance of Quisling and the Nazis.[20]

16. In 1944 a number of articles appeared in a number of periodicals devoted to long discussions of plans for rehabilitation and reconstruction of churches in Germany and the occupied countries. These were carefully drawn up plans, not generalities. Consensus was that the leadership in this program must come from the Confessional Synod leadership.[21]

17. Reports began to appear that the German people were becoming much more interested in religion. Many churches were full. Helmut Thielicke's work in Stuttgart is an example. Brought to Stuttgart by Bishop Wurm specifically to teach and preach as a credible theologian at age 34, he regularly spoke to audiences exceeding 4,000 in the Cathedral Church in Stuttgart. This became known in 1945 when letters he had written as a sort of journal were published in 1945.[22]

18. The Confessing Synod leadership issued a 3,000 word statement condemning the Nazis in the strongest of terms. This was widely reported in the United States in the late summer and fall of 1944. Admiration for these courageous leaders was immense, and clear evidence of the continued resistance of the Confessing Synod. Earlier, a report of such a statement from the Dutch pastors was also reported,

which was read in Dutch churches in spite of Nazi efforts to suppress it.[23]

19. Late in 1944, articles began to appear stating that the Confessing Synod leaders had been meeting in secret to plan for the post-war rehabilitation and reconstruction of churches when the war ended. This plan would form the basis for the conferences that were held in the summer of 1945 that led to a new and reorganized Evangelical Church in Germany.[24]

20. Kaj Munk's murder was reported in January, 1944, as was the increasing calling up of pastors in Norway and elsewhere for military service or labor battalions.[25]

21. The success of the training of laypersons to serve as "substitute" clergy was reported on 1944, as was the removing of Niemoeller to Dachau. There he was given roommates ending solitary confinement, and was allowed to read books. His roommates were 3 or 4 Roman Catholic priests. After the war he stated that he had read over 500 books, mostly in English literature.[26]

22. In 1942 a book had appeared, *I Was in Hell With Niemoeller,* written by a Leo Stein. After the book appeared an investigation was conducted and the book proved to be a hoax. This was reported widely, and *Liberty* magazine, which had published the book serially, published a retraction and interviews with Stein under deposition, in which he admitted that the book was a hoax. After the war Niemoeller was asked about Stein. Answer? I never heard of him; he was not in any concentration camp with me. In late 1944, the *Watchman-Examiner,* a well-known Baptist publication, published an article recommending the book highly, stating that attacks on it were the work of the Nazi propaganda machine in the United States.[27]

23. Things began to change with the successful invasion of Europe at Normandy in June, 1944. One by one as occupied countries were liberated, news of Churches from these countries began to appear, along with the problems these Churches faced. Shortages of Bibles and religious literature, extensive property damage, collaborators with the Nazis, who died and who survived among church leaders, stories of heroic resistance: all were reported. Also, church leaders from these countries were free to travel to the United States. Marc Boegner from France visited the United States; teams of American church leaders were sent to Europe to see for themselves and assess the needs, sent by their denominations or by the Federal Council of Churches. In 1945 these reports became a major part of what was reported to the readers of the

Protestant Religious Press in America. Germany itself, however, was still inaccessible. Lutherans were among the most active in this endeavor, as were those periodicals attuned to the WCC and the FCC. Leadership from these two agencies moved quickly to establish relationships with the newly free Churches, while awaiting the opportunity to enter Germany.[28]

24. Before the war ended two things stand out. The first was that a man by the name of Schoenfeld, a staff member of the World Council of Churches in Geneva, and a German, had maintained contact with the Confessing Synod leaders in Germany, often traveling to Germany and meeting with them in secret. He knew of the plans being drawn up by this leadership for post-war rehabilitation and reconstruction of the Churches in Germany. His articles about all of this began to appear in the Protestant Religious Press in 1945. The second was the freeing of Bishop Berggrav, Primate of the Norwegian Lutheran Church by a daring raid by "patriots" otherwise unidentified (20 of them) from his summer residence where he was under house arrest. This happened before Norway was liberated. He was taken to a safe place for hiding. Berggrav, during his house arrest, had met regularly with his pastors at night in a site very near the Gestapo headquarters in Norway, often aided by his young guards. They were changed frequently because he had such a strong influence over them.[29]

25. When Germany was finally defeated, all church leaders in Germany did not welcome the Americans as liberators, as had been expected. Von Galen is an example. He met with correspondents in his residence in the small village where he had been in hiding, after it was captured. He was dressed in his Bishops attire, was less than friendly and his attitude surprised the correspondents who were present.[30]

26. Niemoeller's liberation was major news. After he was settled under American care in southern Italy in a resort hotel, numerous interviews followed. Dorothy Thompson, Bishop G. Bromley Oxnam of the FCC, numerous Chaplains, including one who was his neighbor, and another whose services Niemoeller attended. These articles/ interviews were published widely. Attacks on Niemoeller were also reported, originating from a young reporter for *Stars and Stripes,* the military newspaper. He said he had been present at a Niemoeller interview/press conference and that Niemoller did not fool him. He was, said the reporter, a proto-Nazi. The attack also came from the War Writer's Board, a semi-official government sponsored group that had served during the war.[31] The secular press and the religious press

picked up these attacks and published them. Niemoeller was defended vigorously by Oxnam, Barth and many others.[32]

27. Stewart W. Herman, Jr was sent by the WCC, as its official representative to Europe. The first clergyperson so accredited to the Allied military, he traveled over 3,000 miles in Germany with permission, a military jeep and escort, and reported back to the WCC on his trip and findings.[33]

28. In July, August and September at Frankfort, Treysa and Stuttgart, the leadership of the Confessing Synod met and reorganized themselves as the Evangelical Church of Germany, made up of Lutheran, Reformed and United Church elements. Wurm and Niemoeller were selected as leaders, and a Council was formed of resistance leaders, Dibelius, Lilje, Asmussen and others to lead this newly formed Church in Germany. Offices were taken back from Nazis, or abolished and clergy who had collaborated with, or became Nazis were dismissed. Herman, already in Germany, attended the Treysa meeting, the only American present. Later, at Stuttgart, a delegation from the World Council of Churches in Geneva surprised those gathered by appearing at almost the last minute.

Niemoeller preached. Visser't Hooft and Cavert remarked that it was the most stirring sermon that they had ever heard.[34]

29. Problems of refugees, displaced persons, imminent starvation for millions, multitudes dying, lack of food, transpiration, need for clothing and food, damage to Church property and Church owned institutions such as hospitals, orphanages and old-people's homes and the need for Bibles and religious literature filled the religious periodicals in the latter half of 1945. As noted in SIWT, the dropping of the Atomic Bomb had a profound effect on American Christians and their leaders. Also, the successful effort of the leadership of the Confessing Synod to assume responsibility, and also their public confession of guilt for failing to confront Hitler earlier and more boldly, and a feeling that present conditions were a punishment from God for such failure, appeared in sermons and official statements from these leaders, widely published in the religious press in America.[35]

30. There was more repentance expressed in genuine humility, and admission of failure to help the Jews in Germany. Leaders spoke of these matter right away. Niemoeller's sermon at Stuttgart has been under-appreciated in this regard, for instance.[36]

31. But the major story in the American Protestant Religious Press remains the plans for action taken and determination to carry out plans

for rehabilitation and reconstruction of German Churches as soon as possible. The main message was to restore fellowship as quickly as possible, not ignoring the past nor being too lenient in judgment for failure of the German Church to confront Hitler, but letting German Christians know that they were not outcasts from the world fellowship of Christians. By late 1945 German Churches under new leadership were welcomed into the World Council of Churches, and tangible evidence in the form of money began to flow to Germany as aid for this immense rebuilding task.[37]

This brief summary hardly scratches the surface. The American Protestant Religious Press reported fully and extensively for the entire Hitler era, but especially from 1938 through 1945 and after.[38] My files are full of such reporting awaiting the next step and the greater challenge, a proposed book, companion to SIWT, but on the American Protestant Press and the German Church Struggle. Every item listed in the citations that follow could be doubled or tripled or more, but enough is enough, at least for now.

Notes

1. Robert W. Ross, "The American Protestant Religious Press and the German Church Struggle: 1933-1937." 25th Annual Scholar's Conference on the Holocaust and the Churches. Brigham Young University, Provo, Utah, March 5-8, 1995.

2. "It's Time to Help," *The Bond*, (May, 1945), p. 4 as an example. There are many more possibilities for citation.

3. "Hungarian Bishops Denounce Nazis," *The Christian Century*, (May 17, 1944), p. 630; "Religion Thrives in Prison Camps," *The Christian Century*, (September 27, 1944), pp. 1113-1114; Both of these articles list Lisbon as sources site; "Kaj Munk: Anti-Nazi Leader Found Murdered in Jutland," *The Churchman*, (January 15, 1944), pp. 21-22. Stockholm is this site of origin.

4. See: Robert W. Ross, "Martin Niemoeller: American Hero," in Hubert G. Locke and Marcia Sachs Littell, Editors, *Remembrance and Recollection: Essays on the Centennial Year of Martin Niemoeller and Reinholdt Niebuhr.* Lanham, Maryland, The University Press of America, 1996, pp. 29-37.

5. "Pastor Niemoeller Free," *The Presbyterian*, (May 17, 1945), p. 8.

6. See: "Thumbs Down on Niemoeller, Letter to the Editor, *The Christian Century,* (June 13, 1945), p. 711; "Don't Bring Niemoeller Here," *The Christian Century,* (June 27, 1945), p. 766; G. Bromley Oxnam, "Why Attack Niemoeller?," *The Christian Century,* (September 12, 1945), pp. 1031-1033; "The Attack on Niemoeller," Letter to the Editor, *The Christian Century,* (November 21, 1945), p. 1290. This is Rex Stout's defense of the attack on Niemoeller, from the War Writer's Board of which he was the head.

7. Henry Smith Leiper, "News of the World Church," *Advance,* (November, 1945), pp. 12-13; P.O. Bersell, "What Should We Do With Germany?," *The Bond,* (June, 1945), pp. 2, 5. He names Berggrav, Munk, Meisser and Thielicke: "They and thousands with them stood heroically....;" S.C. Michelfelder, "Steps in the Rechristianization of Germany," *Lutheran Standard,* (December 1, 1945), p. 11.

8. Karl Barth, "A Letter to American Christians," *Christendom,* (Autumn, 1943), pp. 441-472; Rev. W.A. Visser't Hooft, D.D. "Europe in Agony," *The Living Church,* (March 5, 1944), pp. 12-14.

9. "Greece: Primate Placed Under House Arrest," *The Living Church,* (July 2, 1944), p. 5; "American-Born Clergyman Arrested,:" op.cit.

10. "Kaj Munk: Anti-Nazi Danish Leader Found Murdered in Jutland," *The Churchman,* (January 15, 1944), pp. 21-22; "Kaj Munk, Anti-Nazi Clergyman Found Murdered," *The Living Church,* (January 16, 1944), p. 8.

11. "German Church Gains Prestige," *The Messenger,* (July 11, 1944), pp. 14-15. Reports the 3/4 of German clergy have been mobilized; many killed in action; others imprisoned. Those still at their posts, forbidden to travel.

12. A.L. Warnshuis, "Help for German Churches," *Advance,* (September, 1945), pp. 30-31; "Statement of the Delegation to Germany Representing the Federal Council of Churches," *The Living Church,* (December 30, 1945), p. 8; "With Doctors Behnken and Meyer in Europe," *Lutheran Witness,* (November 20, 1945), pp. 383-384; "For Christ and Humanity," Ibid., (December 4, 1945) p. 401; "Shall Lutheranism In Germany Be Saved?," Ibid., (December 18, 1945), pp. 415-416.

13. "Draft Plans for Reorganization of the German Church," *The Messenger,* (December 26, 1944), p. 27; "German Churches Still Powerful Spiritual Force," Op.Cit., p. 26; "Church Has Wide Reorganization Plan," *The Living Church,* (June 3, 1945), pp. 9-10; "World Council to Study Relationships With Germany," *The Living Church,* (August 5, 1945), pp. 7-8. Noted: that Dr. Hans

Schoenfeld, a German on the WCC staff had traveled freely and often to Germany to meet with German Church leaders of the Confessing Synod during the war.

14. Henry Smith Leiper, "The State of the Church: Wurttemburg Evangelical Synod Makes Unprecedented Decision," *Advance,* (January 1, 1943), p. 14. Lay leaders including women, to be trained as "substitute" clergy.

15. "German Bishops Protest Nazi Treatment," *The Christian Century,* (May 26, 1943), p. 628. Roman Catholic Bishops meeting at Fulda also issued a strong statement of protest.

16. "Behind the German Mask," *Christendom,* (Summer, 1943), pp. 407-408, Review of Herman's book *It's Your Souls We Want,* and Paul Winkler, *The Thousand Year Conspiracy.* Herman's book was widely reviewed and commented on. See: "It's Your Souls We Want," *The Churchman,* (June 1, 1943), p. 17.

17. "Religious Conditions in Germany," *Concordia Theological Monthly,* (January, 1943), pp. 67-68, a speech made by Bp. Wurm sometime in 1941, but just appearing in America, translated from a Swiss periodical, *Schweizer Evangelischer Pressdienst.*

18. "Clergymen Under Arrest," in News of the Religious World, *The Messenger,* (October 5, 1943), p. 28. Arrests in Bohemia-Moravia and conscription of clergy in Estonia, Lithuania and Latvia reported.

19. "British Church Leaders Share Niemoeller Anniversary Service," *Advance,* March 1, 1943), p. 111; "Sermon: Archbishop of Canterbury on Niemoeller's Birthday," *The Churchman,* (February 1, 1943), pp. 17-18.

20. "Leaflet Being Circulated in Norway Secretly," *The Watchman-Examiner,* (December 23, 1944), p. 1222; "And Now the Danish Bishops Protest," *The Christian Century,* (October 20, 1943), p. 1187.

21. Henry Smith Leiper, "Ten Propositions for European Reconstruction," *Advance,* (June, 1944), p. 34; Op. Cit., "How Can We Help Europe's Churches?," (May 24, 1944), pp. 641-643; "Draft Plans for Reorganization of the German Church," News of the Religious World, *The Messenger,* (December 26, 1944), p. 27; *The Presbyterian,* (October 5, 1944), notice of a 44 page booklet released by the American office of the WCC on reconstruction and aid to Europe's churches after the war.

22. "An Evangelical Voice Out of Germany," *The Bond,* (July, 1945), p. 2. Helmut Thielicke's letters written in 1943, but just released.

23. "German Churchmen Denounce Nazis," *The Christian Century,* (August 16, 1944), p. 941. Notes the 3,000 word statement of protest to be read in Churches in Germany; "Denunciation," *The Christian Herald,* (October, 1944), p. 10. "Dutch Pastors Draw Up Denunciation of Nazi Ideology," *The Messenger,* (February 8, 1944), p. 27.

24. See #21 above, *The Messenger;* "Germany: Church Has Wide Reorganization Plan," *The Living Church,* (June 3, 1945), pp. 9-10; the plan was made during the Nazi years, and released to the Religious News Service (RNS) in late 1944.

25. "Fifteen Percent of Clergy Arrested or Exiled," *The Living Church,* (September 17, 1944), p. 11.

26. *The Messenger,* (November 6, 1941), p. 21 reports Niemoeller's transfer to Dachau, which took place July 1, 1941.

27. *The Watchman Examiner,* (February 10, 1944, p. 124, published a statement defending Stein's book, *I Was in Hell With Niemoeller,* which had been shown to be a hoax; see: *The Christian Century,* "A Niemoeller Hoax," (December 17, 1941), pp. 1568-1570. The defense was that the attack on Stein was Nazi propaganda.

28. Extensive coverage begins as Occupied Countries are liberated. American religious leaders immediately traveled to Europe; European leaders came to the United States. Cavert and Oxnam of the FCC; Lutheran leaders: from Europe, Boegner of France, Visser't Hooft of the WCC, etc. Example: "Visitors From Europe," *Advance,* (July, 1945), p. 9.

29. "Bishop Berggrav Liberated," *Lutheran Standard,* (May 12, 1945), p. 14; "Norwegian Church Makes Swift Comeback," *Lutheran Standard,* (June 9, 1945), p. 8. Berggrav was freed on April 16, 1945.

30. "A Warning From an Anti-Nazi," *The Christian Century,* (April 18, 1945), p. 485; Count von Galen's frosty meeting with correspondents after his village was liberated.

31. David L. Ostergren, "An Intimate View of Martin Niemoeller," *Lutheran Standard*, (September 15, 1945), p. 7; "Germany's Hero Pastor Niemoeller," *The Lutheran Companion*, (September 26, 1945), pp. 7-8; there were many other interviews published.

32. "Pastor Niemoeller Free," *The Presbyterian*, (May 17, 1945), p. 8. Widely reported in the religious press.

33. "Impressive Activity of German Church," *Church Management*, (December, 1945), p. 55. Notes Herman's 3,000 mile trip around Germany.

34. "Germany: Protestantism Reverses Policy," *The Living Church*, (September 16, 1945), pp. 7-8. A very long report on Treysa and meetings at Frankfort and Stuttgart. See also: S.C. Michelfelder, "Steps in the Rechristianization of Germany," *Lutheran Standard*, (December 8, 1945), pp. 13-14.

35. The list of statements of confession and repentance by Confessing Synod leaders could be quite long. Examples: "Penitence in German Churches," *The Christian Century*, (August 1, 1945), p. 877; "German Churchmen Repent," *The Christian Century*, (August 29, 1945), p. 988; "Guilty: A German Pastor Urges Repentance for Germans," *The Churchman*, (August, 1945), p. 17; "Niemoeller: Says No German Christian Has a Clear Conscience," *The Churchman*, (November 1, 1945), p. 22; "God has made us dirt and dung ... we have sinned...." *The Churchman*, (December 15, 1945), p. 26; Busstag Day prayer, November 21, 1945 in Berlin; "Church in Germany Confesses Guilt," *Lutheran Standard*, (October 13, 1945), p. 12; "... And Then Stuttgart," *Lutheran Standard*, (December 22, 1945), p. 18; "Berlin," *The Presbyterian*, (November 22, 1945), p. 11 reference to Busstag Day prayers in Berlin.

36. Samuel McCrea Cavert, "The New Birth of the German Church," *The Christian Century*, (December 12, 1945), pp. 1380-1381; Niemoeller made a specific reference to the sin of the German people re: the Jews in his Stuttgart sermon.

37. Numerous articles in late 1945 stressing restoration of German Churches to full fellowship. "German Churches Join World Council," *The Christian Century*, (December 12, 1945), pp. 1356-1357.

38. "Bringing Infamy Home To Germans," *The Christian Century*, (May 2, 1945), pp. 541-542. A prescient statement by the Editor of *The Christian Century*. He stated that having German people brought to the camps, help bury the dead, etc., was a good thing because this all will be denied as propaganda at some future time. Today's revisionism shows how correct Charles Clayton Morrison was.

REFERENCE SOURCES

Arthur C. Cochrane, *The Church's Confession Under Hitler.* Philadelphia, 1952.

J.S. Conway, *The Nazi Persecution of the Churches: 1933-1945.* London, 1968.

Ernst Christian Helmreich, *The German Churches Under Hitler.* Detroit, 1979.

Stewart W. Herman, Jr., *It's Your Souls We Want.* New York, 1943.

_____, *The Rebirth of the German Church.* London, 1946.

Franklin H. Littell & Hubert G. Locke, Editors, *The German Church Struggle and the Holocaust.* Detroit, 1974.

Franklin H. Littell, *The German Phoenix,* Lanham, Maryland, 1992.

Charles S. McFarland, *"I Was in Prison:" The Suppressed Letters of Imprisoned German Pastors.* New York, 1939.

Robert W. Ross, *So It Was True: The American Protestant Press and the Nazi Persecution of the Jews.* Minneapolis, MN., 1980.

Chapter 5

OUR DANGEROUS MORAL SELVES: ON NAZISM'S SPIRITUAL-EROTIC SEDUCTION AND THE EMERGENCE OF THE HOLOCAUST BYSTANDER

James Bernauer

How was it possible for National Socialism to be so successful in capturing the minds and hearts of so many either as committed believers or as tolerant bystanders? Fifty years after the collapse of the Third Reich the question continues to demand raising, especially in this season of Holocaust denial. The Nazi period forces all of us to confront our dangerous moral selves: How we fashion ourselves, or are fashioned, intellectually, ethically, spiritually to appreciate or refuse certain types of moral appeal. This is a perspective complementary to the more typical moral scrutiny which emphasizes isolated moments of decision in the lives of perpetrators, resisters or bystanders. The example of the countless efforts to establish a precise order from Hitler authorizing the Shoah is an example of this focus and expresses the very understandable desire for clear markers on the way to a crime of such proportions. While such a perspective has its place, this factor has too frequently overshadowed the way a personal character has been shaped to do good or evil, apart from specific moments of decisiveness. Such character is the product of what might be called practices of the self, practices which define how an individual comes to feel that a matter warrants moral concern and what steps one is obligated to take in response to that moral signal. Certainly it is the case that National Socialism appropriated a ready-made set of national virtues -- honesty, diligence, cleanliness, dependability, obedience to authority, mistrust of excess.[1] Still, if we are to understand why these virtues came to be so characteristic and why people were so prepared to tolerate evil, we must interrogate the dynamics of the spiritual formation which German culture had passed down. We must question our dangerous moral selves. But why should they be thought of as dangerous? A study of National Socialism brings new insight to this question and not just as an historical matter.

To speak of spiritual life at this time might seem to miss the mark when one remembers the brutal reality of Nazi deeds. What has to be faced, though, is that the beginning of the Hitler regime coincided with a passionate desire among the German people for a spiritual renewal, indeed for a politics of spirit which National Socialism attempted to define. On the eve of Hitler, Germany was haunted by the ghostly presence of a deceased generation still calling for some sort of redemption for its ultimate sacrifice in the Great War. At this distance it is difficult to appreciate how promising a year 1933 was expected to become. In fact, Paul Tillich at the time accused perhaps the most prominent of his theological colleagues (Emanuel Hirsch) of associating the year so closely with 33, the traditional date of Jesus's death and resurrection, that the year of Hitler's coming to power was given the "meaning of an event in the history of salvation."[2] What has to be acknowledged is that there was an intense atmosphere of spiritual transformation that year. Philosophers, above all, felt as though a special invitation had been extended to their talents. What this writer finds so chilling is that the map of night -- Auschwitz, Dachau, Buchenwald, Mauthausen and the other graveyards -- was drawn in part by the moods, ideas and plans which grew in a supposed terrain of day and light -- that extraordinary and proud kingdom of German universities: Berlin, Munich, Frankfurt, Tübingen, Freiburg. In the surrender of German intellectual life to Hitler, philosophers deserve a special mention because they enjoyed pride of place in the university world; they were the guardians of the sciences of the spirit, the conscience of the University. But not then. Of the approximately 215 philosophers who held posts during the Hitler years, 40 left or were forced to emigrate during that period. Of those who remained, 45% became members of the Party, 21% of the others joined official Nazi organizations; of the remaining third there was almost no protest with the great exception of Huber, the supporter of the White Rose student resistance. The Nazi State showed no hostility to the philosophy faculties because they were so eager to contribute to Nazi ideology. One observer of the period spoke of a "Blitzphilosophie," to describe the rapid advance of philosophers toward the mission of supposedly deepening Nazism's spiritual foundations and appeal.[3] The conduct of German philosophers during the Hitler years is sorry and shocking. Perhaps the most thorough analysis of it has been put forward in the 1993 study by Hans Sluga. He claims that the conduct must be seen as another chapter in the interaction between philosophy and politics that has had a troubled history since Plato. More specifically, according to Hans Sluga, Nazi ideology succeeded with philosophers because it fielded a series of categories that, while political, also operated as philosophical. These categories were the notions of crisis, nation, leadership and order.[4]

Although Sluga's work is excellent, this paper will focus upon an issue which he does not treat, namely, that those very categories point to a specific spiritual emergency. He quotes the philosopher Baeumler's conviction that the Nazi political revolution "needed to be accompanied and supported by a 'spiritual revolution' in the universities. This in turn necessitated a new thinking in philosophy."[5] But why was this the case? In fact, there was a very evident sense of spiritual poverty in German philosophy that motivated its receptivity to Hitler; the desire to embrace Nazi thought was also an effort to escape a lifeless, mechanistic, increasingly alienating philosophical discourse. Post-Nietzschean, post-Christian German philosophy carried with it a spiritual emptiness that damaged German theology and invited a salvific Nazi ideology. This claim would have to be justified in terms of concrete analyses of individual philosophers and theologians. Heidegger needs mention.

Why Heidegger? He is the most significant philosopher from that period and some of his students have given the most sustained consideration, explicitly or implicitly, to understanding the Nazi episode in philosophical history. Nietzsche has yielded to Heidegger as the focus for study of this adventure. Heidegger opens an important window into the appeal which National Socialism exercised for the sophisticated -- and into the spiritual poverty out of which his need for fascism emerged. Among the sources for him of that poverty were the parochial culture of early 20th century Catholicism and the superficial, rationalistic intellectualism of German university life. 1933 was the year Heidegger temporarily reversed his earlier philosophical judgment about the usefulness of the category "spirit" (Geist) and began using the term which Nazi culture voiced ubiquitously.⁶ Later he was to say that his intention had been to deepen the notion, to "den Führer zu führen," that is, to lead Hitler himself.⁷ The spiritual depths into which he wished to guide German life can be measured on three axes: the hope for a new sense of community; the desire for a form of post-Christian faith; finally, a changed relationship of ourselves to ourselves. The last is the most important because at the heart of the spiritual crisis in German life was the need for some form of self-esteem, an ability to affirm oneself as worthwhile. The urgency for it, if not the sole source, was the collapse of that German spiritual capitalism which Max Weber explored so well.⁸ This hunger for self-affirmation is the leitmotif operating in each of Sluga's categories: crisis, nation, leader, order.

It was to be a religious self-affirmation. Perhaps the most sinister exploitation of the spiritual realm in which the Nazis engaged was the manipulation of specifically religious symbols, sensibilities and creeds. Theological categories were politicized and ideological perspectives sacralized. Basically a religion of nature, Nazism was very adroit in employing for its own purposes Christian notions of God, redemption, sin and revelation.⁹ Hitler had claimed that intellectuals were not "bearers of faith" and could not measure up to the movement he led. In fact, however, his faith turned out to be contagious, especially for intellectuals. As a result of recent scholarly research, we are now able to see Heidegger's effort to escape Catholicism and, thinking in concert with Nietzsche, to articulate a new paganism focused on Volk and Earth. As a result of this work, it has been claimed that it was his "anti-Catholicism -- not, as Farias would have it, his anti-semitism -- that underlies Heidegger's turn to National Socialism."¹⁰ Just as he urged a transformation of the German Volk from a biological to an historical reality, so Heidegger also tried to articulate a post-Christian faith. This would be a German religion, a Volksreligion, enshrining a spirituality withdrawn from Christian signification.¹¹ He abandoned his Christian origins and accepts the death of its God but still cherishes a sense of the Sacred which is focused on the Fatherland. In explanation of this turn, Heidegger pointed to the ever more apparent weakness of a "dying Christianity," what he called its "historical bankruptcy."¹² This was the background for what he said right after the conclusion of the war. He writes that

> I saw in the movement that had gained power the possibility of an inner recollection and renewal of the people and a path that would allow it to discover its historical vocation in the Western world. Certainly, it was

more comfortable to stay on the sidelines, to turn up one's nose at these "impossible people," and to sing the praises of what had been, without a glance at the historical situation of the western world.[13]

As both philosophers and theologians never ceased to remind us, that historical situation was one of crisis, spiritual crisis. But to speak of spirit in the context of a culture which still possessed deep roots in Christianity is also to discuss flesh; cravings for spirit inevitably connect to a discourse of sin, sensuality and sexuality. This struggle provides the fundamental model for Catholic moral formation. Although many have suggested close affinities between fascism and specific forms of sexuality, these suggestions have rarely been taken up systematically, with the great exception of Marxist thinkers.[14] Here we have, though, perhaps the source of Christianity's greatest weakness in its encounter with Nazism, for spiritual pathology seemed to flourish in modern religious culture's approach to sexuality. Having selected sexuality as the privileged route to moral status, the Churches did not create a very sophisticated palette of insight into it. The broodings of moral theology were isolated from the traditions of Christian spiritual theology and, thus, those interrogations of extreme experiences that might have enabled it to cope better with the psychic forces Nazism was evoking.[15] This writer will not repeat the sad series of Christian statements from this period which denounced the social permissiveness of co-education, and its supposed lack of concern for the lust in children and adolescents; nor those which denounced the immodesty intrinsic to public swimming pools; nor those many warnings about the dangers of nudity and male friendships. This determination to exorcise eroticism reveals such a level of detestation of the body and its desires for pleasure, encourages such a fierce self-hatred that we can understand why one of the major resisters to Nazism, Helmuth James von Moltke, found one thing to praise in Nazi culture: it taught, he said, a reverence for what is below us -- "blood, ancestry, our bodies."[16] The pivotal role which Christian moral formation conferred upon disciplining sexuality had two major consequences.

First, it exposed Christians to a Nazism that could be thought of as either ethically allied with Christianity or as a liberation from religion's inadequacy to the richness of human life. National Socialism found the religious obsessiveness with sexuality in moral formation to be helpful in a variety of ways: it sustained the emphasis on those secondary virtues which made people so compliant; it habituated people to an atmosphere of omnipresent sinfulness which seemed to grow with every step beyond childhood; it educated people into a moral pessimism about themselves and what they might be able to achieve. While it has been frequently acknowledged that an absence of German self-confidence was a precondition for Hitler's successful career, the focus of responsibility has normally been given to economic factors; the moral-spiritual dimensions should not be ignored.[17] This was an education into self-contempt, into a fearfulness which was a paralysis of the inner self. All too often the sexual dimension of the person was treated as an animal instinct. Such paralysis subverted self-affirmation as a Christian practice. It is this subversion which lies behind the primacy given to obedience as a virtue, and the extraordinary insensitivity to the demands of conscience. Many religious and moral practices established a profound alienation from one's self and one's desires. And this self-alienation was also a mode of alienation from the public space: the model for dealing with moral difficulty was set by sexuality: avoidance of danger and cultivation of an ethereal interiority. Often this trained people into a permanent submissiveness or stimulated an intense yearning to get beyond the sexual guilt of Christianity, a state which Nazism held out as one of its promises and, in case after case, accomplishments.

Nazism put forward the bold project of overcoming the dualisms fostered by religion: body versus soul, flesh versus spirit. National Socialism spoke to -- and not just flattered -- the German tradition of and pride in inwardness, the "Innerlichkeit" which advocated a strenuous self-cultivation.[18] So characteristic was this tradition that it tended to cut people off from any relation to politics and history; indeed, at times, it substituted for it: if their neighbors to the West could make a revolution in 1789, the Germans could, and did, point to what could be claimed as a far more significant upheaval, Kant's Copernican revolution and the importance of philosophical idealism in general.[19] But the Nazi revolution bound together this celebration of inwardness, of the German spirit, with a profound affirmation of one's historical moment, of one's own German body, social and personal. It was to be praised for its health, its beauty, its utility and, most of all, as the temple for the transmission of biological life. The depth of its sexual morality could be put forward as what is most distinctive of Aryan ethics.[20] In Nazism we have a psycho-politics which is also an erotic politics. While the erotic dimension of Nazism has often been acknowledged, it has rarely been integrated into the dynamism of Nazism as a cultural movement.[21] And certainly one source for resistance to such integration is the desire to avoid a trivialization of mass murder by suggesting it is due to a cause such as Hitler's sex life.[22] Nevertheless, while acknowledging that danger, this writer finds the success and seductive force of National Socialism to be inexplicable without such an integration.

Its erotic politics was a strategy of sabotage against alternative relations to sexuality. It made a foe of the sexual libertinism of the Weimar Republic and of the Soviet Union. The sexual laxity which had been identified in the past with that ancient enemy, the French, now was tied to Communism's relaxation of legal restraints.[23] After it had replaced the Weimar Republic, the Third Reich mounted a widespread campaign of sexual purification: denunciations of pornography, homosexuality and any eroticism not governed by the desire for procreation, for those would eclipse the central status which sexuality had on the "battlefield of life."[24] This crusade against eroticism was terribly attractive for German Christians -- and made Hitler appear as a force for moral renewal to Christians in this country as well.[25] There was even a tendency to look for supporting arguments for traditional Catholic sexual morality in the ideas of the eugenics movement.[26] Thus, on the eve of the Second World War and the Holocaust, Germany was blanketed with a campaign for decency. But National Socialism was far more cunning than most expected. The campaign for decency was by no means unconditional acceptance of Christian codes. National Socialism constructed a post-Christian erotic. While Church leaders were regularly denouncing the dangers of immodesty, Nazi culture was celebrating the beauty of the nude body and the benefits of exhibiting it -- from galleries of art to the joyful gatherings of youth. The Nazis were very successful in portraying Church views as hopelessly prudish, the Church's sexual teaching as unrelentingly hostile to the joys of sexual life and in encouraging young people to look elsewhere for a wise understanding of their erotic desires.[27] One might have hoped that the long pondering about sexual activities would confer upon Christians a particular sophistication in grasping some of the subtle tones in Nazism's sexual propaganda. This writer has yet to find signs of such proficiency. It is as if the long stress on the natural law had made them deaf to the changing sounds of historically contingent evil. Indeed, there seems a special blindness, a general failure to recognize how demonic the unrelenting stress on eroticism's demonic force could also be.

The catastrophe of this moral formation had a second face. In that endless searching after the reasons why the Jews were so victimized by the Nazis, why so many collaborated in their murder, and especially why so many stood aside and failed to do what could have been done, this writer proposes that this issue of sexuality gives an essential answer. Before the Jews were murdered, before they were turned away from as not being one's concern, they had already been defined as spiritless, on the one hand, and sexually possessed, erotically charged on the other hand. In contrast to that special German inwardness which I mentioned earlier, the Jew was portrayed not only as empty of spirit but as an enemy of it. German philosophers worried about what was called a "Verjudung" of "deutschen Geistesleben," a "Jewification" of German spiritual life.[28] The Jewish intellectual was both a materialist and a pharisaic rationalist in comparison with German depth thinking. Beyerchen has shown how scientists such as Einstein were thought of as saboteurs of the more spiritual Aryan physics.[29] The greatest Jewish criminality was in the area of sexuality, though, for here spiritual realities were transformed into matter, no not just matter, filth. Jews invented psychoanalysis, sexology and perversions such as homosexuality.[30] Deprived of spirit, the Jew was defined in Nazi propaganda as essentially carnal, as excessively sexual, indeed as boundlessly erotic, whose conduct was not under the control of the moral conscience.[31] Lust robbed the Jews of reason and thus reduced them to an animal level.

Certainly some roots of the Nazi portrayal are in Christianity: Heiko Oberman has pointed out that, in accounting for anti-Judaism at certain periods, disparagement of Mary's virginity was more significant than such charges as the stealing of consecrated hosts and ritual murders.[32] Still, the extreme victimization of the Jews by the Nazis comes from the position into which they were placed on the cultural field of modern sexuality.[33] First, with respect to the body: the Nazis opposed their view of a trained, classically beautiful body to the Jewish body, weakened by deviant genitalia and unrestrained sexual appetite.[34] Secondly, regarding children, there was the juxtaposition of an idealized German innocence with the Jewish invention of a childhood sexuality that was believed to reflect both an actual sexual precocity and Talmudic allowance for intergenerational sex.[35] Thirdly, in contrast to the image of the German mother, who delighted in offspring and their care, and yet who felt threatened by the sexual advances of Jewish men, especially medical doctors, there was the Jewish woman, who was inclined to neurosis, attracted to prostitution, and craving emancipation from the home.³⁶ Fourthly, Jews harbored all sorts of sexual perversions, especially homosexuality.³⁷ Finally, within a racial perspective, there was a life and death struggle taking place between the healthy life force of Aryan blood and the disease laden Semitic death substance.³⁸ The German's affirmation of the worth of his sexual life was the ratification of the Aryan's people own biological value as well as the pledge of enmity against that depicted reckless and primitive sexuality into which Jews fall because they are incapable of self-sacrificing love. The saga of history mirrors the story of one's personal struggle with sexual temptation; each person's soul enshrines the clash of biological history itself. The very notion of a German-Jewish assimilation was an erotic nightmare in which both the German's individual and social bodies are penetrated by a foreign, hostile sexual force.

It was in their customary depiction of Jews as an erotic flood that the Nazis spoke to Christian anxieties about the sexual climate of their culture. Jews were sexually dangerous, their printing companies even blamed for producing far too suggestive pictures of the saints which were displayed in German homes.³⁹ If we look for the reasons why so few people were untroubled about standing on the sidelines, why so many failed to get involved with the victimized Jew, practically or even emotionally, this writer would claim that this is certainly a major source of that moral indifference. For the Germans who were proud of that spiritual inwardness which was the legacy of their culture and who were humiliated by the sexual war which was waged in their bodies, the carnal Jew represented a contamination, the destruction of the spiritual sense and the eruption of the uncontrollable erotic body. It was to meet one's end as a moral and religious being. In the light of the predominant Christian style of moral formation, one could have predicted that, even while protests were mounted on behalf of the crippled and the insane, the Jews would be abandoned, at best.

Goebbels, Hitler's propaganda minister, claimed that the Third Reich had changed people inwardly, that it had given people the opportunity to escape the bourgeois epoch and embrace a new ethic of "heroism, masculinity, readiness for sacrifice, discipline."⁴⁰ He is only half-right. Perhaps not since Christianity absorbed pagan religiosity had a radical movement been so successful in absorbing common national virtues, which, at times, were even defended by Christians as particularly appropriate to the religious sensibility.⁴¹ The cultivation of these account for how, in the midst of administering the death camps, SS men could be praised for their decency, their loyalty, their truthfulness.⁴² This is how Eichmann was able to defend himself by claiming that he was a Kantian.⁴³ This is why the Nazis made a sharp distinction between authorized and illegitimate killings.⁴⁴ As strange as it may seem, Hitler's biographer, Joachim Fest seems totally justified when he asserts that National Socialism exercised its greatest appeal among those who had a craving for morality. On the other hand, it is not the intention of this paper to stress this: Goebbels is half-right. One of Nazism's genuine novelties is that it yoked this traditional morality of secondary virtues to an ethic which evoked from the German people an extraordinary willingness to discipline themselves and, in millions of cases, sacrifice themselves physically. And it did this by giving priority to the sexual domain understood as both personal and public. In doing so, it established the opportunity for an intense choice of one's self, in the here and now, an eroticism of one's self in time.

This interpretation runs the risk of duplicating the atmosphere of gloom and pessimism which was so much a part of the climate giving rise to Nazism and to the Church's inadequacy when confronted by this movement. Our dangerous selves has been referred to in those ways we construct ourselves as intellectual and spiritual beings, of how these practices determine our ability to help others and our selves. Perhaps our promising selves needs to be added, because this type of analysis does point to the possibility of transformation. What has been described as terrible poverty: the style of a Christian moral formation which became obsessed with issues of sexuality and of lawfulness over it and which, thus, locked up so many of the resources of its spiritual tradition. But this poverty should remind us of potential treasures. There are many implications for both religious and secular communities of this violent twelve year period. Pope John Paul II's recent call for an examination of Christian conduct during this period, as a way of preparing for the third millennium of Christianity betrays an uneasiness about that conduct.⁴⁵ This writer believes the reason for this uneasiness is that, of all institutions and as inadequate as it still is, the Church has performed the deepest self-scrutiny of its response to Nazism. And, as a consequence, there are some, if conflicting, signs that it is looking for a different model for moral formation, especially in the emphasis so many of its educational institutions are placing on works of justice on behalf of marginalized peoples. Such moral formation shifts from a model in which sex is privileged as the seismographic sign of healthy ethical life to the task of integrating the human needs of the historical moment with a personal self-appropriation stressing one's dignity and the capabilities for meeting those needs. The ideal model for a post-Holocaust moral education might be the formation not of historians, philosophers, economists and so forth but, rather, "seismographers of spirit" who appreciate that spirit dwells in and through the bodily.[46]

Notes

1. See Carl Amery, *Capitulation* (New York: Herder and Herder, 1967) pp. 29-34.

2. P. Tillich, "Open Letter to Emanuel Hirsch" [Oct. 1, 1934] in *The Thought of Paul Tillich,* ed. by J.L. Adams, W. Pauck, R. Shinn (New York: Harper and Row, 1985) p. 364.

3. Martin Ten Hoor, "The Nazis Purge Philosophy," *The Kenyon Review* III, 3 (Summer, 1941) reprinted by the same journal in Winter 1989, p. 173.

4. Hans Sluga, *Heidegger's Crisis: Philosophy and Politics in Nazi Germany* (Cambridge: Harvard University Press, 1993).

5. Sluga, *Heidegger's Crisis*, p. 126.

6. Heidegger's use of the notion has been studied in Jacques Derrida, *Of Spirit: Heidegger and the Question* (Chicago: University of Chicago Press, 1989).

7. Heidegger to Karl Jaspers cited by Hans Sluga, "Metadiscourse: German Philosophy and National Socialism," *Social Research* 56, 4 (Winter, 1989) p. 807.

8. Max Weber, *The Protestant Ethic and the Spirit of Capitalism* (New York: Scribner's, 1958).

9. For National Socialism's use of religion, see Saul Friedländer, "From Anti-Semitism to Extermination" in *Unanswered Questions: Nazi Germany and the Genocide of the Jews*, edited by Francois Furet (New York: Schocken, 1989) p. 30. The work of Uriel Tal is possibly the most distinguished in this field: as examples see his "Aspects of Consecration of Politics in the Nazi Era" in *Judaism and Christianity Under the Impact of National Socialism*, edited by Otto Dov Kulka and P.R. Mendes-Flohr (Jerusalem: the Historical Society of Israel, 1987) pp. 63-95; and his "On Structures of Political Theology and Myth in Germany Prior to the Holocaust" in *The Holocaust as Historical Experience,*

ed. by Yehuda Bauer and Nathan Rotenstreich (New York: Holmes and Meier, 1983) pp. 47-75. Also see Robert Pois, *National Socialism and the Religion of Nature* (London: Croom Helm, 1986).

10. Theodore Kisiel, "Heidegger's Apology," in *The Heidegger Case: On Philosophy and Politics*, edited by Tom Rockmore and Joseph Margolis (Philadelphia: Temple University Press, 1992) p. 34. Kisiel's new work is indispensable for Heidegger's development: *The Genesis of Heidegger's 'Being and Time'* (Berkeley: University of California Press, 1993).

11. See Jürgen Habermas, "Martin Heidegger: On the Publication of the Lectures of 1935" *The Heidegger Controversy*, pp. 195-196.

12. See Kathleen Wright, "The Heidegger Controversy--Updated and Appraised" *Praxis International* 13 (April, 1993) p. 93; Kisiel, "Heidegger's Apology" *The Heidegger Case*, p. 35; Otto Pöggeler, "Heidegger, Nietzsche and Politics" *The Heidegger Case*, p. 129.

13. M. Heidegger, "The Rectorate 1933/34: Facts and Thoughts" *Review of Metaphysics* 38, 3 (March, 1985) pp. 483-484.

14. For example, the work of Wilhelm Reich, *The Mass Psychology of Fascism* (New York: Farrar, Straus and Giroux, 1970).

15. See John Mahoney, *The Making of Moral Theology: A Study of the Roman Catholic Tradition* (Oxford: Clarendon Press, 1987) pp. 28-29, 45.

16. Helmuth James von Moltke, *Letters to Freya : 1939-1945*, ed. by H. von Moltke (New York: Knopf, 1990) p. 110.

17. Waldemar Gurian, "The Sources of Hitler's Power" *The Review of Politics* IV, 4 (Oct., 1942) p. 391.

18. On this topic, see W. H. Bruford, *The German Tradition of Self-Cultivation: 'Bildung' from Humboldt to Thomas Mann* (Cambridge: Cambridge University Press, 1975).

19. See Sluga, *Heidegger's Crisis*, pp. 69-70.

20. See Ferdinand Hoffmann, *Sittliche Entartung und Geburtenschwund* (Munich: J.F. Lehmanns Verlag, 1938), p. 51, and W. Hermannsen and R, Blome, *Warum hat man uns das nicht früher gesagt?: Ein Bekenntnis deutscher Jugend zu geschlechtlicher Sauberkeit* (Munich: J.F. Lehmanns Verlag, 1940).

These are respectively the fourth and fourteenth volumes in the important series directed at German youth and edited by Heinz Müller: *Politische Biologie: Schriften für naturgesetzliche Politik und Wissenschaft* (1936-1940). For a general text on Nazi sexual ethics, see Friedrich Siebert, *Volkstum und Geschlechtlichkeit* (Munich-Berlin: J.F. Lehmanns Verlag, 1938).

21. Umberto Eco's recent study of fascism acknowledges the presence of this sexual feature but I believe misinterprets it. Eco writes: "Since permanent war and heroism are difficult games to play, the Ur-Fascist transfers his will to power to sexual matters." ("Ur-Fascism" in *The New York Review of Books* {June 22, 1995}, p. 15). Sexual matters are the very substance of both permanent war and heroism.

22. The danger of such sexual trivialization appeared most recently with the publication of *Liebesbriefe an Adolf Hitler--Briefe in den Tod*, edited by Helmut Ulshöfer Frankfurt: VAS (Unveröffentlichte Dokumente aus der Reichskanzlei, 1994). For discussion of this theme, see Ron Rosenbaum, "Explaining Hitler," *The New Yorker* (May 1, 1995), pp. 50-70; John Sweeney "Hitler and the Billygoat" *Granta* 51 (Autumn, 1995), pp. 85-90; and Robert Waite's *The Psychopathic God Adolf Hitler* (New York: Basic Books, 1977), pp. 232-243.

23. See Laura Engelstein, *The Keys to Happiness: Sex and the Search for Modernity in Fin-de-Siècle Russia* (Ithaca: Cornell University Press, 1992).

24. Hans Peter Bleuel, *Sex and Society in Nazi Germany* (Philadelphia: J.B. Lippincott, 1973) p. 57.

25. See Frederick Ira Murphy, *The American Christian Press and Pre-War Hitler's Germany, 1933-1939*, a Ph.D. dissertation for the University of Florida in 1970.

26. Michael Langer, *Katholische Sexualpädagogik im 20. Jahrhundert: Zur Geschichte eines religionspädagogischen Problems* (Munich: Kösel, 1986) p. 127.

27. Wilhelm Arp, *Das Bildungsideal der Ehre* (Munich: Deutscher Volksverlag, 1939); Langer, *Katholische Sexualpädagogik im 20. Jahrhundert*, 115. For examples of Nazi denunciations, see *The Persecution of the Catholic Church in the Third Reich. Facts and Documents Translated from the German* (London: Burns Oates, 1940), pp. 440, 464, 472-475. The anonymous editor of this collection was a German Jesuit residing in Rome, Walter Mariaux.

28. As an example see Martin Heideggers's October 2, 1929 letter to Victor Schwoerer, included in Leaman, *Heidegger im Kontext*, pp. 111-112. It is also an expression which Hitler used frequently. For example, see *Mein Kampf* (Boston: Houghton Mifflin, 1971) p. 247. Also see the fine discussion by Steven Ascheim, "'The Jew Within:' The Myth of 'Judaization' in Germany" in *The Jewish Response to German Culture: From the Enlightenment to the Second World War*, edited by Jehuda Reinharz and Walter Schatzberg (Hanover: University Press of New England, 1985), pp. 212-241.

29. Alan Beyerchen, *Scientists Under Hitler: Politics and the Physics Community in the Third Reich* (New Haven: Yale University Press, 1977).

30. Herwig Hartner, *Erotik und Rasse: Eine Untersuchung über gesellschaftliche, sittliche und geschlechtliche Fragen mit Textillustrationen* (München: Deutscher Volksverlag, 1925); Barbara Hyams, "Weininger and Nazi Ideology," in *Jews and Gender: Responses to Otto Weininger,* edited by Nancy Harrowitz and Barbara Hyams (Philadelphia: Temple University Press, 1995), p. 166; Erwin Haeberle's "Swastika, Pink Triangle and Yellow Star--The Destruction of Sexology and the Persecution of Homosexuals in Nazi Germany," *The Journal of Sex Research* 17 (August, 1981), pp. 270-287, and *Anfänge der Sexualwissenschaft* (Berlin: Walter de Gruyter, 1983). This assault upon Jews is repeated, often in the same words, by contemporary Nazis as for example in Harold Covington's "In Praise of the Final Solution: Or, Why I Despise the Jews" *The New Order* (April-May, 1978), p. 11.

31. For a Jewish defense against these charges, see Chajim Bloch's *Blut und Eros im jüdischen Schriftum und Leben: Von Eisenmenger über Rohling zu Bischoff* (Wien: Sensen-Verlag, 1935). On the charges, see Sander Gilman, *The Jew's Body* (New York: Routledge, 1991), p. 258.

32. Heiko Oberman, *The Roots of Anti-Semitism in the Age of the Renaissance and Reformation* (Philadelphia: Fortress Press, 1984), p. 83.

33. My treatment of modern sexuality follows the categories developed in Michel Foucault's *The History of Sexuality I: An Introduction* (New York: Pantheon, 1978). I analyze this history in my *Michel Foucault's Force of Flight: Toward an Ethics for Thought* (Atlantic Highlands: Humanities Press, 1990), pp. 121-184.

34. The most thorough examinations of this theme are: George Mosse, *Nationalism and Sexuality: Respectability and Abnormal Sexuality in Modern Europe* (New York: Howard Fertig, 1985) and the extraordinary series of works by Sander Gilman, especially *Sexuality: An Illustrated History* (New York: John Wiley & Sons, 1989); *Jewish Self-Hatred: Anti-Semitism and the Hidden*

Language of the Jews (Baltimore: The Johns Hopkins University Press, 1986); *The Jew's Body; Freud, Race and Gender* (Princeton: Princeton University Press, 1993). Also see Klemens Felden, *Die Übernahme des antisemitischen Stereotyps als soziale Norm durch die bürgerliche Gesellschaft Deutschlands (1875-1900)*, a 1963 doctoral dissertation at Ruprecht-Karl-University in Heidelberg.

35. Allen Edwardes, *Erotica Judaica: A Sexual History of the Jews* (New York: Julian Press, 1967), pp. 106, 180; Friedrich Koch's *Sexualpädagogik und politische Erziehung* (Munich: List Verlag, 1975) and *Sexuelle Denunziation: Die Sexualität in der politischen Auseinandersetzung* (Frankfurt: Syndikat, 1986), pp. 83-86; Dennis Showalter, *Little Man, What Now? 'Der Stürmer' in the Weimar Republic* (Hamden, Connecticut: Archon, 1982), pp. 189, 198.

36. Otto Hauser, *Rassebilder* (Braunschweig und Hamburg: Georg Westermann, 1925); Guida Diehl, *Die deutsche Frau und der Nationalsozialismus* (Eisenach: Neulandverlag, 1933); Bruno Blau, "The Jew as Sexual Criminal" *Jewish Social Studies* XIII, 4 (October, 1951), pp. 321-324; Mosse, *Nationalism and Sexuality*, p. 17; Koch, *Sexuelle Denunziation: Die Sexualität in der politischen Auseinandersetzung*, p. 53; Erich Goldhagen, "Nazi Sexual Demonology," *Midstream* (May, 1981), pp. 7-15; Gilman, *Freud, Race and Gender* and Showalter, *Little Man, What Now? 'Der Stürmer' in the Weimar Republic*.

37. In addition to Gilman, *Freud, Race and Gender*, see Gunther Runkel, *Sexualität und Ideologien* (Weinheim und Basel: Beltz Verlag, 1979) especially pp. 122-127.

38. Werner Dittrich, *Erziehung zum Judengegner: Hinweise zur Behandlung der Judenfrage im rassenpolitischen Unterricht* (Munich: Deutscher Volksverlag, 1937); Barbara Hyams and Nancy Harrowitz, "A Critical Introduction to the History of Weininger Reception," *Jews and Gender: Responses to Otto Weininger*, p. 4; and Jay Geller, "Blood Sin: Syphilis and the Construction of Jewish Identity," *Faultline* 1 (1992), pp. 21-48.

39. Langer, *Katholische Sexualpädagogik im 20, Jahrhundert*, p. 20.

40. Speech given to NSDAP party members on June 16, 1933. Cited in James Wilkinson, *The Intellectual Resistance in Europe* (Cambridge, MA: Harvard University Press, 1981), p. 112.

41. Jakob Nötges, *Nationalsozialismus und Katholizismus* (Cologne: Gilde Verlag, 1931), especially pages 170-196.

42. As an example see Himmler's speech in *Trial of the Major War Criminals Before the International Military Tribunal,* Volume XXIX (Nuremberg, 1948), p. 145.

43. *Eichmann Interrogated: Transcripts from the Archives of the Israeli Police*, edited by Jochen von Lang in collaboration with Claus Sibyll (New York: Farrar, Staus and Giroux, 1983), p. 288.

44. See Raul Hilberg, *The Destruction of the European Jews*, Volume 3 (New York: Holmes and Meier, 1985), pp. 1012-1029.

45. See John Paul II November 10th, 1994 Apostolic Letter "As the Third Millennium Draws Near" in *Origins* 24, 24 (November 24, 1994) pp. 401-416, especially p. 411.

46. Fritz Stern, *Dreams and Delusions: National Socialism in the Drama of the German Past* (New York: Vintage, 1989) p. 119.

Chapter 6

SELECTIVE RESISTANCE: THE GERMAN CATHOLIC CHURCH'S RESPONSE TO NATIONAL SOCIALISM

Kevin Spicer

Introduction

Unless historians can smell a particular world, they will never catch the scent of its order and nature. Arguing to this effect in 1978, Donald Nicholl rightfully scolded historians for their analysis of the Roman Catholic *Kirchenkampf* during National Socialist Germany.[1] Nicholl believed that historians such as Gordan Zahn and John Conway failed to understand fully the world they sought to grasp in their works. Although these historians carefully chronologized the period with archival documents and eye-witness interviews, Nicholl found that they nevertheless failed to understand the "smell of fear which can transform a superficially comprehensible situation into a nightmare."[2] Nicholl then argued that historians must not only totally master the extant sources of a period, but also must place themselves as far as possible into its world-view. Such action would force historians to ask questions that would necessitate them to examine the period in question from the perspective of the participants. Then and only then, Nicholl argued, would the historians be able to "smell" the atmosphere of National Socialist Germany.

While incorporating his own advice into his article, Nicholl allowed us to see how easily the aura of the Third Reich won the support of millions of Germans, including leading Roman Catholic church leaders.

Unfortunately, in this exercise of "smelling" to understand history, Nicholl totally ignored the intellectual milieu of the 1930's institutional Catholic church. In like manner, most English-speaking historians of the Roman Catholic *Kirchenkampf* have joined Nicholl in either willingly or ignorantly omitting an examination of Catholic ecclesiology and soteriology in their analysis and judgment of the Vatican and the German hierarchy's response to National Socialism. The works of Gordan Zahn,[3] Guenter Lewy,[4] and John Conway[5] are blatant examples of this approach. While Zahn incorporated Catholic church teaching on "just-war" to critique the German hierarchy's zealous nationalism and support for the German war effort, he failed to explore the ideological basis of the bishops' statements. For example, what motivated the German bishops to stress Catholic membership in the *Volk* and encourage the pursuit of war? Zahn attempted to answer this question of motivation when he noted that

> all of the values promoted and supported by the Church must ultimately relate to its institutional function: the salvation of the individual and the redemption of the world. Anything which contributes to the salvation of the individual soul ... is taken over or approved by the Church and its leaders. Anything which interferes is anathematized and forbidden.[6]

Yet, in his response, Zahn failed to explore this point in light of 1930's Catholic theology.

Lewy attempted to answer this same question through his examination of German Catholic history. For Lewy, the fury of anti-Catholicism during the Bismarckian *Kulturkampf* echoed anew during the Third Reich. According to Lewy, many German Catholics, including the hierarchy, attempted to weaken this assault and avoid conflict by stressing both their patriotism and the spiritual role of the church. In a similar vain, John Conway, in *The Nazi Persecution of the Churches,* concluded:

> The Church was unprepared and totally unsuited to cope with this situation. Neither the hierarchy nor the laity had the courage or the means to mobilize the Church against the embattled might of Nazism, and thereby to jeopardize the very existence of their own institutions.[7]

Though he further developed this argument by examining several factors which marked the Protestant and Catholic churches' "meager resistance to Nazism," (i.e., the churches' conservatism and the German readiness to accept the existing political order) Conway failed to explore fully the motivating ideological factors that guided the direction of the Catholic hierarchy to refuse to "jeopardize" its existence.[8]

Recently, however, Robert Krieg, in a study on Karl Adam, has attempted to understand the motivations of Catholics in their response to the Third Reich beyond the important, but often repeated factors of *Kulturkampf,* nationalism, institutional antisemitism, and conservatism.[9] Without diminishing the impact of Karl Adam's embracement of the National Socialist racial ideology articulated in his 1933 essay, *"Deutsches Volkstum und katholisches Christentum,"* Krieg portrayed how Adam reached these conclusions through adoption of the *Lebensphilosophie* of neo-romanticism and the budding "communitarian" theology of Tübingen university. Both these academic impulses stressed an "organic-wholeness" that Adam naively saw lived out in the Nazi ideology of *Volksgemeinschaft.* Donald Dietrich has also sought to understand Roman Catholic's accommodation of Nazism. In *Catholic Citizens in the Third Reich,* Dietrich wrote:

> Catholic responses to National Socialism throughout the Third Reich era were motivated essentially by the pastoral concerns of Church leaders and their responsibility to maintain public worship and the efficacy of the sacraments.[10]

In this regard Dietrich has brought forth the most important ideological motivating factor that framed the Catholic church's response to National Socialism: its soteriological mission to the world by mediating salvation through its teachings and the sacraments. Nothing else has come as close as this position to ascertaining the almost muted response of the hierarchy to the Third Reich. Thus, the Catholic church, believing itself instituted by Christ to mediate salvation in the world, had to do all in its power to continue this divinely ordained mission. Prior to this perspective, however, historians have continually condemned the church for its lack of action against the National Socialist regime without truly understanding the nature of Roman Catholicism. This condemnation need not be lifted since the extant documents from the National Socialist period show how the church failed in its prophetic mission to speak out for the Jews or clearly attack the Nazi *Weltanschauung.* Nevertheless, Dietrich's point, which will be developed in this paper, concretely allows the historian to enter into the historical mind-frame of the 1930's and the German Catholic hierarchy.

Only through this process can historians understand, judge and "smell" the actions of German Catholics during the Third Reich.

The tasks of this essay then are twofold. First, the essay will develop Dietrich's observation on the soteriological mission of the Catholic church in the 1930's through an examination of the theology of the period. After providing a theological foundation, the essay will then show how the Catholic church's dominant self-understanding directed its response to National Socialism as exemplified in the *Sicherheitsdienst* Meldungen.[11]

I. The 1930's Roman Catholic Church

In the first decades of this century, many members of the Catholic faculties of theology throughout Germany produced works that foreshadowed the "communitarian" theology of Vatican II. Two individuals in particular, Karl Adam at Tübingen and Romano Guardini at Berlin, defined the Roman Catholic church, less as an institutional, "perfect society," identified by its hierarchy, and more as a communal "mystical body of Christ" that spiritually united clergy and laity with Christ. In his 1922 work, *Vom Sinn der Kirche*, Guardini wrote:

> the faithful are actively united by a vital and fundamental principle common to all. That principle is Christ Himself ... we are His body, *Corpus Christi mysticum*.[12]

Similarly, in 1924, Karl Adam, in his *Das Wesen des Katholizimus*, incorporated this new theology when he wrote: "The Church as the Body of Christ on earth does not consist merely of the authorities of the church, of the pope and the bishops," but instead includes all the Catholic faithful.[13] Adam and Guardini then offered a new dialectical approach for assessing the Roman Catholic church. While they supported the prominence of the hierarchy and the papacy as the administrative organs of the body, they altered the centrality of the hierarchy with the inclusion of the laity who actively participated in the building up and strengthening of the body of Christ.

The Council of Trent's institutional, hierarchical model of Church, however, did not vanish from Adam and Guardini's theology.[14] Instead, alongside their many passages that offered a communal, organic, "body of Christ" ecclesiology, the rationale for the traditional hierarchical church was always present. Adam wrote,

The whole constitution of the Church is completely aristocratic and not democratic.... The government of the Church is ... in the vertical and not in the horizontal line.[15]

Guardini supported this mind frame when he wrote,

It is the structure of values and standards which he (Jesus) personified and taught and which lives on in the moral and hierarchical order of the Church.[16]

This order of the Church, dominated by the hierarchy, "possesses ... the power which God possesses over the creature; she (church) is authority." While sharing a "direct relation to God," the individual "is notwithstanding subject to the Church as to God."[17]

As the bearer of authority, the church, in turn, administrated by the hierarchy, became the unique mediator of salvation. Guardini wrote: "The Truth on which my salvation depends is a Fact, a concrete reality. Christ and the Church are that truth."[18] The church directed its focus then not on the temporal sphere, but on the spiritual sphere -- preparing Catholics to meet God in the afterlife.[19]

Thus, the primary function of the church was assuring its members salvation. The church accomplished this through the distribution of the seven sacraments believed to be instituted by Christ himself. Adam saw that "the first and chief duty of the church's activity is the sacramental mediation of the grace of Christ."[20] For Adam, this saving power of grace flowed from Christ solely through the Catholic church.[21] In his 1918 book, *Vom Geist der Liturgie,* Guardini argued that salvation especially entered the world through the celebration of the liturgy.[22] Consequently, no matter how eloquently the theologians presented the hierarchy's teaching on salvation, it was still limited primarily to the members of the Roman Catholic church who were without mortal sin. Adam stated this fact when he wrote that the church

cannot admit that men can be saved by membership in other societies established by the side of it in antagonism to the primary Church of Humanity founded by Christ.[23]

Adam then restated Trent's limited understanding of salvation, "Outside the church there is no salvation."[24] After he made this stark pronouncement, however, he attempted to extend salvation to those who were not members of the Roman Catholic church. Clearly pointing out that the Catholic church was the sole mediator of salvation, Adam argued:

> But that does not prevent there being, along this ordinary institute, extraordinary ways of salvation, or hinder the grace of Christ from visiting particular men without the mediation of the Church. ...it holds good, even for those brethren who are thus separated from the visible organism of the Church, that they too are saved through the Church, and not without her or in opposition to her.[25]

Though Adam and Guardini attempted to expand the horizons of Catholics through formulating Church teachings anew and making them more inclusive, the majority of Catholics held views that they had previously learned from priests who had received a strictly neoscholastic Catholic education. In this manner, the majority of priests and bishops studied theology through "textbooks" set in apologetic form.[26] Usually written in Latin, these manuals stated the belief of the Catholic church clearly and succinctly without a great deal of discussion or explanation. Between 1896 and 1902, a French theologian, Adolphe Tanquerey, wrote the widely used *Manual of Dogmatic Theology*.[27] This manual compared equally in content with those used in Germany written by Christian Pesch, Hermann Dieckmann and other German theologians.

Upon examining Tanquerey's manual one does not find the nuances of language used by Adam and Guardini. Tanquerey stated that "Christ established the Church as a society properly called, hierarchical and monarchical"[28] by "bestowing on the Apostles the threefold power of teaching, of ruling and of sanctifying the faithful."[29] As successors to the apostles, the ministers of the Church then are responsible for continuing Christ's ministry through the church here on earth. They are to minister to the members of the Catholic church whose salvation is entrusted to their care. With the exception of those who had no knowledge of Christ, but lived a moral life, Tanquerey clearly pointed out that "Outside the Church there is no salvation."[30] However, in contradiction to Adam, Tanquerey continued, "Whoever culpably remains outside the Church to the end of life cannot be saved."[31]

Elsewhere, Tanquerey agreed with Adam and Guardini that salvation is mediated by the hierarchy of the church through the distribution of the sacraments. Repeating verbatim from the Council of Trent in its pronouncements on the sacrament of penance, Tanquerey wrote

> If anyone denies that sacramental confession *was* either *instituted* by *divine law* or is *necessary* for salvation, or says that the manner of secretly confessing to a priest alone is alien to the institution and the mandate of Christ ... let him be anathema.[32]

The Profession of Faith made at the second session of Vatican I also stressed this point: "that there are seven sacraments of the new law ... instituted by our lord Jesus Christ and necessary for salvation."[33]

Therefore, with this knowledge of theology and church teaching in mind, it may be concluded that the pope, the bishops and the clergy representing the ruling, sanctifying and teaching organs of the church saw themselves as the mediators of salvation for the Catholic faithful. They viewed themselves as divinely appointed and ordained to ensure that the Catholic faithful would continually be cared for until Christ came again. They could not jeopardize the church's mission to carry on the ministry of Christ through the celebration and distribution of the seven sacraments by allowing any temporal event to stand in their way. So, to this degree the hierarchy's primary focus was on the spiritual sphere, not the temporal. However, the church's ministers in reality lived in the world and, therefore, they believed they must do everything in their power to ensure their freedom to distribute the sacraments and thereby offer salvation to the members of the Catholic church. In Germany of the 1930's, this often meant cooperating with or accommodating the Nazis. Historical documents and eyewitness accounts often insinuate that this was done for selfish reasons or out of sympathy for National Socialism. However, this author would argue that in their relations with the National Socialist regime and outside the nationalism that filled the early years of National Socialist rule, the majority of priests and bishops were motivated out of pastoral concern for the institution of the church and the salvation of its members.

The July 1933 concordat between the Vatican and the Nazi government revealed the Catholic hierarchy's main concern -- institutional freedom. The hierarchy wanted the freedom to carry out its pastoral ministry to its faithful. The first article stated:

> The German Reich guarantees freedom of belief and of public worship to the Catholic faith. It recognizes the right of the Catholic church ... to order and administer its own affairs.[34]

Similarly, article five ensured that the "clergy enjoy the protection of the state in the exercise of their spiritual office in the same way as state officials."³⁵ In many ways, as theologian Giacomo Martina pointed out, the Catholic church, identifying itself as a visible "perfect society" through its institutions, ministers and faithful, viewed itself as a state and attempted to assure for itself the same rights endowed in a secular state.³⁶ In turn, this would ensure stability and freedom of worship and celebration of the sacraments.

Essential to the sacramental factor was the denominational school question. The Catholic hierarchy realized the importance of educating children in the faith to ensure a proper understanding of ecclesiology and soteriology. Consequently, the Catholic hierarchy insisted upon freedom for its denominational schools while also requesting the same financial support and rights enjoyed by state schools. In addition, the hierarchy requested the protection and freedom of religious instruction in "elementary, technical, intermediate and high schools" for all Catholic pupils.³⁷

The German concordat was just one of hundreds of treaties concluded by the Vatican with foreign governments to ensure the stability and protection of the Catholic faith throughout the world.³⁸ The prominence of the sacramental factor clearly was revealed in Pope Pius XI's reflection on the Lateran treaties. Commenting on the article that recognized the "civil validity of marriages performed in church," Pius said that "he would have been ready to lay down his life for this one Article 34."³⁹

II. The Church, Salvation and the Sicherheitsdienst

The 1938-1945 *Lageberichte* of the *Sicherheitsdienst* (covering primarily Bielefeld, but also Aachen, Dortmund, Koblenz and Frankfurt) are some of the most unutilized documents of this period for the study of the *Kirchenkampf*.⁴⁰ Uncovered in the mid-1960's, the documents provide a wealth of eyewitness accounts, homily excerpts and discussions of German Catholic literature. Perhaps the 1971 article on the SD reports by Donald Wall, questioning the credibility of the documents, led many historians to avoid their use in research.⁴¹ Wall cautioned historians that SD agents, in order to force action to be taken against the churches, possibly "exaggerated the power and influence of the church."⁴² In addition, he was particularly concerned about the lack of knowledge historians have on the agents who reported their observations to the SD officers. Despite these questions, Wall encouraged historians not to "lightly dismiss" their significance.

While Donald Dietrich made great use of the documents in his chapter on Catholic resistance in *Catholic Citizens in the Third Reich,* he shared Wall's concerns.[43] In addition, he believed that "Himmler's pathological theories of conspiracy, of the secret power of the Church, and of its desire to overthrow the state" shaped the final reporting of events by the SD staff.[44] Even with these cautions in mind, however, this author believes that the documents are of great value to historians of the *Kirchenkampf* and in particular, to this paper's thesis. The reports reveal the response of Catholic clergy and laity to perceived and actual repression of their faith by the SS and the Gestapo. In this manner, Dietrich was correct in his comments on Himmler's perception of the Catholic church. Continually, the SS and SD perceived the church's liturgical celebrations as manifestations of political resistance. In a limited number of cases this was true; however, this author would argue that, for the most part, the clergy and faithful acted out of concern to protect the traditions of their faith and the institution of the church. The church's soteriological mission motivated the hierarchy to resist whenever the SS threatened the church's independence. The Catholic laity, in turn, joined in this resistance whenever the freedom of distribution and reception of the sacraments -- their path to salvation -- was threatened. Similarly, the Catholic religion offered a bond among Catholics that made it possible for many members to transcend national barriers. In turn, this point often became a motivating factor in a Catholic's response to the state and in particular, the war effort. The SD reports revealed how the religious bond shared with Polish Catholics motivated some members of the German clergy to promote peace, to call for a halting of war and to minister to Polish prisoners of war.[45] Also the reports showed how many German Catholic laity also accepted Polish POW's and slave laborers into their homes and parishes.[46]

The first three years of the extant reports, 1938-1940, revealed the motivational factors discussed above. Three documents in particular reiterate this paper's thesis. The most explicit was taken from the 13 June 1940 report on German priests in the *Volksdeutschen* districts. The report's contents highlighted the tension between the German priests' ministerial role and their duty to country. The report stated

> that today some *German priests* do *not muster the courage* any more to acknowledge themselves as Germans and to deal accordingly in pastoral areas. Their understanding (of their duties) already extends to the fact

that in the *first place* they have to care *for the salvation* of believers, while the state would have to look after worldly interests.

The report concluded by noting that other German priests made an honest effort at placing their "*Deutschtum*" before "their feelings and thoughts as priests."[47] It is unclear if the latter group's display of their "*Deutschtum*" inhibited their pastoral care of those they were asked to serve.[48] A second example, taken from a 1939 quarterly report, specifically revealed the importance of the sacraments in the life of German Catholics. Discussing the responsibility of Catholic parents to educate their children in the faith, the report noted that those who failed to comply would "receive a form sent 'by the mandate of the Ordinary' which threatens excommunication and denial of the sacraments and a church burial."[49] The sacraments then were so important that denial of them could be used by the clergy to force parents to offer religious education to their children. In addition, a 28 February 1940 report revealed these same themes when it centered on a Catholic pamphlet "Swastika or Salvation." Challenging the state's persecution of the church, the pamphlet stated,

> under the mission of the so-called "state-welfare," the National Socialist governmental system has recently deemed it necessary to restrict the freedom of its citizens to practice religion and to proclaim God's word.[50]

The pamphlet then continued by encouraging Catholics to resist the state in its repression of the spiritual life of the church.

Was there really a reason for German Catholics to resist the state? Were the sacraments and the ministerial freedom of the church in question? Most of the restrictions placed on Catholics and their organizations were related to the war effort or developed out of the process of *Gleichschaltung*. One of the greatest concerns for the SD agents were feast days that required Catholic workers to leave their jobs and attend mass and participate in religious processions.[51] On 7 May 1940, troubled by the loss of workers in the factories during the war, the government issued a decree prohibiting the celebration of Corpus Christi, normally held on a Thursday, as a state holiday. Though viewing the decree as an attack on Catholicism, the German bishops recognized the prohibition by moving the eucharistic procession to a Sunday. However, the bishops also stated that the faithful were obligated to attend church on the feast day and "the one who did not attend church, commits a sin."⁵² In turn, the SD viewed Catholics' observance of the feast day as political resistance against the state.⁵³ This same pattern repeated itself in the religious school question and in the dissolution of Catholic organizations. The Nazis understanding of *Volksgemeinschaft* did not allow room for separate organizations for each denomination. Instead of separate Catholic and Protestant youth organizations, there was to be one united youth organization -- the Hitler Youth.⁵⁴ Similarly, instead of a separate Catholic schools system, the Nazis Ministry of Education wanted one joined "*Gemeinschaftsschule.*"⁵⁵ Unfortunately, these unified organizations did not include time nor space for traditional Catholic practices and religious instructions. Of course, the state wanted the churches to limit religious practice and education to the confines of the parish and its solely religious organizations. The hierarchy, in turn, viewed this exclusion as religious persecution. Even when the state began to accommodate the hierarchy's desire to reinstate religious instruction in community schools where it had been removed, the clergy and laity together developed religious instruction programs of their own outside of the schools.⁵⁶ Thus, by 1940, if not before, the trust level between the Nazi regime and the Catholic hierarchy and active Catholic laity had been broken. Many Catholic clergy found themselves unable to entrust the children's religious education -- to learn what was necessary for salvation -- to state appointed teachers.

III. Conclusion

This paper has shown that the Catholic church, as administrated by its hierarchy, identified itself as the divine mediator of salvation whose chief responsibility was to administer the sacraments and direct church institutions as their concrete way of continuing Christ's ministry on earth. Promulgating the church's teachings and fostering a ministry to prepare its members for the afterlife, the church's hierarchy was not always able to clearly discern the secular events of the world from the spiritual. In 1933, for example, this factor led the hierarchy of the Catholic church to conclude a concordat with Nazi Germany. Much of what the church believed it had gained through the treaty -- freedom to practice the faith and protection of religious institutions and associations -- was soon deemed as "political" and oppositional to the government. Gradually, however, through state and local decrees, the National Socialist government attempted to force the church to remain within its parish boundaries and concern itself solely with the spiritual welfare of its members. In reaction to this, the hierarchy broadly defined this spiritual realm, including any factor in an individual's life which might prevent him or her from receiving eternal salvation. The church only challenged the state when it believed the state had infringed upon its ministerial freedom and its soteriological mission. As a result, seldom did the church -- the hierarchy and the laity -- resist the Nazi state for any moral or political reason other than to protect itself and to preserve its ministerial and sacramental function.

Did the church, on this account, accommodate Nazism? The answer to this question is yes. The church accommodated Nazism to protect its own divinely perceived mission. In this manner, the church accommodated Nazism to the extent that Nazism accommodated the church. Consequently, while many individual clerics and Catholic laity actively supported the state and participated in the Nazi mechanisms of death, the church as a transcendental institution used Nazism as it did any other form of government that allowed it to exist in a country and fulfill its divine mission. As the theologians in the second section of this paper pointed out, the church therefore saw itself as a "perfect society" equal as a secular state in all areas. Thus, as a "perfect society" with a divine mission, the church only needed recognition of its canon law and freedom to mediate salvation for its members. Beyond this point, the church saw herself free from the state. Thus, when the Vatican signed the concordat with the Nazi state, the papacy claimed a victory for the Catholic church in Germany. Likewise, Dr. Buttmann from the Ministry of the Interior and Hermann Göring, President-Minister of Prussia and special liaison to the Vatican during the early years of Nazism, claimed a victory for the Nazi state. Indeed, the Nazi regime had won recognition by the Vatican and an end to political Catholicism.[57] In the end, however, the political liability of the church and its interference in Nazi policies and programs, i.e., Hitler Youth, community schools, and the racial purity laws (sterilization and euthanasia) hindered the cooperation between the state and the church. Unfortunately, this hindrance never took the form of open political resistance, but remained linked to the preservation of Catholic dogma and institution.

Where then is the blame to be placed for the silence of the institutional church when it was faced with the horrors of the Holocaust and the policies of the National Socialist state? One may choose to condemn the papacy or individual bishops and priests. Ultimately, however, the documents and argument of this essay place the blame squarely on the shoulders of the Catholic self-understanding of the 1930's -- its pre-Vatican II dogmatic teaching on ecclesiology and soteriology. Such a teaching limited the "religious activity" of the church to a purely parochial form of salvation, one that overcharged private salvation over ministerial service; one that put its particular institutional privilege and personal survival above the call to serve all people. Such a teaching ultimately failed to integrate the biblical, liturgical, ecclesial and social dimensions of church life into its structures. That, in turn, would have enabled the church to be the light of all nations and the refuge of all outcasts in the 1930's.

Notes

1. Donald Nicholl, "The Smell of Fear: The Catholic Church and the Nazis 1" *The Tablet* 248 (1994), 914-916, reprint of his 1978 *Christian* magazine article.

2. Nicholl, p. 914.

3. See Gordon Zahn, *German Catholics and Hitler's Wars* (New York: Sheed and Ward, 1962).

4. See Guenter Lewy, *The Catholic Church and Nazi Germany* (New York: McGraw-Hill, 1964).

5. See John S. Conway, *The Nazi Persecution of the Churches 1933-45* (New York: Basic Books, 1968).

6. Zahn, p. 28.

7. Conway, p. 331.

8. See Conway, pp. 334-336. Mary Alice Gallin also followed this pattern when she wrote: [Faulhaber's] opposition was severely limited. Intellectually unable to comprehend the political realities of a totalitarian state, he failed to understand that a defense of ecclesiastical interests alone would ultimately be no substitute for the church's real obligation to the world and to humanity," in her article "The Cardinal and the State: Faulhaber and the Third Reich," *Journal of Church and State* 12 (1970), p. 386. She, however, fails to explore the theological ramifications of her statement "intellectually unable to comprehend." Ethel Mary Tinnemann made similar statements in her articles: "German Catholic Bishops' Knowledge of Nazi Extermination of Jews," in *Holocaust*

Studies Annual 1990, 35-51 and "The German Catholic Bishops and the Jewish Question: Explanation and Judgment," *Holocaust Studies Annual* 1984, 55-85.

9. Robert Anthony Krieg, *Karl Adam. Catholicism in German Culture* (Indiana: Notre Dame, 1992).

10. Donald Dietrich, *Catholic Citizens in the Third Reich. Psycho-Social Principles and Moral Reasoning* (New Brunswick: Transaction Books, 1988), p. 112.

11. Heinz Boberach, ed., *Meldungen aus dem Reich. Die geheimen Lageberichte des Sicherheitsdienstes der SS 1938-1945.* 17 volumes (Herrsching: Manfred Pawlak, 1984). Hereinafter Meldungen.

12. Romano Guardini, *The Church and the Catholic and the Spirit of the Liturgy* trans. Ada Lane (London: Sheed and Ward, 1935), p. 142.

13. Karl Adam, *The Spirit of Catholicism* trans. Justin McCann (London: Sheed and Ward, 1929), pp. 97-98.

14. See chapter two "The Church as Institution" of Avery Dulles, *Models of the Church* (New York: Image, 1978), pp. 15-33 for a discussion of an institutional model of church.

15. Adam, p. 20.

16. Guardini, p. 64. Guardini would continue to struggle between an acceptance of an institutional or a communal or even sacramental model of church. This is evidenced in his posthumous work *Berichte über mein Leben. Autobiographische Aufzeichnungen* (Düsseldorf: Patmos, 1985), p. 88. Here Guardini wrote: "Und nun meinten Karl Neundörfer und ich, das Leben der Kirche müsse vor allem von zwei Seiten her faßbar sein: der soziologisch-juridischen, als Gemeinschaft des Handelns und Kämpfens -- und der liturgischen, als der Einheit des kontemplativen, schauenden, betenden Tuns." And now Karl Neudörfer and I believed, the life of the church must be comprehensible before all on two sides: the socio-juridical, as the community of deed and struggle -- and the liturgical, as the unity of the contemplative, observing, prayerful action. (All translations made in this work are by the author.)

17. Guardini, *The Church and the Catholic and the Spirit of the Liturgy,* p. 42.

18. Guardini, p. 52.

19. Guardini, p. 75. Guardini further clarified this point when he wrote: And we are concerned with man's destiny which depends on this Divine Reality -- the salvation of his soul. That the State should be well ordered is, of course, of great importance, and so is a well-constructed system of the natural sciences; but in the last resort we can dispense with both. But the values bound up with the Church are as indispensable on the spiritual plane as food in the physical order. Life itself depends upon them. (Guardini, p. 50).

20. Adam, p. 179.

21. Adam, p. 169.

22. Guardini, *The Church and the Catholic and the Spirit of the Liturgy*, p. 197. The two essays were translated and published together for the English edition.

23. Adam, p. 159.

24. Adam, p. 161.

25. Adam, p. 170.

26. Michael Fahey offers a discussion of neo-scholastic theology in his article on "Church" in *Systematic Theology: Roman Catholic Perspectives* v. II, Francis Schüssler Fiorenza and John Galvin, eds. (Minneapolis: Fortress, 1991), pp. 30-33.

27. An English translation of the manual appeared in 1959: Adolphe Tanquerey, *A Manual of Dogmatic Theology* 2 vol., trans. John J. Byres (New York: Descry, 1959). A brief biography and description of Tanquerey's life may be found in *The New Catholic Encyclopedia* (New York: Mac Raw-Hill, 1967), p. 934.

28. Tanquerey I, p. 104.

29. Tanquerey I, p. 107.

30. Tanquerey I, p. 138.

31. Tanquerey I, p. 139.

32. Tanquerey II, p. 313.

33. Norman P. Tanner, ed. *Decrees of the Ecumenical Councils* Vol. II, (Washington, DC: Sheed and Ward, 1990), p. 803.

34. Peter Matheson, *The Third Reich and the Christian Churches* (Edinburgh: T & T Clark, 1981), p. 30.

35. Matheson, p. 30.

36. Giacomo Martina, "The Historical Context in Which the Idea of a New Ecumenical Council Was Born" in *Vatican II. Assessment and Perspectives. Twenty-Five Years After (1962-1987)* Vol. 1, René Latourelle, ed. (New York: Paulist Press, 1988), pp. 16-17.

37. Matheson, pp. 31-32.

38. See Anthony Rhodes, *The Vatican in the Age of the Dictators 1922-1945* (New York: Holt, Rinehart and Winston, 1974).

39. Klaus Scholder, *The Churches and the Third Reich. Preliminary History and the Time of Illusions 1918-1934* vol. I (Philadelphia: Fortress, 1988), p. 163.

40. For discussions on the history of the documents see Meldungen, pp. 11-40; Heinz Boberach, ed. *Berichte des SD und der Gestapo über Kirchen und Kirchenvolk in Deutschland 1934-1944* (Mainz: Matthias-Grünewald, 1971, pp. xxix-xliii and Donald D. Wall, "The Reports of the *Sicherheitsdienst* on the Church and Religious Affairs in Germany, 1939-1944," *Church History* 40 (1971), pp. 437-456.

41. Wall, pp. 437-456.

42. Wall, p. 440.

43. Dietrich, pp. 259-293.

44. Dietrich, p. 261.

45. In 1866, a similar bond united German and Austrian Catholics during the Austrian-Prussian War. On this point see Jonathan Sperber, *Popular Catholicism in Nineteenth-Century Germany* (New Jersey: Princeton, 1984), pp. 156-159.

46. Meldungen, 25 October 1939, p. 390; 6 November 1939, p. 422; 11 December 1939, p. 555; 31 January 1940, p. 708; 6 March 1940, p. 843; and 8 April 1940, p. 967.

47. Meldungen,13 June 1940, pp. 1260-1261. "(Anderseits wird jedoch aus volksdeutschen Kreisen auch darauf hingewiesen,) daß verschiedene *deutsche Geistliche* heute schon *nicht mehr den Mut* aufbringen, sich in jeder Hinsicht als *Deutsche zu bekennen* und auf seelsorgerischem Gebiet dementsprechend zu behandeln. *Ihre Auffassung* gehe bereits dahin, daß sie in *erester Linie für das Seelenheil* der Gläubigen zu sorgen haben, während die irdischen Belange der Staat wahrzunehmen habe. (Dies gebe den Tschechen einen enormen Auftrieb hinsichtlich der langsamen aber sicheren Ausschaltung der Einflußnahme der deutschen Priester, die sich erlich bemühen, ihr Deutschtum) voranzustellen dem Fühlen und Denken als Priester voranzustellen."

48. This would not be the first time that such instances have been recorded. See chapter six "Protestants, Catholics, and Poles: Religious and Nationality Conflicts in the Empire's Ethnically mixed Areas, 1897-1914 in Helmut Walser Smith, *German Nationalism and Religious Conflict. Culture, Ideology, Politics, 1870-1914* (New Jersey: Princeton, 1995), pp. 167-205 In this chapter, Smith showed how nationalism encouraged the German Catholic clergy in Eastern Prussian to "Germanize" their pastoral care to Poles. This took the form of the exclusive use of the German language in homilies and church publications and a favoring in parishes of German cultural and religious festivals over Polish ones.

49. Meldungen, 1939 Quarterly Report, p. 230. "(Bei Versäumnissen erhielten bereits verschiedentlich die Eltern) einen Vordruck 'im Auftrage des Ordinariats' zugeschickt, in dem ihnen die Excommunikation angedroht, der Empfang der Sakramente und die kirchliche Beerdigung verweigert wird."

50. Meldungen, 28 February 1940, p. 819. "(Wenn auch in verschiedenen Formen, sowohl das kommunistische) als auch das nationalsozialistische Regierungssystem haben es unter Berufung auf das sogenannte 'Staatswohl' für notwendig erachtet, die Freiheit ihrer Bürger im Hinblick auf die religiöse Praxis und hinsichtlich der Verkündigung von Gottes Wort einzuschränken."

51. See the detailed report on the celebrations and processions accompanying St. Mark's feast day on April 25 in Meldungen, 6 May 1940, p. 1100.

52. Meldungen, 6 June 1940, p. 1232. "(Sein Besuch ist Pflicht;) wer die Kirche nicht besucht, begeht eine Sünde." They added "*Es darf nicht gearbeitet werden.*" (Emphasis in the original.)

53. See similar concerns voiced in Meldungen, 1938 Yearly Report, pp. 32, 33, 37, 43; 1939 Quarterly Report, p. 215.

54. See Lawrence D. Walker, *Hitler Youth and Catholic Youth 1933-1936. A Study in Totalitarian Conquest* (Washington, D.C.: Catholic University, 1970) for the history of the Catholic Youth organizations during the early years of Nazi rule.

55. See Meldungen, 7 November 1940, p. 1742, for the report on how difficult a process it was to keep separate denominational schools open in small villages.

56. Meldungen, 25 July 1940, p. 1417.

57. See Scholder I, pp. 381-413.

Chapter 7

CONTRACT vs. COVENANT IN POST-HOLOCAUST THEOLOGY AND SOCIETY

W. Royce Clark

During the twenty-six years between Richard Rubenstein's first and second editions of his provocatively profound *After Auschwitz*, he expanded his methodology beyond theology and psychology, to include more history, sociology, and political theory. In his second edition, he positions his penetrating theology of the Holocaust within his larger concerns of human nature, genocide in general, and public policy. It is precisely because this rigorously honest book has stimulated this writer to more thought over the years -- about the Holocaust, human nature, religion, and "God" -- than nearly any other, that this brief suggestion toward clarification is offered.

Rubenstein's extensive contact with Japanese culture subsequent to his first edition reassured him of the validity of his emphasis on the *immanence* of God as well as his idea of "God" as "Holy Nothingness." Paradoxically, he admits, it simultaneously deepened his respect for the ideas of *covenant* and faith in the *transcendence* of God,[1] despite his rejection of the Jewish idea of being God's chosen people. He wrote, "My experience in Japan prodded me to reflect on the *functional truth* of the biblical idea of covenant. Unlike the United States with its biblical heritage, Japan has no way of incorporating the stranger within its midst." (xvi)

In a world of diversity it is normal for people to seek others who have similar views or to discriminate against others. Nevertheless, to do so on a grand scale fosters isolationism and a "cognitive monopoly."

A cognitive monopoly, in times of social-economic crises, often motivates a majority to be intolerant of minorities, which can result in genocide. Because a cognitive monopoly promotes the law of the majority, if genocide results, even it is not perceived by the majority as irrational or illegal, but as a logical remedy to preserve order by removing redundant or competitive populations.[2]

To prevent genocide the cognitive monopoly must be eliminated by encouraging diversity and social solidarity, the value of persons rather than particular religious myths and ideologies (ch. 2). This "I-Thou" (Buber) treatment of the "other" must be formalized socially in a "covenant" between the disparate parties. *"Want of a covenant or its functional equivalent has been a moral precondition for genocide in both ancient and modern times"* (149). Since the parties regard each other as equal under the covenant, no one has to prove his or her worth to anyone allegedly in a position of superiority or conversely has to adjust to people presumed to occupy inferior status (14-15). *Without* such a covenant, Rubenstein warns, other motivations for organizing communities such as racism will prevail with sinister dehumanization (147-48).

He thinks the covenant God made with Israel at Sinai stands as a paradigm for uniting diverse peoples by expressing their common interest in ridding themselves of their overlords. The ancestral gods and the god-king of Egypt could be overturned only by a God who was somehow part of the shared experience of this diverse people, later called "Israel." By the emphasis upon their value as free human beings, despite being outcasts or fugitives, this covenant in which God elected them as His people, "overturned all existing social hierarchies, in principle if not yet in fact," by giving priority to ethical concerns rather than racial or political (142-144).

When Rubenstein emphasizes, however, that we must treat each other as persons rather than conform to some caricature based on religious myth, he insists the "rational society of contract" is too abstract. It tends to allow if not spawn depersonalization and dehumanization. The worst example of this is when the vocabulary of mass murder is so sterilized by terms like *Lósungsmóglikeit, Sonderbehandlung,* and *Evakuierung* that it is possible to ignore the fact that human beings are being annihilated" (26). Even in "less pathological forms, such an abstract society runs counter to our earliest and most decisive experiences of social encounter, which are emotionally determined" (26). Rubenstein insists,

Neither the abstractions of a depersonalized secular society nor the dehumanizing myths of a religious society are ultimately conducive to that community of persons which alone offers hope that the fragile human enterprise will not break asunder through its own inner failure (26).

To avoid depersonalizing and dehumanizing citizens, it is necessary to retain the "religious factor," not a mere contract. The source demanding the unity between the parties would be "God" rather than simply human initiative.[3] Rubenstein says "What is needed today is an institution [covenant] similar to that which enabled the Hebrews to unite under God at Sinai, a binding basis for community between men and women who share little but mutual distrust and fear" (152).

There appears to be a problem here since Rubenstein insists that we live in the "time of the death of God" (ch. 14), and "God" -- "Holy Nothingness" (301), or the equivalent to the Buddhist understanding of Sunyata or Emptiness (305) -- although perhaps the general Ground of history, Rubenstein insists, does *not intervene* in history to punish anyone.[4] What does this do to social structures? Human rights do not exist. Only political rights.

In reality, without God there are no human rights; there are only political rights. That is why the question, "Who is to have a voice in the political community?" is the fundamental human question in our era. Membership in a political community is no absolute guarantee of safety. Nevertheless, to the extent that men and women have any rights whatsoever, it as members of a political community with the power to guarantee those rights. This was clearly evident in the fate of the Armenians in Turkey during World War I and the Jews of Europe during World War II. Genocide is the ultimate expression of absolute rightlessness (138).

If Rubenstein is correct, and God is not available to establish human rights in our modern world, then how can the answer to cognitive monopoly and genocide be God establishing a "covenant" between diverse peoples? If "God" is experienced in any way in the covenant process, that would establish "human rights." Or if the covenant is only between the diverse parties and not "God," how does one feel any categorical imperative to honor such a covenant other than fear of the other parties? How is that different from a "contract" that Rubenstein wants to avoid, and how does it prevent dehumanization? If the majority fear neither minorities nor "God," or if the majority's religious imagination conjures up its "God" as demanding the decimation of minorities, such a "covenant" is impotent to prevent the slaughter. Or is the only "transcendent" element reinforcing the covenant a stockpile of nuclear weapons rather than "God" or mutual humane treatment?[5] Whether the binding element is a "covenant" or "contract," the crucial question is what in Rubenstein's view is the matrix which guarantees mutually humane treatment among diverse peoples. To answer this requires clarifying the slight ambiguities within Rubenstein's ideas of "covenant," "religion," and "God."

As we examine these three areas, we will find that the main thrust of Rubenstein's theology, despite his negative view of the modern world of "contract," actually demands more a "social contract" between *all* parties than a mere "covenant" between God and a few diverse peoples. John Rawls' understanding of a fair social contract is that it requires the priority of equality of *all* persons as well as the prohibition of parties to use metaphysical claims to gain personal advantage. If "contract" could be understood this way, it is very compatible with Rubenstein's emphasis on the "I-Thou" relation and the necessity for social solidarity through diluting the religio-mythical caricatures of the "other," and avoids the danger of a "covenant" being made only between a few diverse peoples and their "God."

I. Rubenstein's Analysis of "Covenant"

The primary function of "covenant," according to Rubenstein, is to give political voice to all. In that sense, it operates very much as a "social contract" rather than a covenant merely between God and "God's people." To illustrate how the lack of covenant can lead a majority to annihilate opponents, Rubenstein refers to the Peleponesian wars. A second example he gives of this "might makes right" relationship is ancient Israel's conquest of Canaan. Ironically, however, it was precisely the "covenant" Israel claimed that it had with its *God* that was responsible for the genocide Israel inflicted on these inhabitants of Canaan in the book of Joshua. The ease with which people are able to justify genocide by referring to their covenant with God or gods should have elicited a clarification from Rubenstein. Instead, he only said that we should de-emphasize the negative aspects of covenant:

> [W]e need to place the problematic theological aspects of the biblical covenant in the broader context of the perennial human needs the older covenants were able to meet, at least for a time. The negative aspects of

the biblical covenant are far less important than the example it offered of a way out of unremitting mistrust and destructiveness (153).

But he should have made clearer that while the biblical covenant may have united some peoples to form "Israel," this very covenant made it impossible for Israel and its neighbors to trust each other or live beside each other peaceably because Israel considered itself as God's "chosen." And Rubenstein insists that although most Jews apparently have to think of themselves as the "chosen," it is impossible for him to do so. So what does it mean that Israel's covenant serves as a paradigm? There is no guarantee that if a certain group is persuaded that it has a religious covenant with God that it will voluntarily extend political rights or human rights to other peoples. In fact, history is full of examples to the contrary. Rubenstein himself disparages the treatment Christians gave the Jews in many instances through the ages -- either convert or be killed. Yet the very setting from which Rubenstein derives the "covenant" concept shows the same dehumanization, again, suggesting that the genocide here is God's will and God's war. Had Rubenstein acknowledged the difference between a covenant merely between one people and their God, and a social contract between *all* the parties concerned, then it would have been obvious that a social contract is not as potentially dehumanizing as a religious covenant. Either contract or covenant must have some inherent check to prevent any party from eclipsing the value of others by dehumanizing treatment that silences their political voices or dogmatically diminishes their rights. Dehumanization is not transformed into humanization by mere metaphysical cliches.

Rubenstein implies that the covenant must be voluntary, between the diverse human parties who recognize each other as essentially equal in rights before the other, and who extend to each other the appeal to a law and power superior to both to enforce this covenant. Rubenstein and Rawls both insist that for the covenant or contract to work, the equality of the parties must be one that is not bestowed by one party upon the other, but rather is understood, accepted, or bargained for in the encounter of persons with each other.[6] The nuclear capabilities of Israel referred to by Rubenstein should be taken in the best sense here, as a part of the social contracting or negotiating of the parties rather than simply one party exercising might over the other.[7] But nuclear deterrence seems far removed from the social solidarity and Buber's "I-Thou" relationship that is Rubenstein's norm.

On the other hand, when Rubenstein describes for us the long-term effect of this ancient covenant God made with Israel, he insists that its original displacement of tribal deities or the Egyptian pantheon by a group experience with a single, all-powerful God, paradoxically eventually leads to the same criticism being turned back upon even the idea of this God who brought about this original covenant (145-147). So Rubenstein notes that this very process of "covenant," as essential as it is for uniting disparate groups and helping them to move beyond their former exclusive allegiences, ends up spawning a totally secularized society or atheism. He does not view this as a bad result, since the move beyond "theism" seems necessary to Rubenstein if humans are to have any freedom. He sees the necessity of a transcendent, binding covenant between disparate peoples in order to avoid genocide, yet on the other hand, he adamantly insists that atheism and secularism are not the answers, that human life must retain its sense of the "religious" as well as each group's history. And the "covenant" with God ironically has dislodged "God" from any significant "binding" role in history. Rubenstein has continued to insist that we live in the "time of the death of God," so all the more reason for "religion," but how would a "religion" without God provide a covenant with any protection against dehumanization which he sees as the danger of mere social contract? We must examine how he defines "religion."

II. "Religion" in Rubenstein's Theology

Rubenstein understands "religion" as the sharing within a community of the significant joys and sufferings of life through an identity that involves myth, ritual, and symbols on the unconscious level, and that involves conceptual moral and psychological guidance on the conscious level. Religion is psychologically true for its adherents. It is an identity that supplies the people with a past history and with future hope. Whether one is born into a religion or not is part of the absurdity or "throwness" (*Geworfenheit*) of existence itself; one's choice to affirm or deny that part of one's identity eventually evolves as part of one's finitely free particular choice.

Nowhere, however, does Rubenstein assert that God is responsible for any specific religion as understood and practiced. But one must ask whether Judaism would ever have existed as a "religion" had ancient Israel and later Jews made no claims in retrospect of having experienced God in their lives. If God *is* somehow nevertheless in the world, as the Source of being, as Rubenstein concedes, even that offers little consolation. Criticism has dislodged the ultimacy of the Torah for Rubenstein. He asserts that it is no longer possible for non-Orthodox Jews to have "the security of knowing that their religious acts are meaningfully related to God's will" (234-235). So in the absence of any sense of vital conceptual connection with the Divine, he instructs his fellow-Jew to find meaning in life without requiring it to be superordinate (20), to discover life fulfilling even if it is not eternal (306), to formulate values that guide our lives within the Torah, even if one does not think that much of the Torah is relative to one's present life, and none of it "inspired" as the Orthodox contend (ch. 12).

As Rubenstein sees it, the answer to the human situation is not solved by reducing "religion" to morality, as he tends to fault Reform Judaism (235-236). Morality, which he describes as a "prophetic" religion, only demands, but offers no consolation when one realizes that perhaps one will never be any better person. A religion must manifest also its "priestly" side that offers "atonement" or forgiveness. In rituals connected with atonement, the people of the community cathartically express their aggressive or violent desires to eliminate "God" by their references to the idea of ritual sacrifice, since the ancient animal sacrifice was a thinly veiled surrogate for human sacrifice, which, in turn was a surrogate for the sacrifice of God.[8] People ritually bring to the conscious level the unconscious desires, admit their failures in community with each other, and reinforce a forgiveness they feel comes from "God." To those who think the idea the ritual sacrifice is mere superstition or irrational, Rubenstein replies that humans are not totally rational, and this may be one way of addressing what may be our only choice -- between controlled and uncontrolled violence in society.[9]

Notably what we are dealing with in Rubenstein's definition of "religion" is an individual and communal moral empowering, which, although utilizing rituals and myths to reach unconscious levels, nevertheless is justifiably restrained by social-legal structures from trying to buttress its views or status upon strictly metaphysical claims. This position corresponds exactly to Rawls' insistence that disallows any metaphysical claims from any party in the forming of the "social contract." As a matter of fact, "religion" finally means only "silence" for Rubenstein; he admits that he cannot utter the words at synagogue service but rather must sit silently (200), that he cannot "love God," but is simply "affrighted before Him" and silent (264).

Thus, life is primarily or finally tragic for Rubenstein, and "religion" is only "the absurd, pathetic attempt, for which there can be no substitute, to make a meaningless life meaningful. The attempt is futile but sociologically and psychologically indispensable" (264). Religion, therefore, is not an answer or the answer; it is only the sharing of our human plight, as Rubenstein sees it: "Religion is the way we share our predicament; it is never the way we overcome our condition" (264, 27-28). "It is precisely because human existence is tragic, ultimately hopeless, and without meaning that we treasure our religious community. It is our community of ultimate concern" (19). The ultimate answer to the human predicament, as Rubenstein sees it, is the "Messiah," but "Messiah" can only mean one's death[10] (261-262).

At this point, it is not at all clear what the "religious" element in social covenanting or civilization would be since religion at best still leaves us hopeless in the face of death, yet he insists that extreme atheism and secularism are not the answers. When he says that "religion" is more than a system of beliefs, it is also a system of shared rituals, customs, and historical memories by which members of a community cope with or celebrate the moments of crisis in their own lives and the life of their inherited community" (173), he qualifies this by insisting:

> The need for the sharing is not diminished in the time of the death of God. If it is no longer possible to believe in the God who has the power to annul the tragedies of existence, the need religiously to share that existence remains. In place of the biblical image of God as transcending the world he has created, I came to believe that a view of God which gives priority to immanence may be more credible in our era (174).

This is not to suggest that sitting in silence before the Source of Being or Holy Nothingness is not itself valid, but Rubenstein asserts over and over that while the human community cannot share different and conflicting particular traditions, whether religious or otherwise, it can share doubts, problems, and guilt.[11] But how would there be any doubt to share without there being a common pursuit of truth, any problems without common goals and ideals, any guilt without those humans sharing with each other a common morality? Recitation of one's religious identity through perpetuation of the community's historical traditions, Rubenstein insists, makes religion superior to atheism and secularism. But mere recitation of history or even religious history is not necessarily meaningful. For meaning to adhere to the past, every generation must have a common morality; otherwise, even a negative judgment of the Holocaust could be dismissed as merely the interpreter's preference. Conversely, Rubenstein warns that if religions absolutize their myths that not only impedes meaningful community, it "absolutely preclude[s] it" (25).

Rubenstein follows Hegel in equating human reflection and action with the self-consciousness of God. If Absolute Spirit is manifest through all the spiritual activity of humans so that there is an ontology or system of "continuity" rather than "discontinuity" or "system of gaps" (296), then when one speaks of keeping the "religious" element alive as a vital part of the "covenant" between diverse peoples, that may be saying nothing different from simply suggesting that a human covenant is religious by the very integrated structure of being and specially of rational being, or by the incommensurable nature of the humans involved in the covenanting or contracting process:

> Before this Abyss, we come to intuit something of the holiness of God. When we speak of that holiness we dimly point to the realm of God's utter singularity, uniqueness, and incommensurability with all categories of measurement, logic, or relation. He who intuits, no matter how dimly, the holiness of God, need construct no "God above the God of theism," as does Paul Tillich, to provide a mental hint of that which dwells in its own groundlessness.[12]

While this may be too "humanistic" for some religious people, Rubenstein warned against the depersonalization and dehumanization caused not simply by secular society but also by the myths of a religious society. This seems the natural conclusion of Rubenstein's position also because of (1) his continual rejection of the idea of the Jews being a people "chosen" by God, (2) his insistence that such motif of chosenness is socially and psychologically disintegrating for a society, (3) his note that fortunately we have empowered social-political structures in society to restrain both the religious and non-religious from most unethical or anti-social actions. Rubenstein applauds this feature of American society, emphasizing that for a "genuine meeting of persons" to take place, religious myths must be diluted, and pragmatic concerns of getting along with each other must dictate a "tolerance of ambiguity" in which people learn to live with others whose myths contradict their own (25). This assumes that the common values, the highest of which seems to be the "genuine meeting of persons," are common values of humanity, which should be allowed to overpower, when necessary, the specificity of any and all religious traditions. This

Ground of moral concern which is also the Ground of being and history, is not itself to be equated with any specific moral imperatives, but is discovered in genuine meeting of persons. So the "religious" element needed for civilization, as we clarify these concepts of Rubenstein's, is the shared guilt that humans experience in their dealings with other persons as persons because of the unconditional claim each person's being lays on the other. How does this square with Rubenstein's explicit definitions of or statements about "God?"

III. Rubenstein's Definitions of "God"

Does God "intervene" in history at all in Rubenstein's interpretation? "In truth, the divine-human encounter is totally nonexistent," he answers. If God does not, then how could a covenant be anything more than a social contract between peoples, or at worst, the mere imagination of one party? If God *does* intervene, then does God do so only in superficial ways, so that the tragedy of the Holocaust did not elicit a positive response from God? In Rubenstein's second edition, he emphasizes less the "God of nature" replacing the "God of history," which had served as a partial answer to the traditional Jewish interpretation of the Holocaust in his first edition. In the second edition, he can still no longer believe in the God of history if that means God as the "ultimate actor" in history. Yet he tempers this apparent rejection of the "God of history" and *Heilsgeschichte,* by explaining that through mysticism and dialectic pantheism he can understand that "by virtue of His, or perhaps Its, all-encompassing nature, the God who is the Source and Ground of Being is as much a God-who-acts-in-history as the transcendent Creator God of the Bible, as any reader of Hegel would understand" (174). If one takes "as much" seriously here, Rubenstein would have to accept God's role in the Holocaust also, as the Ground of history, whether the motive was punishment or something else. That does seem to fit his insistence that there is a dark side or destructive side of God as well as goodness and creativity.

At times he seems to abandon only the negative aspects of the theology of the Deuteronomist. He insists that the only thing the "dialectic-mystical" interpretation excludes when looking at the Holocaust, is the notion of guilt on the part of Israel and punishment on the part of God (174). Ironically, however, immediately prior to that he says,

> If it is no longer possible to believe in the God who has the power to annul the tragedies of existence, the need religiously to share that existence remains. In place of the biblical image of God as transcending the world he has created, I came to believe that a view of God which gives priority to immanence may be more credible in our era (174).

Is this immanence only the Power of being that infuses all, the Undifferentiated Source of Being, whose creative as well as destructive nature would be seen more obviously in the cycle of nature than the vicissitudes of history, since Rubenstein thinks God is not responsible for the history of the Holocaust? God is described here as powerless "to annul the tragedies of existence." Or is Rubenstein thinking that the Deuteronomist's understanding of history grounded in God as its Source and Power is parallel or at least compatible to Hegel's view of God as Absolute Spirit, and in which case all Rubenstein finds objectionable in the Deuteronomist's scheme is its attributing to God the *motive* of punishment and to the people the *admission* of guilt. If that is the extent of his objection, his view would accept the idea of God as the Ground of history supporting indirectly the tragic annihilation of human life in the Holocaust. This would correspond with his emphasis on the constructive and destructive powers of this "God."

Yet he states that "God participates in all the joys and sorrows of the drama of creation, which is, at the same time, the deepest expression of the divine life" (302). This sounds like a statement implying that "God" is as upset as humans over injustice. By God's participation God either approves of all the injustices of life, or, disapproving, is either powerless or unconcerned to change the situation. While it may seem that any talk of God either approving or disapproving is far too anthropological, it is not any more so than Rubenstein's description of "God participating" in the joys and sorrows of the drama of creation, unless "participating" in "joys" and "sorrows" does not involve any reference whatever to an emotional sharing, no matter how symbolically he uses the terms. If God cannot approve or disapprove of the Holocaust, then this is a description of an amoral God. When he is summarizing the power of the traditional Jewish idea of "covenant and election," Rubenstein admits that he is convinced "that most religious Jews will eventually affirm faith in the God of covenant and election, even if such an affirmation entails regarding Auschwitz as divine punishment" (197). But he cannot.

> Because of the Shoah, some of us enter the synagogue to partake of our sacred times and seasons with those to whom we are bound in shared memory, pain, fate, and hope; yet once inside, we are struck dumb by words we can no longer honestly utter. All that we can offer is our reverent and attentive silence before the Divine (200).

"God after the Death of God"[13] is for Rubenstein the "ground of feeling, thought, and reflection. Human thought and feeling are thus expressions of divine thought and feeling, albeit in a dialectical form" (296). He contrasts the incorrect "dichotomizing system of gaps" found in Second Isaiah (Isaiah 55:8,9), Calvinism, Kant, Buber, Kierkegaard, and Barth -- with the system of continuities found in Hegel, Lurianic Kabbalism, Jakob Boehme, Buddhism, and in Paul's vision of the consummation of redemptive history. "God," as "Holy Nothingness" is not nothing or non-being, but rather "superfluity of being." God is the "ocean and we are the waves" (299). He explains the difference between Verstand (understanding) and Vernunft (reason) in Kant, but especially Hegel: while Verstand gives incomplete or partial perspectives of discreet phenomena, the reality behind the appearances of such phenomena is none other than the Absolute Geist. Only Verstand or speculative Reason recognizes this, since it is the divinity within the finite that allows it to recognize divinity beyond the phenomenal appearances. This means that "all of nature and history [are] expressions of the self-positing, self-unfolding rational totality," the "Absolute exists only in and through its finite constituents" (297). But if this sounds like "God's" existence is dependent upon human existence, when Rubenstein uses the metaphor of ocean and waves, it is the waves which come from, are not completely distinct from, and which merge back into, the ocean. The latter sounds like human existence depends upon God's existence. More specifically, he emphasizes that

> [W]e simply repeat, each in our own way, a destiny common to billions of other human beings. Admittedly, we possess a measure of freedom to work out our distinctive path in the world. Nevertheless, both the individual and the race are the consequence of vast, nonpersonal forces that transcend yet permeate their every activity and project (299).

Finally, he quotes Hegel to show how God's self-manifestation is our human consciousness:

Spirit alone is reality. It is the inner being of the world, that which essentially is, and is *per se*; it assumes objective, determinitive form and enters into relations with itself -- it is externality (otherness) and exists for self; yet, in this determinateness, and in its otherness, it is still one with itself -- it is self-contained and self-complete, in itself and for itself at once (301).

If the human enterprise is simply God's self-manifestation, then it is not clear why the dialectic of history, with its positive and negative elements, with its constructive and destructive attributes, would be subject to any negative moral judgment. So how could the Holocaust be immoral, which Rubenstein obviously thinks it is? Elsewhere in the book, when trying to explain the Holocaust, he rejects Hegel's view of the Absolute, finds repugnant Hegel's suggestion that "individual injury is overcome in universal ends." Rubenstein insists that

Hegel never faced a situation of universal injury, such as the Holocaust, or the threat of universal extinction in a nuclear Holocaust.... There is a profound difference between a situation in which some persons suffer and perish unjustly but the group survives and one in which an entire group or even all of humanity is obliterated (158).

But a "universal" injury, if we are thinking "universal" as Hegel was, has not occurred. Further, if Hegel's idea of the universal end was something humans would desire, Rubenstein, to the contrary, does not desire the end since the end or Messiah, brings only the elimination of the vicissitudes of life at the expense of having no distinguishable life at all (265, 306). One blends back into "Holy Nothingness," in which there is no individual identity. If "God" is to be conceived as Sunyata, Rubenstein, however, unlike Buddhism, does not welcome that end.

On the question of how this destructive side of "God" is related to morality or virtue, Rubenstein insists that we must accept the "dark side of divinity" or the "demonic aspect to reality and divinity" (208). He continues,

The tragedies, ironies, and ambiguities of existence cease to reflect man's willful rebellion; they become internalized in the self-unfolding of divinity. Virtue ceases to be a choice of discrete alternatives and becomes an overcoming. The contradictory character of existence makes goodness and virtue an overcoming in us as well as in divinity. The very character of life makes the divine source a ceaseless self-striving in which the unending negativities and affirmations of existence follow one another and in which individual forms of life are expressions of the self-construction and self-separation of divinity. Life on life is thrust forward in divinity's ceaseless project to enjoy its hour and then to become the consumed substance of other life. Such a view of divinity makes tragedy and destruction inescapable and ineradicable. Paradoxically, though it ascribes an ontic quality to evil, it possesses far more compassion than the terrible view that makes of evil a free act of will (208).

In his insistence that the "holiness of God" means God's creative and destructive power rather than simply God as moral force, and evil should not be assigned to the free act of will, then it is difficult to understand how anything could be referred to as a tragedy or destruction, or why anyone could object to the Holocaust or any other genocide.[14] That is simply the way life is. Much as Buddhism may allow anything to happen in this world without feeling pain toward it, but Rubenstein expresses moral outrage over the Holocaust. Is there a way in which one does not have to choose between (1) a "God" which is identified with all the good and evil that occurs in this world, a view which makes our moral objections to evil nonsense, and (2) a "God" which is separate from this world, allowing humans freedom enough that they, in a significant way, are able to initiate new causal moral chains of events, which to Rubenstein seems to place too much blame on humans, and feeds the traditional view that God was punishing the Jews in the Holocaust?

IV. The Social Contract Less Metaphysical Claims

If the divine is known only through the finite, or "God" is confronted only in the confrontation with our fellow-human, as we see Rubenstein's emphasis on "I-Thou" relations, as well as other points we have articulated above suggest, then what is the quality that is recognized as "divine," or how does "God" differ from each person or the sum total of humanity and the cosmos? Where is the Unconditioned or "Incommensurability" actually met?

Rubenstein's emphasis upon treating people as "persons" rather than caricatures based on some myths could be extended to suggest that the Unconditioned, the Source of being which is both beginning and end for all of us, confronts us in the person of another, *as person.* This suggests not only the incommensurable nature of each person and the unconditioned claims they lay upon us morally by their presence merely *as persons* since persons are God's self-manifestation and self-consciousness; but it also assumes an equality of voice, as Rubenstein says is necessary for all to have the political rights they should have. So "God" is accessible not in theistic categories but in our human interactions with each other, in our thoughts, feelings, speech, and action -- as persons with persons -- in the process of humanization or essentialization.

This differs from the secular humanism Rubenstein objects to in the sense that individuality is not levelled to some humanistic stereotype. Rather, dialogue and contract honor both the uniqueness of each person (what each is willing to give to the other as "consideration" for the equality desired for the self) as well as the equality of each. But this assumes that the contract or covenant is made between the human parties, not just between one human group and their "God," or religiously-rooted genocide can occur. The very process of reaching this "social contract" is a process of dialogue of equals in which the norms of behavior or moral and civil code are established by this very "meeting of persons." The moral law recognized by civil law is that which the parties hammer out together, and the process cannot allow for either to make metaphysical claims to buttress his or her argument to gain advantage on others. Some aspects of one's moral understandings may not find their way into the civil law since they are incompatible with the civil law that is agreed on.

Under this scenario, one can say that reality (and "God") involves both good and bad, both light and darkness. But that need not dictate a passive resignation to the variety of evils and vicissitudes of existence. "God" may, as the Source of being and Ground of morality, "transcend" actual moral issues and categories, but the particularity involved in the meeting of persons demands that being and morality are honored by the mutuality of moral (hence, also legal) decisions or contracts that are necessitated. Every generation finds itself in dialogue over human behavior, and the implicit contracts under which we live recognize that the normative expectations are based upon the incommensurable nature of all the contracting parties. The contract is continually in process, but moral judgment is justified on the basis of what rightful expectations each party derived from the social contract whether explicitly involved in the actual contracting or only by proxy. No generation decides the extent of the social contract for the next generations, but human society continually must struggle in dialogue to perpetuate this agreement which is able to bring unity to diversity. It is not surprising that Rubenstein's view of his relation to the Torah is precisely this: he himself must decide in dialogue with the community which parts of the Torah are essential for him to live by, but he must pass on the whole since each new generation must be presented the same choices and sense of responsibility. If "God's" will cannot be ascertained as certain in any part of the Torah *per se*, nevertheless, as Rubenstein contends, if human reasoning, or more appropriately human dialogue, is where we meet the claim of the Unconditioned, it is still possible to decide in any given context what is the moral thing. For Rawls, this process of contracting demands equality of voice which can be attained only by hypothesizing ourselves behind a "veil of ignorance," that is, not knowing what status, race, gender, etc. we would belong to. This, of course, is hypothetical. But it corresponds very much to Rubenstein's insistence on (1) the absurdity or thrownness of every human's origin, and (2) using Buber's "I-Thou" category as the norm by which to judge which religious myths and rituals to retain and reinterpret, as well as a paradigm for moral judgment in our encounters with others.

This is only one possible way to smooth out a few of the minor ambiguities within Rubenstein's *After Auschwitz*. The book's profundity will not let us rest until we have struggled with the issues; its prophetic insights and style may suggest, however, that any systematizing of it will reduce its effect which may be experienced in a mystical, paradoxical, dialectical way.

Notes

1. p. xiii. Emphasis mine. All parenthetical page numbers, unless otherwise specified, are to Rubenstein's *After Auschwitz: History, Theology, and Contemporary Judaism,* 2nd ed., (Baltimore: The Johns Hopkins University Press, 1992).

2. As he emphasizes, "*Crime is a violation of behavioral norms defined by political authority.* Homicide, for example, is only a crime when the victim is protected by the state's laws. Even in National Socialist Germany, a very small number of SS officers were punished for the *unauthorized* murder of Jews during World War II." (p. 138)

3. This would be implied especially by chapter 7, although if "religion" is taken here as in other definitions of "religion" by Rubenstein, it may not be possible to assign any particular function of "religion" to God. Then, however, one has to wonder what a "covenant" with God would mean.

4. p. 174. Although Rubenstein is primarily repelled by the Orthodox or traditional Jewish and commonly-Christian explanation of the Holocaust as God's punishment of the Jews, he really repudiates the idea of "God" intervening in history in any way as he faults the idea of God as the "ultimate actor" in history. Since Rubenstein cannot believe in a utopian Messianic age or life beyond death or perfect justice, there would be little incentive to enforce any kind of covenant or contract people make with each other if "God" is at most only the Source or Ground of history. When he later emphasizes the need for "an institution similar to that which enabled the Hebrews to unite under God at Sinai, a binding basis for community," and acknowledges that "it is easier to point to the need than to meet it," he is acknowledging both the need for some transcendent basis of our being as well as our morality which will not eclipse our human freedom.

5. There are points at which Rubenstein seems to emphasize the importance of sheer power or armaments above any covenant or "God" behind a covenant. Cf. 14, p. 138, or "The fact that Israel may possess as many as two hundred hydrogen bombs cannot be separated from the experience of the Holocaust and Israel's perception that she is surrounded by mortal enemies. Having been taught by the Holocaust of the real value of international guarantees, it is hardly surprising that the Israelis have stockpiled an enormous number of nuclear weapons. The capacity grievously to damage or wholly destroy an adversary is, at present, Israel's most credible guarantee of survival. Nor is it likely that, faced with defeat in a war of extermination, the Israelis would go quietly into the dust." (p. 152)

6. Rubenstein insists, "Inequality not only precludes genuine encounter for the client; it also distorts and debases the protector as well.... As Søren Kierkegaard has suggested in his parable of the king who would bestow his love on a servant girl, memory makes a bestowed equality impossible." (p. 15)

7. p. 152. Yet at times, the way he refers to the military power of Israel, it does not seem to be respect for the other as much as sheer power to drive the other to the negotiating table.

8. p. 23. This is elaborated more fully in an article in the first edition that was not retained in the second edition, "Atonement and Sacrifice in the Jewish Liturgy," in *After Auschwitz: Radical Theology and Contemporary Judaism,* 1st ed., Indianapolis: Bobbs-Merrill, 1966, pp. 93-111.

9. p. 240. By expressing these aggressive impulses in a controlled ritual, the irrational results of repressed feelings are avoided. As he says, "Nothing within the domain of human experience escaped its (the Torah) attention. It

understood the paradoxical truth that one can best overcome atavisms and primitivisms, in so far as they are destructive, by acknowledging their potency and attractiveness and channeling their expression to eliminate their harm. *Sublimation has been a perennial Jewish strategy."* (p. 243)

10. pp. 261-262. "Messianism's real meaning is the proclamation of the end of history, which is characterized by the return to nature and its vicissitudes rather than the abolition of nature's tragic and inevitable necessities. History does not conclude with the abolition but with the restoration of ananke (necessity). Now nature's inevitabilities are seen as part of the tragic course of existence itself rather than as God's chastisement for human sinfulness."

11. "For technical society, failure is an incident to be overcome by further effort facilitated by the replacement of older units of manpower with new units. For the human person, failure is of the very essence.

The whole weight of religious tradition, with its insistent and dramatic reinteration of God's holy majesty and the finitude and creatureliness of man, reminds me over and over again of who and what we are. Furthermore, it does more than teach us these lessons at the conscious, intellectual level. It allows us to share these truths in the multiple levels of emotion which religious ceremony at its best can elicit. We have been cast up absurdly and without reason into a world that knows no warmth, concern, care, fellowship, or love save that which we bestow upon one another. Our myths tell us of gifts that await us. We can be far more certain of the need that makes mythical promises alluring than of fullment of the promise. Since we cannot be brothers in promise, let us at least be brothers in need." (pp. 27-28)

12. 244. Yet in another article, he applauds Tillich's movement beyond mere theism for the sake of human freedom, although he says for him the problem of theodicy is more important than mere human freedom in suggesting such a movement beyond theism. (pp. 247-248)

13. The title of the final chapter of After Auschwitz.

14. Rubenstein describes "God" as the power and"dialectic quality of reality" which is not transcendent to nature. Citing Heraclitus, he insists the "[o]nly historical man in his alienation sees nature as devoid of the divine. Humanity at home with itself sees the cosmos as alive with the very same life that infuses its own being ... God will be seen as one, but He will be understood to participate in nature's vicissitudes and necessities rather than to created them outside of His solitary, transcendent perfection.

"A new understanding of God arising out of the return to earth and nature must inevitably confront the issue of the dark side of divinity. The archaic ancients knew that the word holy -- *kadosh-sacer* -- contained a hidden awesomeness that transcends all categories of goodness, virtue, and morality. For the Lord of History there can be no such issue, for all guilt and darkness rests on man's side. Not so, in the religion of nature. Insofar as there is a sense of mankind's unity with nature and nature's source, a demonic aspect to reality and divinity must be accepted as an inescapable concomitant of life and existence. To say that God and nature are at one with each other, that they are alive and life engendering, is to affirm the demonic side not alone in us but in divinity as well. The tragedies, ironies, and ambiguities of existence cease to reflect historical man's willful rebellion; they become internalized in the self-unfolding of divinity.... Life on life is thrust forward in divinity's ceaseless project to enjoy its hour and then to become the consumed substance of other life. Such a view of divinity makes tragedy and destruction inescapable and ineradicable. Paradoxically, though it ascribes an ontic quality to evil, it possesses far more compassion than the terrible view that makes of evil a free act of will." (pp. 207-208)

Chapter 8

THE AUSCHWITZ CONVENT CONTROVERSY: THE CHALLENGE OF REPENTANCE AND RECONSTRUCTION

Susan E. Nowak

This essay will undertake a theological analysis of Roman Catholicism's participation in the Auschwitz Convent controversy in order to examine the theological worldview which shapes the Church's self-understanding. This worldview reveals the framework within which the official teaching Church constructs key theological components, such as covenant and election, memory and memorializiation, and repentance and reconciliation. It also provides crucial insights into the Church's construction of Judaism and the Jewish people. Furthermore, the analysis allows us to examine the relationship between the Church's claims of solidarity with the Jewish people and the positions it adopted during the controversy.

This analysis is crucial because the Convent controversy reveals the aspects of Roman Catholic theology and practice which threaten the credibility of the Church and the viability of Jewish-Catholic relations. The protracted nature of the controversy and the contradictory attitudes, positions, and behaviors adopted by the Church made it clear that the integrity of Jewish-Catholic relations was in jeopardy. As the rhetoric surrounding the controversy escalated, it also became evident that the Church's legacy of anti-Judaism was playing a significant role in the controversy. Despite the publication of important and impressive documents since the promulgation of *Nostra Aetate* in 1965,[1] the influence of this legacy upon Roman Catholic theology and practice continued. Given expression through a theology of supersession, patriarchal projection, and religious triumphalism,[2] anti-Judaism distorted the Church's perception of the critical issues at stake and fostered an acrimonious climate of negotiation.[3] Theological supercessionism, patriarchal projection, and religious triumphalism gave rise to equivocation,[4] contradiction,[5] and inflammatory statements[6] in papal sermons, public statements by ecclesiastical figures, and official Church functions. Furthermore, they blinded the Church to the symbolic centrality of Auschwitz within the Jewish community worldwide.[7] Moreover, these forces enabled the Church to avoid confronting the Holocaust as a Christian catastrophe.[8] This, in turn, allowed the Church to focus upon the defense and rehabilitation of Catholic behavior during the Holocaust[9] and downplay the uniqueness of the Jewish experience.[10] These examples highlight the ways in which theological supercessionism, patriarchal projection, and religious triumphalism cloak the intrinsic interconnection between the perpetuation of theological anti-Judaism, recurrent incidents of antisemitism, and the Church's role in the convent controversy. Catholics and Jews committed to interreligious understanding cannot ignore the consequences of this tragic situation. Three reasons will be highlighted. First, there is the distortion of key theological components, i.e., covenant, election, messianism, and mission. Historically, these deformed components legitimated the Church's construction of itself as the newly elect messianic people, the successor of Israel, and the locus of salvation for all peoples. Furthermore, they formed the basis for the Church's negative construction of Judaism and the Jewish people. The classic analyses of Rosemary Radford Ruether[11] and Franklin Littell[12] and others[13] in this regard are well-known, so what will be highlighted are the tragic consequences of this warped self-understanding and negative construction. The theological legitimacy of Judaism's ongoing covenantal relationship with God is denied. Covenantal relationship and election no longer reside with the "faithless" Jews, but with the Church, the "True Israel." The continued existence of the Jewish people is reduced to one purpose: testimony to the continuation of God's covenantal relationship with Christianity. Jewish suffering, albeit socio-cultural marginalization and/or politico-religious persecution, is understood as a consequence of a willful forfeiture of election and the covenantal relationship. Furthermore, the dualism supporting this distortion allows the Church to project its historical failures onto Judaism. Judaism is constructed as "the purely carnal Israel" and identified with everything unredeemed, evil, and demonic. By presenting Judaism as the theological symbol of unredeemed humanity, an abiding contempt for Judaism and all things Jewish is justified. Moreover, the particularity of Christian historical revelation is reinterpreted as a "universal particularity," thereby legitimating the suppression of religious pluralism.

Second, the impact of the interconnection between theological supercessionism, patriarchal projection, and religious triumphalism is not limited to the past. It continues to shape the Church's self-understanding and its relationship to Judaism as a religion in the present. The convent controversy exposes the ways in which these three elements blunt the Church's sensibilities to the history and experiences of Jewish communities and sabotage its participation in Jewish-Catholic dialogue. In terms of examples, the following will be discussed: the Church's failure to initiate dialogue regarding the convent's establishment, its appropriation of Jewish memory and history,[14] its rhetoric of an equalization of suffering,[15] its indignation that its participation in the negotiations was not received with gratitude,[16] and its tendency to collapse religious and national identities.[17]

Third, the interconnection of theological supercessionism, patriarchal projection, and religious triumphalism promotes attitudes and positions which justify unacceptable and aggressive, if not violent, behaviors. Once again, the convent controversy provides numerous examples: the Church's non-compliance with the timeline of the two Geneva Agreements, the erection of an eight meter cross on the convent building, the publication of accusatory and prejudiced statements, and the physical attack upon Rabbi Weiss and his students outside the convent building. Contemporary Roman Catholic thinkers who have not run from the consequences of the *Shoah* call upon the Church to recognize the intrinsic connection between distorted theological understandings, unjust positions, and violent behaviors.[18] These thinkers are keenly aware that the Church's failure to recognize this connection has exacted a great price from the Jewish people. In the 1930s and 40s, it meant that the Church effectively abandoned the Jewish victims of that era to the Nazi policy of genocide.[19] In the 1990s, it means that their trust in the Church's most recent teachings on theological anti-Judaism and antisemitism may yet prove to be unfounded.[20] This writer contends that the credibility of the Church's identity, witness, and mission rests with its response to this situation. If it publicly acknowledges and redresses the influence of this framework upon its practices, the integrity of Jewish-Catholic relations will be restored. If it refuses, it will be responsible for the ruptured relationships, unjust behaviors, and needless suffering which follow.

Analysis of the dynamics underlying the convent controversy makes it clear that the Church must transform the theological bases which shape its self-understanding, as well as its construction of Judaism, relationship with Jewish communities, and participation in interfaith dialogue. In this paper it is suggested that the principle of solidarity provides a credible and challenging framework for the transformation process. This principle is looked to because it emphasizes the intrinsic connection between theological formulation and right living; the truth of theological statements is inexorably bound to action on behalf of justice and peace. It also supports the reconstruction of identity, witness, and mission according to the principles of justice, inclusivity, and a respect for difference.

The principle of solidarity would challenge the Church to acknowledge the ways in which the separation of theology and practice deforms its self-understanding and fosters an ethos of exclusivity, conformity, and domination. It would also hold the Church responsible for reconstructing its self-understanding, structures, and behaviors in light of those who suffer marginalization, subjugation, and persecution. In terms of the *Shoah*, this means in light of the legacy of Christian supercessionism and the tragic history of Jewish-Christian relations. Theological statements would defend individual and communal rights to religious tolerance and explicitly articulate the relationship between justice and a respect for difference.[21] Ministerial actions would reflect a commitment to those whose "difference" situates them "outside" cultural, political, and/or religious "norms." Together theology and practice would challenge social, political, and religious centers of power which protect their access to privilege and prestige by fostering relationships marked by exclusion, indifference, and oppression. They would expose the systemic connections which perpetuate an oppressive triangle of relationships: ideological definitions of normativity, oppressive location within societal structures, and vulnerability to marginalization and violence.

The future credibility of Roman Catholicism and the viability of Jewish-Catholic relations rests with a crucial choice. Will the Church continue to ground its message and mission in theological supercessionism, patriarchal projection, and religious triumphalism and evade the demands of solidarity as it did in the *Shoah* and convent controversy? Or will it undertake public acts of *teshuvah* for its perpetuation of theological anti-Judaism and antisemitism and submit itself to the transformative power of solidarity?

The hope of the revitalization process depends upon the reinterpretation of covenant, christology, and ecclesiology according to the principle of solidarity. It is important to begin with the notion of covenant because it has shaped decisively the Roman Catholic worldview. Informed by theological supercessionism, patriarchal projection, and religious triumphalism, the concept of covenant became exclusive in scope, dualistic in structure, and divisive in effect. This provided the underpinnings for deformed christological and ecclesiological understandings. Recognizing the extent of the distortion, this paper will attempt to highlight the corrective influence of the principle of solidarity.

Covenant: Disengaged from an understanding of covenant in which Christianity eclipses Judaism as God's elect, the Church could confront the ways in which anti-Judaic teachings and antisemitic behaviors compromise its testimony to God's covenantal promises. In this regard, the Church would face its failure to eliminate theologies which represent Christianity as the "completion" of Judaism or which affirm Judaism's covenantal status only "in principle." Dissociated from the patriarchal ethic of domination-subjugation, Roman Catholicism would be in the position to acknowledge - in theory and practice - the fecundity of Judaism's ongoing witness to covenantal responsibilities, obligations, and rights. The result of this reinterpretation: an understanding of covenant which is able to uphold the validity of both Judaism and Roman Catholicism's covenantal status.

Christology: The reformulation of central christological tenets would be based upon the conviction that doctrinal definitions alone cannot provide a sufficient foundation for christological faith. This faith must embody the insights gleaned from critical praxis if it is to be experienced as a liberating, redemptive reality. Critical praxis would illumine those aspects of traditional christological tenets which sustain oppressive structures within society and religious communities, as well as those aspects which act as a critical force of transformation.[22] The concept of solidarity would challenge traditional constructions of the figure of Jesus, particularly the interrelationship of his life-activity, death, and resurrection. Contrary to traditional theologies which locate the redemptive significance of the Christ event with Jesus' death, a focus upon his life-activity would be emphasized. Christology would address the way in which Jesus' life-activity reveals the nature of God and opens up a way of life. The "profession" of christological faith would demand that the Church stand with humanity in solidarity against the forces of oppression, exploitation, and marginalization.

Ecclesiology: The reconstruction of traditional theologies of God according to the principle of solidarity would present a formidable challenge to Roman Catholic ecclesiologies. It would demand that the Church's self-understanding and praxis reflect the demands of following Jesus, who is in solidarity with God, who is in solidarity with the outcast and marginalized. These ecclesiologies would compel the Church to confront the history of human suffering. It must proclaim the memory of God's solidarity with Jesus, who was in solidarity with all of humankind, as a subversive memory of hope for those who continue to suffer marginalization, persecution and extermination. Empowered by this subversive memory, the Church must challenge every system and structure which threatens human dignity, freedom and peace.

If the Church does submit itself to the transformative power of solidarity and undertake public acts of *teshuvah*, its words and actions will become a source of *teshuvah* as *Tikkun Olam*. Freed from the vision of covenant informed by exclusivism, dualism, and patriarchal projection, it could embrace the demands of solidarity with Judaism and the Jewish people. The two religious traditions would, then, be able to stand together in solidarity on behalf of all who suffer oppression, exploitation, and wrongful death. There could be, in our time, no stronger testimony to the liberating, transformative love of the God of solidarity.

Notes

1. Some of the documents most frequently cited as premier examples of the Church's changed teachings are as follows. The Vatican II document, *Nostra Aetate*, promulgated on October 20, 1965, is hailed as the document which marks the radical shift in the Church's teaching regarding Judaism and the Jewish people. With it came the first official acknowledgment of Roman Catholicism's legacy of theological anti-Judaism and antisemitism. Although the language and scope of *Nostra Aetate* is qualified, i.e. the Council chose not to use the term "deicide" within the final version of the document, the document explicitly condemns antisemitism and states that the Jewish people bear no collective responsibility for the crucifixion of Jesus Christ. The 1975 "Guidelines" statement of the American Catholic bishops charged theologians with the responsibility of re-examining the nature of Judaism's covenantal relationship and Christianity's interpretation of that relationship. It was unprecedented in its call for theologians to achieve an understanding of Judaism

and the Jewish people which reflected Jewish understandings. "Confessions on the Holocaust," the 1975 document promulgated by the German Bishops, is considered by some one of the most moving documents to-date. The 1983 statement issued by the Joint National Commission for Catholic-Jewish Religious Dialogue in Brazil lays down six objectives intended to promote a practical and workable framework of understanding between the two traditions. For articles which raise questions regarding the integrity of the church's participation in interreligious dialogue see: Michael Berenbaum, "The Struggle for Civility: The Auschwitz Controversy and the Forces Behind It," *Memory Offended: The Auschwitz Convent Controversy.* Carol Rittner and John K. Roth ed. (New York, Praeger, 1991), 83-90; Abraham Brumberg, "The Problem That Won't Go Away," *Tikkun* 5, No. 1 (1990): 31-34, 93-94; Deborah McCauley, *"Nostra Aetate* and the New Jewish-Christian Feminist Dialogue," *Unanswered Questions: Theological Views of Jewish-Catholic Relations* R. Brooks ed. (Notre Dame, Indiana: University of Notre Dame Press, 1988), 189-210.; Deborah McCauley and Annette Daum, "Jewish-Christian Feminist Dialogue: A Wholistic Vision," *Seminary Quarterly Review* XXXVIII (1983): 147-190; and Steven F. Windmueller, "The Shoah - Anti-Semitism and Christian-Jewish Relations," *Journal of Jewish Communal Service* 65 (Fall 1988): 3-8.

2. The degree to which theological supercessionism shapes the Roman Catholic theological worldview is given further testimony by the lack of direct participation on the part of the Carmelite nuns themselves in the negotiations. The limitations imposed by their cloistered lifestyle notwithstanding, it is most significant that questions were not raised about the appropriateness of a male superior representing the nuns or that the actual positions held by the nuns regarding the controversy have remained primarily a matter of speculation. For the texts of two interviews with Sister Teresa, the Mother Superior of the Carmelite convent around which the controversy swirled see: Leon Klenicki, *ADL on the Frontline* 2 (October 1992): 16 and Francis A. Winiarz, "We're Not Moving a Single Inch," *Memory Offended,* 259-262.

3. The following authors provide insightful analyses into the various dimensions of this problematic. Stanislaw Krajewski, "The Controversy over Carmel at Auschwitz: A Personal Polish-Jewish Chronology," *Christian Jewish Relations* 22 (1989): 38-39; Burton Levinson, "Winter Chill on a Springtime Visit to Rome," *ADL Bulletin* 46 (June 1989): 2; Daniel Polish, "Catholic-Jewish Relations and the Auschwitz Controversy," *Ecumenical Trends* 16 (October 1987): 169-171; Carol Rittner and John K. Roth, "Introduction," *Memory Offended.,* 1-15.; Ady Steg, "The Jewish-Christian 'Summit,'" *Christian Jewish Relations* 19 (1986): 47-51; David Warszawski, "The Convent and Solidarity," *Tikkun* 4 (November/December 1989): 29-31, 93; Elie Wiesel, "A Year of Blood and Ashes," *Baltimore Jewish Times* September 29, 1989.

4. The 1994 concert at the Vatican commemorating the Holocaust reveals the equivocal nature of the Church's stance toward Judaism and the Jewish people. The initiation and hosting of the concert was itself a momentous event. The Pope spoke movingly of the suffering endured by the Jewish people, honored the courage and tenacity of the survivors, and appealed to members from both traditions to join together on behalf of justice and peace. However, in neither of his public speeches did the Pope admit to the Church's complicity during the *Shoah*. He did not allude to the fact that this commemoratory event was being initiated by the very Church which, not only disseminated derogatory and false teachings about Judaism and the Jewish people, but also chose a cautious and passive posture during the *Shoah* itself. Thus, the concert continued the thrust of *Nostra Aetate* by focusing upon the future of Jewish-Catholic relations in a manner which did not address the tragic particularities marking the history of those relations. As a result, the concert revealed that once again the Church is not yet ready to stand with the Jewish people and confront the failings of that historical relationship. Other examples of the Church's equivocation are readily found in statements made during the controversy by Cardinal Franciszek Macharski of Krakow and the June 7, 1979 and June 24, 1988 papal sermons of Pope John Paul II. For analyses of the statements and sermons see: Karen Adler, "Controversy over the Carmelite Convent at Auschwitz 1988-1989," *Institute of Jewish Affairs: Research Report* No. 7, (September 1989): 9-10; Alan Montague, "The Carmelite Convent at Auschwitz: A Documentary Summary," *Institute of Jewish Affairs: Summary* No. 8 (October 1987): 1-3, 5, 7-8, 12-13; and Elie Wiesel, "Blood and Ashes:" 73. For texts of the statements and sermons see: "Documentation," *Christian Jewish Relations* 22 (1989): 112-140; Alan Montague "The Carmelite Convent,:" 2-3, 7-8, 19; and Carol Rittner and John K. Roth ed., *Memory Offended*, 243; 247-248.

5. A comparison of papal meetings with various dignitaries discloses the Church's contradictory position toward Judaism and the Jewish people. On September 15, 1985 Pope John Paul II met with Jewish leaders and a year later made an historic visit to the Great Synagogue of Rome. However, he also chose to schedule a meeting with Kurt Waldheim, the former Austrian president and World War II German officer who was accused of Nazi sympathies and collaboration, and to award Waldheim knighthood in the 147-year-old Order of Pius IX in July of 1994. Another example can be found in the Pope's willingness to meet with the PLO Chairman, Yassir Arafat, while steadfastly refusing to establish diplomatic ties with Israel until 1994. For discussions of this contradictory stance see: Karen Adler, "Controversy over the Carmelite Convent at Auschwitz 1988-1989,:" 4-5, 9-16; Monty Noam Penkower, "Auschwitz, the Papacy and Poland's 'Jewish Problem,'" *Midstream* Vol. XXXVI, No. 6 (August/September 1990): 14-15, 17-18; A.M. Rosenthal, "On My Mind," *The New York Times* August 12, 1994; Elie Wiesel, "Blood and Ashes:" 73.

6. The inflammatory sermon delivered by Cardinal Jozef Glemp, Primate of Poland, at the shrine of the Madonna of Czestochowa, followed by his interview with *La Repubblica,* an Italian journal, provide tragic, but unmistakable examples. For a complete text of the sermon in English see: "Documentation," *Christian Jewish Relations* 22 (1989): 121-128. Daniel F. Polish offers a compelling analysis of the consequences of the cardinal's sermon for Jewish-Christian Relations. See: Daniel F. Polish, "Catholic-Jewish Relations and the Auschwitz Controversy," *Ecumenical Trends* 18 (December 1989): 169-172.

7. Several authors thoughtfully address the symbolic significance of Auschwitz for the Jewish community, as well as the complexities of the Jewish-Catholic relationship in Poland. See: Gerhard M. Riegner and Stanislaw Musial, "Documentation: Auschwitz Convent - The Second Geneva Meeting," *Christian Jewish Relations* 20 (1987): 53-59 and John Pawlikowski, "The Auschwitz Convent Controversy: Mutual Misperceptions," *Memory Offended,* 63-72.

8. For a discussion regarding the Church's reticence to acknowledge this fact see: Monty Noam Penkower, "Auschwitz, the Papacy, and Poland's 'Jewish Problem,:'" 14-19.

9. Monty Noam Penkower offers persuasive documentation regarding the failure of Popes Pius XII and John Paul II to recognize and honor the uniqueness of the Jewish experience during the *Shoah.* The actions and words of Pope John Paul II provide contemporary examples. For a concise overview of Pope John Paul II's attempts to defend and rehabilitate Pius XII's role in the Holocaust years see: Monty Noam Penkower, "Auschwitz, the Papacy, and Poland's 'Jewish Problem,:'" 15-16 and S.I. Minerbi, "Pope John Paul II and the Shoah," *The Impact of the Holocaust and Genocide on Jews and Christians.* ed. Yehuda Bauer et al. (Oxford: Pergamon Press, 1989), 2975. For papal statements which defend Pius XII's actions concerning for Judaism and the Jewish people during World War II see: "Lessons of World War II," *The Tablet* September 2, 1989: 1011-1012 and "Overcoming Difficulties of the Past," *Origins: CNS Documentary Service* 8. (April, 12, 1979): 691.

10. The Pope's failure to acknowledge the singularity of the Jewish experience during the *Shoah* becomes the opportunity for reasserting the tragedy suffered by Christians in a manner which renders Jewish suffering invisible. The following example provides an example: "When stopping in 1979 before a Hebrew memorial tablet at Auschwitz, he paid homage to the 'sons and daughters of a nation destined for a complete extermination,' only to speak a few moments later, in front of a tablet with the inscription in Polish, of 'six million Poles [who] perished during the last war, one-fifth of a nation.' Three

million Jews were denied their identity in the statistical service of six million Poles. In 1987, visiting the death camp of Maidanek, John Paul II again made no reference to the Jews - who had perished as Jews." See: Monty Noam Penkower, "Auschwitz, the Papacy, and Poland's 'Jewish Problem,'" 16-17.

11. Rosemary Radford Ruether was one of the first Roman Catholic theologians to undertake a comprehensive and critical analysis of the biblical and theological foundations of Christian anti-Judaism and antisemitism. For an examination of Ruether's thesis see: *Faith and Fratricide: The Theological Roots of Anti-Semitism.* (N.Y.: Seabury Press, 1974); "Anti-Judaism is the Left Hand of Christology," *New Catholic World* 217 (January-February 1974): 12-17; "Anti-Semitism in Christian Theology," *Theology Today* XXX (January 1974): 365-381; and "Christology and Jewish-Christian Relations," *To Change the World: Christology and Cultural Criticism.* (N.Y.: The Crossroad Publishing Company, 1983): 31-44.

12. *The Crucifixion of the Jews* (N.Y.: Harper & Row, 1975) is considered one of Franklin M. Littell's most penetrating analyses of the development and justification of Christian anti-Judaism and antisemitism. Littell offers an invaluable examination of the cultural, political, social, and religious factors which have undergirded Christian anti-Judaism and antisemitism throughout the centuries.

13. The writings of Gregory Baum, Alice L. Eckardt, A. Roy Eckardt, Eugene Fisher, Deborah McCauley, and John Pawlikowski figure prominently in this regard. Each thinker has contributed important insights regarding the development of Christian anti-Judaism and antisemitism, as well as to the justification of their devastating behavioral consequences.

14. Pope John Paul II's sermon in Warsaw during June of 1987 not only appropriates Jewish memory and history, but uses Christian categories to interpret its significance and meaning. The Pope spoke of suffering as a purgative experience which engenders hope during his address to representatives of the Polish Jewish community. He evidenced no awareness that he was imposing a Christian understanding of suffering upon his interpretation of the Holocaust. For a complete version of the text in English translation see: "Remarks by the Pope to the Jews in Warsaw," *Origins: CNS Documentary Service* 17 (September 10, 1987): 200.

15. This dynamic was clearly evident in the remarks made by Pope John Paul II during the meeting of the Pope, Jewish leaders and others on April 7, the day of the Vatican concert to commemorate the *Shoah*: "We must be deeply grateful to all who work to secure ever wider and fuller recognition of the 'bond' and 'common spiritual patrimony' which exists between Jews and Christians.

(Dignitatis Humane, 4) In the past these links have inspired deeds of courageous solidarity. In this regard, as a matter of historical fact, one cannot forget that in my own homeland, as in other countries and also here in Rome, in the terrible days of the Shoah, many Christians together with their pastors strove to help their brothers and sisters of the Jewish community, even at the cost of their own lives." See: "Concert at the Vatican: Commemorating the Holocaust," *Origins: CNS Documentary Service* 23 (April 28, 1994): 783-784.

16. These arguments fail to engage a rigorous examination of the issues at play. They primarily give voice to three reactions: concern that the "goodwill" motivating the Roman Catholic participants is not recognized, surprise at the negative reactions of Jewish organizations, and indignation that the Roman Catholic participation in the negotiations was not received with gratitude. The unconscious theology of supersession shaping these reactions is revealed by their dualistic, hierarchical framework. Judaism and Catholicism are placed in a relationship of oppositionality from there can emerge one "winner." Each tradition is also endowed with characteristics which connote their relative power and location within the convent controversy. The Jewish "side" is characterized as "other," "weak," "helpless," and "foreign," while the Catholic-Polish "side" is characterized as "us," "strong," "householder," and "host." Ultimately, these reactions cannot facilitate a just resolution to the controversy because they are grounded in an unacknowledged, but operative interplay of power, dominance, privilege, normativity, and sovereignty. For striking examples of this mode of argumentation see: Waldemar Chrostowski, "Controversy Around the Auschwitz Convent," *Christian Jewish Relations* Vol. 22 Nos. 3 & 4 (1989): 21-36 and Paul Lewis, "Furore Over the Convent Near Auschwitz," *Christian Jewish Relations* 19 (March 1986): 45-48.

17. Stanislaw Krajewski offers a compelling testimony regarding the tragic impact of the collapse of identities upon Jews who claim their identity as Poles in Poland. See: Stanislaw Krajewski, "The Controversy over Carmel at Auschwitz: A Personal Polish-Jewish Chronology:" 37-54.

18. Thinkers not already mentioned who confront the meaning and significance of the *Shoah* in their writing, lectures, and sermons: Archbishop Edward Iris Cassidy, Francis Schussler Fiorenza, Johann Baptist Metz, and Edward Schillebeeckx.

19. For an overview of papal positions regarding the Nazi Regime, the Jewish victims of the *Shoah*, and the Church's role during the Holocaust see: Monty Noam Penkower, "Auschwitz, the Papacy, and Poland's 'Jewish Problem,:'" 14-19. For a recent reference to the repudiation of the documentation's charges

by Vatican historians see: "On File," *Origins: CNS Documentary Service* 24 (June 9, 1994): 50.

20. Although *Nostra Aetate* signaled the Church's readiness on the level of official teachings to affirm the validity of the other major religions, the final version of the document did not include a condemnation of all Christian persecutions or seek forgiveness from the Jewish people for the suffering they endured throughout those persecutions. Instead, the document focused upon fostering future relations characterized by "that mutual understanding and respect which is the fruit above all of biblical and theological studies, and of brotherly [sic] dialogues." See: "Declaration on the Relationship of the Church to Non-Christian Religions," Walter M. Abbott ed. *The Documents of Vatican II* (N.Y.: Guild Press, 1966): 657. It is cogently argued that this focus reveals the problematic which has plagued the reconstruction of Roman Catholic teachings since the promulgation of *Nostra Aetate*. The failure to address concretely and assume responsibility for the behavioral consequences of Roman Catholic theological teachings has allowed the Church to evade the task of a thorough-going reconstruction of every aspect of Roman Catholic theology. Christian Gudorf provides an interesting development of this argument from the vantage point of psychology in her article "Catholics and Auschwitz: Guilt and Beyond," *Christianity and Crisis* 49 (October 23, 1989): 327-328. Claire Huchet-Bishop sets forth a similar analysis in "The New Road," *Memory Offended,* 147-150. There is some hope that the Church is now ready to address this failure. The International Catholic-Jewish Committee called for a deepening of the Church's assimilation of *Nostra Aetate*. The Committee acknowledged that this presupposes not only a systematic uprooting of antisemitism, but also an explicit act of repentance on the Church's part. See: "Uprooting Antisemitism," *Origins: CNS Documentary Service* 20 (September 20, 1990): 235.

21. Rene Girard's mimetic theory offers crucial insights into the pivotal role which the concept of difference plays in the achievement of justice and peace within any given group. Girard's concept of difference is not predicated upon an understanding of differentiation in terms of dichotomous oppositionality. Rather, the acceptance of separation and the promotion of distinctive identities are of quintessential importance if social cohesion and peace are to be achieved. It is the refusal to honor distinctiveness and the eradication of difference which lead to violence and victimage. For a more detailed discussion of this aspect of the Girardian theory see: Rebecca Adams, "Violence, Difference, and Sacrifice: A Conversation with Rene Girard," *Religion and Literature* 25 (Summer 1993): 9-33; Rene Girard, *Violence and the Sacred* (Baltimore: The John Hopkins University Press, 1977); and James Williams, *The Bible, Violence, and the Sacred: Liberation From the Myth of Sanctioned Violence* (San Francisco: Harper Collins Publishers, 1991), 53-54.

22. Roman Catholic analyses of the collusion of traditional christology with oppressive centers of power are indebted to the insights of the Frankfurt School, particularly those of Jurgen Habermas and his notion of a hermeneutic of suspicion. Analyses by the following Roman Catholic theologians illustrate the influence of Habermas' notion within contemporary Roman Catholic theology: Johann Baptist Metz, *Faith in History and Society: Toward a Practical Fundamental Theology* (N.Y.: The Seabury Press, 1980); *Radford Ruether, Faith and Fratricide*; Edward Schillebeeckx, *Christ: The Experience of Jesus as Lord* (N.Y.: The Crossroad Publishing Company, 1977).

SECTION TWO:

HISTORICAL QUESTIONS AND ISSUES OF MEMORY

Chapter 9

JULIUS STREICHER AND NAZI MEDIEVALISM

Frederick M. Schweitzer

This writer first became interested in Julius Streicher (1885-1946) as an important clue to the murderous Nazi regime through the study of medieval antisemitism, specifically Gavin Langmuir's formulation of chimera, as the foundation of German genocide. Chimeria depends upon a capacity to believe as true phenomena for which there is no evidence and which defy empirical observation and common sense. Like Streicher's, medieval Judaeophobia demonized Jews as offspring of Satan and depicted them as guilty of a series of peculiarly Jewish crimes: conspiring on a global scale through an international organization to kidnap and kill Christian children to use their blood for a variety of ritual, magical, or medicinal purposes; to repeat the crucifixion in mockery each Easter-Passover season; to desecrate the holy host of transubstantiation; to induce plagues by poisoning water, food, air, medicine; to contrive the destruction or enslavement of Christendom, kingdom, people; to rob and dominate by usury, magic, and abominations without end. The Middle Ages struck every note in the cacophony of antisemitism, not excluding the racial one. Reflecting on the quotations from his weekly paper *Der Stürmer* that one comes upon in any extensive account of Nazi Germany, their obvious congruity with medieval fixations, particularly his incessant harping on ritual murder is striking. This again confirmed a truism, viz., the indispensability for and continuity with lethal modern antisemitism of age-old Christian antisemitism.

A fundamental shortcoming of Holocaust scholarship is its underestimation of the significance of medieval Christian antisemitism, partly owing to ignorance of a large, complex subject seemingly remote from the twentieth century; partly an apologetic concern for Christianity's reputation; partly from an interpretation of racism as in itself determinative. Racism and racial nationalism, however, would stigmatize any and all groups outside the *Volksgemeinschaft* more or less equally murderously. Clearly that was not the case, indicating that a basic link in the causal sequence is missing. It was the conjunction of traditional Christian antisemitism with modern racial nationalism that proved to be genocidal. It was not by mere chance that chimerical racial antipathy fastened upon the same people as had the chimerical theological kind.

The supposed racial definition of Jewishness in Nazi Germany was actually a religious definition: the misnamed 1935 Nuremberg *racial* laws specify that Jewishness hinges on how many of one's grandparents were members of the Jewish religious community. There is no reference to physical traits or racial features, an inconsistency that helps to explain the wide use of the negative form, "non-Aryan."[1] In significant degree, therefore, the racial terms and concepts employed by the Nazis were transparent veils, a bit of embroidery and embellishment that camouflaged traditional religious and theological antisemitism, secularized and updated in the pseudo-scientific terminology of the modern age. Thus, to Streicher, the purpose of circumcision always was "to assure racial consciousness," and he averred at his trial that until 1933 "the public made distinctions with respect to Jews only on the basis of religion."[2] Typical of his lucubrations on how to identify a Jew was his disquisition in *Der Stürmer* that they were short and small of stature with flat feet, a roll of fat at the neck, speak in a distinctive sing-song cadence, exude a "sharp, sour-sweet odor" (another medieval leitmotif), but no reference to the proverbial Jewish nose that was given much play in his cartoons; Jews also, he said, were over-sexed, have exceptionally large genitals, are irresistible to innocent females, and infect German women with syphilis. In *Der Giftpilz* he explained to children that indeed the Jew is usually recognized by his nose, "crooked" and "bent," but also by his lips, "thick" and "sloppy," and his eyes and "thicker and more fleshy" eyelids; yet the decisive medievalistic "fact" is that "from a Jew's countenance the evil Devil talks to us."[3] Baird concluded that Streicher's ideas of race and of the "Nordic" type as blue-eyed, blond, brave, and creative were so jejune as to be "comical," that he "fused Christian with cultural antisemitism," that "Christian teachings were interpolated into this tangled ideological mess (of racial dogmas)."[4]

Medieval Christian motifs abound much more in Streicher's speeches and writings than the "racial" ones. On Christ-killing he is quite conventional: "Golgotha has not yet been avenged."[5] That meant that "Jewry/Judaism is organized criminality," a much used statement for him as for medieval theologians; Streicher expands on this motif in explaining that the Torah tells Jews – in the Werner Sombart way – to "get all the wealth into their hands," if also "to spoil every country racially."[6] In his medieval medley, Jews have for millennia been guilty of "desecration of churches, of usury, of ritual murders, etc.;" his litany goes on with "Ahasver, the eternal Jew, wandering from country to country" under "the curse laid upon this criminal nation by God" to have no rest anywhere and to destroy peace throughout the world. Rankled by the very idea, the Jews are no chosen people to him, except chosen by God as the only one criminal enough to torture Jesus Christ to death. The "key to world history" - synonymous with "the Jewish danger" - was the implementation of Jewry's conspiratorial plans.[7]

Another medieval avatar is satanization. Streicher was fond of citing its charter text, the Gospel of John (8:42-47) where Jesus excoriates the Jews as no children of God or Abraham, for "your father is the Devil" whose bidding you do in lying and murdering. Hitler, he said, was "liberating the German people from the Devil, so that mankind might again be free from that race ... marked with the brand of Cain."[8] A typical reference is to Jews as the "Devil in human guise;" "the Jew is neither man nor animal. He is the Devil."[9] "The battle against the Devil," he explained, "is to crush the head of the serpent Pan-Juda ... to eliminate the Devil. And the Devil is the Jew." He crusaded to "save humanity from destruction by the Jewish devils." "This satanic race really has no right to exist."[10] Armed with Satan's superhuman powers, the Jews were presumed to be dominant and dangerous, the "menace" so often invoked which made it necessary to destroy the Jews before they destroy us. Many writers note this fear syndrome — Streicher's warnings of "the frightfulness and dangerousness of the Jew" — without grasping its medieval roots[11] or seeing in it a potent source of German aggression.

Ritual murder was at the core of Streicher's antisemitic phobias. All other "Jewish" crimes seemingly stem from that chimerical archetype. He defined the "monstrous" practice of this "strangely fascinating nation" of "criminals, murderers, and devils in human form" in the heinous 1931 special issue of *Der Stürmer* in 1934, although it reads like a twelfth-century text, as follows:

Enticing gentile children and gentile adults, butchering them and draining their blood, [mixing it] into their matzos and using it to practice superstitious magic. They ... torture their victims, especially the children; and during this torture they shout threats, curses, and cast spells against the gentiles.

A tell-tale clue to the perpetrators, ritual murder victims always exhibited the same "gash in the throat" as the "horrifying" incision of kosher slaughter. The blood is eaten in the matzo and wine of Passover with the prayer that all gentiles will speedily die; it is also sprinkled on young married couples, pregnant women, and at circumcision: "The Jew believes he absolves himself thus of his sins." In its first decade, 1923-1933, not less than 19 issues of *Der Stürmer* featured such articles, ranging from medieval "Little Simon of Trent" and "Boy Heinrich of Munich" to numerous modern examples. Most were from Germany — "where [ritual] murder ... has been preached" in synagogues — but he singled out instances from Poland, a country he praised highly (though normally everything Slavic was despicable) for taking ritual murder seriously and pursuing it rigorously: diligent officials were supported by "an alert and enlightened public." Russian Jews have always "celebrated blood orgies."[12]

Typical of Streicher's use of the ritual murder weapon was his 1935 speech to a mass meeting of the Anti-Jewish World League, when he warned of the pending "mass murder" planned by the "whip-swinging" Jews, what would in fact be "the greatest ritual murder of all times" and the prelude to "Jewish domination not just in Germany but final Jewish domination in the whole world." His first public use of blood libel appears to have been spring 1921, when he made several speeches linking it to the annual disappearances of Nuremberg children, for which calumniation he was tried and fined for slander, the precedent of many similar episodes. In 1922 he returned to the charge, asserting that many newspapers reported that on the eve of the 1919 Easter season over 100 German children had disappeared and that the same fate had befallen three Nuremberg boys in the same weeks of 1920. He explained that the Talmud instructs Jews to kill Christians, especially children, and to drink their blood in ritual celebration. One of his favorite proof-texts for this legerdemain was Eisenmenger's treatise *Judaism Unmasked,* 1700, his principal "source" for passages in the Talmud that require all Jews to participate in ritual murder once a year and "permit any crime against gentiles."[13] (We are still in the Middle

Ages when the Talmud was condemned as heretical and burnt by order of popes, councils, universities, monarchs, inquisitors.)

Streicher's fulmination's produced a riot in 1922 in the town of Ipsheim and led again to his being tried, convicted, and fined. In the court proceedings, he said only talmudic Jews(!) practice ritual murder and he submitted a number of books and treatises as "proof." A characteristic gambit of his speeches was to warn that since Easter-Passover was approaching, everyone had to be on guard against Jewish kidnappers. A frequent device in *Der Stürmer* was to list names of children who had, in fact, vanished from their villages in Franconia, and then to "explain" that they were undoubtedly kidnapped by Jews who chained them in dungeons and sharpened their torture instruments in expectation of the Passover event. Again typical of his fixation on ritual murder was his tactic in attacking a Dr. Marcuse who had proposed a law to end the prohibition on abortion; to Streicher abortion was "murder" and proof that Jews wanted the bodies of German girls made available legally to them the better to commit ritual murder. In the same vein was his accusation of one Rauh, a Jewish lawyer said to have murdered two working-class girls who were raped and poisoned by mercury chloride sold to him by a Jewish pharmacist; Rauh was acquitted but Streicher reiterated his ritual murder diatribe.[14]

Jewish doctors were an immense threat, key players in the Jewish world conspiracy in which Streicher equated abortion, venereal disease, white slavery, and ritual murder. Although they ignored him, in 1934 he ordered physicians in his *Gau* to renounce all medical improvements and cures created by Jews, e.g. insulin, the tuberculin test for tuberculosis, salvarsin and neosalvarsin for treating syphilis, and so on; all "impregnations" with serums, lymph, extracts from animals were part of the Jewish doctors' poison plot. Streicher wrote *Stürmer* articles in impassioned condemnation of three bacteriologists, whose breakthroughs in these areas had made two of them Nobel prize laureates, Robert Koch, Paul Ehrlich, and August von Wasserman. The latter's blood test for detecting syphilis was "criminal," simply another element of the Jews' conspiracy to infect Christian womanhood with venereal diseases and their eternal quest for Christian blood. These attacks, typical of Nazi anti-modernism, commended themselves to Hitler who thought to make the *Gauleiter* of Franconia chief of the public health department, but refrained since "Streicher has not the gifts of a great administrator."[15]

Streicher found the blood libel everywhere he sought it: the Exodus was ritual murder which killed off the first-born, "the whole future generation of Egyptians;" Purim celebrates the mass ritual murder of 75,000 Persians. A further variation on the theme was, in the racial lingo, *The Sin against the Blood*, the spurious best-selling novel by Streicher's friend Artur Dinter. (He too was a renegade Catholic, antisemitic fanatic, war veteran, and became *Gauleiter* of Thuringia; demanding a Protestant Nazism and racial *Volkskirche*, he was forced out of the NSDAP by Hitler in 1928.) This is Streicher's rendering of Dinter's "sin," the counterpart in his racial theology of original sin:

> One single cohabitation of a Jew with an Aryan woman is sufficient to poison her blood forever. Together with the "alien albumen" she has absorbed the alien soul. Never again will she be able to bear purely Aryan children, even when married to an Aryan.

They will be "bastards" having a "dual soul," ugly, deficient in character, and illness prone. Christianity being Jewish in Streicher's view, in the 1934 special issue of *Der Stürmer* he pointed up parallels of the Last Supper and Christian communion with ritual murder and kosher slaughter; but when this brought storms of protest from Catholic and Lutheran pulpits (none of it in defense of Judaism), he drew back, reluctant to stir up the church struggle any further than it had already gone, especially in his Bavarian domain. Pounding the ritual murder drum was the order of the day in Nazi Germany, culminating in the 1940 film *Der ewige Jude* and the 1943 "research" by Helmut Schramm, *Der jüdische Ritualmord-Eine historische Untersuchung*, which Himmler found so compelling that he ordered its wide distribution among SS personnel and "especially the men who are busy with the Jewish question."[16] As in Nazi propaganda, Streicher aimed to make Jews the embodiment of evil, transforming the Jew-next-door into a mythological figure, replacing the Germans' acquaintance with Jews as real persons, human as anyone else, with chimeras and mythic beings, collectively guilty of crimes without evidence or witnesses and of the archcrime of ritual murder, abstract and dehumanized the easier to annihilate.

The starting point of Streicher's antisemitism was, at age five, when he first heard the word *Jew* from his mother, crying because a Jewish merchant had cheated her of the cloth she was to make into a suit as a present for his father. Reinforcement came by what he heard in school, out of the mouth of the priest about the "blood bespattered" savior's sorrows and the Jews' demand that he be crucified; "in those religious lessons I learned for the first time that the nature of the Jews was foreign" to everything German. Notable in this connection is the family residence during Streicher's boyhood in the village of Deggendorf. It was one of many locales scattered about Bavaria with shrines of local saints and pilgrim sites celebrating in the most garish way ritual murder, host desecration, and other sacrilegious acts supposedly committed by Jews. One of these was the Church of Gnad at Deggendorf where, in 1338, host desecration and other gruesome acts perpetrated by Jews were punished by massacre and expulsion, to be celebrated ever after as "legitimate zeal pleasing to God" until the bishop of Regensburg called it a pogrom and put an end to it in 1992. In Streicher's time the cult served as "proof" of Jewish criminality. The inscription under the memorial picture prayed God that Germany "be forever free from this hellish scum," and a play written by a Benedictine monk was performed during the annual festival reprobating Jews as "hordes of the devil," "Judas' brood," poisoners, blasphemers, etc.[17]

Having reviewed the standard works on Streicher, biographies and monographs, some articles from *Der Stürmer*, and the abundant material in the IMT volumes, it was no surprise to find that he was a fanatical dogmatist, a repugnant thug and brawler, lecher and pornographer, greedy and corrupt in luxuriating in stolen Jewish property, one of that crowd of sycophantic misfits with their assorted addictions and deformities chosen by Hitler and readily dominated by him in his inner circle and the party. That impression coincides with the conventional view of Streicher in standard histories. Streicher was the most conspicuous preacher of the Nazi antisemitic movement, one of the regime's antisemitic megaphones, speaking, writing, acting in utter conviction, and supremely effective in conveying the Nazi antisemitic ideology to the masses and in reconciling them to genocide. "I stand at the head of the [anti-Jewish] struggle," he crowed in 1933, which was certainly true then when he was in charge of the anti-Jewish boycott, but not for long thereafter. Crowded out of Hitler's circle by Goebbels, Himmler, and Göring until, as of 1940, he was confined to his farm under Gestapo surveillance, not allowed to speak in public or broadcast, deposed as *Gauleiter*, and permitted only to carry on *Der Stürmer* with which he busied himself to the war's end. To Hitler, who alone retained a high regard for him and still read *Der Stürmer* avidly cover to cover, "the Streicher affair is a tragedy [for which] I have a bad conscience;" he "has never been replaced [and] is irreplaceable," for "one could not hope for the triumph [of Nazism] without giving one's support to men like Streicher," although "he *idealized* the Jew. The Jew is baser, fiercer, more diabolical than Streicher depicted him."[18] Even so, their antisemitism was the same ideological brew expressed in the same paranoid terms. There are further striking parallels between these two studies in psychopathology, who were on "Du" terms with each other: both born and reared as Catholics in lower middle class families, the father occupying a low rung in the civil service, a pious mother (both Streicher's parents were fervent Catholics), in their element in war and at the front, fearful of Jewish extraction (and therefore, possibly, more extreme antisemites so as to deny any such extraction), summoned to leadership by an "inner voice," a capacity to mesmerize mass audiences with marathon excoriations against the Jews, and both dabbled in art and literature and confessed regret that circumstances had forced them into politics.

This writer did not anticipate how monotonously simplistic and utterly unoriginal Streicher's antisemitism was. He was a craven copier of Fritsch, Eisenmenger's elegant falsifications, the unfrocked "priest" August Rohling's inelegant fabrications in the *Talmudjude,* what is the most perverse of all these concoctions — *The Protocols of the Elders of Zion,* and most astonishingly the whole stock of medieval antisemitic superstitions. Only in its scatological vileness and venomous crudity was Streicher's antisemitism exceptional, otherwise it is an infinitely boring replication in the most literal terms of age-old Jew-hatred, medieval and Christian in provenance though often expressed in racist jargon. He was king of *Lumpenantisemitismus* and kitsch.

Everything Streicher said or wrote was pitched at an elementary, comic strip level, which was his level. He was at best half-educated and of barely average intelligence (IQ of 102 according to the Nuremberg psychiatrists, the lowest among those tried by the IMT). So one does not have to read much of *Der Stürmer* for a comprehensive grasp of Streicher's antisemitism. In 1945 he said that he utilized gutter sensationalism and banalities to reach a mass audience: the German he addressed

> is in his thinking simple and in his feelings prodigious. He demands that one speak to him the way he speaks.... To that way of speaking and writing I held my colleagues in *Der Stürmer* and in the Party.

His articles were bolstered by "scholarly" citation of books and treatises in a library of Judaica and antisemitica, eventually some 8,000 volumes and manuscripts collected or given to him and, after 1933, confiscated from their Jewish owners. He claimed to use "what the Jews themselves write in the Old Testament, in their history, what they write in the Talmud (and *Zohar*), excerpts from Jewish historical works" such as the famed Heinrich Graetz. In his credulous, ruffian-like way, Streicher repeatedly cited such cults as Deggendorf, miracle plays like Oberammergau, church frescoes and sculptures, and, to him, the huge number of books and treatises produced by renowned theologians and lawyers as "recognized historical sources" testifying to ritual murder. His "sources" for the infamous 1934 special issue of *Der Stürmer* amounted to "a book written in Greek by a rabbi who had been converted to Christianity;" one by "a high clergyman in Milan" known in Germany for 50 years; "court files in Rome" with pictures that show that the church had "canonized 23 non-Jews killed by ritual murder," and so on. This capacity to invoke "sources" ranging over more than 500 years imparted an air of authenticity and scholarly pretension that reminds one of contemporary Holocaust deniers and revisionists.

While his filthy rantings and cribbed fulminations were repugnant to the sophisticated and refined, to the masses they had a convincing appeal. His was, however, the same message that almost everyone in Hitler's Germany willing proclaimed or willingly received. Streicher and the other Nazis, most of whom disdained him, especially those on trial with him, were all of a piece and adhered to the same murderous ideology, except that some were cultured and philosophically subtle and some were brutally crude and primitive. In contrast to his fellow accused whom he dignified as "the spiritual custodian of the movement," Alfred Rosenberg, author of the elaborate treatise *Myth of the Twentieth Century*, Streicher was, as Ian Kershaw noted, "no more than a vulgar racist demagogue of limited intelligence, incapable of extending his obsessive hatred of Jews into a full-scale ideology." Unremarkably, Streicher was most successful in addressing adolescents and in the children's books he put out. There were also special issues (each as many as four million copies) of *Der Stürmer* directed at the Hitler Youth (so named at Streicher's suggestion) "to instill fear of the Jews in the minds of the youthful leaders," by invoking ritual murder and the all-intruding Devil-Jew.[19]

Streicher had early ceased to be a Catholic and became rabidly anti-Christian, since Christianity was Jewish in origin and character and therefore non-German. In his early years as a teacher he was strenuously anticlerical; on his return from the trenches in 1918 he said he "found God again;"[20] whatever that vague spiritualism (which he shared with other Nazis) signified, it is highly likely that he found in the doctrines of racism and antisemitism a surrogate for Catholicism. Moreover, his mystagogue zealotry made him appear religious and enhanced his appeal to many followers, like one in 1922 who hailed him as "the new Luther." Streicher seemed to relish this comparison, as when he said on going to jail in 1926 that he could not do differently nor "recant a single word;" or during the 1933 Boycott that he led, "Strike down the world enemy! And though the world were full of devils, we must yet prevail!" The Protestant Reformer was much hailed in connection with *Kristallnacht*, which occurred on his birthday; a special edition of excerpts from his loathsome transcription of medieval antisemitism, *The Jews and Their Lies* (1543) by Lutheran bishop Martin Sasse exalted Luther as "the greatest antisemite of his time."[21] The Nazis, Streicher in the lead, made much of Luther for obvious reasons, as he indicated in blurting out to the IMT that

> Luther would very probably sit in my place in the defendants' dock today, if this book had been taken into consideration by the Prosecution. In the book ... Luther writes that the Jews are a serpent's brood and one should burn down their synagogues and destroy them.[22]

At Nuremberg Streicher was convicted and sentenced to death on the charge that he had conspired to commit crimes against humanity.

> His 25 years of speaking, writing, and preaching hatred of the Jews ... infected the German mind with the virus of anti-Semitism, and incited the German people to active persecution.

The contrast with Schacht, Von Papen and Fritzsche (all acquitted), Speer and Von Schirach (each 20 years) is stark. Streicher was unsavory and obnoxious to the court, and he alone paraded his loyal belief in Hitler; he convulsed his defense counsel and exasperated the tribunal by insisting – even though it hurt his case — upon the "fact" of ritual murder "up to the present" and the "truth" of antisemitism, demanding that he be able to submit "documentary evidence."[23] No doubt class affiliation and court room demeanor also did much to favor the five defendants mentioned and to vitiate Streicher's standing. His propaganda of hate and fear — as he boasted — intensified the antisemitic atmosphere of the Third Reich. Yet, if the most outrageous, *Der Stürmer* was only one of a great many German antisemitic papers. The extreme antisemitism, paranoid and nihilistic, such as marked Hitler and Streicher and served to integrate the NSDAP, was never grafted upon the German public at large. It was unnecessary to do so, since their traditional antisemitism and apathy — the fate of the Jews "was of no more than minimal interest to the vast majority" — enabled the Nazi regime to carry out the Shoah with impunity. And so Kershaw concludes, "The road to Auschwitz was built by hate [of the Hitler, Streicher kind], but paved by indifference [on the part of a still largely Christian population]."[24] As he proclaimed in 1924, Streicher appealed "particularly [to] you who carry the cross throughout the land."[25] Whether justice was served by his execution or by the non-execution of most of those acquitted or imprisoned is the subject of another paper. This paper has shown Streicher to have been a medieval apparition, chief exemplar of Nazi medievalism.

Notes

1. Raul Hilberg, *The Destruction of the European Jews* (New York: Holmes & Maier, 1985), 65-80; more generally, see Uriel Tal, "Religious and Anti-Religious Roots of Modern Anti-Semitism," The Leo Baeck Memorial Lecture (New York, 1971), #14.

2. Joseph E. Persico, *Nuremberg* (New York: Viking, 1994), 228f.; International Military Tribunal, *Trial of the Major War Criminals*, 42 vols. (Nuremberg, 1947-49), 12:312; hereafter IMT.

3. Office of United States Counsel for Prosecution of Axis Criminality, *Nazi Conspiracy and Aggression*, 8 vols. and 2 supplements (Washington, D.C., 1946-48), 4:358; hereafter *NCA*.

4. "Das politische Testament Julius Streichers," ed. Jay W. Baird, *Vierteljahrshefte für Zeitgeschichte*, 26 (1978): 664, 666.

5. *NCA*, 8:21.

6. *NCA*, Suppl. B:1433-35.

7. *NCA*, Suppl. A:1211-12.

8. IMT, 5:111.

9. IMT, 5:97; Randall L. Bytwerk, *Julius Streicher* (NY: Stein & Day, 1983), 168.

10. *NCA*, 8:6-7; *NCA*, Suppl. A:1209; IMT, 12:370.

11. Showalter, 58-59, 129-31; Bytwerk, 121; quote in IMT, 5:113.

12. *NCA*, 8:28 and 5:372-73; Showalter, 158; *NCA*, Suppl. A:962.

13. IMT, 38:111-12; *DS*, 1936 sp. is. #4, Leo Baeck Institute, NYC.

14. William P. Varga, "Julius Streicher: A Political Biography, 1885-1933," Ph.D. diss. (Ohio State University, 1974), 154.

15. Robert E. Conot, *Justice at Nuremberg* (New York: Harper & Row, 1983), 292; *Hitler's Secret Conversations, 1941-1944*, ed. H.R. Trevor Roper (New York: Signet Books, 1961), 170.

16. Hilberg, 1021-22.

17. Kershaw, 229 n. 14; Guenther Lewy, *The Catholic Church and Nazi Germany* (New York: McGraw-Hill, 1964), 272-73.

18. *Secret Conversations*, Dec. 1941, 168-70; cf. Apr. 1942, 393.

19. IMT, 12:328 on Rosenberg; Kershaw, *Hitler* (London: Longman, 1991), 31; Varga, 226.

20. Baird, 672.

21. Robin Lenman, "Julius Streicher..." in Anthony Nicholls, ed., *German Democracy and the Triumph of Hitler* (London: Allen & Unwin, 1971), 131 n. 1; Varga, 167; Eliot C. Wheaton, *The Nazi Revolution, 1933-1935* (New York: Anchor, 1969), 309; on Sasse, Mark Edwards, "Luther and the Jews," unpublished lecture, 1980.

22. IMT 12:318.

23. IMT, 12:336-38; *NCA,* Suppl. B:435, 456, 458.

24. *Popular Opinion*, 277, 359, 372; Kershaw refers to "a deeply Christian ... moral sense" as an effective barrier to Nazi threats to the church, but ignores Christian antisemitism when he notes "the reluctance of the church hierarchies, for whatever motives, to oppose the inhumanity towards the Jews," ibid., 274f.; exploration of the "motives" and of "latent anti-Jewish feeling" prevalent in Germany and instrumental to the Nazis would find that it was largely traditional antisemitism, Christian and chimerical.

25. IMT, 5:92.

Chapter 10

CHOSEN CHILDREN: THE JEWISH IDENTITY OF JEWISH CHILDREN DURING THE HOLOCAUST

Leora Saposnik

In the past ten years Holocaust scholarship has broadened its scope of inquiry to include many previously unexplored aspects of this period.[1] Conspicuous among these, is the experience of Jewish children during the Holocaust. Up until very recently, the experiences of Jewish children during the Holocaust were thought to be included by the overall examination of Jewish life during the Second World War. Little thought was given to the unique situation of children in society, much less to the unique situation of children in a threatened community. As the field is being opened to more detailed examination, scholars have been able to redress previous omissions in representation. For example, historians no longer utilize Nazi terminology unequivocally to describe the events which took place during the Holocaust. This paper proposes that a similar reevaluation must take place in expropriating Jewish identity during the Holocaust from the pages of the Nuremberg Laws.

In concurrence with this inclination toward closer examination of Holocaust history, this research sought to challenge the Nazi premise that Jewish identity could be clearly defined by a set of arbitrary, externally imposed guidelines. In order to challenge this premise, this writer chose to look specifically at children, who are assumed to be the least rooted in their communal identity, and who would therefore further defy such facile categorization. Furthermore, this research sought to hold scholars accountable for the accuracy of definition and representation. For, in some measure, we as scholars of this time period have allowed for the Nuremberg definitions to hold, and have accepted the causal relationship between that definition and the ensuing persecution.

Scholars who have researched the Holocaust have to date assumed that one's Jewish identity tied one to the collective Jewish fate. However, by doing so, we have (perhaps unwittingly) allowed the Nazis' definitions of Jews, which resulted in deciding who wore the "Jewish star" and who was to be targeted for death, to determine our own definition of Jewish identity. What this paper proposes is that Jewish identity during the Holocaust was already a difficult notion to define; that Jews were rapidly transforming their identities in the modern era, and that therefore many of those defined as Jews by the Nazis would not have defined themselves as Jews. The Jews of Europe were not a monolithic, highly segregated group. Furthermore, the Nazis' definition of Jews was based on a rather artificial "racial" classification alone, and did not encompass the other social, cultural, religious and national elements embodied in Jewish identity. Moreover, the process of determining whether one was Jewish or non-Jewish was quite an arbitrary act, often dependent on an official's opinion or mood, rather than the "science" the eugenics movement suggested. The nature of Jewish identity has long eluded scholars. Jews have been variously classified as an ethnic group, a religious affiliation, a people, and a race. In studying the systematic persecution of this group during the second World War, contemporary scholarship has not yet addressed the difficulties in describing exactly who those six million victims and the remaining survivors were. Although this point may seem self-evident, our presuppositions that those who were persecuted were persecuted based on their "race," are in effect based on Nazi definitions of Jewishness.

The question of identity becomes all the more compelling when we examine the pivotal role identity played in Nazi classification and the consequences those classifications carried for their victims. The Nazis made identity a key issue in their racial ideology. One of the first decrees specifically aimed at the Jewish community was an attempt to define them in order to confine them. It became increasingly clearer that the Nazis desired to "strip"[2] the Jews of their former identities, and reclassify them according to Nazi perceptions. The Reich Citizenship law (which formed part of the Nuremberg Laws) reads:

Jew is he who is descended from at least three grandparents who are fully Jewish by race.... Also to be considered a Jew is a partly Jewish national who is descended form two fully Jewish grandparents and who belonged to the Jewish religious community, upon adoption of the [Reich Citizenship] Law, or is received into the community thereafter, or who was married to a Jewish person upon adoption of the law, or marries one thereafter, or who is the offspring of a marriage concluded by a Jew (as outlined in paragraph 1) after the entry into force of the Law for the Protection of German Blood and Honor of September 15, 1935..., or who is the offspring of an extramarital relationship involving a Jew (as defined in paragraph 1) and who is born out of wedlock after July 31, 1936.[3]

As it has been pointed out previously, this Nazi attempt to uniformly categorize a widely diverse population was absurd when it came to adults, but was even more so when it applied to children, who by and large were still forming their identities. Children, a segment of society which is normally provided a chance to develop personal and group identities as a result of a gradual process of observation and deliberate education by the family unit; were in this case compelled to suppress their individual and communal identities without proper explanation. By and large, these critical elements of identity development during childhood, were expropriated from Jewish children living in Nazis occupied Europe. In this light, this research also sought to examine how children reacted to their group identity in the total or partial absence of these traditional tools. Furthermore, the research is intended to pose a paradoxical question: was or to what extent was the children's own Jewish identity reinforced by external Nazi definition of them as Jews? Did it in fact, in an odd turn of events, in some cases make it easier to identify as a Jew because one had already been recognized as such?

In examining the relationship of Jewish children to their Jewish identity, this study will look at that identity as it was carried and transformed by the children through various settings. That is, most often the children's situation did not remain static throughout the war; rather, as the adults around them struggled to preserve them and their world for as long as possible, Jewish children were often ferried from setting to setting in an attempt to save their lives. By examining the children's changing self-perception in each setting, one can observe their continual struggle to come to terms with their Jewish identity, even as that identity became increasingly more threatening.

I. Pre-War Life

As the Nazis first rose to power in Germany, this chapter primarily reflects the changes confronted by German Jewish children. However, as Nazi domination spread throughout much of Europe, the children's lives and fates were impacted by the objective factors of their home countries. While each individual child was affected by a unique set of circumstances, children were equally affected by such factors as: the timing of German invasion and occupation of their country (and by which branch of the German army), the geographical location of their home country (significant in both attempts at rescue and self-preservation such as emigration and resistance), the prevailing attitude of the local non-Jewish population toward increased victimization of the Jewish population (which often determined the severity to which the Nazis implemented discriminatory legislation),[4] the stance of Church leaders, and the history of Jewish-Gentile relations in the home country.

As these factors illustrate, there was great variety in the timing and fervor of Nazi victimization, however, what must be stressed is that despite these distinctions, all Jewish children under Nazi occupation underwent a measure of ill-treatment which altered their sense of self and sense of security.

At first Nazi anti-Semitic propaganda, rather than specific legislation, signaled the changing world for German Jews. Children were confronted with negative images of their community in everything from textbooks, to children's rhymes, games and movies. The continued barrage of Nazi governmental decrees and societal attitudes challenged the children to interpret their position vis-à-vis their Jewish identity. As children were stripped and distanced from their national community they began to question their position in that commonwealth as well as in their other communal affiliations (such as family, ethnic or religious group, peer group and others). The final blow for children came when the Nazis introduced the racial definitions embodied in the Nuremberg Laws, which facilitated the children's banishment from all that had once been their domain of learning and playing. Children were no longer allowed to attend school with their gentile friends, nor were they allowed to play in public parks, or swim in public swimming pools. Werner Angress points out in his book: *Between Fear and Hope: Jewish Youth in the Third Reich*, that in this case, it was children who were far more affected than adults; for while some adults could continue in their daily routine of work,

Conversely, education and vocational or professional training for Jewish youth were restricted on all levels nearly at once.... Thus the prospects of young Jews for a normal life in Germany were negated step-by-step nearly from the outset of Nazi rule.[5]

It goes without saying that all Jewish children under Nazi occupation experienced this same separation and denial of rights to an extremely similar degree, however the timing of these institutionalized decrees differed from one country to the next. The institutionalization of such isolationist decrees, must be considered the pivotal point in reconstructing the children's perceptions of themselves as Jews.

This violent separation from the community they shared with their gentile friends raised two distinct but obviously related sets of issues, and engendered a two-part reaction. The immediate response was related to the trauma of ostracism and expulsion. Suddenly, from one week to the next, a basic structure of their experience collapsed – and collapsed for them alone. Their subsequent reaction centered on the question of Jewish identity. For the first time in many of these children's lives, they were forced to confront the concept of what being a Jew meant to them and to the society in which they lived. They had no choice but to understand that they were thrown out of school solely because they were Jews. It was a legal and societally accepted sign that they were marked as different. No longer members of the community, they were strangers.[6]

Coming to terms with how one perceived one's self provided an enabling mechanism for self protection. Once the children themselves understood what their own feelings toward Judaism were they could then confront the anti-Semitic propaganda which was becoming part of their daily lives. One child survivor describes her frustration at having not been handed any tools to counter the negative images that met her at every turn:

I would see posters ... horrendous caricatures.... At first when I saw it, it filled me with real loathing and also tremendous anxiety. I was not quite sure how to cope with it ... I did not know how to counter the growing anti-Semitic propaganda and the caricatures and the attacks made on Jews on many fronts, because I had so little positive identification as a Jew from my own background and experience.

While the initial stages of differentiation were difficult, and were indelibly branded in the minds of most children old enough to remember the visual and audible assault on Jews, these incidents were but fragments of disruption in an otherwise normal child existence. As the survivor recounts, the actual impact of the restrictions on an 11½ year old child, were far more emotionally burdensome than physically injurious.

> As far as I was concerned ... [the impact] was much more psychological than it was physical.... Obviously, there were many restrictions on our lives ... but, on the whole it was the psychological effect that was really indelible [because] I had never developed a positive Jewish image, I found it so terribly difficult to respond to any attacks that were directed against me or against the Jewish people....[7]

The irony that resulted from this situation is that as the Nazis endeavored to define and confine the children's lives, many Jewish children reacted by undertaking to know more and become more enmeshed in the world to which they now willingly or unwillingly belonged. Unexpectedly perhaps, the feeling of being shunned from one society led the children to embrace their newfound (or for some children already) existent solidarity with the people whom externally they were to belong to, and now internally desired to belong to. Thus many children relate their excitement at attending the compulsory Jewish schools, after being forcibly expelled from state schools. By 1935-1936, conditions in the state run public schools were increasingly unpleasant for Jewish children; many had experienced ostracism from former friends and teachers, public humiliation, unfair grading and even blows, thus suddenly to find themselves among other peers with similar backgrounds and an understanding teaching staff elated the children.

> How insignificant were the difficulties [I] encountered with foreign language in comparison to the positive changes which this Jewish institution of learning brought into my life. Gone was the evil nightmare of Jew hatred. There was no longer a picture of the Fuhrer; there were no more Sieg Heils, no unfair brawls, and no Nazi fighting songs. Liberated, I was allowed to breathe freely.[8]

As Werner Angress points out, the Jewish schools served the function of providing an alternative educational resource for Jewish children who could otherwise not further their education, but more significantly they provided a meeting place and refuge for Jewish children. Additionally,

The Jewish schools did not merely dispense knowledge. Beyond this primary task, they also tried to strengthen the pride and raise the Jewish self-awareness of their young charges.[9]

As their surroundings were increasingly hostile, the all Jewish environment enabled the children to acknowledge their feelings with others who shared their fears and confusion, and struggle with their peers to provide answers to what being Jewish really meant. This process of self-analysis and communal coping also engendered a restoration of pride and integrity to badly wounded egos. In a sense, it is fairly ironic that the Jewish schools reacted to the Nazi decrees by emphasizing the positive nature of Jewish identification. One might wonder why the Jewish schools desired to increase the Jewish content of their curriculum precisely at a time when it was so uncomfortable to be a member of the Jewish community. The report of the Central Committee for Aid and Development in Germany, December 1933, outlines the perceived goals of Jewish education:

> We can state in general that the Jewish schools are attempting to make the overall instruction more [consciously] Jewish in nature in order to convey to the growing youths the degree of emotional support that they will require for their future life....[10]

The document further stated that every child was to

> acquire a healthy awareness of ... [his or her] Jewishness, ... [he or she] was to learn gladly what this meant, with every bit of pride and sacrifice this entailed. For this reason, "things Jewish" were to be made "the core of all subjects suited for them," thus notably in religion, Hebrew, biblical and Jewish history.[11]

Perhaps Martin Buber and others who were responsible for drafting the guidelines, recognized that for the children "this was not ... a political measure, a law passed by others, an edict published in the papers. This was personal."[12] While the exclusionary measures constantly forced the children to confront questions of community and identity; their new schools provided them with the sanctuary from which it was safe to confront these issues.

Many children describe their flowering as individuals during this interim period prior to the start of the war, and while emigration was still a viable option. While identity formation is presumed to be a gradual process of learned and observed identification with parental role-models, it is at this stage when the first signs of the deterioration of that assumed model appear. Oftentimes, it was precisely those children who had been provided very little previous knowledge of their Jewish roots who now became determined to discover what was embodied in their Jewishness, and how they could participate. What is also true is that some children endeavored to rebel against their parents for preparing them so poorly for their current circumstances that they embraced everything Jewish and joined Zionist and other Jewish Youth organizations, because they knew that their parents would think ill of such "overtly" Jewish activities. The children themselves took on the presumed parental role by educating themselves on the meaning of their Jewish heritage. The children strove to move beyond that model provided by their parents and find other role models perhaps better suited to their current circumstances. Thus:

> We asked: "who are we? What does it mean to be Jews?" They who had been assimilated before and lived among Catholics all their lives faced these questions when they were together. And they learned that Judaism was not a religion alone. "This was the great discovery of the Jewish school when we began to understand that to be Jewish was not only to be of the Jewish religion. A Jewish culture existed, a Jewish civilization existed, that, in other words, all that is meant by Jewish existence. All this was very important. In my opinion, the Jewish school was like the opening of a book for us, and we began to read in this book which had been completely closed to us before.[13]

This new found consciousness,

> coupled with the relief of being with peers their age and exposed to the same hardships, lent to many of these young people an inner strength that their parents by then were no longer able to give them.[14]

As the sphere of life in childhood and adolescence is generally limited to the two primary areas of education and social groupings, the devastation caused by separation from these spheres was significant. The fact that the Jewish schools and youth movements provided the opportunity to participate in these once again, furnished necessary guidelines for Jewish youth during the Holocaust.

> As children and adolescents, they generally suffered more under the discriminatory practices they encountered than did their elders. The latter

were able in many instances to maintain their relations with non-Jewish friends and acquaintances of long-standing, or if these relations started to disintegrate, to deal with the reasons for such a development rationally. Conversely, many youngsters, notably those at the age of puberty, reacted purely emotionally and more violently than their parents did. And as they were now shunned by their peers as pariahs, they became receptive to new circles of friends and thus often joined a Jewish youth group.[15]

Like the Jewish schools, the Jewish youth movements opened up a whole new world to European Jewish children. Not only did the youth groups provide a rare opportunity to hold discussions, dance, and play with complete abandon, they also provided a safe place from which to dream of the possibility of flight from the present circumstances. At a time in which the world seemed more fractured, these youth had the opportunity to experience a measure of solidarity with other children who were undergoing similar feelings and experiences. Children from assimilated and more Jewishly aware families suddenly were brought together by a shared sense of fate, and a desire to understand what it meant to be marked as a Jew. Socio-economic differences were also bridged by this process, in which Jewish children re-grouped based on their Jewish identification rather than other social distinctions. The diaries, letters, memoirs and oral testimonies of survivors frequently recount the feeling of solidarity granted by this sense of belonging:

> I was not brought up with any kind of Jewish background.... The Youth group met on Saturday afternoon ... we used to do a lot of *hora* dancing and we used to have a lot of intellectual discussions ... I loved it ... I felt tremendous. I mean this really gave me a lot of strength.[16]

As Werner Angress affirms, the Jewish settings of youth groups and schools provided a host of benefits for Jewish youth under Nazi occupation.

> A further consequence of the new situation after January 1933 was the discovery of things Jewish and of Jewish values.... The fact that they had suffered discrimination simply because they were Jewish awakened their self-consciousness and forced them to accept the affiliation with this religious community and its history dating back over 2000 years.... Primarily the Zionist youth groups did their part to impart Jewish traditions and knowledge frequently all but forgotten or never even known by the boys and girls, and to bring these to life.... The objective

was to strengthen first and foremost their awareness as Jews and their pride in being part of a larger community.[17]

As the circle of life for children became more constricted, the adults around them endeavored to hold back the ill effects of the shrinking sphere of life, by replacing the lost institutions with replicas of those institutions. Just as there had been public schools, now there were Jewish schools, just as there had been youth groups, now the children had their own Jewish youth groups. As discussed previously, the fact that the German Jewish community reacted rather quickly to each Nazi decree limiting the sphere of life for Jewish children, by replacing the state-run programs with internal communal programs, meant that Jewish children did not feel the full weight of their exclusion from their national grouping, as it was rapidly replaced by a cultural/religious community. These substitutions revived the self-esteem of Jewish children and entrenched them in their Jewish identity. An interesting example of a direct mimicry of the German youth groups comes from a distortion of the Hitler Jugend cry: "The Fuhrer we thank you!" which was reconstructed in the Zionist Youth groups as: "Herzel and Trumpeldor the Jewish Youth thanks you!"[18] followed by singing the Hatikva. The critical element which seems to have provided the glue which kept Jewish identity strong was that at this point families were by-and-large intact, as were the newfound Jewish social circles. Thus, despite the hardships of life under Nazi rule and scrutiny, the children generally experienced a sense of physical and social security. This sense of security engendered largely by a normal continuance of expected societal groupings, was a pivotal aspect of the maintenance of the self-esteem of Jewish youth.

The disintegration of the independent functioning of the Jewish community and its ability to shield German Jews from some of the hardship dictated by life under the Nazis really came with two pivotal Nazi decisions: the first ended the possibility of emigration, and the second compelled Jews to be visibly distinct from the rest of the German population by the Nazis adding the name Sarah or Israel to one's name, by stamping one's identity card with a bold, red "J" and finally, by compelling all Jews over the age of six (in different places there were other age limits) to wear the "star of David" on their outer garments. This pattern was repeated elsewhere in areas occupied by Germany after 1939, only in all other places the process of destroying the independent functioning of the Jewish communities advanced much more rapidly. This in the final analysis, was the final "stripping" of the

Jews of Europe, which left them little hope to escape the next phase of Nazi policy, as yet unknown to them. As they were stripped of viable options, of hope for rescue, and of a chance to be unrecorded, and undistinguished, children expressed a variety of reactions to their new situation. The physical "branding" exemplified by the compulsory "Jewish star" seems to have occupied many of these children. Yitzhak Arad testifies to his own conflicted feelings, as a 13 year old boy obliged to wear the yellow star:

> On the first of December all Jews aged 12 and over were ordered to wear a blue and white ribbon on their right hand, and upon it was a blue *magen david* on a white background.... When I went down to the street adorned with the ribbon, I felt a mixture of pride and humiliation at once. ...I convinced myself that it was incumbent upon me to wear this symbol on my arm with pride. However, the fact that I was compelled to wear this symbol by the Nazi occupiers, degraded me. I was sure that many others felt similarly to me, as they first put the ribbon on.[19]

Yitzhak Arad came from a very observant Polish Jewish family, in which his father was a cantor. Subsequently it may have been easier for a child who understood that he was essentially linked to his Jewishness to accept the fact that now others could also identify him as a Jew. Arad found sanctuary instead in the Zionist movement which endowed the *Magen David* he was wearing with an alternative meaning to that imposed by the Nazis. In effect, the youth movement allowed him to come to terms with this degradation by thoroughly reversing the intent of the Nazis and wearing the "Jewish star" as a sign of Jewish national pride. Other children from more assimilated Jewish backgrounds had greater difficulty understanding why they suddenly had to be marked. Renee Roth-Hano recalled her childhood in Germany and later in France and her reaction to the compulsory donning of the star:

> Fourteen major anti-Semitic decrees were passed by 1940, when we arrived in Paris, and 1942, when we had to go into hiding. The one that bothered me the most was the one that said I had to wear the Star of David. I was 10 years old. I had always been a very inquisitive, outgoing kid, but wearing the star was like the final straw, the most damaging of all; it made me feel ashamed. I became very withdrawn.... I felt so incensed by the decrees which were telling me, "you are a Jew" even though I didn't feel like a Jew and hadn't been raised as one.[20]

As the Nazis pursued their ideal of creating *Lebensraum* for Germany and began occupying, first Poland, and later many other countries across the European continent, their restrictive measures directed against Jews, traveled with them and were implemented with great speed. As the report appearing in "Congress Weekly" a journal of the World Jewish Congress, demonstrates, the victimization of Jews in occupied Europe was abrupt and immediate.

> The process of subjugating the occupied European lands to the Nazi ideology with anti-Semitism as the capstone of the "new order" is proceeding at almost a feverish pace. Anti-Semitism has reached the blitzkrieg stage. The Germans have learned to be deft at it. What required years even in Germany to put through in the way of anti-Semitic restriction and proscription is now being put through in a few months in the Nazi occupied lands.[21]

As a result, most children in these newly conquered areas did not have the same amount of time to become accustomed to their changing status, nor did their communities have the same luxury of time to institute "replacement" communities for them, as had happened in Germany. Hence, these children were severed from their two primary spheres of existence, education and social groupings, quite suddenly (in fact in some cases they were forcibly separated from these spheres by their local authorities, even prior to actual German occupation).

Indeed the next phase of life brought little security to these children's lives. Many lost families and friends and the necessary stability and guidance that correspond with societal structure as they entered periods of ghettoization, life in hiding, or death.

II. Children In Ghettos

The ghetto was a place in which the multitude of definitions and identifications which existed both prior to the war, and during, surfaced and remained highly observable. Jewish life within the ghetto was not divorced from Jewish life as it had existed outside the parameters of war. The ghetto not only reflected these pre-existing divisions, it often accentuated them. As numerous diaries and eyewitness accounts affirm, the ghetto was also a site in which Jewish learning and life took place in quite a concentrated form. For Jewish youth, the outcome of living within the confines of an entirely Jewish "city" of sorts, took on three major characteristics. The first, was a renewed sense of Jewish identity, precisely because these Jewish children were now being forced to confront their own people and their connection to these people on a very basic level of daily existence. This bolstering of young Jewish identification was a conscious tool on the part of some sectors of the Jewish community who understood that Nazi occupation was bringing with it an unparalleled sense of threat to Jewish existence in Europe. The second consequence of ghettoization, was an ambivalent opinion toward Jewish identity. Many children (and adults alike) reacted to legal and physical measures which separated them from their former world and their former freedom to choose who they were and how they desired to present themselves, by outright rejection of compulsory identification. Many maintained that their national identities took precedence over their communal identification, and were distraught at the sudden rupture in their sense of self. This trend was assisted by the fact that the majority of European Jewry was already severely effected by the increasing trend of assimilation in language, dress, politics and culture. The third and most drastic manifestation of Jewish children's identities in the ghetto was a rejection of Jewish identity for the purpose of survival. Some Jewish children who had little time to gain an affinity to their Jewishness saw no viable reason for attachment to the principles of Judaism, nor to a dying people. In these cases, Jewish children wished to be transformed and disconnected from the community, so that they might be in a position of power, in which they could choose to be a member of a group not being victimized. These outgrowths of ghetto life will be explored more fully in the course of this chapter.

At first, many children have described the initial relief of sorts at having been forced into the ghetto. The ghetto, like the Jewish schools described previously, enabled Jewish children and youth to live among other Jews and avoid the (by then) almost daily taunts and unpleasant environment which existed outside the ghetto walls. In a sense, not knowing what the future would bring for the ghetto inhabitants, some children related the excitement of being moved to a new place, where they hoped for a relative serenity, and acceptance among peers. Nelly Toll recalls:

> It was different playing in the ghetto rather than in the Christian part of town. In a strange way the ghetto was our territory. No one here called us bad names, and there were plenty of kids to play with.[22]

On the one hand and especially in the early years of ghettoization, children gained a sense of their Jewish identity through a myriad of cultural and educational activities which were consciously set up by the community precisely in order to bolster their sense of self; while on the other hand, the constant danger to which these children were exposed, moved them to ask: "why me?" and in the larger context, "why us?," why the Jews? The ghetto was at once a prison and a haven of sorts. In the ghettos, Jewish children found themselves in an all Jewish atmosphere, which though it was compulsory, afforded them an opportunity to explore their Jewish heritage. Unlike children who went into hiding on the "Aryan" side, these children understood that at the moment, the reality of their present lives afforded them no options of escaping their Jewishness and becoming anyone but themselves, as they were locked into it in quite a literal sense. Thus, the ghetto, at least for a time was a haven from the barbaric and hostile world lying on the other side of the wall. Feivel Podeh, a youth involved in the Ha Shomer Ha Tzair Zionist Youth Movement, in the Lodz ghetto wrote about the sealing of the ghetto, on April 30, 1940,

> Precisely then an easing of life for Jews occurred -- because in the city they suffered from a sense of vulnerability -- at any moment they could be caught by a German and be killed or tortured. Suddenly, after the initial shock of forced removal to the ghetto, a new period began: the period of "independence" for the Jews of Lodz.[23]

In this setting, everyone was Jewish, and therefore wearing the "yellow star" was no mark of shame, rather it was the norm. Ultimately, however, Jewish children were placed in increasingly more dangerous positions, and Jewish life within the ghetto became constricting, defeating, and finally a way-station towards doom.

Numerous cases of what is often termed, "spiritual resistance" have been recorded in the ghettos. That the Jewish community as a whole endeavored to exist and maintain some semblance of normal life is evident through the surviving documentation, both visual and oral. As in the pre-war period, the Jewish youth groups offered an outlet for Jewish children to be together and to temporarily block-out the world in which they were mired. Feivel Podeh, who wrote down his testimony in 1945, which is based on the notes, letters and diaries kept by members of his Zionist youth group which he collected after surviving the last *Aktzia* in the Lodz ghetto, describes the enhanced importance of the youth groups in the context of the ghetto.

> We met often and one can say with full assurance that our lives were eased only because of these meetings. There were moments, and even hours, when we forgot about everything. And it seemed to us that we were back in the [pre-ghetto] home of our troupe, on 110 Pietrovska Street.[24]

These children did not merely rely on their families to provide them with Jewish content; rather they turned toward their peers in a desire to see other young and vibrant people who did not carry the gloom of the ghetto on their features. Haviva Dembinska, who was six years old in 1939, testified in 1946 to the important role the youth of the ghetto played:

> Every house arranged its own hidden "corner" where the children came to learn to read and write. I went too. Our teacher was a 17 year old girl named Sokolowska. She talked to us about Palestine and told us stories about the history of our people.[25]

On the other hand, Jewish children in the ghettos also experienced starvation, apathy, loss and death. One cannot say that all Jewish children viewed the ghetto as a place where one could finally breathe free; on the contrary, many Jewish children began to realize that the rules of the game were changing, and that survival in this context was dependent less on faith and community, then on power and might. In their despair, the children chose the values which operated their world, in which those who had uniforms, boots and weapons controlled the move of those without these. Emmanuel Ringelblum depicts several instances in which very young Jewish children became so overwrought about being helpless to change their conditions, that they began to emulate the behavior of the oppressor.

> An eight year old child went mad. Screamed "I want to steal, I want to rob, I want to eat, I want to be a German." In his hunger he hated being Jewish.[26]

Under these conditions the children became more savvy, more aware of what the rules of their world dictated. Ringelblum recounts a discussion the children were having about what will happen to the Jews, in a February, 1940 entry he writes:

according to [my son] Uri, the children tell one another: "the old people will be shot, the middle aged will be sent to the camps, and the children will be baptized and passed out among Christian families."[27]

Of course, however aware the children were of the changing laws of existence, they could not have anticipated that Nazi racial ideology saw no salvation for the Jew other than death. The children had no way of knowing that for the Nazis, baptism provided no shield against the supposed "racial pollution" that these small children were capable of.

As the ghetto began to be dismantled and liquidated by the Nazis, it became increasingly clear that it was no longer a viable option, for even the skeletal form of existence it offered was now being demolished. One 14 year old boy wrote: "We are like animals surrounded by the hunter. The hunter is on all sides: beneath us, above us, from the sides.[28] Thus, special efforts were made to ferry Jewish children out of the ghetto. Jewish children were dispersed in a variety of settings. Some children went into hiding on the "Aryan" side, others fled to the woods to join family camps, or partisan guerrilla units, and still others had no avenues of escape and were deported to concentration camps and death camps. The following chapters will explore the unique situations in which Jewish children were placed.

III. Hidden Children

In the inter-war era, approximately 1.6 million Jewish children lived on the European continent. After the Holocaust, 1.5 million of these Jewish children had been murdered. Of those who did survive, the majority were children who were hidden.

Hidden children can be grouped into two categories: those who were hidden "invisibly" tucked away in an attic, a pantry, a closet or sewer, and who remained shut off from the world they once knew; and those who remained "above ground" on false documentation, extending their lease on life by assuming a new identity. The stories of children in hiding hold particular relevance to the topic at hand, because their Jewish identity was at the root of their concealment.

Hidden children's group identity was placed under tremendous strain; first because they were most often hidden alone, with no adult role-models to help them sustain their sense of self, and secondly because they were frequently very young. Those hidden above ground on false documentation, were told to assume every aspect of that new identity: name, nationality, cultural and religious origin, age and ancestry. Therefore, to recall or to mention who one truly was, would have put the child and the hosts in grave danger. Thus, it should not be surprising that many children, particularly those who were hidden "above ground" on "Aryan" papers, felt a dire need to escape this identity and fate. For though the Nazis posited that this identity could not be shed, the children simply deduced that by changing a few artificial components of their identities, they could in fact completely transform themselves and their circumstances. Children who were hidden without papers, that is in a variety of enclosed settings, may have felt an equal desire to break away from an identity which tied them to unbearable circumstances and unbearable tension in which they were constantly hanging on the fine line between life and death. However, since transforming themselves into "Aryans" was not a viable option for many of these children, they may have more likely accepted that they were inextricably linked to their Jewish roots, but may have struggled no less with the consequent implications of this at the time. These children felt tremendous rejection from the larger society, since their very presence could engender such harsh reactions. Consequently their sense of self became quite bruised.

Visible but Invisible: Hidden Children Under an Assumed Identity

These children understood that their lease on life was extended only because they ceased to be themselves. This meant that any friends who played with them or any neighbors who were kind to them, treated them in such a manner on the condition that they remain someone other than themselves. Though these children may have benefited from the occasional suspension of their anxiety, in which they acted like any other children, the key element to this construction is the verb "act." In essence these children endured a double life, one of which included pretending to be happy playful children, while the other included the knowledge that not only had they (in most cases) been separated from family and friends, but the very fact of what their true identity represented could imperil their entire existence. While children who were physically hidden could at least remain themselves, precarious a situation though it may have been, children who lived on borrowed documents, had to assume the personality, the name and the history that so arbitrarily became their new selves. Therefore, for many children the solution became obvious: "These children tried to shed their Jewish identity by living illegally in the forbidden Christian world."[29]

Defying Nazi orders they lived, but not as themselves. Children living on borrowed documents were constantly reminded that those documents were the reason they were being allowed to stay alive. The outside world was emphasizing to them that their own identity was an inadequate ticket to life. Thus, it would be almost absurd to find children who viewed their Jewish identity as a positive addition to their life; for they were receiving unambiguous messages that being Jewish was not only detrimental, but was highly disregarded by the larger society to which they now belonged.

Many children wrote about their struggle to comprehend why they were so reviled as Jews. Many also wrote or have written after the war about their acute sense of anger toward God, and their consequent belief that the Jewish God must not be taking care of his children, and thus to be Jewish was not as advantageous as to be protected by the Christian God. As such, Eva Nisenzweig testifies to a desire to escape her ethnic identification: "I did not want to be Jewish. I wanted to be a Catholic so that I could be protected by their God."[30] The children's rejection of their God and their allegiance to the "covenant" of Israel was, in a sense a necessary defense mechanism. That is,

> The danger that the children felt from being associated with a people undergoing such terrible hardships led many to the conclusion that they stood to profit most in distancing themselves and severing all links to Jews and Judaism. This tendency was further abetted by the rather strong anti-Semitic sentiments of many segments in Polish society, which could not but affect the tender minds of these children cruelly estranged from their own kind.[31]

As these hidden children were restored to society by virtue of altering some minor details of their identity, namely anything that tied them to their Jewishness, many Jewish children now felt the need to repay their hosts for "reinstating" them, by fully embracing the identity which brought them this "salvation." Some children felt that fully embracing their new identity and their new "family" would give them an added sense of security, so missing from their daily lives. By choosing to identify with the group which obviously seemed "stronger," the children were able to feel that they were allying themselves with the side which guaranteed the greatest odds of survival. Furthermore, they may have wished to repay their rescuers by exhibiting zeal for their way of life. Additionally, lacking the role models usually provided by parents, some children naturally chose to identify with an alternative adult model.

The constant tension between the two lives and selves and the danger involved in being one's true self, may have led many hidden children merely to abandon their former identities and histories. If they were very young and had begun the war with the uncertainty of their relationship to their Jewish faith and people, then the likelihood of abandoning these certainly increased.

> To give up who they had been and to become who they were supposed to be; to hide their Jewish identity not just from the Germans and their allies, or their new friends and neighbors, or even their host families, but from themselves was a wonderfully direct way to resolve their anxieties, conflicts and tensions.[32]

To live as a gentile in a world which for a period, valued this above life, to adopt a new people and history and to renounce the past, became a goal of many who as a result were lost and often irretrievable.

Invisible: Children in Hiding

Undoubtedly the most famous hidden child during the second world war was Anne Frank. As her example demonstrates, children hid in any setting that was available to them; some hid alone and by their own resources, while others hid with families or with some portion of their family. The experiences of these children are tremendously varied. However, the shared sense of fear of discovery and the imposed restrictions on any semblance of child life are common elements. These children lived in a preposterous situation: they lived a clandestine existence in a world which did not tolerate them. As a result, the children learned to live without being noticed, they made no sounds which would endanger them, left no traces, had no outside contacts, and often saw little of the world in which others lived.

Because for the most part these children were not compelled to change their whole selves for the benefit of others, many children's personalities and sense of self remained intact. Equally important, once the children arrived into hiding, they were now largely shut off from the anti-Semitic climate existent outside their walls, any may have consequently been less prone to internalize that projection of negative attitudes toward Jews. Although much of the children's protection from the loss of self was dependent on the circumstances in which they were hiding and the people sheltering or assisting them, these children were less prone to the dual existence that the "aryanized" Jewish children had undergone.

Nonetheless, the trauma of disappearing or ceasing to exist cannot be underestimated. The emotional vacuum this created for children who were in their prime years of growing and becoming aware of themselves as individuals and who suddenly had no one and nothing to turn to, is incomprehensible. Virtually "ceasing to exist" created emotional and physical strains on children who were undergoing both physical and emotional maturation, but whose existence was hidden and confined. Obviously, in many cases this created a very severe breakdown in the child's sense of cultural and personal identity. Anne Frank confided to her diary, Kitty, while in her secret annex:

> We have been pointedly reminded that we are in hiding, that we are Jews in chains, chained to one spot, without any rights, but with a thousand duties. We Jews mustn't show our feelings, must be brave and strong, must accept all inconveniences and not grumble, must do what is within our power and trust in God. Surely the time will come when we are people again, and not just Jews.[33]

The inexplicable nature of confinement cries through Anne's words. Why, she wonders, must this be her fate? Anne's frustration with her confinement eloquently expresses what thousands of other Jewish children in hiding asserted at the time and since that time.

> Who has inflicted this upon us? Who has made us Jews different from all other people? who has allowed us to suffer so terribly up till now? It is God that has made us as we are, but it will be God, too, who will raise us up again. If we bear all this suffering and if there are still Jews left, when it is over, then Jews, instead of being doomed will be held up as an example. Who knows, it might even be our religion from which the world and all peoples learn good, and for that reason and that reason only do we have to suffer now.[34]

While she is acutely aware of her identity as a Jew, and is not prepared to deny it, Anne nonetheless attempts to contextualize her persecution as a Jew within the confines of a larger mission. She optimistically searches for a reason, a purpose for her own confinement. At the same time, Anne also gives rise to her ambivalent relationship to Judaism; for while she does not deny her connection to the Jewish people, she subordinates Jewish identity to human identity hoping for a time when they will not "just be Jews." However, it is nonetheless astonishing that a fairly assimilated child spent a significant portion of her diary attempting to wrestle with her Jewish identity and its place in her life. By struggling so openly and eloquently, Anne demonstrates why her words have attained such power and resonance.

Children who spent a number of years (between 1-4 usually) in hiding often escaped their confinement by imagining themselves elsewhere. Anne Frank used her diary as a substitute friend. She also invented other friends who came to life in her many short stories. Several other children used the pen or the brush to express their despair, or to flee their loneliness. Nelly Toll attests to this desire to confide the injustice of her existence to someone or something. She began keeping notes at age six and began painting at age eight while in hiding.

> The journal was my place for recording the frightening realty of my existence during those dark days -- unlike the paintings that I created at the same time, which provided me with an escape into a fantasy world.... Once I started to paint, a new world opened up for me. It was as if the little box of watercolors made a bright path straight through the apartment walls to the outdoors.... In my pictures there was no war, no danger, no police, and no tears. Everyone liked each other in my make-believe land, and all the people were as free as kites in the sky.[35]

Despite the fact that by the time she had entered into hiding with her mother she had already underwent life in the ghetto, a failed attempt at escape, and life on the "Aryan" side as a Christian, Nelly does not express anger at being Jewish. Undoubtedly, her mother's presence and ability to remind her young child of positive associations with Judaism enhanced Nelly's sense of pride in her Jewish roots, despite the fact that this was precisely the component which tied her to a life of confinement and constant exposure. In fact, quite the opposite was true, she relates that her mother taught her Jewish ethics and ethnic pride and reminded her often of the family gatherings and communal events.

As mentioned earlier, when children were not completely isolated from their past and from adult role-models, many were able to grow into an understanding of their communal identity as part of a gradual process of observation and deliberate education by the adult model. Where the children were hiding on their own, either as "legitimate Aryans" or alone amongst non-Jewish rescuers, they were much more likely to become ambivalent about their Jewishness, and may have even actively tried to shed their identities in the absence of any proof that it was essential. Of course, these factors also hinged on the age of the child, the amount and quality of formal and informal Jewish education, and the pressure brought upon the child to conform by the host family or institution. Although feelings of inadequacy and pressure to conform were certainly brought to bear on a hidden child, and one's ability to conform often determined one's eligibility for life, nonetheless, children did not always choose to forfeit this portion of themselves. Even for those children who did not previously place their Jewish identity in high regard, the very irony of compulsory external classification, now created a situation in which they themselves had to clarify who they were.

Not all Jewish children were able to find shelter with gentile friends, acquaintances or strangers who were willing to take the risk of concealing them. Similarly, even those children who managed to find secure homes, often found these to be temporary; rescuers became frightened and refused to keep the children, non-Jews betrayed the children and led to their incarceration, Nazis and their collaborators staged raids and children who had temporarily been "safe" were now brought back into the stark reality of life for Jews. Those children who had no opportunity to hide, were forced to continue along the lifeless path of the "final solution to the Jewish problem" designed and honed by the Nazi bureaucracy.

Children in the "Holocaust Kingdom"

The concentration camp existence was set up precisely and purposefully in order to rob human beings of any measure of their identity. Since it was the intent of the Nazis to create a brutal environment where one's sense of self would vanish at the entrance to this "unparalleled universe," where a number became a name, and where a person was divested of his past and all that he had brought with him; it would indeed be surprising to find vestiges of positive sense of self. Rather, the concentration camps were intended to break a person's spirit, to humiliate him, to starve him, to over-work him, and ultimately to kill him once his usefulness was maximized. The possibility of survival was not planned.

Any children left in this arena were the exception. The concentration camp was not set up for life -- much less child life. By and large children never entered the concentration camp world -- they were immediately "selected" for death. Generally, children under the age of 15 never made it inside the concentration camp. Those children who managed to lie about their age, or who looked sufficiently healthy upon arrival to be exploited for slave labor were allowed the "privilege" of entrance. Thus, no child life existed in concentration camps, because any children who were admitted, were admitted as adults and no special provision were made for them.

One of the only remaining records of children and youth who were initially not selected for death comes from the "model" concentration camp (*Vorzugslager* or "preferential camp" as the Nazis called it) of Terezin. As the Nazis had intended to use this camp as their "showcase," in order to keep up the illusion that Jews were being "resettled in the East," Terezin included a much larger proportion of children than any other camp. Although Terezin was made slightly more palatable for foreign eyes, one must remember that the fate of those incarcerated in Terezin was no different than that of other Jews slated for death. Terezin and Westerbork, which also was unique in interning whole family units, were in fact as Philip Mechanicus wrote in 1943, merely "another word for purgatory."[36] These camps functioned as way-stations to Auschwitz, but the destination was clear. In the Nazi mind the children were merely pieces in the game of illusion they were creating for the public eye. When that eye was not fixed on the game board (as was often the case), the pieces were moved and were replaced by others, all the while feeding the constant cycle of death.

Camps such as Terezin, Westerbork and to some extent, Bergen-Belsen,[37] which served the dual purpose of concentration camps and transit camps, tended to involve far more structure for children than any other camps.

> As camps Westerbork and Theresienstadt occupied a paradoxical yet unique position in the Nazi camp universe. Although neither possessed extermination facilities, both exhibited, to a large degree many of the horrors and cruelties of concentration camps.... While ghetto councils faced grave difficulties in creating a livable environment, however tenuous, for the children, it was an even greater wonder that Auschwitz, Bergen Belsen, and other camps (among them Theresienstadt and Westerbork are especially noteworthy) possessed some rudimentary system of child care.[38]

Here children were still treated as children, adults strove to shelter them from fully entering the devastation of life occurring all around them. In Terezin it was still possible to paint a picture, to play outside, to dream of the world beyond the fortress walls. Although this was far less true in Belsen (which became increasingly run-down as the war progressed), a young survivor, Gabor Czitrom describes his awakening interest in the Jewish religion and civilization while at Bergen-Belsen. "There was quite a series of [lectures by] young rabbis....

> There [in Belsen], I had a glimpse of how highly interesting biblical exegesis could be. There was a fascinating series of lectures by these young rabbis on various chapters of the Bible, putting it into historical context. I do not recall the facts, but I do exactly recall the huge interest of it, and that I discovered quite a new perspective.[39]

The traditional institutions of stability, such as family and school were maintained to the best of their ability, despite their mostly clandestine nature. In this sense, the adult community attempted to re-construct a model of child life, in this subverted model of life. As has been discussed throughout this work, Jewish identity of children is assumed to be in part tied to such factors as: parental role-modeling, educational efforts, and social participation in the community. Nowhere were these factors of stability so stretched pulled, challenged and disfigured as in the concentration camps. Families were not intended to remain a unit. Education was reduced to learning to adapt to an illogical universe, governed by its own set of rules. And yet, in Terezin the adults strove to impart a sense of normalcy to the children's days. To this end, the Council of Elders set up a Youth Welfare Department. The department provided for recreational activities, artistic endeavors, musical and theatrical performances, and clandestine schooling:

> The most outstanding work of the Department ... was its support of clandestine classes. Secret study circles were established, and many of the *Betreuerinnen* or *Betreueren* (child care workers) in the homes were devoted to the cause of education. For them, as for the children it was an act of faith in the future.[40]

Interestingly enough, though the children were subjected to a stark environment, in which many "never saw another butterfly," and were aware of the connection between victimization and their Jewishness, the clandestine curriculum focused on things Jewish nonetheless. Rather then distance the children from the "cause" of their incarceration, the adults endeavored to imbue the "star" with meaning. As they attempted to support the children in alleviating the many shortcomings of their life in camp, they undertook to provide them with all that the Nazis had taken away from them. These included: toys and playgrounds, physical freedom, identity, laughter, and imagination. From the adult perspective, the hope for the future was pinned not merely on the desire to outlive the war, but equally, on the desire to outlive the culmination of the "final solution to the Jewish problem." That goal could only be achieved if some Jewish children remained.

Similarly, and quite paradoxically, some children relate that they greeted their arrival in the concentration camps with a sense of relief; after years of trying to avoid deportation, the "game" of hiding and avoiding expulsion was over. Children survivors have recounted that being thrust into an environment (particularly those which existed in Terezin or in "Family Camps") which was entirely Jewish after years of hiding or debasement, permitted them to feel more at ease and to regain a stronger sense of themselves as Jews. Helga Pinsky-Pollack who was 12 at the time of her incarceration in Terezin recalls that

> the Betreuerinnen promoted an intellectually, culturally, and emotionally nurturing environment. "They taught us a lot about Zionism and other things. We had a choir ... [and sang] usually in *Ivrit* [Hebrew] or in Czech.... We were playing theater and celebrating Jewish holidays.... Everything which had to do with Israel [Palestine] was looked upon as something fantastic, and something everybody wanted to do was go to Israel and be in a *kibbutz*.[41]

Despite the horror of the conditions, life did continue to the extent that that was possible in the concentration camps. One cannot forget that young people in the camps, were nonetheless, young adults, who needed, as Anne Frank wrote: "to have lots of fun ... for once, and to laugh until my tummy aches." By providing us with such accounts, survivors are able to modify our image of concentration camps as valleys of death, and fix our gaze on the living instead.

However, these descriptions of children learning, and in some sense finding a renewed interest in, and connection to their own Jewish background, were obviously the exception. Most Jewish children did not think about their connectedness to their cultural and religious identity; their place had been decided for them, and their paramount priority was obtaining food and surviving. Elie, who was 14 at the time of his liberation from Buchenwald, recounted how:

I met Martin, a Hungarian, who was my age and we occasionally recited the *Gemarah* together. Those were always special days. Most of the time however, I thought of nothing but food.[42]

Thus, as Deborah Dwork confirms,

the educational and cultural activities we have discussed so far were exceptional events in the ordinarily dreary and dismal days in a transit [or concentration] camp. Most of a normal day's events were dictated by the conditions of camp life, and they were paltry and petty indeed.[43]

Children in concentration camps were subjected day in and day out, to beatings and curses, in which Jews were demeaned and degraded. As this process was hardly new to Jewish children who had been living for years with increasingly vicious anti-Semitic propaganda, it often combined to form an accumulated affect of self-loathing, or at the very least, self-doubt. To children and adults alike, the reason, the crime, that had brought them into this "universe" was inexplicable. The only "reason" provided, was that they were Jews. In a recent interview with a survivor of eight concentration and death camps, N. recounts how he himself began to feel that he was worthless, that maybe he was an "untermensch." Upon arrival to Auschwitz, N. was 14 and was selected for forced labor,

when they told us to undress, in my naiveté I left my glasses with my clothes, thinking that I would go back and get them later. A few days later I entered the latrine, and because I could not see well, I evidently entered the latrine reserved for the SS. An SS spotted me. He ordered me to remove my cap and clean the latrine with my hat. After such an experience, you begin to feel you are not worth much.[44]

While N., who had been educated in the traditional Jewish schools of the *cheder*, at least knew that he was Jewish and had some conception of what that encompassed, other children may have little to no sense of what they were being killed for.

As the research has indicated, even within the bounds of the concentration camp which was to serve as the "final" road for the soon to be "extinct race," some Jewish children were able to gather strength from their communal bond. Instances of smuggling in Torahs, or small prayer books were not uncommon, celebration of festivals were recorded across the board in all concentration camps. Nonetheless, at the same time, children in the camps were degraded and they, in turn internalized that degradation and believed it to reflect their own worth.

Conclusion

Jewish children during the Holocaust came from remarkably diverse backgrounds, which differed in nationality, level of religious observance, cultural identification, and ethnic awareness. The Nazis did not see these distinctions. However, as this paper has sought to demonstrate these distinctions are central to the question of who really was a Jew, and how each Jew perceived his own Jewishness.

What is significant to this research is that the children's experiences be personalized and individualized, and that their identity as Jews must not be taken for granted. Historians have yet to upset each bedrock of the Nazi system. Scholars must still examine the linguistic acrobatics of the Nazis, in which words for murder were couched in digestible phrases such as "resettle," "deport," "cleanse."[45] Scholars must also overturn definitions, categorizations, and other remnants of Nazi tenets which subvert reality, and permit, even in small measure, for Nazi success at desensitizing us to the true nature of their ideology and actions.

Notes

1. See for example: George Eisen's *Children and Play in the Holocaust* (Amherst, MA: University of Massachusetts Press, 1988), or Christopher Browning's *Ordinary Men: Reserve Police Battalion 101 and the Final Solution in Poland* (New York: Harper Collins, 1992). Both these books twist the realm of our expectations of the Holocaust by portraying the "ordinary" within the extraordinary. Recent publications which have dealt primarily or exclusively with the fate of Jewish children during the Holocaust include: Deborah Dwork's *Children With a Star*, Azriel Eisenberg's *The Lost Generation: Children in the Holocaust*, Jane Marks' *The Hidden Children*, and Marie Rut Krizkova et al's *We Are Children Just the Same*.

2. As Helen Fein has termed it in her book, *Accounting For Genocide* (New York: Free Press, 1979).

3. Raul Hilberg, ed., *Documents of Destruction* (Chicago: Quadrangle Books, 1971), pp. 20-23. Exemplifying the equivocal nature of such unnatural delineations, Hilberg quotes a case in which the Nazi authorities attempted to

decide whether two Jewish girls were to be considered Jewish or *Mischlinge* (as the parents requested). The text follows: The Jewish Community List (critical date, October 1, 1935) drawn up by the Jewish Community in Elberfeld and available to my branch office in Wuppertal carries the *Mischlinge* of the 1st degree Eva and Mally Heimann as members of the Jewish religious community. Moreover, their Jewish father, Wilhelm Isr. Heimann designated them as "Israelite" in the yearly registrations of 1931 and 1932. On the basis of these records the decision with respect to racial classification was that these *Mischlinge* of the 1st degree were to be regarded as Jews within the meaning of article 5, section 2a of the First Ordinance to the Reich Citizenship Law and that accordingly they had to wear the Jewish star. The Heimanns deny that they registered their children as members of the Jewish community in Wuppertal or that they permitted them to take part in Jewish religious instruction. During the examination of the records of the Jewish community in Wuppertal it was established that the Jewish community list was put together on the basis of the community's consolidated household list by the Jew Sussmann, now deceased, then employed in the community as a teacher. Sussmann, however, added Jews and *Mischlinge* who were known to him, but for whom there were no household lists, to the community register.... As to the Heimann family as well as seven other persons, there is neither a household list nor any note prepared by Sussmann. It is therefore not possible to provide an incontestable answer to the objection of the Heimanns that their children were included in the Jewish community list without their knowledge.... However ... I request that the appeal of Mrs. Heimann be rejected and that the *Mischlinge* of the 1st degree Mally and Eva Heimann be classified as Jews ....

4. As Helen Fein demonstrates in a model of victimization arranged according to the level of "stripping," the more comfortable the local populace became in seeing a minority among them slowly lose rights through discriminatory legislation, the easier it became to ruthlessly persecute that population. States which introduced such discriminatory measures, had f*our times as many victims. See: Accounting For Genocide* (New York: Free Press, 1979), p. 63.

5. Werner T. Angress, *Between Fear and Hope: Jewish Youth in the Third Reich* (New York: Columbia Press, 1988), p. 1.

6. Deborah Dwork, *Children With a Star* (New Haven, CT: Yale University Press, 1991), p. 15.

7. Josey G. Fisher, *The Persistence of Youth: Oral Testimonies of the Holocaust* (New York: Greenwood Press, 1991), pp. 4-5.

8. As cited in Werner T. Angress, *Between Fear and Hope: Jewish Youth in the Third* Reich (New York: Columbia Press, 1988), p. 13.

9. Angress, p. 14.

10. *Ibid.*, p. 14.

11. *Ibid.*, p. 16.

12. Dwork, p. 21.

13. Taken from an interview with a survivor recorded by Dwork, p. 17. Additional notes outside the quotation are Dwork's, material in quotes taken from survivor testimony.

14. Angress, p. 21.

15. *Ibid.*, p. 20.

16. The testimony of a woman who grew up in Germany and who was later interned in Westerbork, as cited in Fisher, p. 44.

17. Angress, p. 20.

18. As cited in Yehoshua Ivshitz, *Be Kedusha Uvegevurah: Pirkei Kiddush Ha Shem Umisirut Nefesh* (Tel-Aviv: Defus Hadkal, 1976). My translation.

19. Yitzhak Arad, *Neurim Be Lechima: Mi Gay Ha Churban Le Har-El* (Tel-Aviv: Marachot Tzahal, 1977), p. 21. My translation.

20. Jane Marks, *The Hidden Children* (Columbine, New York: Fawcett, 1994), p. 35.

21. Henry Friedlander & Sybil Milton, *Archives of the Holocaust: An International Collection of Selected Documents* (New York: Garland Press, 1990), p. 149.

22. Nelly S. Toll, *Behind the Secret Window* (New York: Dial, 1993), p. 29.

23. Feivel Podeh, "Ken Ha Shomer Ha Tzair Be Ghetto Lodz," *Yalkut Moreshet*, v. 28, 1979, p. 11.

24. *Ibid.*, p. 8. My translation.

25. Azriel Eisenberg, *The Lost Generation: Children in the Holocaust* (New York: Pilgrim Press, 1982), p. 102.

26. Emmanuel Ringelblum, *Notes From the Warsaw Ghetto*, ed. by Jacob Sloan (New York: Schocken, 1958), p. 39.

27. *Ibid.*, p. 15.

28. Yitzhak Rudeshevsky (Vilna) as quoted in Eisenberg, p. 82. During the war he wrote a diary from June 1941-April 6, 1943. He did not survive. The diary was found after the war by a friend.

29. Nechama Tec in the appendix to Jane Marks' *The Hidden Children* (New York: Columbine, 1994), p. 273.

30. As cited in Mordechai Paldiel, "Fear and Comfort: The Plight of Hidden Children in Wartime Poland," *Holocaust and Genocide Studies*, v. 6,1991, p. 403.

31. *Ibid.*, p. 403.

32. Dwork, p. 104-105.

33. Anne Frank, *The Diary of a Young Girl* (Otto Frank, 1952), p. 34.

34. *Ibid.*, p. 34.

35. Toll, pp. ix & p. 94.

36. Philip Mechanicus was a very respected journalist who was interned in Westerbork before being deported to Auschwitz where he was killed. As cited in George Eisen, *Children and Play in the Holocaust* (Amherst, MA: University of Massachusetts Press, 1988), p. 45.

37. Bergen-Belsen was officially established as a concentration camp only in April of 1943. Initially it was intended to serve as a detention center (*Aufenthaltslager*) for those Jews who held papers (*Promesas*) from other countries such as South American certificates or Palestinian passes, or for those Jews who were set aside for possible "exchange" (such as the Kastner group). Later conditions vastly deteriorated as inmates from other concentration camps were deported to Bergen-Belsen while no provisions were made for their addition to the camp. These prisoners were given no shelter, no blankets, no medical attention, and very little food even by concentration camp standards.

Anne Frank and her sister, Margot were among a group of prisoners transferred her in March of 1944. They, like hundreds of others died just prior to liberation from typhus, which under the conditions in the camps, was rampant.

38. Eisen, p. 44.

39. As cited in Dwork, pp 131-132.

40. *Ibid.*, p. 120.

41. *Ibid.*, p. 128.

42. As cited in Judith Hemmendinger, *Survivors: Children of the Holocaust* (Bethesda, MD: North Press, 1986), p. 120. The author had escaped to Switzerland during the war, but returned to Paris in 1945 to work for the Organization for the Assistance of Children (O.S.E.). During that time she met and cared for some of these children and youth who had survived.

43. Dwork, p. 132.

44. Interview conducted by author, April 3, 1995.

45. These terms correspond to the German: *Aussiedlung* ("evacuation"); *Umsiedlung* ("resettlement"); *Sauberung* ("cleansing").

Chapter 11

DISSENTING VOICES: U.S. GENTILE RESCUERS IN SERVICE ORGANIZATIONS DURING THE HOLOCAUST

Barry Trachtenberg

The young are more important.
~ Juliet Kulka[1]

In the United States, from the early 1930s until 1945, a movement of activists, writers and scholars dedicated itself to rescuing European Jewry from persecution and systematic extermination. While historians have examined the efforts of Jewish Defense Organizations to change United States refugee policy, considerably less attention has been paid to their non-Jewish counterparts – Gentile rescuers.

As distinct from Europe, in the United States there were no direct perpetrators or victims of Nazi atrocities. While antisemitism was virulent in the U.S., Nazi persecution was confined to Europe, thus leaving the United States to choose whether or not to come to the aid of European Jewry. The choice facing the country was either to act as bystanders or rescuers.

As most students and scholars of the Holocaust agree, the United States government did little to help European Jewry.[2] Indeed, a majority of U.S. citizens were opposed to assisting Jews with even temporary refuge. Many factors were present in this refusal: rising antisemitism, concerns for maintaining political power, nativism, isolationism, a threat of increased unemployment, fears of Axis spies and an unwillingness or inability to believe the reports from Europe.

David Wyman has remarked that the assault on the Jews was a "terrible tragedy" that affected all people: Jews, Gentiles, indeed all of Western Civilization and humankind. Yet as he has stated, few non-Jews "recognized that the plight of the European Jews was their plight too."[3]

There were groups outside of the Jewish community, however, who disagreed with such sympathies and actively aided the Jews marked for destruction. This paper examines the role of one such organization, the Women's International League for Peace and Freedom (WILPF). The WILPF fought the immigration barriers erected by the United States government, which had set upon a policy of actively prohibiting the immigration of European Jewry to the United States.

Working with other service organizations, the WILPF was engaged in refugee work throughout the 1930's and 1940's. Through contacts with prominent individuals, intensive lobbying efforts, securing affidavits for refugees and by raising the country's awareness, the WILPF's refugee committee worked unceasingly to save European Jewry.

The non-Jewish side to the overall movement for Jewish rescue spanned fifteen years, originating with warnings of Hitler's threat to the Jews as early as 1930 and ending with the last days of the war. The convictions of the activists were clear: they claimed that it was abhorrent for a democratic country such as the United States not to use its vast resources and power to end the suffering of European Jewry.

Combined with the alternative press and other non-Jewish service organizations, the work of the WILPF clearly demonstrates the existence of a non-Jewish component to the overall rescue movement. Often working in tandem with Jewish Defense Organizations, activists processed countless numbers of refugee claims, organized temporary shelters around the country, lobbied Congress and President Roosevelt for changes in the immigration laws, and repeatedly tried to convince the public that this issue affected all of humanity rather than being an issue for Jews alone.

The scholarship exploring the question of responsibility for the Holocaust has often minimized the issue of rescue. Most scholars have chosen to focus their attention on the people who either suffered from persecution, caused the terror, or allowed it to occur. The political scientist and historian Raul Hilberg has developed the three categories of perpetrator, victim and bystander to classify the people involved and determine levels of responsibility for the Holocaust.[4] With these divisions, Hilberg has shed considerable light onto the activities, mindsets and motivations of the millions involved in this colossal tragedy. For example, in his *Destruction of the European Jews,* Hilberg documents with meticulous detail the roles of the various figures at all levels of the Nazi machine.[5] In his more recently published *Perpetrators, Victims, Bystanders,* he gives the reader a guide to those in charge of the massacre, the histories of the Jews destroyed, and the deadly indifference of those who stood by.

While an awareness of these three categories is crucial to understanding the event itself, the divisions are insufficient to encompass fully the even broader spectrum of people involved. While it may be a relatively easy task to determine who should be classified as either perpetrator or victim, the grouping of bystander is far more ambiguous. Not surprisingly, this group is the largest, as nearly the entire world sat silently and permitted the Holocaust to occur. However, instead of there being criteria for determining entry into this category, the term bystander is often used to define the remaining people who do not fit in the first two. It is unfortunate, therefore, that within this third category are placed those who were the Jews' rescuers and allies.[6] Although rescuers were certainly fewest in number in compared to the others, they deserve a category of their own. For in a time of horror and unimaginable evil, they point to alternative paths of action.

One may reason that the category of bystander can only exist with the opposite category of rescuer. Bystander means – quite literally – "to stand-by" to chose not to engage one's authority and thereby allow events to happen unhindered. As historians, we cannot classify people and nations as bystanders if we do not point out the alternatives available to them. Only by establishing that people had a choice to behave otherwise can we begin to consider their tolerance of and indifference to the Nazi attempt at genocide. In any discussion on the role of the United States during the time of the Holocaust, we must point to the options available to those invested with the authority to determine refugee policy.

Although only mentioned in passing in David Wyman's *Abandonment of the Jews,* and not at all in the other texts on the United States rescue movement, the Women's International League for Peace and Freedom played an important role in the overall refugee effort. Working with other organizations, the WILPF was actively engaged in refugee work throughout the war. Through contacts with prominent individuals, intensive lobbying efforts, securing affidavits for refugees and by raising the country's consciousness to the plight of European Jewry, the WILPF's refugee committee, led by its Honorary International President, Emily Greene Balch, worked unceasingly to save Europe's Jews.

The Women's International League formed as a result of the peace movement during World War I.[7] The League was and is dedicated to "universal disarmament, the abolition of violence ..." and working towards an "ultimate goal [of] the establishment of an international economic order founded on meeting the needs of all people and not on profit and privilege."[8] The U.S. section of the WILPF originated with the Women's Peace Party, which after the First World War helped to found the WILPF under the direction of Jane Addams, (later the winner of the 1931 Nobel Peace Prize). In working to protect the rights of political prisoners, protesting the deportation of suspected Communists, and countering the spread of U.S. imperialism, the U.S. WILPF had grown by 1940 to 13,000 members with over 100 branches.[9]

During World War II, the refugee committee of the WILPF tirelessly struggled to get its members out of Europe and to provide for the wellbeing of refugees once they arrived. As part of an international organization, WILPF members were often singled out and persecuted by the nationalistic Nazi regime. The attempts to secure the release of two such Jewish refugees, Ella Kulka and Suse Siebenschein, best illuminate the tireless work of the WILPF's staff and their dedication to easing the pains of war. The story of the rescue attempt is told primarily via dozens of letters between the WILPF's Ellen Starr Brinton and Juliet and Rosa Kulka during 1939 to 1942.[10] By understanding the bureaucratic maze through which the Kulkas hoped to gain sanctuary for their two nieces, Ella and Suse, one can begin to comprehend the struggle which existed for hundreds of thousands of Jews hoping to escape persecution in Europe.

Ella Kulka was born on 23 July 1913 in Banská-Bystrica, Slovakia. After the death of her father in 1925 and her mother a year later, she was taken into the care of two aunts, Rosa and Juliet, and moved to the town of Brno, in the Moravian portion of Czechoslovakia, still retaining her Slovak citizenship. Trained as a "dispensing chemist" at Karlova University, she earned her degree with honors and by the age of twenty-five had learned to speak English, French, German, Czech, Slovak and Hungarian. Additionally, her aunt, writing on her behalf, praised her as "a very capable worker, ... tall and slender, fair and goodlooking. She can do all household work, cooking, sewing underwear, knitting fancy needlework, etc."[11] With the annexation of

Bohemia and Moravia and with Slovakia a German satellite late 1938, Ella joined the ranks of the tens of thousands of Jews who sought to make their way to the United States hoping for a life free from fear.[12]

Ella's aunt and foster-mother, Juliet Kulka, had a connection in the United States with Ellen Starr Brinton, an officer of the WILPF and the curator of the Jane Addams Peace Collection at Swarthmore College. As a member of the Czechoslovakian branch of the WILPF, Juliet had met Brinton a year earlier at the reception desk of the WILPF conference held in Luhacovice.[13] Juliet hoped to utilize this prior contact by soliciting Brinton's help to secure safe passage and quick entry into the United States for Ella.[14] Juliet's sister Rosa was Chairman of the WILPF's German group in Bron from 1924 to 1938. In early 1939, Brinton enthusiastically responded that not only would she be eager to take up the case and begin gathering the appropriate papers, but she offered to welcome Ella into her home through the coming summer or until she could find employment. Brinton also suggested that if Juliet and her sister Rosa had anyone else they would like to send, she would be more than willing to assist that person also.[15] Taking up the offer, Juliet and Rosa requested that their other niece, Suse Siebenschein, also be helped, stating "Young Jewish girls here have really no great prospects"[16]

In early 1939, Juliet and Rosa informed Brinton that Suse had been born on 17 April 1916 to Jean and Anna Siebenschein (née Kulka), matriculated in 1938 with honors in modern languages, and had become a licensed dressmaker in her mother's shop.[17] After a brief, impetuous marriage and divorce from another man, Suse became "unofficially" engaged to Dr. Jan Broch when they were both very young. Before the necessary formalities had been arranged, Broch went to Italy and after difficulties there, took sanctuary in San Domingo. Suse hoped to join her fiancé as soon as possible and escape the growing turmoil in Czechoslovakia.[18]

Just three months after Brinton received the requests from the Kulka family and offered her help – a sign of hope – the case also received its first setback. Because of the strict quotas and the growing number of refugee applicants, Ella wrote to say that she would be placed on a waiting list over three years long. Before this process could even begin, however, she would have to receive affidavits from persons within the U.S., willing to sponsor her application. The affidavits required that the sponsor take personal responsibility to provide for the refugee if unable to secure employment or be financially self-sufficient. It was possible at times to circumvent the list by gaining support from "a member of the Congress or another high personality."[19] Later that year, Rosa Kulka wrote to Brinton that they were considering going to England, but they were aware that the situation there was already overburdened by the costs of the impending war and the influx of refugees. Citing her belief that "the young are more important than we are," Juliet asked Brinton to press on and try to speed up the process.[20]

By December of 1939, Brinton had secured two affidavits of support, one from Mrs. Lena Lewis of Cambridge, Massachusetts and a second from Mrs. Francis Curtis (address unknown), both of whom were friends of Emily Greene Balch, President of the WILPF and head of its refugee committee.[21] They even secured a letter of support from Massachusetts Senator Henry Cabot Lodge, Jr.[22] With these important backers, it was reasonable to hope that Ella could gain entry sooner than expected. Rosa wrote to say they were pleased that these "supplementary papers will make it possible to Ella to accept your very kind invitation much sooner than we had anticipated."[23] Additionally, Rosa mentioned that "every day brings a new care" as she now had to worry about her brother's family in the former Poland.

It seemed that with these important backers, Ella's now year-long wait would come to an end and she would soon be in the United States. Yet a month later, these new hopes were dashed when the American Consulate General wrote to Senator Lodge informing him that no exception would be granted and in perfect "offical-ese" stated:

> Your interest in the matter has been noted and you may be assured that the case of Miss Kulka will receive every consideration consistent with the law and regulations governing the entry of aliens into the United States.[24]

In March of 1940, the application suffered a severe reversal when it was discovered that Mrs. Lewis's affidavit of support for Ella had not been correctly completed.[25] This became a new source of worry as the affidavits were a crucial element for refugees seeking entry. The confusion with the affidavits would continue throughout Ella's wait as it later turned out Mrs. Lewis could no longer support the case, (the reason was never stated), and Brinton had to demonstrate that she could support Ella herself, a risky endeavor with the limited salary she received from the WILPF and Swarthmore College.[26]

The situation for the Kulkas became more and more strained as 1940 continued. In July of that year, Rosa wrote to Emily Greene Balch to update her on the status of Suse's attempt to find sanctuary. Rosa stated that "Circumstances have really made me a 'beggar poor in thanks,' and "I have become old, without needing to receive help and now I do not know how to acknowledge it."[27]

Even more depressing news came later when in November of 1940, a letter to Brinton arrived from the American Consulate General in Vienna, expressing,

> ...regret to inform you that this Consulate General is unable to approve the documents of support which you have submitted on behalf of Miss Kulka. Your income and resources must be considered to be insufficient to warrant your undertaking to guarantee the support to this applicant to the United States.[28]

While the Consulate General said the office would reconsider the application should new information be sent, the office also warned,

> You will understand, ... that all questions regarding the final settlement of visa cases must be viewed in the light of the current transportation difficulties being encountered by persons domiciled in Europe who desire to emigrate to the United States.[29]

While Ella Kulka was trying to get to the United States, Suse Siebenschein was attempting meet her fiancé in San Domingo. In early 1941, she was able to leave Czechoslovakia to travel to Berlin, in the hopes of obtaining an American Transit Visa which would allow her to begin her journey. The Dominican Republic Settlement Association, (Dorsa), had secured a Dominican visa for her,[30] traveling by way of Cuba.[31] But in June, she was denied the Transit Visa.[32] The delays forced her ticket from Lisbon to New York to be sold to another passenger and any hope of getting out of Czechoslovakia was lost. Yet Suse did not despair. As she wrote to Miss Curtis, "These difficulties cannot last for ever and perhaps I shall have the pleasure one day of thanking my kind benefactors in person."[33]

While Suse's attempts to leave Czechoslovakia were effectively finished, there was still some hope left for Ella as 1941 approached. It was now getting closer to the end of the three year wait and because of the past difficulties, her case was sent to the AFSC's Refugee Section. But the situation in Europe had grown more dire, as the AFSC's Louise Clancy wrote to Brinton informing her that the experiences of people seeking to leave Moravia were increasingly difficult. The only advice she could give was to strengthen the original affidavit as much as possible, and perhaps be willing to set aside money each week to ensure that Ella would be taken care of properly if she should reach the United States.[34]

By the summer of 1941, Germany had conquered most of Europe and begun its massive assault on the Soviet Union. The situation had grown desperate, and Brinton wrote to the Kulkas that she feared the recent "international crisis" would stop the flow of refugees altogether and that little hope remained.[35] She and the AFSC would keep working as hard as possible to secure their nieces' rescue. To help ease the sense of isolation experienced by her European friends in the WILPF, Brinton sent books of American Literature to the Kulkas and planned to send others to friends in Denmark.[36]

As the doors to refuge were quickly shutting, Rosa's letters to Brinton began to take on a more desperate tone as there was little progress to report. Simple communication became important in and of itself. As Rosa Kulka wrote to Brinton in late June, 1941, "Whether this letter can be posted, when and if it may reach you, seems a matter of History." Rosa beseeched Brinton: "Do not forget us, dear friends and be assured that we shall always, whatever happens, be alive to feelings of love and gratitude to all our dears."[37] Additionally, Rosa sent along the curriculum vitae of another niece, Liselotte Fretig and her husband Paul, as well as Suse's fiancé, to support their applications.

The news that the American Consulates in Germany had closed in late July only lessened any hope that remained. The State Department announced that it would no longer consider or approve visa applications from persons residing in Germany, the German-occupied regions or in Italy, since applicants were unable to apply in person to an American Consulate.[38]

By September, the letters from Rosa took on an urgent, pleading tone:

> ...on October 1st or 31st, Slovak Citizens are to have new Pasports [sic] and then there may or rather will come the moment when Ella has no citizenship at all. This has always been a tragedy, how much more in these days? ...Ella is single. She has never been involved in any political activity. Her parents being dead, [she] has no place or abode on this side of the grave. That at least may be believed. Needless to say this we all appreciate everything that yourself and our other friends on your side the Ocean have done for us. We are very grateful, indeed and very much averse to troubling you with ever repeated requests,....[39]

Brinton's reply was equally distressed:

> Your letter of September 13th, fills me with deep concern about you and your family. I am so sorry that Suse did not get off to San Domingo as planned. ...All travel has ceased between this country and central Europe – and no visas are being issued in either direction. Thousands of persons are still coming in from other parts of the world, and these are being given every possible assistance. I hope that mail communications will continue regardless what might come next. ...Some day it will be different, and we will all live again like intelligent human beings.[40]

This final letter was never received by Rosa Kulka, for in August of 1942, Brinton sent her a Red Cross telegram stating:

> Greetings to you and family. Sorry our correspondence cannot be continued. My last letter to you just now returned. Write when you can.[41]

At the end of the war, and with the terrors of the Nazi machine being exposed to all, Ellen Starr Brinton began requesting information through the Central Location Index as to the fate of the Kulka family.[42] She received the following letter from Lola Hanousková of Praha-Orechovka (Delostrelecka), Czechoslovakia on 11 June, 1946:

> Only today I am in the position to answer your letter of February 19th, which contained the inquiries about Rosa and Juliet Kulka, both from Brno.

The results of my investigation were sad: Rosa Kulka died at the beginning of November 1942 in the Concentration Camp in Terezín, Julia Kulka and her niece Ella were moved from Terezin to Poland into the district of Lublín, and what that meant we know by now only to [sic] well. They have not returned. ...It is all so dreadful. We have lost so many good friends, we miss them very much.[43] The fate of Suse is unknown.

The Kulka case well exemplifies the roadblocks refugees had to endure in seeking to escape the Nazi regime. While the United States was certainly not to blame for the Nazi atrocities in Europe, the decision by the U.S. government to toughen the immigration process for European Jews seeking even temporary refuge is one of the country's worst failures and remains an indelible stain on its collective conscience.

Additionally, this case also reveals important aspects about the rescue movement in the United States. It shows the dedication of Gentile service organizations groups such as the Women's International League for Peace and Freedom, the American Friends Service Committee and the Dominican Republic Settlement Association, the courage and resolve of individuals like Ellen Starr Brinton and Emily Greene Balch, (who, for her efforts, won the Nobel Peace Prize in 1946), along with the sponsors, the affiants, and countless other Gentiles struggling to transform the United States into a safe haven for Jewish refugees.

Notes

* I am indebted to the Holocaust Studies Program at the University of Vermont for the funding the research for this project.

1. Juliet Kulka, Letter to Ellen Starr Brinton (ESB), 10 April 1939, Swarthmore College Peace Collection (SCPC), Ellen Starr Brinton Papers (ESBP), Kulka Case, DG51, Box #1.

2. Most notably, Richard Breitman and Alan Kraut, American Refugee Policy and European Jewry, 1933-1945, (Bloomington: Indiana University Press, 1987); Henry Feingold, The Politics of Rescue, 2nd ed. (New York: Holocaust Library, 1980); Saul S, Friedman, No Haven for the Oppressed: United States Policy Toward Jewish Refugees 1938-1945, (Detroit: Wayne State University Press, 1973); Arthur D. Morse, *While Six Million Died,* (New York: Hart Publishing Company, Inc., 1967); Monty Noam Penkower, *The Jews Were Expendable,* (Chicago: University of Illinois Press, 1983); David Wyman, *The Abandonment of the Jews: America and the Holocaust 1941-1945,* (New York: Pantheon Books, 1984); Wyman, *Paper Walls: America and the Refugee Crisis 1938-1941,* (Amherst: University of Massachusetts Press, 1968).

3. David Wyman, *Paper Walls: America and the Refugee Crisis, 1938-1941,* xi.

4. Raul Hilberg, *Perpetrators, Victims, Bystanders,* (New York: Harper Collins, 1992).

5. Hilberg, *The Destruction of the European Jews,* (New York: Holmes and Meier Publishers, Ltd., 1961, revised 1985).

6. Hilberg, "Helpers, Gainers, Onlookers," *Perpetrators,* Victims, 212.

7. Gertrude Bussey and Margaret Tims, *Pioneers for Peace: Women's International League for Peace and Freedom 1915-1965,* (Oxford: Alden Press, 1980).

8. Catherine Foster, *Women for all Seasons: The Story of the Women's International League for Peace and Freedom,* (Athens: University of Georgia Press, 1989), ix.

9. Eleanor M. Barr, "Records of the WILPF, U.S. Section, 1919-1959, Guide to the Scholarly Resources, Microfilm Edition," (Wilmington, DE: Scholarly Resources, Inc., 1988), 6.

10. I am indebted to Wendy Chmielewski, SCPC curator for introducing me to these documents.

11. "Curriculum Vitae" of Ella Kulka, SCPC, ESB, Kulka Case, DG51, Box #1.

12. Juliet Kulka, Letter to ESB, 18 Dec. 1938, SCPC, ESBP, Kulka Case, DG51, Box #1.

13. *Ibid.*; ESB, Letter to George Warren, 9 June 1941, SCPC, ESBP, Kulka Case DG51, Box #1.

14. Juliet Kulka, Letter to ESB, 18 December 1938, SCPC, ESBP, Kulka Case, DG51, Box #1.

15. ESB, Letter to Juliet Kulka, 6 January 1939, SCPC, ESBP, Kulka Case, DG51, Box #1.

16. Juliet Kulka, Letter to ESB, 24 January 1939, SCPC, ESBP, Kulka Case, DG51, Box #1.

17. "Curriculum vitae" of Suse Siebenschein, SCPC, ESBP, Kulka Case, DG51, Box #1.

18. Rosa Kulka, Letter to ESB, 23 June 1941, SCPC, ESBP, Kulka Case, DG51, Box #1.

19. Ella Kulka, Letter to ESB, 7 March 1939, SCPC, ESBP, Kulka Case, DG51, Box #1.

20. Juliet Kulka, Letter to ESB, 10 April 1939, SCPC, ESBP, Kulka Case, DG51, Box #1.

21. Eva Wiegelmesser, Letter to Emily Greene Balch, 8 March 1940, SCPC, ESBP, Kulka Case, DG51, Box #1.

22. Irving N. Linnell, American Consul General, Letter to Senator Henry Cabot Lodge, Jr., 20 Jan. 1940, Copy, SCPC, ESBP, Kulka Case, DG51, Box #1.

23. Rosa Kulka, Letter to ESB, 30 Jan. 1940, SCPC, ESBP, Kulka Case, DG51, Box #1.

24. Irving N. Linnell, American Consul General, Letter to Senator Henry Cabot Lodge, Jr., 20 Jan. 1940, (Copy), SCPC, ESBP, Kulka Case, DG51, Box #1.

25. Eva Wiegelmesser, Letter to Emily Greene Balch, 8 March 1940, SCPC, ESBP, Kulka Case, DG51, Box #1.

26. ESB, Affidavit of Support for Ella Kulka, 30 April 1941, Copy, SCPC, ESBP, DG51, Box #1.

27. Rosa Kulka, Letter to Emily Green Balch, 8 July 1940, (Copy), SCPC, ESBP, Kulka Case, DG51, Box #1.

28. Harry E. Carlson, American Consul, Letter to ESB, 20 Nov. 1940, SCPC, ESBP, Kulka Case, DG51, Box #1.

29. *Ibid.*

30. Mrs. Rebecca Hourwich Reyher, Dorsa, Letter to ESB, 10 May 1941, SCPC, ESBP, Kulka Case, DG51, Box #1.

31. ESB, Letter to Rosa Kulka, 8 June 1941, SCPC, ESBP, Kulka Case, DG51, Box #1.

32. Suse Pollack, (neé Siebenschein), Letter to Mrs. Francis Curtis, 18 June 1941, SCPC, ESBP, Kulka Case, DG51, Box #1.

33. *Ibid.*

34. *Ibid.*

35. ESB, Letter to Rosa Kulka, 1 July 1941, SCPC, ESBP, Kulka Case, DG51, Box #1.

36. *Ibid.*

37. Rosa Kulka, Letter to ESB, 23 June 1941, SCPC, ESBP, Kulka Case, DG51, Box #1.

38. Marjorie Page Schauffler, Letter to ESB, 24 July 1941, SCPC, ESBP, Kulka Case, DG51, Box #1.

39. Rosa Kulka, Letter to ESB, Sept. 1941, SCPC, ESBP, Kulka Case, DG51, Box #1.

40. ESB, Letter to Rosa Kulka, 2 Nov. 1941, SCPC, ESBP, Kulka Case, DG51, Box #1.

41. ESB, Red Cross letter to Rosa Kulka, 3 Aug. 1942, SCPC, ESBP, Kulka Case, DG51, Box #1.

42. The Central Location Index was a service organized to make possible the "re-establishment of contact between persons here and abroad." The service was a cooperative effort among various refugee organizations including The American Jewish Joint Distribution Committee, the American Friends Service Committee, the National Council of Jewish Women and others. (Guide to Central Location Index, SCPC, ESBP, Kulka Case, DG51, Box #1.)

43. Lola Hanousková, Letter to ESB, 6 Jan. 1946, SCPC, ESBP, Kulka Case, DG51, Box #1.

Chapter 12

WHY DID HITLER PERMIT A JEWISH HOSPITAL TO FUNCTION THROUGHOUT THE WAR? A PERSONAL AND HISTORICAL PERSPECTIVE

Gerda Haas

I am examining here the phenomenon of a Jewish institution in the heart of Berlin which was never closed by the Nazis and indeed exists to the present day, namely the Jewish Hospital on Iranische Strasse. I was a nurse at the Hospital from October 1941 to March 1943. From there, I was deported to Theresienstadt and stayed there until February 1945, when I was released to Switzerland. I wrote down my recollections of Berlin and the Hospital. My remarks in this paper, as far as they concern the Hospital from October 1941 to March 1943, are based on these notes and I call that part of my paper: Part I: Personal Perspective.

Part II, the historical section, deals with events at the Hospital from after my deportation in March 1943 to the liberation of Berlin by the Russian Army in May 1945. Information about this period comes from conversations and letters with nurse friends who had remained at the Hospital and whom I met again here in the United States; as well as from sources identified in footnotes.

In conclusion, I have a suggestion to make why Hitler never ordered the Hospital closed when Germany, and especially Berlin, were supposed to be "Judenrein."

Part I: Personal Perspective

I began my training as a pediatric nurse at the Kinderheim in Niederschoenhausen, a suburb of Berlin, and advanced to the Jewish Hospital midway through the training. In October 1941, I graduated with a degree in pediatric nursing. My diploma stated: "Restricted to the care of Jewish babies and children." I was delighted when the Hospital's director, Dr. Walter Lustig, personally offered me employment at the Kinderstation; I was overjoyed staying at the Hospital where I made friends, having meaningful work when Jews in Germany and Berlin were fired or deported and earning a little money. I, a religious girl from *Unterfranken*, barely 19 years old, was now a nurse at the Hospital, I was even able to join the "Kosher Kitchen" for my meals. For the moment I was happy and felt secure in the Hospital.

The Hospital was a complex of 7 buildings on a large corner lot between Iranische Strasse and Schul Strasse in the district of Wedding. The front buildings were Administration and a large nurses residence, the central structure was the actual 600 bed hospital with all its different departments, and behind this main structure were maintainance buildings and, bordering on Schul Strasse, the ivy covered pathology house. Pleasant green walkways connected the buildings above ground while spacious underground tunnels linked all the parts of the large complex. The whole was enclosed by a wall so that upon entering through the gate at Iranische Strasse one got the feeling of being in one's own world and quite protected from the rest of Berlin. The sunny room in the nurses quarters which I shared with Schwester G. increased that feeling.

But the sense of security was a deception. My employment at the Hospital in October 1941, coincided with the first transports out of Berlin. These transport were conducted in secrecy, they were called "Arbeitstransporte," labor trans- ports, or "Umsiedlung," resettlement, or simply "Osttransporte" and we had not the slightest inkling of their sinister nature. We believed what we were told, namely that our friends were being relocated in labor camps somewhere in the East and that we would see them when our turn came to go there. Even when the destination "East" was replaced with a specific location called "Auschwitz" it meant nothing to us then.

Soon there was an increase in admission of suicide patients at the Hospital and although we at the Children's ward were not directly involved, we had serious discussions about the absurdity of being forced to bring these people back to life and then to deliver them to the collection center at Levetzow Strasse for the next transport.

We, the nurses, were involved, though, when we found our nursing director one morning dead in her bathtub, having committed suicide during the night. Frightened, we clustered in the halls and rooms for whispered discussions. What would we do without the stern guidance of Frau Oberin? Going back home was no option - most cities and towns in Germany were either already "Judenrein" or in the process of evacuation; hiding in Berlin, going underground, was a possibility. There were decent Germans who offered Jews an attic or a backroom to live with them illegally and many people I knew had already gone that route - alas only to be caught in the Gestapo nets or denounced by an active informer network made up of despicable Jews who worked for the Gestapo. But we didn't know that then. I very seriously considered the underground option when a kind woman who barely knew me, offered to hide me; I still remember her name: Ruth Sasha. In the end, I stayed at the Hospital.

We were now overworked and undernourished, dreaded the frequent air raids when we had to get out of our warm beds after a few short hours of dead-like sleep and rush to the wards, take our patients down into the underground tunnels. My memory is vivid about a delivery that was performed there while the sirens howled. Daytimes, regularily now, we were called to duty at collection centers and at railways stations, especially on Sundays when we were supposed to be off. We no longer felt secure or protected.

Another vivid memory: my friend Schwester G. and I looked out of our windows in the nurses residence one sunny day in May 1942, and watched in disbelief as on the street below Jewish men were picked up by Gestapo and SS, wives and children handwringing behind them. What was going on? Eventually, Dr. Lustig was ordered by the Gestapo to inform us that 500 men had been arrested and 250 already been shot because there had been a hostile rally at the Soviet exhibition in the Lustgarten; it was simply taken for granted that the Jews were behind the demonstration and needed to be punished for it.

In September 1942, a directive came from the Gestapo via Dr. Lustig that all Jewish personnel had to be at the meeting room at Oranienburger Strasse at 6 AM the next morning. What now? My friend G. and I dressed quickly and went with the employees. We stood at attention from 6 till 12 in the big meeting room, when, finally, Eichmann and Guenther appeared, accompanied by a third SS man in shiny uniform, also young and arrogant, cigarette between his lips: Alois Brunner from Vienna.

In his own good time Brunner informed us that from now on the Gestapo would no longer put up deportation lists or collect Jews. We, the Jews were to be the agents of our own destruction. Each department head would have to fill the lists with people from his own department and we, the employees of the Jewish Community and the Hospital, would do the collecting. He called several officials to step forward and make up a list right then and there, to appear at collection center the next day. One of the men, Dr. Kraindl, suffered a heart attack and fell dead to the floor; eight others were taken prisoner. Brunner assured the assembly that these men would be shot if we didn't cooperate. We cooperated but the eight hostages were shot anyway. Among them were Drs. Blumenthal, Lange, Goldstein, Herr Selbiger and Herr Loose. Their families went to Auschwitz. How could anyone think of disobedience under such circumstances?

We nurses were given white armbands to wear for collecting and deporting our own Jews. We were ordered never to disclose to anyone what we were doing.

More and more now, transport lists included personnel from the Hospital. Patients, physicians, nurses, orderlies, people from the kitchen, the laundry, cleaning personnel, no one was safe anymore. The positions that opened up were filled with *Mischlinge,* half Jews who were protected from deportation because of an Arian parent; and with "protected Jews," Jews living in mixed marriages. We, the "Volljuden" were now in the minority at the Hospital.

"Fabrik Aktion" of February 1943, the relentless collection of all Jews working in factories, thousands of Jews were loaded into trucks directly from their supposedly safe factory jobs and were brought to centers around Berlin. Schwester K. and I were assigned to the barracks at Rathenauer Kaserne. We put on our white armbands and went there, not at all sure that we wouldn't be loaded into the freight trains along with the multitude. When the "Fabrik Aktion" was over, 20,000 Jews had been shipped to the East; several hundred persons, having been able to proof either the status of a Mischling or partnership in a mixed marriage, had been taken prisoner at Gestapo headquarters at Rosen Strasse; and we Jewish nurses were sent back to work.

That week Hitler was treated to the first, and probably only, act of rebellion of his whole twelve-year reign of terror: the German wives of Jewish partners and the German parents of Mischlinge held prisoner, demonstrated openly at Rosen Strasse, right outside the windows were their families were captives. "Gebt uns unsere Männer wieder!" Give us our men back! was the cry that was heard at high Nazi places around Berlin, and it was successful: the men and other prisoners were released. We heard about it and wondered. Did news of the plight of Jews begin to reach the ears of Berliners inspite of all the secrecy with which these manuvers were carried out?

At the Hospital, weekly now, doctors, nurses and patients were removed for deportation. Friends we had worked with, were torn away. We still fantasized that they would be safe "in the East" and that we would see them soon. We did wonder, though, why we never heard from our friends, why nobody ever wrote from those mysterious labor camps where they were supposed to be working.

At the Hospital, the empty positions, as well as the empty beds, were immediately filled with *Mischlinge* and "protected Jews" who were reasonably safe; for most the rest of us, it was only a matter of time.

On March 17, 1943, my name was on the list and I was picked up by Gestapo, right in my room at the nurses residence. Many of my nurse friends were on the same list. I had a few minutes to gather my bags and another minute to hug friends and then an armed SS man walked me out of the Jewish Hospital.

Part II: Historical Perspective

The Jewish Community in Berlin, the *Juedische Kultus Gemeinde* or JKG, was originally housed at Oranienburger Strasse, with Dr. Paul Eppstein and Phillip Kozover as functionaries. (Jews could no longer call themselves "leaders" or any other noun that denoted superiority). The JKG was part of the *Reichsvereinigung der Juden in Deutschland* (National Association of Jews in Germany) which had its offices at Kantstrasse with Rabbi Leo Baeck as its head. The Hospital was a part of both these organizations under Dr. Walter Lustig. All of the above, it will be remembered, were subject to *Reichshauptsicherheitsamt*, Amt IVB, the Gestapo at Rosenstrasse, which dealt with the "Judenproblem." The two men most feared at Rosenstrasse were Adolf Eichmann and Rolf Guenther.

In June 1943, the Gestapo ordered the Reichsvereinigung and the JKG to close their offices on Oranienburger Strasse and Kantstrasse respectively. Dr. Eppstein and Rabbi Baeck, their chief administrators, had been sent to Theresienstadt in February of 1943, and most of the other dignitaries were deported to the East. The Jewish staff was set adrift to be deported with the next train load. Such personnel as was urgently needed was replaced with protected Jews or Mischlinge. And any remaining documents were sent to the Hospital where a few rooms in the Administration building were designated offices of the "Neue Reichsvereinigung" as it was refered to. In June of the same year, SS Rolf Guenther told Dr. Lustig that he was now in charge of this new organization, in addition of course to his duties at the Hospital, responsible for social aid, cemetery and burial matters for Jews remaining in the Reich and for "Sonderprobleme" which meant people in the Reich who couldn't be deported such as half Jews and *Mischlinge.*[1]

Who were the people that presented Hitler with this *Sonder problem*, this special problem that remained a thorn in the Nazi hide to the very end? These were the people who were "neither black nor white, neither Jew nor German."[2] According to the Nuremberg Laws of November '35, the "Rassengesetze" there were two categories of persons: Arians and non-Arians. Non-Arians were again subdivided into Jews and *Mischlinge. Mischlinge* could be half-Jews or quarter-Jews, depending of their parentage and grandparentage and were designated accordingly into 2 categories: *Mischling* 1st degree or *Mischling* 2nd degree. Now another problem came up: do *Mischlinge* have to wear the yellow Star of David? And once that was resolved the big question was: can they be deported. Finally, if they can't be deported, what do we do with them. How do we protect our pureblooded Germans from these part-Jews? And, wait, there is another dilemma: what do we do with Jews living in mixed marriages? According to records from the Wannsee Conference of January 20, 1942, there were at that time 125,000 *Mischlinge* in the Reich and the Protectorate, and 28,000 Jews in mixed marriages.[3] Since many of these marriages were never dissolved, either for personal reasons or because of church policy, Jewish partners who had to wear the Star, constituted yet another problematic category. Could the Nazis let these Jews walk around Berlin with their bright yellow Stars visible to everyone, when Goebbels had already told his fuehrer that the German capital was free of Jews?

The Jewish Hospital on Iranische Strasse seemed to be the answer. While there was never a ghetto created in Berlin, this Hospital had the characteristics of such a place: a hermetically sealed Jewish environment separated from its German surroundings by a wall and gates that could be locked; inhabitants identified by the Star; administered by a Jew who had all the attributes of a ghetto "Aeltester," a Jewish Elder, subordinated to the Gestapo.

It was the Hospital then, which could hold - and conceal - the Jews of Berlin, and even of the rest of the Reich.

In February 1945, there were 162 full Jews in Berlin[4] and most of them lived at the Hospital, either as patients or because they had been bombed out and could not gain lodging anywhere in the city because of the Star; or they were the Jewish partner of mixed marriages whose German wives continued to oppose deportation; or they were foreign Jews who could not get home; there were Jewish patients who were under Gestapo supervision until they could be deported and healthy Jews who for one reason or another were waiting for deportation. Some "Sonder" cases came from all of Germany to live freely at Iranische Strasse. Also living freely at the Hospital were Jewish informers who took their orders from Gestapo, searching and hunting for "underground Jew" in and around Berlin. According to Rivka Elkin, from the Spring of 1943 to Liberation two years later, the Hospital had about 800 patients and inhabitants.

By November of 1944, there were about 13,00 Jews left in the the Reich, half of them in Berlin; these were mostly Jews in mixed marriages and offsprings of such marriages defined as Jews, whose fate had not been determined by Nazi law.[5] (Hilberg puts their number at 28,000).

At a nurses' reunion in the Summer of 1946 in New York I met some of the nurses who had remained at the Hospital throught the War. My former colleague Schwester A. told me of the hardship of those years. SS Oberscharfuehrer Walter Dobberke had been put in charge and lived at the Hospital; Dr. Lustig had to obey his orders; SS harassment increased; so did the bomb attacks. The Hospital was severely damaged at several raids: in the daytime, Jewish personnel had to clear and clean the damages of the night. Scarlet fever broke out and many of the nurses, Schwester A. included, were deathly ill. There was a shortage of food and coal. Three of the seven hospital buildings were closed and the remaining four were seriously damaged. From her also came the information that the vine-covered pathology house on Schul Strasse was converted into a collection center in the Spring of 1944 and that transports were taken from there directly to the cattle trains at Putlitzer Strasse and other side stations. When Liberation finally came, she reported, Dr. Lustig and SS Dobberke were arrested by the Russians and shot. The Jewish Hospital had survived, but at great cost to human lives and at great distruction to its buildings.

Conclusion

Hitler was successful in his fixation to root out the Jews from his Reich and from great parts of Europe and, incredibly, had done it without anyone realizing what was going on in those ominous "labor" camps in the East. But he never was able to solve the question of the "half" Jews, *Mischlinge* and other "Sonder" Jews. In the half Jew problem, forced divorce or legal separation from the Arian partner was considered but dropped for fear of opposition from the Church; also, the experience of March 1942 when German wives demonstrated at Rosen Strasse, counciled against it. In the case of the *Mischlinge,* sterilization was debated at several conferences but was never implemented. At the Wannsee Conference of January 20, 1942 when the Jewish question was decided upon, the "Sonder" Jews were defined and categorized but no decision was reached on their fate. In two subsequent conferences, March 6, and October 27, again none was reached. The Gestapo was getting impatient and Hitler was asked for a final decision, but he declined.[6]

In the end, with no one knowing what to do with these special cases and no one willing to take on the final decision, the Jewish Hospital seemed the logical catch-all point for them. Hilberg is right when he states that "it simply didn't pay to jeopardize the secrecy of the whole extermination process for the fate 28,000 [Sonder] Jews ..."[7] (translation mine)

Notes

1. K.J. Ball-Kaduri, "Berlin is "Purged" of Jews. Yad VaShem Studies V, (1963) p. 303.

2. Raul Hilberg, Die Vernichtung der Europaeischen Juden. Olle & Wolter, 1982, p. 294 (translated).

3. *Ibid.*, p. 294

4. Rivka Elkin, Das Juedische Krankenhaus muss erhalten bleiben! Edition Hentrich, 1993, p. 60.

5. *Ibid.*, p. 72.

6. Hilberg, Die Vernichtung der Europaeischen Juden, p. 301-2.

7. *Ibid.*, p. 302.

Chapter 13

THE POLITICIZATION OF HOLOCAUST SURVIVORS IN CANADA 1945-1985

Franklin Bialystok

Philip Weiss came to Winnipeg from Europe in 1948. He was born in Poland in 1924, and was survivor of Auschwitz. He recalls his first years in Canada.

They were hard years. We had full freedom, but still from a point of spiritual satisfaction, there was a lot to be desired. You had to start anew, you were an immigrant. We didn't have relatives. We were strangers in a strange land. You were not fully accepted, even in Jewish circles. There were barriers between Canadian citizens and those who survived. We were all considered to be *greener* (green horns), and we were to a certain degree.... For a certain period of time everything was dark, you could not be as happy as the Canadian who didn't go through the experiences of the Second World War. It was a tremendous burden which a former inmate carried for a lengthy period of time. Eventually the barriers broke. For me it took a minimum of twenty years.[1]

Cyril Levitt is a third generation Canadian Jew, born in Toronto in 1946. He remembers that growing up, "the Holocaust was never broached directly in my house. It was kind of a disease that one didn't talk about." Regarding the survivors, he recalls that

they were the butt of jokes. At the same time there was this sense that they were all a little bit crazy, that you couldn't really treat them as normal people. (It was) due to partly fear, partly pity, partly a sense of stigma. We called them "greenies...." The Holocaust was constantly being swept under the rug. It wasn't until post 1967 that the established community came onside.[2]

Philip Weiss and Cyril Levitt represent two of the faces of post-war Canadian Jews. Born in different generations, one a European survivor and the other a child of middle class Canadians, they describe the dilemma of the survivor from contrasting viewpoints, and yet arrive at essentially the same conclusions. In the first decade after the arrival of the survivors to Canada there were two Jewish communities, in psychic, if not always geographic terms. In the 1960s, the more vocal survivors tried to enter the Jewish community's mainstream organizations. Nevertheless, for most Canadian Jews their collective memory of the Holocaust was that a tragedy had befallen fellow Jews in a different place that was outside their scope of comprehension and experience. In the 1970s survivors cracked the barriers of the established structures and emerged as the catalyst for Holocaust remembrance and education. Consequently, by the mid 1980s the Holocaust had become one of the pillars of ethnic identification for most Canadian Jews as a response to the changing collective memory of the community about the event. An analysis of the process of politicization by survivors within the ethnic community is the focus of this study.

Canada is an enormous country, the second largest in the world, but one of the least populated. The proportion of Jews in Canada's population has remained relatively static at 1.5 per cent since the 1920s. Today, there are 360,000 in a population approaching 30 million. In the decade between 1947 and 1956, approximately 35,000 Holocaust survivors and their families immigrated to and remained in Canada. In absolute terms, this influx was small in comparison to the estimated 250,000 who went to Israel, and the overall figure or 137,500 Jewish immigrants (survivors and non-survivors) who went to the United States. In relative terms, however, the number was extremely high. It represented 13 to 15 per cent of the total Jewish population by the mid 1950s, far greater than the proportion of survivors who made up American Jewry in the same period (approximately 4 per cent).[3]

In the immediate post-war era, the Canadian Jewish community was led by the children and grandchildren of settlers who had made their way to Canada during the great wave of immigration between the 1880s and 1914. The leaders' most pressing agenda was integrating Canadian Jewry into the Canadian polity. Stung by the federal government's reluctance to open the gates to Jews trapped in Nazi occupied Europe, by the venomous displays of antisemitism in the inter-war period, and sensitive to the divisions within the Jewish community, individuals such as Samuel Bronfman, President of the Canadian Jewish Congress (CJC) and Saul Hayes, Executive Director of CJC, were most concerned with cementing a diverse community into a unified body. At the national level, this commitment to forging an effective voice representative of Canadian Jews was necessary to deal with federal politicians and bureaucrats on issues most pertinent to the community - the establishment of a Jewish state in Palestine and the easing of immigration restrictions for Jewish refugees in Europe. To a large measure this effort proved fruitful, due more to domestic needs and international developments than to pressure from the community.[4]

At the local level, the community was in a state of transition. The established Jews (defined as those who lived in Canada before World War II) in the largest cities (Montreal, Toronto and Winnipeg, which housed three out of four Jews) were preoccupied with advancing from the fringes of the Canadian mosaic into the mainstream of Canadian society. Whereas the pre-war Jewish neighborhoods were located in the inner-city cores, the post-war exodus to the suburbs was reflective of changes within the community. The most significant transformation was the emergence of an upwardly mobile professional and business class. Its members distanced themselves from the working class origins of previous generations. They considered themselves to be Canadians and were increasingly accepted as such. Community structures were expanded and moved to the suburbs. Thus, at both the national and local level, from 1946 to 1960 the Jewish community succeeded in articulating a national voice and gaining acceptance as "ordinary" Canadians.[5]

During this period of transition, the concentration on creating a unified voice and gaining recognition by the majority of English and French Canadians left little opportunity for established Jewry to comprehend the experiences of the refugees who inundated the community, and even less appreciation of the destruction of European Jewry. The established community, rightly, was most preoccupied with the immediate needs of the survivors, namely relief, restitution and absorption. Canadian Jews felt secure in a tolerant and prosperous post-war nation. They did not feel that the Holocaust was part of their world. Major community organizations were ill-disposed to pressure the government about the entry of Nazi war criminals or sympathizers, or to campaign against hate propaganda. The relative quietude of anti-Judaism in Canada together with the corresponding tranquility of antisemitism abroad reinforced the mood of ethnic comfort.[6]

For the survivors this was also a period of transition. Many had created new lives for themselves in the refugee camps and cities of war-ravaged Europe prior to immigration. Some had married or re-married, bore children, resumed their education or learned new skills, and prepared themselves for integration into North American culture and society before they set sail. Upon arrival to Canada, they were consumed with finding accommodation and employment and establishing communal networks with other survivors. For the most part, they were not concerned with relating their experiences with established Jews, especially since their memories were so fresh, so painful, and bespoke of their rupture from their families and homes. For those who did speak to established Jews about their experiences, the response ranged from shock to incomprehension to derision. Many of the survivors interviewed reflect on this period. For Philip Weiss,

> The majority of the survivors did not open up, and the Jewish community carries a certain responsibility because it wasn't interested, which is human. People in good situations under good conditions don't always like to listen to sorrow and tragedy, which is exactly what survivors brought. They didn't come here to discuss other things. The only thing they brought as their baggage was their tremendous tragedy, and they could not unload it. They had to carry it within themselves.

Mike Englishman, when asked about that period and whether he spoke about his experiences, recalls that,

> no, not even in the house [even though his wife was a survivor]. You could say something about the concentration camps [he was in Auschwitz] and people would look at you as if you were stark, raving mad. They couldn't comprehend. [Moreover] English is not your mother tongue. To express a thing like that in your own language is next to impossible; now try it in another language.

Nathan Leipciger came to Toronto and belatedly entered high school and then university.

> I never told anyone my story. I never told anybody where I came from. In university, I spent four years with guys who had absolutely no inkling. I didn't wear short sleeved shirts because I didn't want them to see my number. This was the price I paid.

Donia Clenman came to Toronto, married a Canadian Jew, and raised a family. She recounts that period in one of her poems.

> Sometimes
> I am a stranger to my family
> for I bring Europe's ghosts
> into the well-lit living room
> of Canadian internationalism...
> I was no child on arrival
> and yet, so well assimilated.
> even my verses are native,
> and I dream in good English too.

Ultimately their experience created a gap, as evidenced by their separation in neighborhoods, community organizations, and most important, in the articulation of ethnic identification.[7]

The community's relative contentment with its position in the Canadian mosaic became increasingly undermined in the 1960s. Domestic events and international developments unmasked the vulnerability of the community to anti-Jewish elements at home and abroad. Established Jews and survivors differed in their responses to these threats. The former tended to maintain the *sha shtil* (keep quiet) approach of earlier times, while the latter, now more emboldened by its success in establishing a foothold in its newly adopted country, advocated a more dynamic response to threats to Jews in Canada and abroad.[8]

Five sets of events, in close proximity to one another during the 1960s and early 1970s swung the mood of the Jewish community from its comfortable perch within the Canadian social fabric to a fear that a re-emergence of anti-Jewish forces was primed to restrict its gains. The first development was the capture, trial and execution of Adolph Eichmann. In Canada, the months of testimony and the picture of the average man in the glass booth transmitted on television screens did more to inform and alarm both Jews and other Canadians than any other occurrence.[9]

Concurrently, a re-emergence of neo-Nazi activity contributed to the growing unrest in the community. This second development was the most significant factor in the politicization of Holocaust survivors. This phenomenon began in the winter of 1959-60 when a widespread, spontaneous outburst of swastika daubings occurred in Jewish communities world-wide. In Canada scores of daubings, including

smaller towns with few Jews, outraged Canadians. Joan Seager, writing in the small town newspaper *The Burlington Gazette* remarked that:
I occasionally received chain letters and other garbage from anonymous sources which "proved" that the Jews were responsible for - among other things - all the wars in history, the weather, strikes, Edward the Eighth's abdication, sexy movies and cancer.... I could feel the hate dripping off the paper. I could hear the sick mind vomiting its filth.[10]

In Quebec a fledgling Nazi party was started that had minimal support, but succeeded in gaining widespread publicity. CJC was lackadaisical in publicly decrying this development. In response, a small group of vocal survivors created the first organization of survivors in Canada that crossed the lines of the *landsmanschaften* (societies composed of immigrants from the same region or city in Europe). The Association of Survivors of Nazi Oppression staged a public march in opposition to the Nazi party in May, 1961. It printed a newspaper, *The Voice of Survivors,* which focused on antisemitic groups in Canada and Europe, and called upon the Jewish community to denounce these elements and to pressure on government authorities to restrict their activities and publications.[11]

Widespread dissemination of hate literature, largely anti-Jewish, but also aimed at Afro-Canadians, native Canadians, and Catholics, became pervasive in Toronto in 1963. Its source came from neo-Nazi and white supremacist groups in the United States; its distribution by their Canadian acolytes. Survivors pressured CJC to take an active and public opposition, and while CJC together with the Royal Canadian Mounted Police (RCMP) did undertake surveillance of these groups, and while the leaders were unmasked at the Warsaw Ghetto commemoration in 1964, some survivors remained critical of the established community for not being sufficiently strident. As a consequence an umbrella organization of survivors and their supporters, dubbed N3 (after Newton's Third Law) was created to militantly respond to the local hatemongers. This fringe group of fascists formed the Canadian Nazi Party on April 20, 1965 and declared that they would hold a rally at a park in downtown Toronto. On May 30, the would-be rally deteriorated into a violent demonstration, instigated by a small group within the five thousand anti-Nazi protesters. The event was dubbed the Allan Gardens Riot. The response by the established community organizations, notably Canadian Jewish Congress, was to denounce the rioters, some of whom were survivors. This fuelled the already wide gulf between Jewish communal leaders and the Holocaust survivors. Ultimately the neo-Nazi party was proven to be minute, while Congress was spurred to create an anti-Nazi committee that soothed some of the survivors' opposition to the hitherto quiescent response. This was the seminal event in the post-war Jewish community in Toronto. For the first time survivors gained a foothold in the established organizations because of their independent actions.[12]

The third development was the rise and prominence given to American Nazi organizations, such as the American Nazi party led by George Lincoln Rockwell. Rockwell was among the most visible racists in the United States during the backlash to the Civil Rights Movement. He had links with Canadian neo-Nazis. His organization's literature, together with the bile produced by scores of other white supremacist organizations, flooded Toronto mail boxes and infuriated both established Jews and survivors. Interviews with Rockwell were aired on the publicly funded Canadian Broadcasting Corporation (CBC), which infuriated the community. During one broadcast, survivors, including members of N3, protested and picketed the CBC studios in Toronto. When Rockwell appeared in Montreal, demonstrators outside his hotel forced him to leave the country. [13]

The fourth factor in disquieting Canadian Jews was the emergence of German Nazis in the mid 1960s as a potential force in West German politics. The emergence of the National Democratic Party (NDP) and proposed legislation to invoke a Stature of Limitations on war criminals alerted Canadian Jews to the anti-Jewish climate still alive in Germany. When the interview with Eric Von Thaden, the leader of the NDP was aired on CBC, its studios were picketed once again. The disclosure that Von Thadden might visit Canada (he ultimately cancelled the trip) led to a protest rally in Toronto on January 29, 1967 that drew 3,000 Jews. The event was jointly organized by survivor and established organizations, helping to bridge the gulf between them. [14]

Fifth, the Israeli wars between 1967 and 1973 rattled Canadian and world Jewry. The swift victory in June 1967 only underlined the threat that Israel faced from its immediate neighbors and the Islamic world. The rise of the Palestine Liberation Organization, the anti-Israeli resolutions at the United Nations, the War of Attrition, the consolidated attack by Syria and Egypt in October 1973 and the subsequent oil embargo were all instrumental in informing Canadian Jews of the reality that the existence of Israel was precarious. For many Jews these threats, coming on the heals of the preceding developments, led credence to the feeling that they were imperilled once again. Some survivors who had not been politically active beforehand now came to the fore as fund raisers and community activists. During this period, therefore, the main agenda of the community became the survival of the state of Israel, and by extension the survival of the Jewish people. This development helped solidify the Canadian Jewish community, and was a precursor to the community's decision to appropriate the Holocaust as point of ethnic self-identity.[15]

The community's response to these developments was manifested in two ways. First, communal organizations pressured the federal government to enact legislation to ban hate propaganda. Spurred by the accusations of associations of Holocaust survivors that the established community was not responding sufficiently to these developments, the CJC resolved in 1962 "to bring about amendments to the Criminal Code which will make it a criminal offence to practice genocide and race hatred." In 1965, a bill to that effect was tabled in the House of Commons. The Minister of Justice appointed Dean Maxwell Cohen to head a committee on the issue, a committee which included the future Prime Minister, Pierre Elliott Trudeau. Its report in 1966 led to the passage, in June 1970, of a law prohibiting the espousal of racial hatred.[16]

The second path was the unfolding of a concerted program of commemoration and education about the Holocaust within the community. At its plenary session in November, 1971, the CJC resolved to "establish a permanent national memorial to the Holocaust," and to "intensify its efforts to motivate the interest to learn about the Holocaust and develop appropriate programs...." This led to the creation of the National Holocaust Committee in 1973.[17]

With the formation of the renamed Holocaust Remembrance Committee (HRC), the appropriation of the Holocaust as a defining point of ethnic identity by Canadian Jewry was underway. Since the late 1970s, a new generation of leaders from both established and immigrant backgrounds has been instrumental in advancing this process.[18] Three events in 1985 were indicative of the impact of the Holocaust on the Canadian Jewish community: legislation to prosecute Nazi War criminals resident in Canada; the trial of Ernst Zundel for publishing anti-semitic materials, notably Holocaust denial literature; and the gathering of Holocaust survivors and their children in Ottawa on the fortieth anniversary of liberation.

The evolution of the survivors as a force within the Jewish community was of central significance in this process.[19] Whereas there were no survivors on the CJC National Executive and whereas survivor organizations had no input on the resolutions presented at Congress plenaries until 1965, a decade later they were accepted, albeit grudgingly, by the mainstream organizations. Survivors who have been active in this process are not of one opinion as to why this took place. Lou Zablow, the first survivor to become a member of the CJC National Executive states:

> When we (the Association of Survivors) started, they [CJC] hated our guts but they started to respect us in 1965 because of the bill (on hate propaganda). We had marched four times in Montreal, we had just come back from Ottawa on the twentieth anniversary [of liberation] where we met with Prime Minister Pearson. They let us talk at the Plenary. Very simply they didn't want trouble. It was better to have a Lou Zablow in than out. It was strictly a practical political decision.

Nathan Leipciger has a more balanced view.

> Even in the 1970s the influence of the survivors was very weak, although stronger than before when it was non-existent. It wasn't necessarily Congress' fault. It was that a lot of survivors were working hard to establish themselves, to make a living. It's a chicken and egg situation. I didn't start working for the community until 1972, only after my kids were in high school. Did the community hold them out or did the survivors not come forward? I know there are many survivors who feel that the community didn't give them the opportunity. I'm not convinced of that.[20]

The impact of the politicization of the survivors was most evident in local federations. Survivors in Montreal pressured the local Jewish theater to stop the production of *The Man in the Glass Booth* in 1972.[21] Later in the decade, survivors together with young, Montreal born Jews convinced the federation to allow fund raising for a Holocaust education and memorial center in the newly built community center. It was not an easy process. Abba Beer was the chairperson of the National HRC. He remembers that "one VIP said, 'OK, but I don't want horror chambers.'" Lou Zablow states that "it took years before the thing was designed, and only occurred by having young people working with us." One of them was Stephen Cummings, a third generation Canadian Jew. He recalls that:

> There was a Holocaust Committee not accomplishing its goals. I said "look we'll do it." Together with a group of younger people combined with the members of the Association of Survivors we essentially told the powers that be in Federation that they had to let us run the committee. We determined that what we wanted was a living memorial, that this

should be an on-going educational experience, not simply a monument, a mini Yad Vashem.

The Montreal Holocaust Centre opened in 1980.[22]

Similar developments occurred in the 1970s in Toronto. There, a local branch of the HRC emerged. By the end of the decade it had ten subcommittees, including ones dealing with the annual *Yom Hashoah* commemoration, student education, community education, and documentation. The Yom Hashoah commemoration attracted more than two thousand people and was one of several such observances held in the city. Survivors had also made headway in congregations and other organizations such as B'nai B'rith Canada, the friends of the Simon Wiesenthal Centre, and the Holocaust Remembrance Association, which split from the HRC. In education, an annual student seminar was begun in 1979, attracting six hundred children, while inroads were made with boards of education and the provincial Ministry of Education to include Holocaust in the curriculum. Specific curricula were written by members of the HRC for two of the boards. The Holocaust Education Week subcommittee exposed the wider community, both Jewish and non-Jewish, to the topic, with a series of lectures, movies and seminars. By 1985, there were some thirty programs presented. All these endeavors necessitated a collective effort from survivors, Canadian Jews, and non-Jews. In 1982 plans for the construction of a Holocaust Education and Memorial Centre in the Jewish community complex were underway. Under the direction of survivors Nathan Leipciger, the chair of the local HRC and Gerda Frieberg, who eventually became the president of CJC Ontario Region, $800,000 was raised, and the center opened in 1985.[23]

Local committees emerged in other cities as well. Holocaust education programs were introduced in the mid-sized Ontario cities of Ottawa, Hamilton, Kitchener and Windsor. In western Canada activity was centered in Winnipeg and Vancouver. In the former, a Holocaust memorial was erected on the grounds of the provincial legislature, while a city block was renamed "Avenue of the Warsaw Ghetto Heroes" by city council during Yom Hashoah commemorations. In the latter, three major initiatives were launched. The original Warsaw Ghetto Commemoration, begun in 1953 by survivors, was integrated into the Vancouver Jewish Federation. The Standing Committee on the Holocaust began an annual seminar for secondary students at the University of British Columbia in 1976 that soon spread to two days and attracted over one thousand participants. A long-standing campaign

The Politicization of Holocaust Survivors in Canada 1945-1985 203

to erect an education center within the community complex finally reached fruition in 1993. As in Toronto, these efforts were initiated by survivors but depended upon the active contributions of other members of the community as well.[24]

A second impact made by Holocaust survivors since the 1970s has been as speakers. From coast to coast hundreds of survivors have shed their cloaks of anonymity in classrooms, church basements, seminars and other public gatherings. This was one by-product of their politicization. Having entered the community domain as activists for their cause, many had gained the assurance and confidence to speak publicly. Moreover, the structures that they were instrumental in creating within the local federations offered them the opportunity to tell about their experiences. Another reason was their revulsion by neo-Nazis masquerading as deniers of the Holocaust. Survivors felt that it was their mission to expose the calumny that their experience was a fraud.

Perhaps the most compelling factor was the response that they received from their listeners, especially from non-Jewish youth. Leo Lowy came to Canada as a war orphan with his twin sister. He spoke for the first time at the initial student seminar in Vancouver in 1976, and has been doing it ever since.

> The inner feeling was that I had a story to tell. I just had to describe to these kids the emotions, the feelings, the behaviour that I had at that age, to be woken up,[marched] to the brick factory, to the cattle cars, to the Mengele experiments. We are treated like celebrities by the students. The last time I did it, it just strengthened my belief to continue doing it and being involved because these kids are so green, so moved by the issues.[25]

Philip Weiss relates that

> Holocaust survivors had to become involved in the educational process, they had the responsibility for those here and for those who perished. The youth accept us with open arms, they listen, they want to know, they are passionate.

Professor Musia Schwartz is a survivor who has become involved interviewing other survivors.

> We should have more interviewers who are survivors because it's a painful enough experience to open the wounds, and if you have any

doubts if this person is capable of empathy, then this person (the interviewer/survivor) is of some consolation (to the interviewee).

Approximately forty thousand students and their teachers annually visit the education memorials in Toronto, Vancouver and Montreal. All of them meet survivor speakers. Thousands of others learn about the survivor experience through the documentary projects undertaken in many communities which have videotaped more than one thousand people.[26]

Three events in 1985 demonstrated the influence of survivors. The first was the trial of Ernst Zundel, a publisher, author and rabble-rouser, who was accused by the Ontario Attorney General of spreading "false news" in his assertion that the Holocaust did not happen. Zundel's influence was far-flung. Based in Toronto, he was one of the largest purveyors of Holocaust denial literature in the world.[27] Following years of pressure from the Holocaust Remembrance Association, the Crown laid charges against Zundel. The Crown's case was prepared with input from the CJC and the League for Human Rights of B'nai Brith Canada. He was convicted, although two years later his conviction was overturned due to legal technicalities. He was tried again, convicted, but this decision was overturned by the Supreme Court of Canada. Nevertheless, the process was demonstrative of the leverage that survivors had gained in the body politic.[28]

The second event was the creation of the Deschenes Commission on Nazi War Criminals by the Federal Government. CJC had been passing on information about suspected war criminals who immigrated to Canada to the RCMP since the 1950s, but no action had been taken. In the plenary sessions held every three years, the National HRC consistently raised the issue, and resolutions were adopted to pressure the government to take action. During the Liberal administration of Pierre Elliott Trudeau (1968-1979, 1980-1984), indications were given that some public policy would be forthcoming, but the Jewish community was never granted a guarantee, and little ground was gained despite intense lobbying on the offices of the Minister of Justice and the Solicitor General. It was not until the election of the Progressive Conservatives led by Brian Mulroney in 1984 that a change in policy took place. The Commission recommended that suspects should be tried in Canada. To date, only one trial resulted in a conviction, and that was overturned by the Supreme Court. The key consideration, however, as with the Zundel trial, was the ability of the survivors to force the CJC to take more concerted action, and the public exposure that was given to the issue.²⁹

The third event in 1985 was the gathering of Canadian Holocaust survivors and their families. The germ of the idea occurred in 1983 during the gathering of American survivors in Washington. Leaders of the HRC attended that event and decided to launch a Canadian version. Although the gathering had the imprimatur of the CJC, all of the fund raising and programming was done by a separate committee composed of survivors, their children and other Canadian Jews. The organizers anticipated the registration of one thousand people for the three day event at the newly built National Convention Centre in Ottawa, but were astonished when four thousand attended. At the *Yom Hashoah* commemoration on Parliament Hill speakers included the Minister of Finance, the leader of the Opposition Liberal Party, the leader of the New Democratic Party, and Elie Wiesel. The Gathering was the culmination of almost four decades of adaptation, involvement, and influence by survivors. The gathering was the marker of the Holocaust as a pillar of identification in the collective memory of the community.³⁰

Every historical event is the result of circumstance and context. In their first decade in Canada survivors were preoccupied with creating a new life. Their memories and experiences were closeted, only to be shared, if at all, with other survivors. To Canadian Jews, the Holocaust remained outside their realm of experience and comprehension. Their preoccupation was in gaining the acceptance of their countrymen after decades of wearing the tag of foreigners. It was only due to the perceived threat of antisemitism by local hatemongers, and the rise of fascism and anti-Zionism abroad in the 1960s, that the community was alerted to its vulnerability. By this time, many survivors had established themselves, and some had gained the self-assurance to challenge the mainstream organizations to respond with vigor and determination to this threat. Had the events of the 1960s taken place a decade earlier all of the actors in this study maintain that the response would have been muted because of the circumstances of the two communities. Those circumstances had changed by 1965. Emboldened by their success at gaining the attention of the community and establishing links with politicians federally and provincially, survivors were brought into the mainstream in the 1970s. Their impact within the Jewish community and on the public agenda created a new level of consciousness for many Canadians by the mid 1980s. Their influence in community politics can be seen tangibly in memorials, education centers and curricula, but more significantly, in the appropriation of the Holocaust as a pillar of ethnic identification by most Canadian Jews.

Notes

1. Interview, Philip Weiss, Chairperson, Winnipeg Holocaust Remembrance Committee 1979-1991, Winnipeg, Man., November 21, 1995.

2. Interview, Prof. Cyril Levitt, Toronto, Ont., May 9, 1995.

3. J. Torczyner and G. Goldmann, "Demographic Challenges Facing Canadian Jewry" in *The Canadian Jewish News,* December 12, 1993, pp. 1-2. Joseph Kage, *With Faith and Thanksgiving - the Story of Two Hundred Years of Jewish Immigration and Immigrant Aid Effort in Canada (1760-1960),* Montreal: Eagle, 1962, p. 261 (extrapolated), 262. John J. Sigal and Morton Weinfeld, *Trauma and Rebirth: Intergenerational Effects of the Holocaust,* New York: 1989, p. 6. William Helmreich, "The Impact of Holocaust Survivors on American Society: A Socio-Cultural Portrait" in *Remembering for the Future: Jews and Christians During and After the Holocaust,* Oxford: Pergamon, 1988, p. 363.

4. Irving Abella and Harold Troper, *None Is Too Many: Canada and the Jews of Europe 1933-1948,* Toronto: Lester and Orpen Dennys, 1982. David J. Bercuson, *Canada and the Birth of Israel: A Study in Canadian Foreign Policy,* Toronto: University of Toronto Press, 1985. David J. Bercuson, "The Zionist Lobby and Canada's Palestine Policy 1941-1948" in David Taras and David H. Goldberg, eds., *The Domestic Battleground: Canada and the Arab-Israeli Conflict,* Kingston, Ont.: McGill-Queen's University Press, 1989, pp. 17-36. Michael R. Marrus, *Mr. Sam: The Life and Times of Samuel Bronfman,* Toronto: Penguin, 1992. Interview, Ben Kayfetz, Executive Director of CJC Joint Public Relations Committee, Central Region, 1947-1985, Toronto, November 7, 1995.

5. Irving Abella, *A Coat of Many Colours: Two Centuries of Jewish Life in Canada,* Toronto: Lester and Orpen Dennys, 1990, pp. 209-223. CJC Memo #524, November 15, 1968, Ottawa: *National Archives of Canada* (NAC), B'nai Brith Canada Papers, MG 28, V 133, 36/21.

6. Kayfetz Interview. Interview, Ben Lappin, Executive Director, CJC, Central Region, 1947-1958, Herzliya, Israel, August 20, 1994.

7. Weiss Interview. Interview, Mike Englishman, Member of the CJC Anti-Nazi Committee, 1966-1970, Toronto, May 8, 1995. Interview, Nathan Leipciger, Chairperson, Holocaust Remembrance Committee, Toronto Jewish Congress, 1980-1988, Chairperson, National Holocaust Remembrance Committee, 1989-present, Toronto, November 10, 1995. Selections from "I Dream in Good English Too," Dr. (Hon.) Donia Blumenfeld Clenman, *I Dream in Good English Too,* North York, Ont: Flowerfield and Littleman, 1988, p. 14.

8. Irving Abella, "Jews in Canada: A Look at the Past," *Viewpoints,* January 1990, p. 1. Abella, *A Coat of Many Colours - Two Centuries of Jewish Life in Canada,* p. 226. Myra Giberovitch, "The Contributions of Montreal Holocaust Survivor Organizations to Canadian Jewish Communal Life," unpublished M.A. Dissertation, McGill University, 1988, pp. 96-102. Montreal: Canadian Jewish Congress (CJC) National Archives, Association of Survivors of Nazi Oppression, ZC1, ZC2, ZF Publication File.

9. Toronto: Ontario Jewish Archives (OJA), Joint Community Relations Committee Papers, MG8S, 1961, 12/13A, 1962, 14/14, 1963, 15/15, Eichmann Files. Montreal: Jewish Public Library Archives (JPL), Canadiana Collection, "Holocaust and Canada," Box 3.

10. Joan Seager. "The Fatal Disease of Anti-Semitism" in *The Burlington Gazette,* reprinted in *The Toronto Telegram,* January 23, 1960. OJA, JCRC Papers, 1960, 12/32.

11. CJC Archives, ZC 1, Organization Files, Association of Survivors of Nazi Oppression, ZF, Publication Files. JPL Archives, Canadiana Collection, Box: CJC National Holocaust Committee. Interview, Lou Zablow, founder and first president of the Association, Montreal, May 29, 1995. Interview, Isaac Piasetski, founder of the Association, Montreal, July 19, 1994.

12. OJA, Minutes of the Executive of the Central Region of Canadian Jewish Congress. June 24, 1965, July 8, 1965. JPL Archives, Association of Former Concentration Camp Inmates Survivors of Nazi Oppression, Open Letter, June 6, 1965. Mark R. MacGuigan, "Hate Control And Freedom Of Assembly: The Canadian Nazi Party In Toronto, 1965-1966," *Saskatchewan Bar Review,* 1966, 31, pp. 232-250. Kayfetz, Englishman, Levitt Interviews. Interview, Judge Sydney Harris, Co-Chairperson, CJC Joint Public Relations Committee, Central Region, 1962-1968, CJC President, 1973-1976, Toronto, May 10, 1965. Interview, Judge Phillip Givens, Mayor of Toronto, 1963-1966, Toronto, May 10, 1995. Interview, Mike Berwald, founder of N3, Toronto, May 7, 1995.

13. Kayfetz, Piasetski, Zablow Interviews. OJA, JCRC Papers, Montreal: CJC Confidential Memo, November 24, 1964. Toronto: CBC Film Archives, "This Hour Has Seven Days," Interview with George Lincoln Rockwell, October 25, 1964.

14. OJA, JCRC Central Region, Minutes, January 13, 1967, March 23, 1969. Interview, Larry Zolf, CBC Reporter and interviewer of Von Thadden, Toronto: November 19, 1995. CBC Film Archives, "Sunday," Von Thadden Interview, January 22, 1967.

15. Interview, Sam Rothstein, President Vancouver Jewish Community Centre 1972-1974, Vancouver, November 28, 1993. Interview, Professor Moe Steinberg, Chairperson, CJC Pacific Region 1977-1980, Vancouver, November 29, 1993, stated that "Israel and Holocaust awareness are inseparable." Interview, Professor Sid Olyan, director of the Jewish Federations in Vancouver and Seattle in the 1960s, Toronto, November 14, 1993, on the impact of the 1967 War.

16. CJC National Archives, Ab, Plenary Sessions, 1962, 1965, 1968, 1971. Maxwell Cohen, et. al. *Report of the Special Committee On Hate Propaganda In Canada,* Ottawa: Queen's Printer, 1966. Interview, Justice Mark MacGuigan, Justice of the Federal Court of Canada, Member of the Cohen Committee, Federal Minister of Justice 1982-1984, Ottawa, September 13, 1995. William Kaplan, "Maxwell Cohen and the Report of the Special Committee on Hate Propaganda," *Law Policy and International Justice: Essays in Honour of Maxwell Cohen,* William Kaplan and Donald McRae, eds., Kingston, Ont.: McGill-Queen's University Press, 1993, pp. 243-274.

17. CJC National Archives, Ab, Plenary Sessions, 1971, 1974. JPL Archives, Canadiana Collection, CJC Holocaust Memorial Committee File, Minutes of Holocaust Memorial Committee, April 26, 1973.

18. Les Scheininger, a child of survivors, was President of Ontario Region and then National President. Gerda Frieberg, a survivor, was President of Ontario Region. Ralph Snow, a Holocaust survivor, was President of B'nai Brith Canada.

19. Interview, Dr. Robert Krell, Chairperson Vancouver HRC, November 28, 1993. Giberovitch Dissertation. Jean Miriam Gerber, *Immigration And Integration In Post-War Canada: A Cast Study Of Holocaust Survivors In Vancouver 1947-1970,* unpublished M.A. Dissertation, University of British Columbia, 1989.

20. Zablow Interview, August 28, 1995. Leipciger Interview, January 25, 1996.

21. Giberovitch, pp. 99-100. Zablow Interview. Articles in *The Montreal Star, The Montreal Gazette, La Presse, Le Devoir, Canadian Jewish News,* courtesy of Lou Zablow Personal Papers.

22. Zablow Interview, August 28, 1995. Abba Beer, Interview, Montreal, July 19, 1994. Stephen Cummings, Interview, Montreal, August 31, 1995.

23. OJA, JCRC Papers, Toronto Jewish Congress Papers, HRC Papers. Leipciger Interview, November 10, 1995. The two curricula are: Alan Bardikoff and Jane Griesdorf, *The Holocaust,* North York Board of Education, 1982; Franklin Bialystok and Barbara Walther, *The Holocaust And Its Contemporary Implications,* 3 vols., Toronto Board of Education, 1985.

24. For summaries of the activities of local committees see *Zachor,* the newsletter of the National HRC, published quarterly, commencing in December 1976, in the JPL Archives, Canadiana Collection, Institutions File. For Winnipeg, selected press clippings from *The Jewish Post,* Winnipeg: Jewish Historical Society of Western Canada *Archives.* Winnipeg: Provincial Archives of Manitoba, Winnipeg Jewish Community Council Papers, P3542, P4641, CJC Papers, P3535, Abraham J. Arnold Papers, P5108, P5138. Philip Weiss Interview. Interview, Harry Gutkin, Chairperson, Jewish Historical Society of Western Canada, Winnipeg, November 20, 1995. Interview, Sol Kanee, CJC President 1970-1973, Winnipeg, November 20, 1995. For Vancouver, CJC Pacific Region Papers, and Mark Silverberg Papers, Vancouver: Jewish Historical Society of British Columbia Archives. Krell Interview. Interview, Sophie Waldman, Chairperson of the Warsaw Ghetto Memorial 1953-1986, November 26, 1995.

25. Interview, Leo Lowy, Vancouver, November 24, 1995.

26. Philip Weiss Interview. Interview, Prof. Musia Schwartz, Montreal, May 29, 1995.

27. Deborah Lipstadt, *Denying The Holocaust: The Growing Assault on Truth and Memory,* New York: Penguin, 1994, pp. 157-163.

28. NAC, B'nai Brith Papers, Vols. 79, 98. Gabriel Weimann and Conrad Winn, "Hate on Trial: The Zundel Affair, The Media, Public Opinion in Canada" in R. Brym, et. al., eds., *The Jews In Canada,* Toronto: Oxford, 1993, pp. 97-111. Manuel Prutschi, "The Zundel Affair" in Allan Davies, ed.,

Antisemitism In Canada: History and Interpretation, Waterloo, Ont.: Wilfred Laurier University Press, pp. 249-278. Kayfetz and Leipciger Interviews.

29. CJC Archives, Plenary Sessions Resolutions, 1968-1986; OJA, JCRC *Papers,* War Criminals Files, 1962-1986; Kayfetz, Harris, MacGuigan (Minister of Justice, 1982-1984) Interviews. Judge Phillip Givens, Member of Parliament, 1968-1971, Interview. Harold Troper and Morton Weinfeld, *Old Wounds: Jews, Ukrainians and the Hunt for Nazi War Criminals in Canada,* Toronto: Viking, 1988. Papers on War Criminals and the Deschenes Commission in Irwin Cotler, ed., *Nuremberg Forty Years Later: The Struggle against Injustice in Our Time,* Kingston, Ont: McGill-Queen's University Press, 1995, pp. 45-96, 212-220.

30. Beer, Krell, Leipciger Interviews. Interview, Mendel Good, co-chair of the Gathering, Ottawa, September 13,1995. CJC Archives, 1983 Plenary Resolutions. JPL Archives, Canadiana Collection, Box "Holocaust and Canada," File "Gathering of Jewish Holocaust Survivors."

Chapter 14

ANDRE STEIN: THE CATEGORY OF DIALOGUE

Harry James Cargas

The dialogue form has a long history, of course, and goes back even beyond Plato. As a literary form, the oldest known are Sicilian mimes, written some 2,500 years ago in rhythmic prose by Sophron of Syracuse. Since none of them have survived we know of them only by inference from the verse mimes of Herodas about three centuries before the Common Era. These are limited, short, realistic scenes of common life with common character types. Plato was an admirer of this form but his adaptation of it for his purposes of philosophical exposition in about 400 BC was such that he can be considered as having advanced the form in his own way as a unique literary invention. In no way static like that which preceded them, Plato's dialogues are much more dramatic and render characterization in a newly emphasized way.

Lucan, who flourished about six centuries after Plato, is credited with giving a new tone and function to dialogue in his "objectively" satirical *Dialogues of the Dead.* The influence of this work lasted for many centuries and can be seen in the 17th century French writings of Bernard de Fontenelle and the 18th century's Francois is Fenelon. But well before those authors the interest in the dialogue form was renewed when Plato became repopularized in the Renaissance from the mid-16th century to the mid-17th. Nor were the topics for which this form was employed restricted to philosophical inquiries. For example in Spain, Juan de Valdes used it to explore philological problems; Vincent Carducci thus investigated theories of painting; and others who wrote dialogues included Torquato Tasso, Giordano Bruno and, perhaps most surprisingly to some, Galileo. It was even used as a method of language instruction.

Controversial political, economic and even religious ideas were presented in what may have been considered this "safer" form. Other writers who should be cited here include philosophers George Berkeley (*Three Dialogues Between Hylas and Philonous*) David Hume (whose *Dialogues Concerning Natural Religion* was much influenced by Cicero's use of the form), and Walter Savage Landor's *Imaginary Conversations,* up to Andre-Gide's *Interviews Imaginaires* published just over a half century ago.

And yet Andre Stein writes not so much in the tradition of dialogue as in the category of dialogue. Let me explain. Traditionally, the dialogue form as employed by the masters of that genre share certain literary characteristics, some of them clearly found in Stein's book *Broken Silence.* We can extrapolate from what appeared before. First, dialogue includes a way of advancing actions rather than being perfunctorily ornamentation. Next, it reflects the character of the speakers, their social positions, idiosyncrasies, jobs, psychological states, backgrounds, aspirations, etc. Third, there is a certain naturalness of discourse implied (and presented) even though the reader will know that what is being rendered is fiction, not a word for word account of a historical conversation. Here, we understand, is a literary reality rather than a verbatim record. Fourth there is a give and take among the participants in the dialogue rather than a mere collection of paragraphs or oral essays presented by each "side" of a question posed. Fourth, the speech of each of those engaged in the dialogue must be such that it is so appropriate to the speaker that the "listener" can identify who is talking without that person being identified by the author. Good readers of William Faulkner will understand this as will those of Claude Mauriac's magnificent tetralogy, beginning with *All Women Are Fatal,* in which not a single speaker is identified by Mauriac in any of the four volumes. These are major factors in judging the "success" of the dialogue form and readers can see how Andre Stein's "Dialogues from the Edge," as his book *Quiet Heroes* is subtitled, approximates meeting these arbitrary but not therefore dismissable standards.

One major difference in Stein's approach is his emphasis on dialogue as a means to intimacy rather than in distancing himself from his topic. This was, perhaps, not consciously done, at least initially by the author. But this comes through, in what follows. It is appropriate that, given the style employed by Stein in his books, that the dialogue stratagem be employed with him to allow him, with some prompting, to speak for himself. Here, then, is an edited version of a St. Louis to Toronto telephone interview taped on February 16, 1996. This interview began by asking Stein why he did not write in his native Hungarian language.

AS: I have found the Hungarian language alienating and I associate the Hungarian language with trauma. At that time, when I started to write, I felt the need to be as far from it as possible.

HJC: As you of course know, you are not the only survivor to write that way. This distancing is replicated in the dialogue form you use -- is that correct?

AS: Yes, and there was another reason for the dialogue. At the time I sat down to write *Broken Silence* I essentially had no one to engage in a dialogue with. I could not unleash this on my family; my colleagues could not and would not want to cope with it -- in fact I was hit on the head in many different ways for even attempting to deal with something in the first person singular so I needed another voice. There is another reason for the dialogue forms. This process was for me an attempt at making sense of not only my experience but I had to fantasize in most of the dialogues what the other person's experience might have been. I thought that I could put it across in a clear way and also I would experience it in a clearer way if indeed I made my voice separate from that of my interlocutor.

HJC: So imagination played a great part in what you did.

AS: Imagination in a sense of creating a voice that actually did not really exist, yes. Imagination especially in the dialogue with the torturer and the dialogue with the victim, had to play a part because I did not have either my mother who was the victim nor the torturer who was my torturer available to dialog. So I had to posit their voices and at the same time -- it wasn't entirely imagination. I wrote *Broken Silence* in six or seven weeks. (It was more like it wrote me rather than the other way around.) But what went into it was about three years or more of reading survivor testimonies, reading essays, research papers on all the experiences of all the persona involved in the Holocaust: the perpetrator, the victim, the survivor and the bystander. In a way a lot of the material that went into the other voice was a composite of a lot of people's experiences.

At this point I spoke to Stein about how he went forward with his work. I knew he had contacted Elie Wiesel and me (neither of us had known Stein prior to his initiating this contact in which he kindly felt we had, perhaps, something to offer him).

AS: I reached out to four people: You, Robert McAfee Brown, Gregory Baum and Elie Wiesel. All were total strangers to me and yet I felt a greater affinity with all of you than anybody whom I was actually acquainted with -- just through the writings.

HJC: Three Christians and one Jew.

AS: I reached out to Wiesel not primarily because he was a Jew but because he was a survivor; a child survivor at that.

HJC: And all four responded to you?

AS: And all four responded to me and all in extremely encouraging, supportive and wise ways. I'll never forget the responses of any of you. That has been really important to me. The one who has had the greatest effect on the development of my subsequent writing and also my Judaism was Wiesel.

Stein then explained how initially he could only communicate with Wiesel through Wiesel's agent, how Wiesel called him and suggested that instead of Stein coming to New York, they meet during Wiesel's next speaking engagement in Toronto a few weeks hence. They met and two things stand out in Stein's collection of their relatively long encounter. One was regarding Stein's attitude toward his Judaism. He says that he was either ashamed of it or had disowned it. Wiesel told him that being a Jew was not like having an American express account -- you can't lose your membership: "At worst you are a lapsed Jew." That, Stein says, was "incredibly helpful for me." Then was the question of belief in God. Stein said "We haven't been on speaking terms. My Communist training in Hungary allowed me to live on an ideological level what I was living on a personal level." If there was a God, it could not have allowed what happened to me and to my family and to other Jews. When Stein answered in the affirmative Wiesel's question about whether he had ever hated God or wanted to put God on trial, he heard that he was in very good company. In Judaism we can love God, hate him, argue with him. The only thing we are not allowed to do is to be indifferent. Stein was told he was anything but indifferent because he had spent so much energy against God, to deny his existence. "That really opened the door for me to go on the very long road to contemplate the question of finding a possible way to accept God."

HJC: Throughout all of this is the question of what language means to you. I take it you are rather comfortable in Hungarian, French, Spanish and English.

AS: I studied quite a bit of Italian, Russian for 12 years. I studied Japanese for three years.

HJC: I want to talk about the adequacy and the inadequacy of language for you in what you have to say.

AS: Prior to the Nazis coming into my life -- I come from an old fashioned, fairly primitive Hungarian Jewish uneducated family where the rule was for the children to speak only when spoken to. So for me it was never safe to speak about how I felt. Then came the experience of hiding, then came the experience of rape that I could not talk to anyone about -- I had no language to talk about it. I didn't know the word "rape." I didn't know any of the words for what happened to me. I was eight years old, I didn't have the linguistic sophistication of children today. So silence came natural to me. But about two years after liberation somehow, through opera, (there is a very big opera culture in Hungary) I found the opera world so full of fantasy and I loved the music so I decided that I wanted to learn Italian. I actually saved my pocket money to be able to get Italian lessons. It was not through school but through my need for one area where I could actually experience beauty. And an area which was just mine in my family, that nobody could interfere with. That was my private domain -- at age 10. I became proficient in Italian in a year. And I continued with it. Then at school I had to learn German and Russian. I liked language. I also loved the Hungarian language. I was the only kid in my class who loved grammar. Language allowed me to deal with the outside without having ever to attend to my feelings. Once I had these foreign languages available to me or the whole of domestic Hungarian grammar, it really allowed me to create worlds other than the one in which I lived. Especially emotionally. Socially as well. I also studied Hebrew for three years and then when they closed down the yeshiva then Hebrew dropped out of my life.

Then in 1956 I escaped to France. There my knowledge of Italian became extremely useful because there were no Hungarian-French language books but we could find Italian-French language books. I taught myself French in six weeks. I got to Paris November 7, for the Christmas party at the

Sorbonne for Hungarian refugees I was the interpreter. I had not known a word of French before. For me at that point when I got to France it was a second birth. French allowed me to free myself. I threw myself into the study of the language with a fervor that I haven't done with anything else since. It was the opportunity for me to integrate, for the first time, where I lived in body and in intellect. To this day, very often, when I need to deal with matters of the soul, I write in French.

Then I went to North America, to Berkeley. English did not come to me as naturally. I didn't feel at home in California, I felt at home in France. But language has always allowed me to be child-like, in terms of playfulness: I am an incorrigible punster. I love all kinds of word games. The first time I used English for experiencing feeling and dealing with my past was with *Broken Silence*. I was fully aware of how frustrating it was because of what you call the inadequacy of language. I couldn't even fathom if whether in English or any other language I could find words to correspond to what I experienced. Even more so, I thought it was morally wrong to try to label the experience with inadequate words and thereby give a distortion to what really happened.

HJC: So you approach now the subject of the literature of silence.

AS: Yes, and at the same time it's a huge paradox. On the one hand I'm aware of the necessity of speech, of testimony, of telling one's story and at the same time I'm dismayed by the impossibility of doing justice to that.

HJC: Have you found that your writings have been purgative in some way?

AS: The last book, *Hidden Children,* I would say has most obviously had that effect. At the same time I am fully aware that I would never have written *Hidden Children* had I not written *Broken Silence* and *QuietHeroes*. Gregory Baum said something to me after *Broken Silence*. He said he hoped that writing this book had healed me and that my next book would heal my readers. He told me that after he had read this book he felt damaged. Somebody else wrote in a review that she found that my language was so private that there was nothing universal in it for her and therefore reading *Broken Silence* was not a useful experience for her to the extent that *Night* was because of the universal language that Wiesel used.

HJC: Was it useful for you, though? That's an awful word but I'm just repeating what you used.

AS: Was it useful? That wasn't my word, it was hers. But I had no choice. I said earlier that book wrote me. Otherwise you don't write a book like this in six or seven weeks. Or maybe the other way around: you maybe can write something this only if you allow it to gush.

HJC: Did you find an element of revenge as well as an expression of anger?

AS: Rage, yes, anger, yes, revenge was never my experience. I don't think revenge could do anything for me because under no condition can I see myself healing myself at the expense of inflicting pain on anybody and thereby becoming a torturer my own self. But there is another issue: if you want to take revenge, you have to know specifically what for. That to me would be reductionist and it would mean for me that I know exactly what I want, let's say in terms of robbing me of my mother. I can't do that. It's just as I could never bring myself to apply for a penny of war reparations money. It would, again, feel like I'd have to put my losses into a paradigm that would be reductionist. I jut can't do that.

HJC: How is it you feel you could have waited 40 years to "unblock" the silence?

AS: There are a couple of ways to look at that. One is that for a long time I was too busy trying to come alive, and writing is the opposite of living. I can't live and write at the same time. You either record or you live. For me writing would be another instance of deadening myself. I had had enough of that, thank you very much. So I was just too busy to try to resuscitate whatever was left of my life. I threw myself into the everyday activity of being, doing, discovering. Then I escaped from Hungary and had to start again (the rebirth I mentioned) and the pragmatics of learning a new language, going to school, of creating for myself a new community, falling in love for the first time. All of those were very much grounding me in the present moment and the present place. Then once again leaving another country and coming to North America, going to Berkeley, starting all over again -- a new language, a new community, new studies, getting married, becoming a father. And then shortly after picking up again and leaving for another country (Canada). So there was no time, no room, no energy.

But also there was no safety. I really didn't feel that what I had to say would be honored and the impetus that in fact I actually needed to get going was a spontaneous recovery of a repressed memory of the sexual assault on me by those Arrow Cross militiamen. I had no memory of that whatsoever until 1978. The process began during a training session at the Gestalt Institute of Toronto. We all had to give our autobiographies and I began to speak a bit about my memories from the war and a colleague gave me a copy of Terence Des Pres' book *The Survivor*. That began to open things for me. Then I began to search. And one day, in another training workshop I went to with my wife Vickie, at the same Gestalt Institute, all of a sudden from nowhere the memory just gushed open. After that it took me about a year to say now I must understand. I can no longer just hide from the reality. I need to somehow reconstitute myself, become whole.

For years, prior to dealing with my story, the story of the Jewish people, I had the sense of being a stigmatized outsider. My first areas of study and clinical work, my first writings were about beggars and criminals in France. Then I spent four years in working with the clinically obese. Then I gave my time, energy and interests to helping young gay men to come out. It is only after I had attended to all of these different other groups' needs and stories and tainted identity that I finally got to me and I realized that once I got to looking at my story, with each of these different populations, I was looking at my story, but metaphorically. I started to deal with and write about my experience at the very first opportunity that I had at the emotional and intellectual means for it.

HJC: While you were talking I couldn't help thinking of the patient you wrote about in one of your reports. You took him to a cemetery to help him to come to terms with his experience as a survivor.

AS: Once I had begun this kind of work for me I realized that where I could be the most useful, the most efficient for others, is in helping others to tell their story and begin to heal themselves. That's why much of my therapeutic practice has been with Holocaust survivors and also with survivors of torture victims in Argentina and Chile.

HJC: You have gone from concentrating on yourself, in a sense, in *Broken Silence,* to others in *Quiet Heroes* (about rescuers) to *Hidden Children.* There seems to be a pattern. Can you say what is next?

AS: Yes, there is a pattern, There will be no more books that I can foresee on the Holocaust. At the time I begin, in *Broken Silence,* I identify four persona: the perpetrator, the victim, the survivor, the spectator. Then you and Wiesel invited me to that gathering in Washington at the State Department honoring rescuers. I was asked to speak on behalf of the six million who were not rescued. That was at the very beginning of the conference. I did what I had to do and then there was no usefulness for me. The people who had the attention were the rescuers and I sort of just stepped back and felt extremely abandoned, extremely sad and out of place because I had no rescuer to honor. Nor could I ever conceive of anyone willing to risk his or her life for me. Then an elderly couple came up to me and told me I looked very lonely and upset. They said they liked my talk and a few other compliments and I was so touched. They noticed me, all by myself and came up to me and reached out to me. At that point I said to myself that I have to understand what makes these people tick. What makes them so different? So by the time I came back from Washington I was committed to writing a book, I talked to my publisher and three days after that gathering I had the contract for the book (*Quiet Heroes*). I found a lot of solace. In thinking about what Gregory Baum said about healing myself with *Broken Silence* and hoping to heal my readers with the next one -- actually, he was off. *Broken Silence* opened the wounds and I felt like there was no way to heal myself. The feedback, the echoes to the book, confirmed that. The response from much of the Jewish press for sure and some of the metropolitan press was that this is a dangerous and toxic book by a very damaged person. It was banned from the Jewish education system here and so I thought I made a mistake, I shouldn't have spoken out. But with *Quiet Heroes,* meeting the rescuers that I interviewed, the process of healing began because it was the first time in my life that I felt that good does exist. It gave me some hope that, if indeed it does exist, perhaps I should rethink my own history and look for instances of good in my life.

I was quite absorbed with that process when I learned of the gathering of hidden children in New York. For me the real healing began at that gathering -- seeing sixteen hundred people, all of them with similar histories to mine. Many of them were looking like me: sort of battered by time but yet energetic and enthusiastic. And Abe Foxman, in his plenary address, said something that really got me going. He said what, if not anger, is the proper response of a child who had been abandoned and abused. I thought that finally, finally, it's now safe. Coincidentally, the woman from the Canadian Jewish Congress who had requested that my book be banned from the Jewish education system, was standing next to one. I said to her "Does that remind you of anything?" And she said that now, I was right. Back then it didn't. At that point I was already just past being riveted on my own story. Now I wanted to know everybody's story. Meeting all these people, and doing my sister's story (it is hers that appears in *Quiet Heroes* not mine), I did it for me. I felt that now, everything has been said, I've said what I had to say. So the book I'm now working on, I've gone beyond. I began with myself, then the rescuers, then the hidden children -- the next book I'm working on deals with all of the children in the world. It is a book about child-sacrifices as taught to us by Genesis.

HJC: You have also written fiction, some very interesting short stories.

AS: I do like fiction. I wish I had more time for it. I don't want to be an absentee father like my father was.

HJC: A final question: Do you have hope?

AS: If I didn't have hope I would be dead. But what do you mean by hope?

HJC: You talk about Camus in *Broken Silence*. One of his ideas was about the greatest problem of our time having to do with whether or not to commit suicide. You note he said it is up to man to make his own history. Is that enough? Is there something more that you see that is attainable?

AS: Well I thought of *The Myth of Sisyphus*. How can we imagine that Sisyphus can go through with this endless chore? Camus' answer is that you must imagine Sisyphus hopeful on the way up. Each time. That's my model. Regardless what else, you have to imagine that this time it has to be better. If not, how could I go on and have five children?

HJC: Well, in the end, Prometheus, who is condemned to eternally have his gut plucked by a bird, he gets out of that situation. I feel that in the end Sisyphus is going to make it.

AS: If that were not possible then I'd say that my reading of all our civilization would be just unintelligible and we would already have had a nuclear holocaust.

HJC: One of the things your books are showing is that while Sisyphus may not make it alone, he'll make it with us. It's a community thing.

AS: Absolutely. And that to me has become so clear. That's why the world of *Broken Silence* was to me a suffocating one because it was a world without community; by the time I get through *Quiet Heroes* and *Hidden Children* I am a member of a community. Without that community I would be a profoundly pessimistic and deflated man, a paradigm of Jean Amery -- not necessarily the intellect but certainly I probably would have committed suicide.

HJC: I am pleased that we are members of the same community.

Chapter 15

LAWRENCE LANGER AND "THE HOLOCAUST EXPERIENCE"

Gary Weissman

In 1964 Lawrence L. Langer was a professor of American studies teaching in Austria on a Fulbright fellowship. At this time war-crimes trials were being conducted in Germany, and as Langer followed them he developed an abiding interest in the Holocaust. "I knew a little before, but not much," he says; "I had never been much involved."[1] Today Langer is the preeminent literary critic working in the interdisciplinary field of Holocaust studies. His standing is attributable to the success of his fourth Holocaust-related book, *Holocaust Testimonies: The Ruins of Memory*, which won the 1991 National Book Critics Circle Award in Criticism. In 1995 he published two more books: an anthology of Holocaust-related texts, most of them written by survivors, titled *Art from the Ashes*, and a collection of essays titled *Admitting the Holocaust*.

This collection occasioned a *New York Times* article on Langer. Titled "A Scholarly Call For a Realistic View of the Holocaust," it reports:

> A retired professor of English at Simmons College in Boston, Mr. Langer says that psychologists, scholars and writers who have not been through the Holocaust have difficulty fathoming bottomless evil and tend to seek some redeeming message even — perhaps especially — in tales of annihilation.[2]

This statement encapsulates Langer's "realistic view" of the Holocaust, a view he has expressed repeatedly in books and essays written over the course of two decades: namely that we avoid facing the Holocaust by clinging to a language of redemption. No doubt it is important and necessary to criticize feel-good approaches to the Holocaust which stress heroism and the triumphant human spirit; but while repeating this criticism throughout his work, Langer has done little to move beyond it. He does not address the question of *why* psychologists, scholars and writers seeking a redeeming message would be drawn to studying the Holocaust. Nor does he elaborate on what it means to fathom bottomless evil. And he does not explain what, contrary to "some redeeming message," he and other scholars tend to seek in the Holocaust, or in what he calls "the Holocaust experience."

Langer criticizes Terrence Des Pres, author of *The Survivor*, for "creating a collective identity called 'the survivor'" when "[a]nyone conversant with the thousands of separate testimonies of survivors knows what an *un*common catastrophe it was for each of them."[3] Nevertheless, he consistently refers to a collective experience called "the Holocaust experience" without reflecting on the similar problems posed by this phrase.[4] What does Langer seek in the Holocaust experience? Rather than taking up this question, he reproaches those who look for redeeming messages. In doing so, he targets not only those who have *not* been through the Holocaust, but those who have, the survivors themselves. In one striking instance he refers to the survivors participating in an event commemorating the fiftieth anniversary of the liberation of Auschwitz as "those 'holocaust deniers.'" To Langer's mind, this name-calling is warranted because the *brochure* for this event contains the most hackneyed "redemptive rhetoric," including references to "heroism, hope, and healing" and "the triumph of the human spirit in the face of unspeakable evil."[5]

The title of Langer's collected essays plays off the title of Deborah Lipstadt's well-known book on Holocaust denial, *Denying the Holocaust*.[6] *Admitting the Holocaust* suggests that one is either an "admitter" or a "denier;" there is little room for a more nuanced understanding of how survivors and nonsurvivors relate to the Holocaust. In this formulation, all those who seek some kind of redeeming message in relation to the Holocaust fail "to admit disturbing evidence"[7] and thereby contribute to Holocaust denial. Herein lies what I take to be the greatest danger of Langer's work: that other scholars may be roused to see themselves as "admitters" like Langer, taking on all those Holocaust scholars and survivors who are "in denial." To caution against such a move, this essay presents a critique of Langer's writings which explores terms, strategies, and motivations which have gone unexamined in his work.

1. History, Imagination, Memory

"One of the most striking events in Holocaust studies in recent years," notes Langer in a 1993 essay titled "Memory's Time," "has been the proliferation of titles focusing on a single theme: memory."[8] Indeed, the word not only appears routinely in titles, but pervades the rhetoric of Holocaust studies. With tedious regularity, we refer to "memory" where we might otherwise speak of remembrance, commemoration, consciousness, knowledge, history. A Holocaust museum is said to preserve memory, Holocaust memorials are said to generate memory, and visitors to these sites are called memory-tourists, while "Holocaust memory" itself is subdivided and categorized into an ever-increasing number of types.[9] After Langer illustrates this focus on "memory" with a list of titles featuring the word, including his own 1991 book *Holocaust Testimonies: The Ruins of Memory*, he writes:

> Perhaps this means we have finally begun to enter the second stage of Holocaust response, moving from what we know of the event (the province of historians), to how to remember it, which shifts the responsibility to our own imaginations and what we are prepared to admit there.[10]

This explanation for the prevailing focus on memory is most striking in that Langer attributes the act of remembering not to memory but to our imaginations, indicating that how we "remember it" is analogous to how we imagine the Holocaust. Whereas at one point in *Holocaust Testimonies* Langer reckons that those of us who are not surviving victims are "witnesses to memory rather than rememberers themselves," here our imaginations enable us all to be rememberers.[11] While it may be appealing to imagine that we are rememberers in the sense that survivors are rememberers, we do so at the risk of obscuring vast differences between survivors' memories of past experiences and our own imaginings of what these experiences may have been like. Even as "witnesses to memory," we read and watch and listen to *testimony*, which transmits some part of what some survivors remember about some of their experiences.

Langer finds in the focus on "memory" some indication that we in Holocaust studies are entering a so-called second stage of Holocaust response. The first stage appears to have been dominated by historians and their project of determining "what we know of the event" — what our historical knowledge and understanding of the Holocaust might be;

the second stage involves moving from what we know to "how to remember it." By this Langer means not how are we to remember this history which we know from historians, but rather: how are we to remember (imagine) what it was like to experience the Holocaust as a victim? Clearly, Langer's answer is not that we remember by being good historians or students of history. Indeed, historians are ill-equipped to "remember it," as they know only history, which Langer equates with "Holocaust facts."[12] To "remember it," it seems that we must turn not to history but to memory, and not to historians but to our own imaginations.

The inadequacy of "the historian or reporter of mere facts" is already pronounced in Langer's 1975 book *The Holocaust and the Literary Imagination*.[13] There he explains that while Holocaust literature may be "no more satisfactory than history for solving the desperate and by now persistent questions of how and why the Holocaust occurred," it is far more able to evoke the "atmosphere of the Holocaust" and confront readers with the "exact details of the experience."[14] Literature succeeds where history fails because whereas the historian is bound by fidelity to fact, the survivor-writer is able to draw not only on historical fact (by virtue of his or her memory), but on "the power of the imagination."[15] Holocaust literature relies on imagination no less than memory, as it is the survivor's *imaginative* literary rendering of remembered events that makes the Holocaust experience accessible to our own imaginations — hence the importance Langer places on "the literary imagination."[16]

However, with *Holocaust Testimonies* Langer seeks to undo this conjoining of memory and imagination. More specifically, he seeks to remove "the literary imagination" as a mediating factor, facilitating a more direct connection between survivor memory and our imaginations. To accomplish this he turns from literature to a non-literary form of testimony: videotaped interviews with survivors. Explaining this move in his book's preface, Langer writes,

> Holocaust *literature* ... challenges the imagination through the mediation of a *text*, raising issues of style and form and tone and figurative language that — I now see — can deflect our attention from ... the event itself. Nothing, however, distracts us from the immediacy and the intimacy of conducting interviews with former victims (which I have done) or watching them on a screen.[17]

Langer implies that "the immediacy and the intimacy" of interviewing survivors or watching video testimonies directs our attention to the event rather than to its textual representation. But what lends this immediacy and intimacy? He explains that "[o]ral testimony is distinguished by the absence of literary mediation:" whereas most written survivor testimonies abide by literary conventions, including "above all, perhaps, the invention of a narrative voice," in oral testimony we encounter the immediate, intimate voice of memory.[18] Implying that there is no mediating factor present in oral testimony, Langer treats the video testimonies as if they constitute this voice of memory, directly conveying the event. Therefore he does not differentiate between "conducting interviews with former victims" and "watching them on a screen," for it seems that in either case the event is conveyed not by a medium — not by the interview process, not by the spoken word, and not by video — but by memory itself.

In *Holocaust Testimonies* Langer touches on his earlier work, writing that the survivor-writer employs various literary devices in an effort to narrow "the vast imaginative space separating what he or she has endured from our capacity to absorb it." Yet he does so only to note that we, as readers, are often left with "the uneasy feeling of the literary *transforming* the real in a way that obscures even as it seeks to enlighten."[19] In this way the survivor's imagination becomes associated with literary devices that transform and obscure the reality of the Holocaust. Given this, the imagination no longer works with memory but against it, as a contending voice in testimonies. What then of "the power of the imagination" which enables the survivor-writer to make his or her Holocaust experience accessible to nonsurvivors? Without explanation, Langer transfers this power from the survivor-writer to nonsurvivors. Although those events survivors relate to as *memory* we relate to as *history*, Langer believes that our own imaginations enable us to cross the "vast imaginative space" that separates the province of historians from the memory of survivors.

2. *The Question of Accessibility*

A greater sense of why Langer is interested in moving past a supposed first stage of "Holocaust response" associated with history to a second stage associated with memory may be gained by considering a passage in which historian Christopher Browning expresses the limits of the historian's response. Browning writes:

> [T]he Holocaust is not an abstraction. It was a real event in which more than five million Jews were murdered, most in a manner so violent and on a scale so vast that historians and others trying to write about these events have experienced nothing in their personal lives that remotely compares. Historians of the Holocaust, in short, know nothing — in an experiential sense — about their subject.[20]

Historians lack precisely the knowledge — that is, the experience — which Langer most desires; what they do know, by comparison, are "mere facts."

Browning refers to this limit on knowledge as an "experiential shortcoming." Since Langer shares this shortcoming, since he too can never know the real event or the history in an experiential sense, he turns to the Holocaust-as-abstraction, writing of "the Holocaust universe" through which one may travel as a "Holocaust voyager."[21] This is the Holocaust not of history — that is, neither of historiography nor of past reality — but of "memory." Although it may be noted that our "experiential shortcoming" extends to memory, Langer believes that through a convergence of survivor memory and our own imaginations, Holocaust testimony can be translated into "a shareable experience."[22]

In thinking of the Holocaust as something of a shareable experience, Langer rejects the widely-held notion that the Holocaust is an *unimaginable* event for all of us who were not "there." This view has been popularized by Elie Wiesel, in such statements as:

> Those who never lived through this time of death will never be able to grasp its magnitude of horror. Only survivors of Auschwitz know what it meant to be in Auschwitz.[23]

It is also expressed by several survivors whose video testimonies Langer discusses in *Holocaust Testimonies*. In this book's preface he presents an excerpt from the video testimony of Magda F., in which she contends: "[T]o understand us, somebody has to go through with it. Because nobody, but nobody fully understands us. You can't. No [matter] how much sympathy you give me when I'm talking here." Moreover, she hopes that "nobody in the world comes to this again, [so] they *should* understand us."[24]

In response to Magda F.'s testimony, Langer comments:

> A statement like "to understand, you have to go through with it," however authentic its inspiration, underestimates the sympathetic power of the

imagination. Perhaps it is time to grant that power the role it deserves.[25]

Langer announces that we nonsurvivors have the "power" to understand survivors — even those who claim that we cannot understand them. In calling ours a "sympathetic power," he picks up on Magda F.'s claim that no matter how much sympathy you "give" her, you cannot get understanding in return; in reply, he seems to be saying that Magda F. fails to realize just *how much* sympathy our imaginations are prepared to give.

In fact, Langer argues that Magda F. underestimates not only our ability "to understand," but also our ability "to go through" the Holocaust, for we can do both by virtue of our imaginations. Thus he does not exactly refute the idea that "to understand, you have to go through with it;" rather, Langer imaginatively stretches the range of what "going through with it" might include. In Magda F.'s usage it is fairly clear that this "going through with it" refers to having lived through the Holocaust — in her case, deportation to Auschwitz, Plaszow, Leipzig, Theresienstadt — if not also living with having lived through it — in her case, surviving while her brother, three sisters, parents and husband were all killed.[26] What then constitutes the imaginative equivalent? To approach an answer, I will look at how Magda F.'s two interviewers utilize "the sympathetic power of the imagination."

Langer, who was one of the two interviewers, writes of a moment near the end of her testimony when Magda F. turned to the other interviewer and "in genuine amazement" exclaimed, "You're crying!" This "amazement" is offered as proof of her underestimation of the imagination's "sympathetic power," while the interviewer's tears take on a greater burden of meaning. "They were tears of pity, to be sure," Langer reasons; "but they may also have been tears of fear and despair, resulting from a direct encounter with the melancholy universe that had consumed most of Magda F.'s family."[27] The intriguing distinction between these two kinds of tears, and the comparative insignificance accorded to tears of pity, calls our attention to the shades of meaning that differentiate pity from sympathy.

The relevant distinction may be that whereas pity is a feeling felt for another, sympathy is a sharing of another's feelings. In pity, we feel a certain way towards another; in sympathy, another's feelings become our own. Treading a thin line between compassion and appropriation, sympathy raises questions of what another *wants* to share with the sympathizer and what the self-interest of the sympathizer might be. This brings us back to Magda F., who resists sharing full understanding with her sympathizers. How then does the imagination engage its sympathetic power to overcome her resistance? With reference to "tears of pity" and more meaningful "tears of fear and despair," Langer suggests that whereas pity enables us to feel *for* the survivor, the "sympathetic imagination" enables us to feel *like* the survivor. The tears of fear and despair do not appear to be felt for or with Magda F., but result from what Langer imagines might have been the interviewer's own "direct encounter" with the Holocaust (imagined as a "melancholy universe"). In the supposed directness of this encounter — and what makes this encounter *direct* is left unstated — we lose sight of Magda F. In Langer's description, her testimony becomes, or is displaced by, a directly encountered, directly "understood" Holocaust universe.

What then of Magda F.'s other interviewer, Langer himself? In his case we find nothing as unguarded as tears, but rather a more radical translation of the survivor's story into one's own Holocaust experience. For Langer, understanding appears to be gained not by identifying with individual survivors like Magda F., but by amassing and assessing their testimonies. Thus he remarks: "In spite of Magda F.'s misgivings, listening to hundreds of witnesses' stories is a form of 'coming to this again.'"[28] What are we to make of this? By couching his words in Magda F.'s awkward phrasing, Langer obscures the significance of his remarkable statement. For when Magda F. says, "I hope nobody in the world comes to this again," what does she mean by "com[ing] to this again" if not coming to experience another holocaust — not a simulated, audio-visual "Holocaust," but actual genocide?

My sense is that Langer borrows her wording in order to muffle his claim that watching hundreds of video testimonies is in some way comparable to ("a form of") living through the Holocaust. Whereas Christopher Browning observes that historians and others trying to write about the Holocaust have experienced nothing in their personal lives that remotely compares, Langer wants to believe that putting himself through the experience of "listening to hundreds of witnesses' stories" does compare. Based on his comparable "Holocaust experience," Langer claims the kind of understanding that Magda F. attributes only to survivors. What is more, based on the difference between his experience and that of survivors, he claims a *greater* degree of understanding; for whereas each survivor sees her or his experiences as "an isolated private ordeal," Langer finds himself in a position to "assess their experiences from a superior vantage point," noting a pattern of behavior during the Holocaust that individual survivors, drawing only on their own experiences, may not recognize or understand.[29]

In yet a third move, Langer maintains that this understanding is readily available to any of us who do not avoid confronting the Holocaust. In this vein he argues that

> the more we listen, the more evidence we have that the question of accessibility may be our own invented defense against the invitation to imagine what is perfectly explicit in the remembered experience before our eyes and ears.[30]

His argument fails to acknowledge or account for why the inaccessibility of the Holocaust has been asserted most forcefully by survivors. In addition, Langer begs the question: does oral testimony really make "perfectly explicit" how we should imagine survivors' remembered experiences? Is the remembered experience really there "before our eyes and ears?" If so, what need is there to *imagine* the experience if it is already right there before us?

Langer's phrasing recalls words he has quoted from the video testimony of Chaim E. Describing the experience of telling his story, this survivor of the Sobibor death camp explains, "I see the picture *in front* of me; you have to *imagine* something." Langer's description collapses this very distinction, as he writes that what we imagine is this picture — it is not only in front of the survivor, but "before our eyes." Chaim E. goes on to say,

> The one that listens has to imagine something. So it has a different picture for me than the one that imagines it. At least I think so, because sometimes I hear telling back a story that doesn't sound at all the same what I was telling, you see.[31]

Unlike Langer, Chaim E. describes steps involved in the story-telling process: the survivor tells a story; we listen to it; we imagine it; we retell the story. The discrepancy between Chaim E.'s story and the story his listeners tell back to him emphasizes the gap between the remembered experience and the experience as we imagine it. Although this gap is often referred to as an abyss, it is not a space of radical emptiness, but an expanse traversed by layers of mediation.

While I find fault with Langer's argument, my intent is not to answer the question of Holocaust accessibility by siding with Magda F. against Langer. My interest lies instead in exploring how Langer's project is shaped by an aggressive desire to make the survivors' experiential understanding one's own. How else might a nonsurvivor attempt to get "close" to the experience of the Holocaust? I am reminded of a comment made by Kenneth Jacobson during a panel discussion of Langer's work held at a 1996 Holocaust studies conference.[32] Jacobson, who interviewed hundreds of people persecuted by the Nazis and wrote a book which features the life stories of fifteen of these survivors, remarked that he was often asked what he had learned most from talking with survivors. His answer was unexpected: "What I learned most is that I was not there."

He explained that once he realized this — that the experience of persecution was not *his* experience, despite his identification (as a Jew) with the survivors — he was able to see more clearly and feel more vividly the experiences being recounted. Instead of projecting himself into these experiences, coloring them with his own needs and feelings, he strove to perceive the experiences from the point of view of the teller. In short, survivors' Holocaust-related experiences became more accessible only when Jacobson came to terms with the larger sense of their inaccessibility. Jacobson's remarks suggest a more complicated response to the question of accessibility, one which negotiates not only the boundary between the Holocaust and those of us who were not there, but the boundary between self and others.

3. Determining "The Way It Was"

Langer brings to his assessment of videotaped Holocaust testimonies two terms, "common memory" and "deep memory," which appear briefly in a passage by Auschwitz survivor Charlotte Delbo.[33] Delbo writes that deep memory "preserves sensations, physical imprints. It is the memory of the senses." These preserved sensations of being in Auschwitz are separated from Delbo's "present self," suppressed within what she calls "the skin of memory." As Delbo imagines it, this skin separates the traumatic sensations of deep memory from a larger, out-lying region of common memory. At times this skin ruptures and deep and common memory meet, as when Delbo dreams of being in Auschwitz. In these dreams she sees herself as she was in Auschwitz and relives the pain she suffered there; she writes: "the suffering I feel is so unbearable, so identical to the pain I endured there, that I feel it physically, I feel it throughout my whole body." When she awakens, Delbo remembers what it was like to relive these bodily sensations in her dream, and this remembering — unlike the sensations themselves — is not suppressed but part of her common memory. Whereas deep memory *preserves* and *suppresses* the past, common memory *remembers* and *narrates* it, puts it into words, tells it as a story, and in this way attempts to work through trauma. "When I talk to you about Auschwitz," Delbo writes, "it is not from deep memory my words issue. They come from ... intellectual memory, the memory connected with thinking."

Through dreams, sensations preserved in Delbo's deep memory come to be verbalized by way of common memory. As readers, we can begin to imagine what Delbo undergoes in her dreams, and through that what she underwent at Auschwitz; however, we cannot experience her "sensations" of being in Auschwitz ourselves. We cannot translate the words of common memory back into the sensations of deep memory. This being the case, Delbo's distinction between deep memory and common memory does not help Langer in his efforts to access the unmediated memory of the Holocaust. Instead, the distinction speaks to how much of Delbo's experiences in and memories of Auschwitz *cannot* be shared with her readers. It stresses that our understanding of the Holocaust will always be intellectual and common, rather than experiential and deep. Yet, perhaps because what Delbo locates in deep memory is so enticing to Langer, he takes up her terms and interprets them in such a way as to make "deep memory" accessible, in some way shareable.

After Delbo describing dreaming of Auschwitz, she writes,

> I cry out. The cry awakens me, and I emerge from the nightmare, exhausted. It takes days for everything to return to normal ... for the skin of memory to mend itself.

Langer writes:

> The cry that awakens her also awakens us to the astonishing realization that Delbo, unwittingly or not, has herself pierced the skin of memory through her description, using the dream as an 'excuse' to do so.

To come to this "astonishing realization," he dismisses the dream as a literary device, neglecting to consider how the dream mediates between deep memory and Delbo's written description. In her description Langer detects

> the voice of deep memory struggling to displace the milder tones of common memory as we read, in spite of her insistence that this is not possible.[34]

For Delbo this is not possible because deep memory does not speak or think as such. But in Langer's reformulation, deep memory, like common memory, is "connected with thinking," albeit with a difference: unlike common memory, it has access to the preserved sensations of Auschwitz. For this reason, deep memory knows "what common memory cannot know but tries nonetheless to express." In short, deep memory remembers and common memory imagines that it remembers.

By transforming Delbo's lyrical phrases into pseudo-analytic terms that may be applied to video testimonies, Langer enables himself to distinguish between the survivors' deep memories, which accurately recall "the way it was," and their common memories, which — through devices analogous to those in literary texts — distort "the way it was" by imposing traditional (pre-Holocaust) or present day (post-Holocaust) values on the description of the past.[35] Qualifying his claim that oral testimonies are uniquely characterized by an absence of literary mediation, Langer recognizes the presence of such mediation, but only to relegate it to common memory while safeguarding a preserve of pure, unmediated deep memory — so that, in effect, deep memory is memory proper, whereas common memory is tantamount to "the literary imagination." Consequently, it is Langer who ultimately determines "the way it was" as he separates out unauthentic "traditional memory" from authentic "Holocaust memory," in a quest for what he calls "the uniquely imprisoned persistence of a Holocaust event in a witness's memory."[36] In the search for this "Holocaust event," the survivor's "present self," and this self's memory of the event, become obstacles to the event itself.

Langer's treatment of a moment from the video testimony of Abraham P. is illustrative. When his family arrived at Auschwitz, Abraham P.'s parents were sent to the left, to death, while he and his three brothers were sent to the right. Abraham P. then instructed his younger brother to go with his parents, and in the interview he says, "Little did I know that I sent him to the crematorium. I am ... I feel like I killed him."[37] According to Langer, at this moment in Abraham P.'s testimony, "[a]s memory seeks to recapture the details of what happened *as* it happened, inappropriate guilt intrudes." This guilt is inappropriate because it supports "the idea of the individual as responsible agent for his actions" when "the law of systematic caprice that governed the selection process" deprived him of moral agency.[38] Thus, Langer suggests, Abraham P. could not have felt guilt then, and his expression of guilt now only serves to distort "the way it was."

The evidence in these testimonies,

Langer states,

> indicates that guilt, both as label and concept, is totally inadequate and indeed misleading as a description of the internal discomfort of surviving victims.[39]

Here his failure to mention the psychological term "survivor guilt" is remarkable. Shamai Davidson, a psychiatrist who worked with survivors and their children, describes "the well-known phenomenon of survivor guilt" as the first step in a working-through process by which survivors regained a sense of individual identity, restored "lost human values" and began "the postponed process of mourning."[40] This working-through process has no place in Langer's work; he appears interested in survivors' "Auschwitz selves" to the detriment of their present-day selves. In his drive to imagine the Holocaust "the way it was," Langer wishes survivors to remain the way they were, fully within trauma.

Geoffrey Hartman, director of the Yale Video Archive which provided Langer with the video testimonies he analyzes, writes that when giving testimony, "the survivor is more than a victim, more than the living carcass to which the camps systematically reduced every inmate."[41] Alas, this is precisely the problem for Langer, who observes that for the survivor, "[t]he fact of having survived ... *interferes* with a convincing portrayal of events."[42] By contrast, Hartman values video testimony for presenting "not ghostly voices from the past," but "a living person whose story, however painful, is part of that person." Rather than holding out the prospect of a "direct encounter" with the Holocaust, Hartman remarks that video testimony brings us closer to the people who bear witness to the Holocaust. He comments, "Videotaped testimony, which adds body to voice, so that we *see* the witness reliving his memories, is the closest we will ever get to the person." Such a sentiment is foreign to Langer's work. He desires to get close not to the person, but to "the Holocaust experience" that may be extracted from the person's story. As a result, Langer presents testimony in a processed form: excerpted and transcribed, moments taken from various video testimonies are removed from the context of life stories to appear as a series of illustrative anecdotes.

4. Langer Against the Holocaust Commentators

In a striking passage from *The Holocaust and the Literary Imagination*, Langer refers to a question posed by George Steiner in his essay on Sylvia Plath. Steiner concludes his discussion of her poetry with a reading of "Daddy," a poem which includes the lines: "An engine, an engine / Chuffing me off like a Jew. / A Jew to Dachau, Auschwitz, Belsen." After writing that with this poem "Sylvia Plath *became* a woman being transported to Auschwitz on the death trains," Steiner asks:

> Was there latent in Sylvia Plath's sensibility, as in that of many of us who remember only by fiat of imagination, a fearful envy, a dim resentment at not having been there, of having missed the rendezvous with hell?[43]

Langer's response to this question is intriguing. He writes:

> These are perhaps the most honest words spoken on the subject by Steiner, who in another moving essay calls himself a 'kind of survivor;' but they represent autobiography, not literary criticism.[44]

Strangely enough, Langer notes the honesty of Steiner's words only to dismiss them for being autobiographical and therefore falling outside the apparently unself-reflective or objective domain of literary criticism. Although Steiner attributes what he terms "a fearful envy" first to Plath and then to *many of us* who, "not having been there," can only imagine the Holocaust, Langer relegates this envy to Steiner alone. He does so by insinuating that Steiner is really talking only about himself — that in his honesty, he gives himself away — hence the charge of "autobiography," leveled at someone who tellingly calls himself a "kind of survivor." With this move, the very opposite of Steiner's sympathetic approach to Plath, Langer distances himself from the implications of Steiner's honest words. In any case, Langer seems to be saying, even if one were to feel "a fearful envy, a dim resentment" at not having gone through the Holocaust, recognizing and reflecting upon this feeling is not part of the literary critic's task.

The absence of such reflection in Langer's work requires the suppression of what motivates his on-going project to translate the Holocaust into a shareable experience. For instance, in his essay "The Literature of Auschwitz" he quotes a poem by Delbo which reads: "As for me / I'm still there / and I'm dying / back there / every day a bit more / I die again / the death of all those who died." He then claims: "Delbo's doom-laden line 'I die again / the death of all those who died'... stretches the circle of recruits to include its audience as well."[45] Here we find no analysis of *how* the line includes the poem's readers among those dying the death of Auschwitz victims; nor is there consideration of what such inclusion might mean or feel like; nor is there reflection on *why* one might want to join the so-called circle of recruits by reading oneself into the poem's first-person "I." What then identifies this claim as "literary criticism" rather than "autobiography?" My sense is that Langer presents as criticism a fantasy that will appeal to his readers if they too want to join the circle of those "still there" in Auschwitz, reducing the difference between actual Auschwitz victims and themselves.

Following his reading of the "doom-laden" line in Delbo's poem, Langer concludes that much as "[t]he experience of Auschwitz, like all of the Holocaust, cannot be left behind" by the survivors,

> [n]or do we return from our encounter with its literature unblemished. Instead, like [Auschwitz survivors] Delbo, Levi, and all the rest, we face the necessary burden of adjustment.... We pay a price for learning how to imagine what happened.[46]

While Langer is committed to reminding his readers "how much of our language is designed to console instead of confront the Holocaust,"[47] he never considers how, for those who *do* seek confrontation (like Langer himself), he offers another language of consolation. Certainly many readers would *like* to imagine that there is enough of a correspondence between the Holocaust and its literature, between their reading experience and a Charlotte Delbo or a Primo Levi's Holocaust experience, that they too might gain what Delbo has called "knowledge at the price of suffering."[48]

Langer describes this knowledge as if it were accessible to all readers or viewers who learn "how to imagine what happened" from Holocaust testimony, arguing against the notion that "an impassable chasm separates the seriously interested auditor and observer from the experiences of the former Holocaust victim."[49] Nevertheless, he tends to describe the work it takes to cross this chasm in terms that virtually only he has fulfilled. When Langer claims that "listening to hundreds of witnesses' stories is a form of 'coming to this again,'" we might wonder: is it enough to be a "seriously interested auditor and observer," or must one (like Langer) spend years watching hundreds of video testimonies? Similarly, when he asserts that "[a]nyone conversant with the thousands of separate testimonies of survivors knows what an *un*common catastrophe it was for each of them," we might ask: can one gain a sense of how diverse victims' experiences were by reading a handful of accounts, or is this knowledge only available to *anyone* (like Langer) conversant with thousands of accounts? Given Langer's prolonged encounter with hundreds and thousands of Holocaust testimonies, can anyone ever learn "how to imagine what happened" as he has?

Langer repeatedly distinguishes between those who are capable of imagining what happened and those who are not. "It seems that two forces are at work in Holocaust commentary," he writes in an exemplary passage:

> what we appear to have is, on the one hand, a historical consciousness determined to distort or at least alleviate the harshest truths of the Holocaust, and, on the other, a historical consciousness resolved to confront its implications wherever they may lead.[50]

The correspondence between these two forces and the two voices of memory, common and deep, is striking. Indeed, Langer conceives of Holocaust memory, testimony, and commentary alike, all in terms of two competing sides: a courageous *good* side, devoted to facing the worst of the horror "without flinching;" and a contemptible *bad* side, devoted to "sweetening" the horror, denying harsh truths, and falsifying the "the way it was."[51]

Throughout his writings, Langer pits one side against the other: deep memory against common memory, the true witness against the false witness. In his books he pits Elie Wiesel against Anne Frank, Jean Améry against Viktor Frankl, Pierre T. against Leo P., etc.[52] Finally, Langer sets himself apart from the mass of Holocaust commentators — "they are too numerous to list" — who inevitably betray a "need to make the Holocaust appear more harmless than it was" by heroicizing the victims and finding some redeeming meaning in atrocity.[53] Ultimately, only Langer seems free from this need; even Elie Wiesel occasionally falters, and "[i]f Wiesel himself is not immune to such temptations," Langer warns us, "how careful must we be in assessing the interpretations of other commentators, survivors and nonsurvivors."[54] Here being careful does not mean exercising caution in one's *own* interpretations; rather, it denotes a readiness, if not an eagerness, to expose *other* commentators' lapses and failings in the face of the Holocaust.

We can see this in Langer's description of how even Wiesel "occasionally is victimized by his own illusions." Based on his interpretation of a passage in one of Wiesel's essays, Langer faults this survivor-writer for believing that had the Hungarian Jews been forewarned about Auschwitz, they might have saved themselves. Langer comments:

> To expect starving and frightened men, women, and children, however forewarned, to flee through the barbed wire surrounding Birkenau (to say nothing of SS bullets), to run miles to distant mountains, to survive there without food, clothing, or shelter, not knowing Polish, subject to the hostility of a suspicious native population — is bizarre and absurd.[55]

However, this illusion belongs strictly to Langer, for Wiesel's point is decidedly *not* that the Jews from Transylvania could have orchestrated a mass escape upon arrival at Auschwitz-Birkenau, had they only known what awaited them there. Rather, he claims that had these Jews known about Auschwitz *before* being deported from Transylvania to the death camp, they could have fled from the poorly guarded ghetto into the surrounding mountains.

Given that Langer's misinterpretation is based on a confusing passage,[56] what is striking here is not the possibility of misreading Wiesel, but the unhesitating zeal with which Langer attributes to Wiesel a conviction that is so "bizarre and absurd." Rather than questioning the accuracy of his own interpretation, Langer focuses on drawing out the scenario of the Jews' escape from Auschwitz to full effect, as if he is scoring points with each detail: the barbed wire, the SS bullets, the distant mountains, the suspicious Poles. At such moments — and they are prevalent in Langer's work — the critic seems more interested in berating others for their failure to face the Holocaust's "harshest truths," than in confronting "its implications, wherever they may lead."

Missing in Langer's work is some recognition that these implications may eventually lead us back to *ourselves*, to an examination of our own work which raises the very questions and concerns he would dismiss as "autobiography." In contrast to Langer, Holocaust scholar Alan L. Berger writes,

> There are reasons both conscious and subconscious that impel the attempt to confront the kingdom of night. Autobiography is at least as important as intellectual concern. Or is it the other way around?[57]

In fact, autobiography is inseparable from intellectual concern and for this reason must be *of intellectual concern*. That is, we need to reflect upon our reasons for confronting the Holocaust, as they shape our intellectual endeavors in significant ways that elude conscious understanding. This means asking ourselves what it is we seek *in* and *from* the Holocaust, what "harshest truths" relevant to our own lives we hope to find there.

Ironically, the importance placed on confronting the Holocaust may be utilized to dismiss the relevance of confronting questions of this kind. In the introduction to a 1988 volume of essays titled *Writing and the Holocaust*, Berel Lang concedes that

> it may be objected that to call attention to the *writing* in writing about the Holocaust must have the effect of distancing readers and writers from the subject of the Holocaust itself. Surely, this objection goes, what ought to be central are the issues raised by the events of the Holocaust, not the manners of its representation.[58]

In the same way it may be objected that a concern with "autobiography" diverts us from the real work of confronting the Holocaust itself.

Berel Lang justifies the focus of *Writing and the Holocaust* by explaining that "without an understanding of the means by which a subject is 'written,' access to the subject itself is unavoidably impeded."[59] This conception of writing as an obstacle to be dealt with is taken to a further extreme by Langer in his essay which appears in Lang's volume. There Langer notes that when it comes to written texts, such as survivor memoirs, "we are dealing with represented rather than unmediated reality." He then explains:

> This led me to an inquiry into whether an unmediated text about the Holocaust experience is ever achievable. And this in turn roused my curiosity about the nature of the difference between written memoirs and oral testimony, particularly videotaped testimony.[60]

This in turn led Langer to write *Holocaust Testimonies*, the book which would incorporate his essay in *Writing and the Holocaust* as part of its second chapter.

This story of the genesis of Langer's book is also the story of his quest for the "unmediated text" — that paradoxical text which would enable him to encounter the Holocaust in some way other than "through the mediation of a *text*."[61] This text would not *represent* the reality of the Holocaust, but would somehow *be* this reality. In short, the imaginary "unmediated text" would enable Langer to *experience the Holocaust* itself, for himself. We need to think critically about the desire for such a text, as it too mediates our relation to the Holocaust — and complicates our relations to other "Holocaust commentators," both survivors and nonsurvivors. Indeed, as troubling aspects of Langer's work demonstrate, criticism of other commentators' failures to confront the Holocaust in what we deem to be meaningful-enough ways cannot be a substitute for critical self-reflection regarding our own methods and motivations.

Notes

* This essay has developed out of a paper delivered at the 26th Annual Scholars' Conference on the Holocaust and the Churches in March 1996. I wish to thank Richard Prystowsky for inviting me to be part of a panel on the work of Lawrence L. Langer at that conference; Jane Gallop for invaluable commentary and conversations; Stephen Brown, Eric Hayot, Ken Jacobson, Anna Kisby, Laura Micciche, and Laurinda Stryker for their helpful feedback at various stages of the writing process; and the United States Department of Education for the Jacob K. Javits Fellowship which enabled me to attend the Scholars' Conference.

1. Quoted in Lynn Karpen, "Distorting the Holocaust," in *The New York Times Book Review*, January 29, 1995, p. 2.

2. Diana Jean Schemo, "A Scholarly Call For a Realistic View of the Holocaust," in *The New York Times*, February 20, 1995, p. B1.

3. Langer, "What More Can Be Said About the Holocaust?," in idem, *Admitting the Holocaust: Collected Essays* (New York: Oxford University Press, 1995), p. 183. Terrence Des Pres, *The Survivor: An Anatomy of Life in the Death Camps* (New York: Oxford University Press, 1976).

4. While this phrase is not restricted to Langer's work, his excessive reference to "the Holocaust experience" is noteworthy. See, for example, *Admitting the Holocaust*, pp. ii, 4, 6, 25, 68, 163, 177, 181; and his *Holocaust Testimonies: The Ruins of Memory* (New Haven, CT: Yale University Press, 1991) pp. 59, 61, 201.

5. Langer, "No Cause for Celebration," in *Tikkun* Vol. 10, No. 3 (May/June 1995), p. 16.

6. Deborah Lipstadt, *Denying the Holocaust: The Growing Assault on Truth and Memory* (New York: Plume, 1993).

7. Joseph Brodsky quoted in Langer, "Introduction," in *Admitting the Holocaust*, p. 5.

8. Langer, "Memory's Time: Chronology and Duration in Holocaust Testimonies" (1993), in *Admitting the Holocaust*, p. 13.

9. These examples of the reification of Holocaust memory are drawn from Langer, *Holocaust Testimonies: The Ruins of Memory*; James E. Young, *The Texture of Memory: Holocaust Memorials and Meaning* (New Haven, CT: Yale University Press, 1993); and Edward T. Linenthal, *Preserving Memory: The Struggle to Create America's Holocaust Museum* (New York: Viking, 1995). In the closing panel of the Lessons and Legacies conference on the Holocaust held at Dartmouth College in October 1994, Michael Marrus noted that whereas ten years ago Holocaust scholars spoke about knowledge, information, and lessons, today the keyword is memory; and he noted that the two other speakers on the panel, James Young and Edward Linenthal, had written new books with this word featured prominently in their titles. Marrus' question — Why "memory?" — was not addressed in the discussion that followed his remarks. Of course, one might argue that the word "memory" is so much in use at present because of the importance Jews have placed on memory since biblical times. However, this explanation overlooks the degree to which this keyword, as routinely employed by Holocaust scholars, has little or no connection to the group memory of the Jewish people. Langer himself is not so much interested in "a Jewish view of the past," but in a more "universal" view of "our inhuman past." Langer, "What More Can Be Said About the Holocaust?," p. 184.

10. Langer, "Memory's Time," p. 13.

11. Langer, *Holocaust Testimonies*, p. 39.

12. Langer, "Fictional Facts and Factual Fictions: History in Holocaust Literature" (1990), in *Admitting the Holocaust*, p. 75.

13. Langer, *The Holocaust and the Literary Imagination* (New Haven: Yale University Press, 1975), p. 29.

14. *Ibid.*, pp. 29-30, 79.

15. *Ibid.*, p. 79.

16. *Ibid.*, see pp. 8, 12, 92.

17. Langer, *Holocaust Testimonies*, pp. xii-xiii.

18. *Ibid.*, pp. 57, 41.

19. *Ibid.*, p. 19.

20. Christopher R. Browning, "German Memory, Judicial Interrogation, and Historical Reconstruction: Writing Perpetrator History from Postwar Testimony," in Saul Friedlander, ed., *Probing the Limits of Representation: Nazism and the "Final Solution."* (Cambridge, MA: Harvard University Press, 1992), p. 25.

21. Langer, "Beyond Theodicy: Jewish Victims and the Holocaust" (1989), in *Admitting the Holocaust*, pp. 26, 28.

22. Langer, "The Literature of Auschwitz" (1994), in *Admitting the Holocaust*, p. 91.

23. Elie Wiesel, "Does the Holocaust Lie Beyond the Reach of Art?," in *The New York* Times, April 17, 1983: Section 2, pp. 1, 12.

24. Bracketed words in the original. Langer, *Holocaust Testimonies*, p. xiv.

25. *Ibid.*, p. xv.

26. *Ibid.*, p. 73.

27. *Ibid.*, pp. xiv-xv.

28. *Ibid.*, p. xiv.

29. *Ibid.*, pp. 143-44.

30. *Ibid.*, p. 82.

31. *Ibid.*, p. 62.

32. The 26th Annual Scholars' Conference on the Holocaust and the Churches, held in Minneapolis, MN, March 5, 1996. Kenneth Jacobson is the author of *Embattled Selves: An Investigation into the Nature of Identity Through Oral Histories of Holocaust Survivors* (New York, The Atlantic Monthly Press, 1994).

33. Charlotte Delbo, "Voices," trans. Rosette Lamont, in Langer, ed., *Art from the Ashes: A Holocaust Anthology* (New York: Oxford University Press, 1995), pp. 78-79.

34. Langer, *Holocaust Testimonies*, pp. 6-7.

35. *Ibid.*, p. 13. Langer differentiates "'the way it was' from how we think it was (and how [the survivor] thinks it *should* have been) from the vantage point of the present." *Holocaust Testimonies*, 65. In other words, "the way it was" means the way it *really* was — but exactly what "it" was or refers to remains abstract. "The Way It Was" appears as a section heading in Langer's *Art from the Ashes: A Holocaust Anthology*, where it is conspicuous amongst the other, more generic headings ("Fiction," "Drama," "Poetry," etc.). This eclectic section of nine "accounts of 'the way it was'" includes postwar testimonies by surviving victims and perpetrators, as well as one account by a historian, while journals and diaries written in the Warsaw, Lodz, and Kovno ghettos appear in a separate section titled "Journals and Diaries." Langer, "The Way It Was," in *Art from the Ashes*, p. 11.

36. Langer, "Memory's Time," pp. 14, 16.

37. Langer, *Holocaust Testimonies*, p. 185.

38. *Ibid.*, pp. 186-87.

39. *Ibid.*, p. 144.

40. Shamai Davidson, "Mourning and the Holocaust Survivor: Bereavement in Israel from War, Holocaust, and Terror," in Israel W. Charny, ed., *Holding on to Humanity - The Message of Survivors: The Shamai Davidson Papers* (New York: New York University Press, 1992), p. 187. This reference to Davidson is but one example from an immense body of work in Holocaust studies on "survivor guilt." For a critical overview of the concept of survivor guilt, see Paul Marcus and Alan Rosenberg, "A Philosophical Critique of the 'Survivor Syndrome' and Some Implications for Treatment," in Randolph L. Braham, ed., *The Psychological Perspectives of the Holocaust and of Its Aftermath* (New York: Columbia University Press, 1988), pp. 53-78, as well as other essays in this volume. While one can only wonder why in *Holocaust*

Testimonies Langer does not recognize the category of "survivor guilt," this omission is indicative of his book's overall unwillingness to engage with, much less acknowledge, work done on trauma and memory in psychoanalysis, psychology or Holocaust studies.

41. Geoffrey H. Hartman, "Preserving the Personal Story: The Role of Video Documentation," *Dimensions* 1.1 (Spring 1985), p. 14.

42. Langer, *Holocaust Testimonies*, p. 188.

43. George Steiner, "'Dying is an Art'," in idem, *Language and Silence: Essays 1958-1966* (London: Faber and Faber, 1967), p. 330. Misquoted as "by fiat or imagination" in *The Holocaust and the Literary Imagination*, p. 19.

44. Langer, *The Holocaust and the Literary Imagination*, pp. 19-20.

45. Langer, "The Literature of Auschwitz," p. 106.

46. *Ibid.*

47. Langer, "Introduction" (1994), in *Admitting the Holocaust*, p. 5.

48. Langer, "The Literature of Auschwitz," p. 107.

49. Langer, *Holocaust Testimonies*, p. xiv.

50. *Ibid.* For related descriptions of "the two planes on which the event we call the Holocaust takes place in human memory" and the "two masters" of "Holocaust writing," see *Admitting the Holocaust*, pp. 33, 169.

51. While Langer harshly criticizes commentators for heroicizing the victims, he does not shrink from applying a rhetoric of heroism to those who have the "courage" to confront the Holocaust "without flinching" — as if "flinching" when contemplating this event is a shameful sign of cowardice. For references to flinching, see *Admitting the Holocaust*, pp. 4, 8, 166, 183.

52. The Holocaust and the Literary Imagination, pp. 76-77; "The Literature of Auschwitz," p. 91; *Holocaust Testimonies*, p. 88. Langer's ventriloquism may be most pronounced in *Holocaust Testimonies* when he imagines one survivor (whose video testimony he has watched) responding to a statement made in the video testimony of another. Langer writes: "If Pierre T. could respond to this 'insight' [made by Leo P.], he would argue that the witness has allowed language to impede his vision of the past."

53. Langer, "What More Can Be Said About the Holocaust?," pp. 182, 184.

54. Langer, *Versions of Survival*, p. 145.

55. *Ibid.*, pp. 144-45.

56. This passage appears in "The Guilt We Share," in Wiesel, *Legends of Our Time* (New York: Holt, Rinehart and Winston, 1968), p. 166. A related, more clearly stated passage appears in "Sighet Again," in Wiesel, *From the Kingdom of Memory: Reminiscences* (New York: Schocken, 1990), p. 128.

57. Alan L. Berger, "How My Mind Has Changed" in Carol Rittner and John K. Roth, eds., *From the Unthinkable to the Unavoidable: American Christian and Jewish Scholars Encounter the Holocaust* (Westport, CT: Praeger, 1997), pp. 73-4.

58. Berel Lang, "Introduction," in idem, ed., *Writing and the Holocaust* (New York: Holmes & Meier, 1988), p. 3.

59. *Ibid.*, p. 4.

60. Langer, "Interpreting Survivor Testimony," in *Writing and the Holocaust*, p. 26. See also *Holocaust Testimonies*, p. 41.

61. Langer, *Holocaust Testimonies*, p. xii.

Chapter 16

"THEY FORCED ON ME ANOTHER WOMAN'S LIFE:" THE IMPACT OF THE HOLOCAUST ON HEBREW WOMEN'S FICTION

Nurit Govrin

1. Hebrew Women's Fiction

One of the most prominent and refreshing phenomena in Hebrew fiction of recent decades is the entry of many women authors into the circle of Hebrew fiction. The number of women authors is already close to half the total number of authors, almost proportionate to the number of women in the total population. But we are speaking more about quality than quantity, though the latter is important too. The prose written by women is perhaps the most refreshing thing in Hebrew fiction of the present. It offers a vibrant, living, bold and original voice.

The historical reason for the almost total absence of women authors in modern Hebrew fiction in the late 19th and early 20th centuries is mainly because in traditional Jewish society women did not receive a traditional Hebrew education as men did, and did not know Hebrew as a mother-tongue. And where there is no language there are no authors. This is in addition to other historical, social, cultural and traditional reasons beyond the scope of the present survey. Only with the inception of equal education for boys and girls in the Hebrew school of Eretz-Israel and the State of Israel did the ranks begin to fill, although slowly. The full results of this change have become apparent only in the recent decades.

In women's fiction of previous generations, the endeavor to write like male authors and to be equal to them is more prominent. Feminine characteristics, to the extent that they were present, appeared beside the more general ones, and were submerged by them, mutely, almost apologetically.

As stated, what matters is the fact that the fiction being written by women in the State of Israel today is fiction of the first order and meets all the artistic criteria. It seems that it is in this fiction that the important developments in innovative writing are occurring: in style, subjects and characters. Thus, for example, women have a large part in the postmodernist trends, in concentration on the characterization of women as central figures, in their relationships with their families, in the emphasis on the feminine point of view, in the introduction of a reflexive humor together with blatant and violent writing as a counterpoint to the earlier trends and an antithesis to the earlier image of women as gentle, polite and passive.

2. The Theme of the Holocaust in Women's Fiction

These developments in Hebrew fiction as a whole also include fiction dealing with the Holocaust. The number of women authors who wrote on the Holocaust during the '50s, '60s and '70s was very small. I'm speaking of fiction as such, as distinct from documentary literature or memoirs. With the rise in the number of women authors in general, the number of those for whom this theme has become an inseparable part of their work has grown, especially since the '80s.

Furthermore, the fixed image about fiction by women was that it steers away from the great themes, from the central national, social and cultural questions, and limits itself to the sphere of the individual and the family. One reason for this is that women do not take part in Israel's wars and remain in the rear, and therefore can describe this central theme as wives and mothers, but not as part of the major Israeli collective memory.

The increasing treatment in recent years of Holocaust themes by women authors is restoring women to the center of the literary and cultural stage, as authors of works which deal with one of the most sensitive intersections of Israeli identity. The impression is that the number of women writing on the Holocaust is as great, or at least equal, to the number of men writing on this theme. Holocaust fiction which has been written by women, like that which has been written by men, can be divided, firstly and simply according to the biography of the author, between those who lived through the Holocaust and those who were not "there." One of the prominent women authors in the first group, which is not large in number, is Yonat Sened, who writes all her books with her husband Alexander Sened (she was born in Poland in 1926, and came to Israel in 1948).

The second group, which is steadily growing in numbers and is at the focus of our present discussion, is comprised mainly of women of the second generation and now also the third - the children of parents both or one of whom are Holocaust survivors. The parents transmitted their ghastly experience to their sons and daughters in various ways; the children experienced it at home since their infancy, and were condemned to bear it with them throughout their lives.

There are also other groups, such as members of the first generation who did not physically experience the Holocaust, because they were born in Palestine or immigrated before the war, and experienced it from afar, such as Anda Amir (born in Western Galicia, 1902; immigrated in 1935), Lea Goldberg (born in Kovno, Lithuania, in 1911; immigrated in 1935). Then there are those who were born and raised in Eretz-Israel to parents born in the Diaspora who immigrated as pioneers before the war, but learned about the Holocaust through encounters with survivors, or through contacts with Europe after the war. Among these are Naomi Frenkel (born in Berlin in 1920; immigrated in 1933), and Yehudit Hendel (born in Warsaw in 1926; immigrated in 1926).

As is the case with fiction in general, it is not possible in the present state of research, and certainly not in the framework of this paper, to deal with the question of whether Holocaust fiction written by women has distinctive characteristics that differentiate it from that written by men. It may be assumed that the conclusions will be identical to the general trends: there is a group of women authors whose Holocaust fiction has conscious and distinctive feminine traits, and beside them other authors, whose writing on this theme has no distinctive feminine character.

Since this issue has not yet been the subject of comprehensive research, and it is possible that this research is one of the first references to it, I will attempt here to isolate the narrative fiction that has been written by women, and to foreground what is contained in it. At this preliminary stage I have chosen a sample of four authors, and some 30 works. My aim here will be to characterize the components, the central motifs and the distinguishing features of these works.

I will not make any comparisons here with Holocaust fiction written by men, and the emphasis will be on what there is in Holocaust fiction by the women authors selected. Such comparative study should be done in the next stage of the research, after the characteristics of each group have been described separately in a broader sample.

3. Common Themes, Differing Dosages

Psychological research is divided not only on the question of whether there are real differences between the second generation of Holocaust survivors and the second generation in an ordinary population, but also on the question of whether there are differences between women and men in the second generation of survivors. Those who think that the problems confronting survivors and their children are not different from those of an ordinary population claim that researchers who do not share their view set out from self-confirming presuppositions. Without taking a stand on this argument, the fundamental premise here, in the sphere of fiction in general and in the study of Holocaust fiction in particular, is that in fiction which by nature closes and opens circles, tremendous weight is given to the biography of the characters and to the past that feeds the future. Hence, since the authors describe the first and second generations in distinctive ways, the reader should relate to them accordingly. Since the authors see their heroes as a distinctive group, the researcher and the reader should follow suit.

On the question as to whether Holocaust fiction written by women has distinctive characteristics, all we can do at this early stage is to offer impressions. If to sum up these impressions, we could be so bold as to say that *the first impression* is that what is common is greater than what is divisive and unique. The visible trend is that the major themes, components and motifs that characterize the stories in the sample are *common* to Holocaust fiction in general by both women and men. Among the themes are: to remember/to forget; the question of identity; the attitude to the past and the confrontation with the present.

The second impression is that although there are no characteristics found exclusively in Holocaust fiction written by women that are not present in the Holocaust fiction written by men, there do exist differences in *dosage,* that is, in the degree of intensity of certain themes, characters and motifs which are more frequent in fiction by women than in fiction by men, and vice versa.

The reason for this, which is for the time being partly based on stereotypes, until proven otherwise, is, perhaps, that a girl spends more time at home, and therefore knows its secrets (closets, drawers, boxes, attic or basement, picture albums and photographs) better than a boy does. She is less independent and more vulnerable, as a woman, and is therefore more susceptible to "over-protection" by her parents. She perhaps feels herself more committed to her parents, and is therefore more connected to the "secrets of the family," which was more interested in discovering their past and the secret of their survival, and leads to her wondering about her own identity. She perhaps occupies herself, more than a boy does, with her capacity to marry and to bear children.

The multiplicity of women characters as central heroines, or as the object of wonder of the central hero, almost certainly stems from the fact that the woman author intimately knows the feelings of a woman heroine, and it is easier for her to enter her character.

The multiplicity of particular motifs in Holocaust fiction written by women also stems from the fact (which still awaits proper scientific proof) that the sensitivity of girls in certain spheres is greater than that of boys in these spheres. Examples are: the body (hair, cleanliness, washing, perfume); clothes (shoes, dresses); accessories (purse, bag); outer form (fingernails, manner of walking, general appearance); food (various kinds of food, especially bread and meat).

Quite a number of these common motifs shift from the peripheries to the center, and become a central theme in the stories. For example, hair ("Cutting," by Savyon Liebrecht); a picture-album ("Mother's Album," also by Liebrecht); suitcases ("Suitcases," by Nava Semel); meat ("Horses," by Ruth Almog); photographs (*The Name* by Michal Govrin).

Because of this greater sensitivity (if it is indeed based on research and not on conventions) the frequency of these motifs and others like them is very great in stories by women on the Holocaust, much greater than in stories by men, although they are present there as well.

These impressions, formed from examining 30 stories by 4 authors, still await a double confirmation by research: in the sphere of all Holocaust fiction written by women, and in the comparison of the latter with Holocaust fiction written by men.

If these impressions formed from the stories in the sample are indeed valid, it may be assumed that the similar results will be received from the examination of other works on the Holocaust that have been and will be written by women.

The four authors studied in this sample did not experience the Holocaust physically, but they do have a biographical connection with the subject. All of them were born (or almost born) in Eretz-Israel. The eldest and best-known is Ruth Almog, who was born in 1936 in Petach-Tikva, during the British Mandate period, to parents who were born in Germany and arrived in Palestine when Hitler came to power. The three others are Savyon Liebrecht (born in Berlin in 1948, and arrived in Israel the same year), Nava Semel (born in Tel Aviv in 1954), and Michal Govrin (born in Tel Aviv in 1950). They are in their forties, and one or both of their parents are Holocaust survivors.

These four are part of a growing group of women authors who write on the Holocaust in prose fiction, some of them from the "second generation," such as Leah Eini, Orly Castel-Bloom and Yehudit Katzir, to mention only three. They form part of a still larger group of women authors and poets of the second and third generations.

Out of the wealth of themes and problems that recur in Holocaust fiction in general and in the stories in the sample in particular, I have isolated six feminine motifs: "angles of vision;" "the name;" "the reincarnation" and "a private Holocaust." Under each subject I refer to only very few examples out of a great many.

4. The "Catch" in the Literary Confrontation

The subject of the Holocaust is by its nature an impossible one: to express in words the inexpressible; to remember in order to forget; to forget in order not to remember; to sever oneself and to be connected; to comprehend the incomprehensible; to live a normal life after the seven circles of Hell; and to raise a new family after the original family is no more.

It is fiction that expresses this paradoxical set of contrasts, by depicting the impossible situations of the survivors and their children. This complexity of contrasts characterizes all of the themes, descriptions and motifs of Holocaust fiction, with all of the "great" problems presented in it and all of the "little" details that demonstrate it.

Hence, while each theme, with all its details, will simultaneously express contrasts, there will be a simultaneous double framework of time and place, of "then" and "there" and of "now" and "here." Each object will have a dual and contrary set of roles; each word will have a double meaning, derived from the two realities it represents: the "other planet" of the horrors of the Holocaust and the world of sane reality after it. Each character will live a double life. In the first generation, the survivors will live their dreadful past that continues into the present and refuses to let them be. In the second generation, the children will inherit their parents' memories, and their lives will be a reincarnation of the lives of the dead whose lives they continue. Many among the "second generation" will experience a "private holocaust" of their own, which will contain a fraction of what their parents experienced, in order to feel, understand, come closer, and sense the feeling of being "victims."

5. Angles of Vision: From Restraint to Over-Boldness

Holocaust fiction is constantly occupied with developing modes of expression for a literary grappling with the subject which is beyond verbal expression, yet needs to be expressed. It involves an incessant quest for new and unconventional angles of vision, to the point where there is a danger of slippage into seeking novelty at any price and making such fiction not only vulgar but also "immoral." Most of the stories do preserve the maximal restraint and caution required by the subject, and from the horrors and the fate of the individual, readers learn indirectly about the millions.

In the present sample, the most frequent angle of vision in most of the stories is that of the first or second generation survivor, in the first person or by narrators linked to their consciousness. This is true for both children and adults. These angles of vision are generally restrained and implicit. The impression is that if there are differences here between men and women authors, in the stories by women there is a greater frequency of women characters whose angle of vision is that of the narrator. There is almost no story in the sample without a woman character as the central figure, or as a secondary figure, in her roles as a mother, a Holocaust survivor, or as a daughter of Holocaust survivors. Very frequently the story describes the relationship within the family, between the son or daughter and the mother, or the wife and the husband.

The story "Hayuta's Engagement Party," by Liebrecht, combines the angles of vision of the generations: to remember/to forget. The grandfather, at every family dinner, obsessively tells about the horrors he underwent, as a "final release," and when he is not allowed to do this he collapses. On the other hand, the generation of children and grandchildren do not want to hear him, because the dreadful memories "spoil" their celebration. The grandfather "kills the festival for me," his daughter says.

There are also some hard and unconventional angles of vision, as presented in several stories by Almog and Liebrecht, who have dared to touch upon the horrors directly. To my own taste, some of these descriptions arouse recoil and repulsion and are out of place. Are women authors more bold than men? For the time being, the comparative question remains open. What is clear that they are undoubtedly bold.

Liebrecht's story, "The Strawberry Girl," is narrated from the point of view of the wife of a Nazi officer, one of the commanders of the Auschwitz concentration camp. She knows nothing about what is going on. The horrors transpiring behind the fence of her home become revealed to her only gradually when she leaves the camp. It may be assumed that the story was born after a visit to the extermination camp, where as a part of the tour, visitors are shown the homes of the families of the Nazi officers who lived "normal lives" with their wives and children. The visitor finds it difficult to understand how this could be.

6. *The Name Makes the Person*

The child bears the name of the relative who died in the Holocaust, and must therefore live all his or her life in two realities -- the past and the present: to continue the life of the person she is named after and at the same time to live her own life in the present; and to fulfil her parents' expectations with regard to the dead person instead of developing her life according to her own inclinations and wants. The children's attempt to satisfy and compensate their parents, together with their efforts to evade this "task" or "mission," their guilt feelings together with their feelings of anger and frustration, all force them into the psychological "catch" they are trapped in.

This theme arose, perhaps for the first time, in Aharon Megged's story "Yad Vashem" (1955), in an inter-generational struggle about remembrance and forgetting. It was to take an entire generation until the bearers of the names themselves matured and attained the capacity to bear witness about the hard and complex psychic reality they had grown up in, as persons who were expected to be a constant reminder of the past, a living memorial.

"They Forced On Me Another Woman's Life," wrote Semel in "And What's an Outing," thus formulating most acutely one of the difficult problems of the second generation, as it appears in Holocaust fiction in general and in the stories of the sample in particular. The girl's father - whose sister committed suicide after her baby boy was "smashed against the railway-carriage door and his blood burst out," continues to seek for her and believes, "in his madness" that "one day she'll appear," and therefore "named his daughter after her." Each time he "moved around her in the rooms, or called her to come home from the yard, he would writhe, because this name stretched out to the girdle of the heavens." The girl rebels against the life of the other woman that has been forced on her and tries to bring him back to reality: "Your sister's dead;" " She's dead and I'm alive," and in the end, because of the dead sister, "she has no children and no man," because her father "has managed to keep her in a frozen pattern of childhood."

The Name is the central hero of Govrin's novel, as its title indicates. Its meaning also includes that of "*HaShem,*" the Name as referring to God, the quest for God, and of "*tikkun*" (spiritual repair) and the meaning of life. The father names his daughter Malinka after his first wife, the pianist, and demands that she be like her namesake and relive her biography: "Only you can bring Malinka back to us." You're our second Malinka, you bring Mala back to us! You!" And the girl wonders: "How will I have a life, thanks to her death, if I have the same name as hers?!" Her other names express her numerous attempts to extricate herself and to adapt to other ways of life to which she unsuccessfully attempts to escape.

7. Reincarnation

The shared name forces its bearer to live the life of the person whose soul has been reincarnated in his or her body, and determines the course of her life. The character is the *reincarnation* of the dead soul. This is how her parents and their friends see it, and this is also how the character sees herself, after wondering about her own actions which seem inexplicable. On discovering the "reincarnation" the character attempts to escape this fate, generally without success.

One point of view may be that of the second generation, which sees itself as a "reincarnation," as in Semel's story "Hunger," where the daughter continues her mother's life and hoards food as she did, and as in most of Semel's other stories.

Or it may be that of the first generation, those who see their sons or daughters as "reincarnations" of dead family members (as in Liebrecht's

"Pigeons"). It may also be a mixed point of view of all those involved, (Govrin's *The Name*).

Life as reincarnation is generally expressed in the stories of the sample by means of several recurrent motifs, such as music, outward form, or a journey. The characterization of it by means of music is the most common, to the point that the motif has become a stereotype. Music represents the harmonious Jewish life "there," and the spiritual wealth and qualities of the dead character, as in Almog's "A Good Corner"and "A Little Coat;" Liebrecht's "Sonia Muskat;" and Semel's "But the Music Doesn't Cover," which is written from the point of view of a Christian German woman who converted and married a Jew.

The "reincarnation" theme is most often expressed in the musical talent of the character from the past and the parents' desire to coerce the character in the present to play her music.

In Almog's "A Good Corner," the son repeats the course of his father's and mother's lives. Like his mother in the past, he leaves his family, travels afar, plays a harmonica on a street corner and begs alms. Like his father, he earns his livelihood by watching the dead, and is attracted to skin.

In contrast, Shaul-Paul, the hero of Almog's "A Little Coat," whose parents and their friends from the past do all they can to finance his music studies as a compensation for their lost lives, does actually learn music, but manages to escape the fate of the "reincarnation" by not earning his living from music as a performer but as a researcher.

The reincarnated character recalls the character from the past *in outward form*, to the point that both the close and the distant environment mistake one for the other.

In Liebrecht's "Pigeons," the son David resembles the beloved brother: "When his hair grew and his facial features became clear she could see him as her beloved brother David. As she matured, he copied the bodily gestures and the tones of voice and the inquisitive look of her dead brother. At times the resemblance was so great that she called him aloud, 'David'."

The "reincarnated" character feels an inexplicable and uncontrollable urge to travel to the place where one or both of his parents were born, not only to become acquainted with his roots and to understand himself and his identity better, but mainly in order to re-experience the life of the dead person and to ground it anew as personal experience. There are stories in which the journey is one among several motifs (Semel's "A Hat of Glass," Govrin's *The Name*), and others in which it is the central motif (Almog's *Don't Hurry the Journey,* Semel's "Journey to Two Berlins," and Liebrecht's "A Celebration of the Two Worlds").

8. *"A Private Holocaust"*

In Holocaust fiction in general, and in most of the stories of the sample in particular, there recurs the situation of "a private holocaust" - a "phantom pain" (as defined by Presco, 1984) undergone by a second-generation hero, or by which he explains difficult experiences he has gone through. Second generation heroes in the stories have copied, reconstructed and transferred to themselves the traumas of their parents, and have adapted them to their own lives. The characters suffer the pain of situations they have never known, as a secondary experience passed on to them by their heritage. The fiction describes the "private holocaust" of second generation characters mainly as a private family experience, but at times also as part of the collective historical memory of the entire Jewish people. The heroine of Almog's novel *Don't Hurry the Journey* has a nightmare in her journey to the past, when she sleeps in the house where she was born. In this dream, following the format of the biblical story of "the concubine on the hill" (*Judges* 19-20), a mob surrounds the house to kill her.

In Semel's story "A Private Holocaust," the rape of the heroine in London is experienced as a recurrence of the horrors undergone by her parents, and despite all the recoil from rape, there is the feeling that the daughter longs for it, in order to come closer to her mother in this way and to understand more what she went through. The scene of the rape is described using a vocabulary specific to the Holocaust: *"Raus! Raus!* The *Akzion* has begun. Go straight to the *Platz!"*

In the stories of the sample, descriptions of scenes of "private holocaust" often include a disease, generally shortness of breath and coughing. These appear in extreme states of pressure and excitement, in which the character is constrained to confront the parents, past. Thus Shaul, in Almog's "A Little Coat," Amnon in "Pigeon," the heroine of Liebrecht's "A Wife" and the heroine of Govrin's *The Name.*

The Holocaust does not release its victims and their families, and accompanies them wherever they go, in Israel or abroad. It recurs by means of references to churches, the pealing of bells, furnaces, smoke, trains, meat, whips and other Holocaust "accessories" present in the Israeli reality.

9. Family Secrets

The survivors speak very little about their experience, and the children grow up with a dim knowledge about "family secret." They sense that there exists a terrible secret in their past, which weighs heavily on their parents and their friends from "there." The child obsessively tries to uncover these secrets, especially the secret of their survival. He senses that he has a strong and hidden connection with these secrets and that they influence him and his relations with his parents and their friends. He lives with the feeling that if he discovers the secrets he'll understand them and (especially) himself better, and will be able to change his parents' lives and his own. He blames these secrets for his failures in relations with others and in his difficulties in establishing a family.

The stories deal mainly with families where parents are silent: "We never spoke about it with Arlette!;" "It's better that they shouldn't know. And anyway, they don't care. They're too busy with other things" (Govrin, "La Promenade"). Even when the children dare to ask, they are told "This isn't a story for children" (Almog, "Dwarfs on the Pajamas").

The recurring motifs in these stories are *family secret objects,* which the child repeatedly goes through: bags, suitcases, purses, closets, drawers, boxes, photographs and albums. He spends a lot of time in attics or basements. These objects, appearing in the present reality of Israel, recall the presence of the past, and hint at identification with their owners.

There are stories where these objects become the story's central theme, as in Semel's "A Woman from Fayoum" and "Suitcases," or Liebrecht's "Mother's Album," or the women's purses in Govrin's "La Promenade," which the heroines never part from for a moment. In Govrin's *The Name,* the pictures and photographs are one of the novel's major motifs.

The *professions* of the second generation are oriented towards discovering the secrets of the past. The following are all women: an archaeologist (in Almog's *Don't Hurry the Journey*); a doctor (in Semel's "Hunger"); a psychiatrist (in Liebrecht's "Mother's Album"); a field-security officer (in Liebrecht's "A Celebration of the Two Worlds"); a photographer (in Govrin's *The Name*). The latter profession expresses the tension between recording the past and seizing the moment in the present. Even the English word "shoot," in the photographic context, connects with shooting in the camps.

The parents' connection with *friends from "there"* stems from the terrible experiences they shared, the secret of their survival and the feeling that whoever was not "there" will never understand. Their children who try to decipher their secrets also have to decipher their relationships with their friends.

Govrin's story "La Promenade" is entirely based on connections from the past, which have linked the group of friends over the years. The friend from the past sometimes supports the parents and their children for reasons known to the parents alone, which they don't speak about: "There's no money? There's Ishtvan." (Almog's "Dwarfs on the Pajamas").

The most developed example is Stein in Govrin's *The Name,* who loved the narrator's father's first wife, and sees the latter's daughter as her "reincarnation" as well as the daughter who might have been his. He "adopts" her, and tries to direct and even control her life.

The family that was: The child senses that his family had a past which he has no part in, though it influences his life, and he tries to discover it. *There was a family,* which is his family too, but it is also his rival, and he tries to grapple with something he has no idea about. He ferrets incessantly through the hiding-places in the home and repeatedly looks at photographs from the old days. The boy in Almog's "A Gentile Woman" hunts through "an old file of papers" on top of a wardrobe and finds a picture of a boy whom he can't connect with his life; "Who is this boy?" the wife asks her husband in Semel's "A Woman from Fayoum."

The child senses that there is a terrible secret in his parents' past, and in the fact that they managed to survive. Faced with the silence of the parents and their friends, the secret grows to threatening proportions. The greater the silence, the stronger grows his determination to discover the secret of their survival, as well as his fear of what he might discover.

It is not surprising to find the use of the "opening up Pandora's box" motif in this context (Semel's "A Woman from Fayoum"), or of the modern image of "the black pit" (Govrin's *The Name*). "My mother never told me." And when she came back to us she didn't speak again: muses the hero of Semel's "A Woman from Fayoum"). In a "journey" that the hero makes to his parents' past there is no escape from the thought: "and what price did Anna Wagner pay for your little gesture" (Semel's "Voyage to Two Berlins"). The drive to discover the "secrets" leads to the absurd act of seeking the company of the murderers or people close to them in order to understand (*ibid.*)

One "answer" to these quests to discover the secrets appears in Almog's "A Little Coat," which describes one of the only heroes in the stories of the sample who manages to rehabilitate his life. His success stems from his ability to do what he was taught by Farkasz, the Hungarian barber and Holocaust survivor, who repeatedly claims that one must give up trying to "understand," because "it's impossible to understand everything, and whoever thinks he can understand everything is a sinner."

10. Feminine Motifs

The three examples that follow all have to do with the body and associated accessories: hair, shoes, food (bread and meat).

Detailed descriptions of the body, and especially of the hair and the shoes, are perhaps the most distinctive characteristics of Holocaust fiction written by women. Other accessories and contrasts appear quite frequently: beautiful freshly-pressed clothes and rags; well-manicured as against chewed nails; perfume and bad smells; exaggerated cleanliness and washing opposed to neglect and dirt. The excessive care of these things is an expression of efforts to sever oneself from the horror of the past.

The *hair* is probably the part of the body that is dealt with most frequently. There is almost no description of a character, man or woman, without it. The function of the hair as a metonymy for the Holocaust and its horrors is not mentioned directly; the reader is left to sense it himself.

Hair recurs in several constant forms. *Fair hair* attests to its owner's capacity to survive, while dark hair hints at the difficulty of this. An example is the fair hair of "The Boy" in Almog's story by this title, and his memory of his mother is also a memory of her hair touching his.

The heroine who has survived the Holocaust keeps looking among the children for her lost child, with a pomegranate blossom stuck in her "yellow hair: (Almog's "Enana"). Women with dark hair who survived paid the full "hair-raising" price. Thus Aphrodite, whose "face is white and long, surrounded by a halo of black hair" (Almog's "A Little Coat").

Conflict between the second generation of the murderers and their victims occurs by means of descriptions of hair. It operates as a hint of what happened between them in the past. The hair-do of a Nazi girl is metonymic for evil, cruelty and inhumanity. The Nazi girl in Liebrecht's "A Celebration of the Two Worlds," who travels by train to celebrate the release of one of the Nazis, has "fair hair cut in a straight line which looks like hair made of plastic threads, with the parting, straight as a ruler, precisely marking the middle of the crown." The Jewish girl, in contrast, has "terribly disheveled hair."

In these stories there are contrasts of disheveled hair and neat hair, short hair and long hair, which attest to the characters' confrontations with their past.

In Liebrecht's "Cutting," hair is the hero of the story. The grandmother, a Holocaust survivor regresses to her life "there" as a consequence of a note she received from the nursery school teacher about lice in her granddaughter's hair. In an emotional outburst which she can't control she crops the child's beautiful hair in order to protect and rescue her, as they had done "there." She learns a harsh condemnation from her son-in-law, recoil from her granddaughter, and the helplessness of her daughter who is torn between her mother and her family.

Shoes of various kinds are a constant item. Their appearance, like that of the hair, arouses hard associations with the past and also relates to the attempt to shape a different reality in the present. They appear in characterizations of both men and women.

Boots, together with a *whip*, are the most distinctive accessories representing the Nazis (Semel's "A Private Holocaust," and Almog's "A Gentile Woman"). The heroine of Liebrecht's "A Wife," who cannot sever herself from her obligation to the past and thus makes herself miserable in the present, supports herself and her husband as a saleswoman in a shoe store.

Pointed, *elegant* shoes with stiletto heels are the contrast to the worn but, functional shoes from the past. The orthopedic shoes worn by the heroine of Govrin's "La Promenade" attest to her scarred past, while the other survivors in the group take excessive care of their elegant shoes as a compensation for the past.

Food: The feeling of revulsion is likened to "a pantry full of food in an abandoned apartment" (Almog, *Don't Hurry the Journey*). Gluttony appears as a compensation for the hunger experienced "there" (Govrin, "La Promenade"); tables laden with quantities of good food recall the terrible lack of food "there" (Liebrecht's "Rochele's Perfect Bridegroom"); some characters equip themselves with food wherever they go, "a bag with four loaves of bread in it" (*ibid.*).

In Semel's "Hunger," food moves from the periphery into the center and becomes the story's hero. The story contains most of the components of the attitude to food of both the first and the second generation: the mother hoards food - "they'll never break in on me again without my being prepared," and her daughter continues the process, and hoards food too. The children are ordered to have a special respect for bread: "You must never dishonor it, because it is vengeful. To this day I don't dare to throw the old bread away." The children have to finish the food and the drink served to them and not to leave anything. They have to eat even if they're not hungry, and they therefore develop a resistance to food: "I used to vomit when I was a child."

Appendix 1
Women Authors and their Holocaust Stories

Ruth Almog was born in Petach-Tikva in 1936. Her parents, both doctors, migrated from Germany in 1933 and settled in Petach-Tikva.

"A Gentile Woman," Margerita's Night Graces. Stories. Tarmil Publishers, 1969, pp. 53-60. Story dated: "June 1969."

Don't Hurry the Journey, Am-Oved Publishers, 1971.

"The Boy" *After Tu B'Shvat: Six Stories,* Tarmil Publishers, 1979, pp. 94-156. Reprinted *Artistic Mending.* Keter Publishers, 1993, 49-84.

"Henia Isn't Blue Any More," *Women,* Keter Publishers, 1988, pp.61-67.

"Dwarfs on the Pajamas;" "Enana;" "Horses;" "A Good Corner;" "A Little Coat," *Artistic Mending,* Keter Publishers, 1993.

Michal Govrin was born in Tel Aviv in 1950.

"La Promenade. A Triptych," *Hold on to the Sun: Stories and Tales.* Siman Kriah and Hakibbutz Hameuchad Publishers, 1984.

The Name. Siman Kriah and Hakibbutz Hameuchad Publishers, 1995.

Savyon Liebrecht was born in Germany in 1948, and was brought to Israel in the same year.

"Pigeons;" "A Man's Wife;" "Hayuta's Engagement Party," *Apples from the Desert,* 1986

"Cutting;" "Sonia Muskat;" *Horses on the Gehah Road,* 1988.

"Mother's Album;" "A Celebration of the Two Worlds;" "The Strawberry Girl;" "Morning in the Park, With the Nannies;" "Grace;" *It is Chinese I'm Speaking to You,* 1992.

"Rochele's Perfect Bridegroom," *On Love Stories and Other Endings,* 1995.

Nava Semel was born in Tel Aviv, in 1954.

A Hat of Glass: A Collection of Stories of the Second General, Sifriat Poalim Publishers, 1985. Dedication: "To my mother who survived, to my father who accompanied."

Remarks:

1. The number of authors: four. All were born in Israel (Savyon Liebrecht was born in Germany but arrived in Israel at the age of one.)

2. Ruth Almog: a daughter of the most veteran generation, born during the Mandate period; the other three were born after the establishment of the State and are in their '40s.

3. Age in 1996: Ruth Almog (1936: 60); Savyon Liebrecht (1948: 48); Michal Govrin (1950: 46); Nava Semel (1954: 42).

4. 31 works were examined: 28 stories and 3 novels (2 by Ruth Almog and 1 by Michal Govrin).

5. Division of the stories: 7 by Ruth Almog; 11 by Savyon Liebrecht; 10 by Nava Semel; 1 by Michal Govrin.

6. Only the stories and books on the Holocaust by these authors have been mentioned here.

Appendix 2:
The Stories in Chronological Order

Ruth Almog

"A Gentile Woman," *Margerita's Night Graces: Stories.* Tarmil Publishers, 1969, pp. 53-60. Story dated: "June 1969."

Don't Hurry the Journey. Am-Oved Publishers, 1971.

"The Boy," *After Tu B'Shvat: Six Stories,* Tarmil Publishers, 1979, pp. 94-156.

Michal Govrin

"La Promenade. A Triptych," *Hold on to the Sun; Stories and Tales.* Siman Kriah and Hakibbutz Hameuchad Publishers, 1984.

Nava Semel

"A Hat of Glass;" "A Private Holocaust;" "A Woman from Fayoum;" "Fonda - One Journey;" "Suitcases;" "So What is an Outing;" "Hunger;" "A Voyage to Two Berlins;" "But the Music Doesn't Cover;" "Epilogue;" *A Hat of Glass: A Collection of Stories of the Second Generation,* Sifriat Poalim Publishers, 1985.

Ruth Almog

"Henia Isn't Blue Any More," *Women,* Keter Publishers, 1988, pp. 61-67.

Savyon Liebrecht

"Pigeons;" "A Wife;" "Hayuta's Engagement Party;" *Apples from the Desert,* 1986.

"Cutting;" "Sonia Muska;" *Horses on the Gehah Road,* 1988.

"Mother's Album;" "A Celebration of the Two Worlds;" "The Strawberry Girl;" "Morning in the Park, With the Nannies;" "Grace;" *Is it Chinese I'm Speaking to You,* 1992.

Ruth Almog

"Dwarfs on the Pajamas;" "Enana;" "A Good Corner;" "A Little Coat;" *Artistic Mending,* Keter Publishers, 1993.

Michal Govrin

The Name. Siman Kriah and Hakibbutz Hameuchad Publishers, 1995.

Savyon Liebrecht

"Rochele's Perfect Bridegroom," *On Love Stories and Other Endings,* 1995.

Appendix 3:
Studies in Psychology: On the First Generation of Holocaust Survivors and their Children

Note: All the studies listed here are final theses for the Master of Arts degree at Tel Aviv University.

1. Eizenberg, Krina.
   The Social World of the Second Generation of Holocaust Survivors: Values and Beliefs about Interpersonal Relations.
   Under the supervision of: Arie Nadler and Sophie Kav-Venaki. TAU, April 1982

2. Haver, Dali.
   Life-Span consistency and Efficiency of Personal Coping Style in Holocaust Survivors.
   Under the supervision of: Jacob Lomranz and Dov Shmotkin. TAU, September 1993.

3. Tal, Ido.
   Separation-Individuation and Capacity for Intimacy in Children of Holocaust Survivors.
   Under the supervision of: Aviva Mazor and Yolanda Gampel. TAU, November 1992.

4. Zechovoy, Amnon
   Time Orientation and Interpersonal Relations among Holocaust Survivors, First and Second Generations.
   Under the supervision of: Jacob Lomranz and Dov Shmotkin. TAU, January, 1986.

SECTION THREE:

CONFRONTING THE PRESENT AND FUTURE

Chapter 17

RIGHT-WING EXTREMISM AND THE CHRISTIAN DEMOCRATS: THE ADENAUER AND KOHL ERAS

David A. Meier

Introduction

Ralf Dahrendorf's perception of Germany *before* Hitler offers an intriguing beginning for discussing German political problems *after* Hitler. Postwar right-wing extremism and radicalism, a by-product of German nationalism, links Hitler's National Socialism with right-wing extremist solutions to contemporary German problems. Two Christian Democratic chancellors, Konrad Adenauer and Helmut Kohl, dismissed right-wing extremists as fundamentally anti-German and acted to minimize radical right activities and growth. Under Helmut Kohl, however, the right-wing extremists scored unprecedented electoral successes and right-wing radicals (Skinheads and Neo-Nazis) were involved in violent acts numbering in the thousands. What had changed in Kohl's Germany? By comparing elements of right-wing extremism and radicalism during the Adenauer and Kohl eras, an answer may emerge.[1]

Serious observations are already on the table. Diethelm Prowe observed three features common to both eras, namely, "democratization, economic reconstruction, and coping with a past of terror." In practice, democratization gave way to a focus on more authoritarian leaders as an outlet for revenge against a hated regime and economic reconstruction became an outlet for denying difficult historical issues. Postwar political reconstruction, consequently, took place gradually and in an atmosphere of increasing prosperity and outside pressure. After unification, the Kohl government provided economic assistance in much the same fashion as the United States did through the Marshall Plan. Overall, this West German benevolent occupation could provide a path to further democratization and integration on all levels. On the other hand, Horst Moeller, director of Munich's *Institut fuer Zeitgeschichte*, rejected most comparisons between postwar West Germany and unified Germany as ahistorical when placed outside the context of European history. For example, postwar Germans rejected a revived German nationalism -- a former component of discredited National Socialism. Unified Germany, however, confronts revived European nationalism celebrating a more traditional national pride and its victory over Communism. Nevertheless, Germany's "decoupling of historic developments today is as impossible today as they were in 1945 and 1989."[2]

These authors offer, by unfolding the layers of right-wing extremism and radicalism, a merging of historical, political, and socio-psychological analyses. Post-war right-wing extremism blended various socio-political orientations, namely, authoritarian, conservative-nationalist, folkish socialistic, and monarchical orientations, into fundamentally authoritarian anti-democratic programs and party structures with clear links to Nazism (except for German monarchists). During the Adenauer era, right-wing extremism revealed a more regional character. Supported by a protestant middle class, northern groups favored an authoritarian-conservative nationalism. Within southern groups, lower middle class elements rejected traditional monarchical inclinations in favor of a more nationalistic orientation. During the Kohl era, right-wing extremism lost its more regional influences. While similar to the Adenauer era in its nationalistic anti-democratic folk-socialistic orientation, Kohl era right-wing extremism and radicalism, whose origins lay in former West Germany, assumed a more violent form and with clear parallels to Hitler's National Socialism. This brand of radical right-wing emotional authoritarian nationalism generated increased national appeal as mainstream parties appeared out-of-touch with the electorate, with the rising tide of anti-foreigner sentiment and unemployment, slow economic growth, and the heightened sense of nationalism following unification. While the Adenauer government kept extremism under control, the Kohl government found it necessary to take extraordinary steps to bring right-wing fringe elements and violence under control.[3]

Political Groups in Western Germany, 1945-1949

Overall, Allied support for moderate political parties in the post-war era laid a stable foundation upon which a sovereign West German state would subsequently be built. All three Western Allies actively worked to eliminate reactionary groups, including, the Bavarian Homeland and Royalist Party in the American zone, Heinrich Leuchtgen's National Democratic Party in the American and French zones, and the German Conservative Party-German Right Party in the British zone. Generally, undesirable political groups were either prohibited, purged of politically unacceptable personalities, forced out of existence, or fused with existing parties. Although the Allied presence cast a strong shadow over the developing party system, Allied policies on political parties forced Germans to rethink long-held notions of political parties and move towards the notion of *catch-all parties*, which had not been part of a German political consciousness before 1945. Popular acceptance of these measures is supported by various postwar opinion polls.[4]

Nevertheless, right-wing political groups/parties dotted the political landscape in postwar western Germany. While most Germans were preoccupied with survival, small secretive Nazi groups were active through 1947. Collectively, these groups represented small loosely organized groups with little financial support, no outside assistance, and with no future. Right-wing political movements, on the other hand, emerged in the British zone -- with the DKP-DRP eventually the leading the pack. Rooted in Weimar's German National People's Party (*Deutschnationalen Volkspartei* or DNVP), the German Conservative Party (*Deutsche Konservative Partei* or DKP) registered its first successes in Schleswig-Holstein, Hamburg, the Rhineland, and Westfalen (modern Nordrhein-Westfalen). Similarly, the German Construction Party (*Deutsche Aufbau-Partei* or DAP) attracted former supporters of the German People's Freedom Party (*Deutschvoelkischen Freiheitspartei* or DVFP), which broke with the DNVP in 1922 and subsequently absorbed Hitler's National Socialists. Guided largely by Adolf von Thadden in 1946, the DKP and the Party of the German Right (*Deutsche Rechtspartei* or DRP) merged (DKP-DRP) to create a "uniform large right-wing party, in which all conservatively, Christian and nationalistically inclined Germans may find their home." The DKP-DRP scored its greatest success in local elections in Niedersachsen in 1948 -- taking almost 70% of the vote in Wolfsburg. Preparing for the August 1949 national elections, the DKP-DRP pulled onto its election list Dr. Fritz Dorls, organizer and head of the Community of Independent Germans (*Gemeinschaft unabhaengiger Deutscher* or GuD) and former Nazi, and Otto Ernst Remer, the former commander of the Berlin Watch Battalion. Although these efforts were intended to draw the attention of former members of the NSDAP, the effort, however, failed as both Dorls and Remer rejected the overwhelmingly nationalistic and conservative path pursued by the DKP-DRP. In national elections in August 1949, the DKP-DRP took 8.3% within Niedersachsen but only 1.8% of the national vote. As a consequence, three new parties were created, namely, the *Deutsche Partei* (DP) espousing a conservative-authoritarianism within the German-national tradition, the *Niedersaechsiche Landespartei* (NLP) promoting a radical socially oriented program, and the Socialist Reich Party (*Sozialistische Reichspartei* or SRP).[5]

The Adenauer Era, 1949-1963

When the German Federal Republic was established in 1949, Konrad Adenauer (1876-1967), heading the Christian Democratic Union (CDU), won the chancellorship and remained chancellor until 1963. During his chancellorship, Adenauer produced a political miracle: the establishment of a stable democratic political system. In his first speech to the new government on September 20, 1949, Adenauer fundamentally rejected left and right extremist politics. Adenauer feared German political passivity, one consequence of National Socialism, had left Germans susceptible to calls from both political extremes. Adenauer's domestic policies, consequently, were directed at reviving German confidence in their capacity for democratic self-government. Similarly, the CDU (and Bavaria's Christian Socialists) criticized National Socialism as a materialistic anti-Christian movement emanating from a failed Marxism. As such, Christian Democrats and Christian Socialists viewed National Socialism as the antithesis of traditional German society and values. Shortly before leaving office in July 1963, Adenauer confidently declared German democracy alive and well: "For the German people, the failure of the National Socialism was so striking along with its crimes, that a German dictatorship today has become something completely impossible."[6]

There were some, however, who were uncertain about the new state and society being created. Lower middle class elements feared so-called Guest Workers (*Gastarbeiter*) from Italy, Greece, and Spain, and later Turkey, threatening overall job security. Upper class elements watched traditional lifestyles give way to a sexually liberated, materialistic, and egocentric society. In January 1953, Werner Naumann (former State Secretary in the Reich Ministry of Propaganda) and other former Nazis leaders were arrested for planning a second Nazi putsch and for threatening the safety of Allied troops. Although not underestimating right-wing extremists' and radicals' potential to stir-up social discontent, Adenauer, nevertheless, viewed such extremists as less a domestic threat than as an impediment to effective international relations. For example, paralleling the Eichmann trial in Israel from 1960-1962 (made possible because of West German assistance in finding Eichmann), Nazis swastikas and the words "Juden raus" reappeared scrawled on Koeln's rebuilt synagogue on December 24, 1959 (the work of East Germany's Ministry of State Security). Leading German newspapers asked how any German could remain anti-Semitic after Germany's Jews had been almost totally annihilated. The Adenauer government assured world opinion that "nowhere is the indignation over the heinous deeds as intense and general as in the Federal Republic." On the practical side, these acts complicated sustaining the Hallstein Doctrine, support for German rearmament, and strong ties with the West. Publicly, the *Einsatzgruppen* trials in 1956, events in Koeln and elsewhere Eichmann's trial, and the Auschwitz trials of the 1960s all generated intense public discussions of the evils of National Socialism and the dangers emanating from right-wing extremist groups. In short, West Germans experienced an intensive review of Nazi atrocities, furthering their resistance against militarism, fascism, and right-wing extremist propaganda.[7]

Post-war German intellectuals also had their doubts. Divided over the strength of in western culture and the Enlightenment in German society, for example, Friedrick Meinecke and Karl Jaspers, their writings and debates complimented growing public awareness of Nazi crimes and pushed many West German youth to embrace a pacifist-left orientation. In pursuit of balance, conservative thinkers placed their faith in a rapid process of reconstruction and modernization, and a strong blending of rationality and Christian morality. More liberal groups, for example, the New Left, represented by *Group 47*, Heinrich Boell, Guenter Grass, criticized society for turning away from the Germany of *Dichter und Denker* (poets and thinkers) to operators and profiteers in an era of political reaction and authoritarian oppression.[8]

Right-Wing Extremist Parties

Until new legislation was passed in 1964, state ministries of the interior were responsible for banning radical groups and parties threatening the domestic order. All told, state agencies banned 328 right and left-wing extremist groups and alleviated the need for federal intervention. After 1964, this responsibility passed to the Federal Ministry of the Interior. Extremist groups, consequently, sought to remain on the fine edge between constitutionality and prohibition. Accomplishing that goal demanded minimizing apparent links with National Socialism and violence. Thus, a small handful extremist groups survived under the watchful eyes of state authorities.[9]

When Dorls and Remer broke with the DKP-DRP on October 2, 1949, they also founded the *Sozialistische Reichspartei* (SRP). The SRP's platform and party structure clearly emulated the National Socialist ideology and internal anti-democratic party structure. Opposing the western-oriented *Parteien-Demokratie*, the SRP's ideological foundations included a sense of community (*Volksgemeinschaft*), respect for the German state (*Reichsgedanke*), and "German Socialism" (*Deutscher Sozialismus* or *Volks- und Reichs-Sozialismus*). The SRP also opposed the occupying powers' interference in German economic and political affairs, for example, executing German war criminals and German rearmament to defend the hated republic. Furthermore, the SRP's affiliated organizations, *Reichsjugend*, *Frauenbund*, and *Reichsfront*, emulated former Nazis organizations. With these tools, the SRP attracted a variety of discontented elements, including, former and active Nationalists, the unemployed, and recent emigres.[10]

The SRP found its greatest number of supporters in the Protestant north, namely, Niedersachsen, and entire DKP-DRP county level organizations. By January 1950, the ranks of the SRP rose to some 6000 members. As the ideological stance of the SRP did not sit well with the ruling parties in Bonn, in late 1950 the Adenauer government declared membership in the SRP to be incompatible with public service and in November 1951 the Constitutional Court agreed. Nevertheless, the SRP took 11% of the vote and sixteen seats in Niedersachsen's state parliament in May 1951 and 7.7% of the vote and eight seats in Bremen's October state elections. Concerned about West German relations with the Allies, Adenauer said on September 6, 1951, that he would welcomed an Allied statement on intervention should the radical right threaten the democratic order. Adenauer did not, however, expect such a situation would arise. However, both Britain and France suffered from what Adenauer called "nervous jitters in response to people like Remer."[11]

On October 23, 1952, the West German Constitutional Court declared the *Sozialistsiche Reichspartei* unconstitutional, revoked its only seat in the Bundestag, and confiscated its property. According to the court's final report, former National Socialists held

> key positions in the party to such an extent as to determine its political and intellectual image.... In addition, the speeches and activities of party leaders demonstrated the party's ... acceptance of the idea of an authoritarian Fuehrer state

which was accompanied by the "revival of a vicious anti-Semitism." Thus, the court declared it to be neo-Nazi in character whose goals threatened the democratic order and the existing multi-party system. The court clearly signaled that images or policies reminiscent of National Socialism would not be tolerated.[12]

Right-wing radicals, consequently, sought more cautious paths through which to exert their influence. Many shifted their allegiance to the *Deutsche Reichspartei* (DRP). Hessen's DRP entered political affairs in January 1950 through the union of the Niedersachsen branch of the DKP-DRP with Hessen's 300 member *Nationaldemokratische Partei* (NDP). Through their union, both hoped to blend nationalistic and national-socialistic traditions in a "citizen's oriented" (*Buergerblock*) right-wing political movement. Electoral success was not forthcoming. DRP never united behind the new ideological mixture and the electorate used the DRP as little more than a vehicle for a reserved protest. At the national level, the DRP's 300,000 votes (or 1.1% of the popular vote in 1953, 1.0% in 1957, and 0.8% in 1961) stood well below expectations as well as the newly established "5% hurdle" to keep such groups out of the Bundestag. In addition, those votes came heavily from Niedersachsen (44.7% in 1953, 28.8% in 1957, and 24.1% in 1961) but counted for only 1951 2.2% (three seats) of Niedersachsen's overall vote in 1951 and 3.8% in 1955. Lacking a "5% clause" to prevent entry into the state parliament (*Landtag*), Niedersachsen's *Landtag* included six DRP representatives in 1955. Losing ground, the DRP lost all its seats in 1959.[13]

The poor electoral elections undermined centrist elements in favor of those on the right. German neutrality, modeled after the Austrian

Treaty of 1955, became the DRP's foreign policy position regarding Germany's path to reunification. Fused with the *Deutsche Nationalpartei* (DNP; founded in 1950) under Herbert Freiberger, DRP positions assumed more radical overtones. Freiberger, chairman of the DNP in Niedersachsen, made his opinions clear during the 1956 party convention in Celle and during the DNP's national convention in Wiesbaden. Freiberger encouraged the party to reject Germany membership in NATO, military service in a divided Germany, and identified the Christian Democrats under Konrad Adenauer as the DNP's main opponents. As for the Soviet Union, Freiberger stood on the side of rabid anticommunism and against any talks with Soviet authorities.[14]

The litmus test of the DRP's new platform failed in the 1957 federal elections as the ruling conservative CDU/CSU coalition came away with an absolute ruling majority. Seeking political allies, Mainberg and von Thadden first favored an alliance with the centrist *Freie Demokratische Partei* (FDP) and the center-right *Gesamtdeutscher Block/Block der Heimatvertriebenen und Entrechteten* (GB/BHE) while forcing Freiberger out of the party in 1957. Cooperation between the center and far right proved superficial and short-lived. The FDP and GB/BHE broke with the DRP in 1958. The DRP's neutral and nationalistic platform had generated little support outside the party and inspired change from within. Party leaders, von Thadden, Hans-Heinrich Scheffer, Wilhelm Meinberg, and Waldemar Schuetz, the editor of the *Deutschen Wochenzeitung*, pushed a pro-West position against Heinrich Kunstmann's neutral-nationalistic stance allowing for German unification. Torn in two during the December 1961 *Northeimer Parteitag*, the conference ended with von Thadden as the new party chairman and Kunstmann and his followers forming the new *Deutsche-Freiheits-Partei* (DFP) in January 1962. (Three years later the DFP united with the *Aktionsgemeinschaft Uabhaengiger Deutscher* (AUD).) The remodeled DRP became evident during the 1962 Frankfurt party convention. The older neutral-nationalistic platform gave way to a "Europe of Fatherlands," which underscored the need for military strength, an authoritarian-conservative social order, and continued its anti-communistic stance. Failing to break the 5% hurdle in state elections in Rheinland-Pfalz and Niedersachsen in 1963, the DRP allied itself with Bremen's *Deutsche Partei* (DP) (thus, *Gesamtdeutschen Partei* (GDP)) resulting in an electoral success: 5.2% of the vote (and four seats) in Bremen's 1963 state elections. However, the DRP's political position became increasingly difficult. Aligned with the DNP in Niedersachsen, it leaned away from a more socialistic orientation and towards a more traditionally conservative position. In Bremen, on the other hand, its fusion with the DP took it more towards the center-right.[15]

The Interregnum and the NDP, 1963-1982

Moving from the 1960s into the 1970s, right-wing political parties were confronted declining political support. Beginning in 1964, the DRP announced its desire to take part in a *National-Demokratische Union*. Smaller parties and groups from the radical right, remaining elements of the failed *Gesamtdeutschen Partei* (GDP), Thielen's *Deutsche Partei* (DP) in Bremen, and the *Deutsche-Nationale Volkspartei* (DNVP; founded in 1962 in North Hessen) answered DRP's call. Gathering in Hannover, some seventy splinter groups founded the *Nationaldemokratische Partei Deutschlands* (NPD) on November 28, 1964, and from 1966-1972 reached levels of success never seen by the DRP. Supported largely by Protestant middle class and agrarian elements, NPD ranks grew after 1966 from 25,300 to almost 28,000 while sixty-one NPD delegates sat in seven state parliaments. With poor returns during federal elections in 1969, NPD membership declined from 27,900 in 1971 to only 17,300 in 1979. Concurrently, the Interior Ministry's investigations revealed a "party engaged in anti-constitutional goals," and as a "danger to the democratic order." The Constitutional Court, however, refused to declare the NDP unconstitutional.[16]

The Kohl Era, 1982-1996

Christian-Democratic rule returned in October 1982 under the leadership of Helmut Kohl. Despite the banning of several right-wing extremist groups, membership in right-wing extremist groups grew from 20,300 in 1980, 28,300 in 1988, 35,900 in 1989, 39,800 in 1991, and 42,400 by 1994. In 1992, Kohl's government finally cracked down on the radical right and eased domestic concerns by passing new legislation to resolve the "foreigner problem." Throughout these years, German politicians carelessly dealt with Germany's unique historical roots and mainstream political parties appeared unreceptive to public needs at a time of rising inflation, rising unemployment, waves of foreigners seeking jobs, and a growing insecurity about the future (thus, *Parteiverdrossenheit*). The so-called Historians' Debate

(*Historikerstreit*) added to the confusion. German intellectuals debated the nature of German identity, criticized CDU/CSU policies, the legitimacy of two German states, undermined the government's credibility, and fueled more radical responses. These public debates revealed deep divisions within German society. In addition, right-wing extremist elements benefited from the highly politicized discussion. Highly public events, for example, Ernst Nolte and David Irving's Holocaust revisionism, Ernst Juenger's 100th birthday, and Bitburg, helped both state and society drift further towards the political right. Tapping this sentiment, Schoenhuber's "We want to become a self-confident people again" attracted supporters by rejecting the guilt felt by most Germans over the Holocaust. As the final straw, *die Wende* (the Transition) of 1989 broke postwar Germany's traditional link with its past.[17]

Christian-Democratic Leadership

As for Germany's right-wing extremists and radicals, Kohl, echoing Adenauer's words, called rising international concerns "absolutely unjustified." Critics charged Kohl with failing to aggressively respond against the neo-Nazi threat. But Kohl did not intend a revival of German militarism or to justify the past. Rather, Kohl pursued a revived sense of *historical normalcy*. The quest for *normalcy* also led to mistakes with few parallels in the Adenauer era. Kohl's actions at Bitburg in 1985 and again in 1991 with his presence at reburial of Frederick the Great at Sans Souci Palace in Potsdam presented alarming signals. Similarly, President Richard von Weizaecker's May 8, 1985, speech, which admonished all Germans to accept responsibility for the Holocaust, was falsely interpreted to be an endorsement for the concept of "collective guilt." Three years later, the President of the Bundestag, Philipp Jenninger, commemorated the 50th anniversary of the Night of Broken Glass *(Reichskristallnacht)* on November 10, 1988, but was victimized by poor television and press coverage and criticized for his lack of emotional commitment to his subject matter. Jenninger was forced from his position within a few weeks. In pursuit of *normalcy*, Kohl detached rising xenophobia and attacks against foreigners by skinheads from his vision of German society. What Kurt Biedenkopf feared in 1989 in the rise of extremism, Kohl simply rejected in 1994 with, "That is not Germany."[18]

The Problems of Normalcy

Fifty years after Germany's surrender, a unified Germany remembered its defeat, liberation, and the victims of Hitler's Nationalism Socialism. In Bonn, conservative political circles departed from Adenauer's vision of May 8, 1945, as a gloomy day in German history. Parliamentary President Rita Suessmuth and Chancellor Kohl underscored their belief in *May 8* as *the* day of *liberation* from Nazi tyranny -- which to others implied a *detachment* from the past as well. Meanwhile, the news media ran hundreds of articles and programs on life in Germany shortly before and after its surrender in 1945. Hamburg's *Die Zeit* published a series dealing with such issues as the German resistance to National Socialism, the occupation, memories, dictatorship, liberation, expellation, and the Holocaust. Nevertheless, according to a survey conducted by *Der Spiegel* magazine in early 1995, less than 40% -- but only 27% of those between 18-34 years of age -- of all Germans were aware of the actual date when the Second World War ended. Worse yet, half of the last war generation still held Poles responsible for starting the Second World War. Of individuals experiencing the end of the war as a child, roughly fifty percent condemned the forced expulsion of the Germans from the East as "just as bad as the Holocaust of the Jews." In addition, the American Jewish Committee determined in 1994 that most Germans (68%) were uncomfortable with the idea of Gypsies residing in their communities while a large minority also objected to Arabs, Poles, Turks, and Jews (47%, 39%, 36% and 20% respectively).[19]

The Extreme Right Raises Again

The most prominent German right-wing extremist and Neo-Nazi, Michael Kuehnen, began his activities distributing leaflets for the NDP. Periodically jailed for his activities, Kuehnen merged his *Aktionsfront Nationaler Sozialisten* (ANS) with other extremist groups to form the NS/NA in November 1983. After 1989, Kuehnen directed his efforts at eastern Germany where he founded the *Deutsche Alternative*. Kuehnen's organizations were all quickly banned by the government. After dying from AIDS in 1991, his organization disintegrated. Nevertheless, right-wing extremist parties did score major gains in Bremen in 1987 (*Deutsche Volks-Union/Liste D* (DVU/LD) and *Die Republikaner* (REP), 4.68%), Baden-Wuerttemberg in 1988

(*Nationaldemokratische Partei Deutschlands* (NDP), REP, and *Oekologisch-Demokratische Partei* (OeDP), ca. 6.7%), and in Berlin in 1989 (REP, 7.5%). Campaigning for Bremen's state elections in September 1991, the Gerhard Frey's ultra right-wing *Deutsche Volksunion* party employed simple anti-foreigner slogans, "The Boat Is Full" and "Germany for the Germans." When the final vote was tabulated the *Deutsche Volksunion* moved from three to six seats in Bremen's state parliament. In Schleswig-Holstein, the DVU also held several seats in Kiel's *Landtag*. Kiel also proved quite inhospitable for DVU representatives. When Ingo Stawitz and the DVU fraction relativized National Socialist crimes in October 1992, *Landtag* delegates passed Legislative Bill 13/471, stating:

> The DVU seeks to identify itself with right-wing forces, attempting to undermine the legitimacy and respect of all democratic institutions and encourage anti-democratic thinking as well as violence against memorials devoted to the victims of National socialism.[20]

But the *Deutsche Volksunion* did not stand alone. The *Partei der Arbeit* (PdA) entered German political life in the early 1970's. After breaking with the NPD, Friedhelm Busse founded the PdA in Krefeld in 1971. After the PdA fused with the *Volkssozialistische Bewegung Deutschland* (VSBD/PdA), its neo-Nazi character drew the attention of West German authorities, who banned the VSBD/PdA in 1982. Inspired by the Strasser brothers ideas from National Socialism's formative years, former NPD party activist Meinolf Schoenborna pushed forward the *Nationalistische Front* (NF) in 1985. The NF ten-point program was a call for revolutionary action. The NF called for German resistance against an imperialistic West determined to keep Germany divided while destroying the German nation. The NF program also advocated expelling foreigners and reasserting "der Volksindentitaet, der Lebenswerte und der Wesensart der Deutschen Volkes." German society, under NF leadership, would realize an "Antimaterialistische Kulturrevolution" and an "Antikapitalistische Sozialrevolution" (linked with a domestic campaign against organized crime, the child prostitution, treason, corruption, and anti-social behavior or *Gemeinschaftszerstoerung*) allowing the emergence of a free healthy Germanic people (Germans and Austrians) within a "Volksstaat" capable of defending itself without the economic and military coalitions forced upon Germany since 1945. Furthermore, the NF intended to put an end to the one-sided attempts to explain the origins and character of

National Socialism and to punish those guilty of collaborating with the occupying powers.[21]

Neo-Nazi activities were equally characteristic of the *Freiheitliche Deutsche Arbeiterpartei* (FAP). A resuscitated version of Michael Kuehnen's 1983 *Aktionsfront Nationaler Sozialisten/Nationale Aktivisten* (ANS/NA) forced underground once declared illegal, the FAP ranks swelled to roughly 500 members in 1987. The FAP's 1986 political program (*Aktionsprogramm*) showed more restraint than its associated publications. The *FAP-Nachrichten*, the monthly *Deutscher Standpunkt*, as well as numerous leaflets included calls for racial pride and a revived sense of community ("Rassenstolz und Volksgemeinschaft"), articles, for example, *Aryan's Highest Good* ("Arier hoechstes Gut"), and the condemnation of miscegenation as murder ("Voelkermord"). Acting on this belief, FAP members assaulted victims physically and through arson. Led by Martin Pape until November 1988 when replaced by former-PdA chairman Friedrich Busse, the FAP entered state elections (1985-1988) and federal elections (1987) but without any notable success.[22]

As the European Workers' Party (*Europaeische Arbeiterpartei* or EAP) collapsed near the end of 1974 in Wiesbaden, Hegla Zepp-LaRouche organized the Patriots for Germany *(Patrioten fuer Deutschland)*, who entered the national political arena in August 1986 at Ruedesheim and by early 1987 claimed some 2000 members. As the *Patrioten* prepared for federal 1987 elections, their more right-wing orientation took more concrete form. The *Patrioten* accepted the policy of anchoring Germany to the West but justified western defense policies as a reflection of the continued legal existence of the German Reich as defined by the borders of 1937 by appealing to German history and pride. Miserable electoral returns in Niedersachsen (1986), Rheinland-Pfalz (1987), during federal elections (1987) and in Baden-Wuerttemberg (1988) signaled their political collapse.[23]

As the Social-Liberal coalition fell apart in 1982, a new political entity on the political right arose: the *Republikaner* or Republikans (REP). Founded in 1983, it drew from the ranks of dissatisfied members of Bavaria's CSU and found a spokesperson in Bavaria's popular television moderator of the series "Jetzt red i" and former Waffen-SS soldier, Franz Schoenhuber. The Republikan Party entered its first electoral campaign in Bavaria in 1986. Unified behind their slogan "Ja zu Deutschland," the Republikans were especially successful in northern Bavaria receiving 3.0% of the overall vote. During the campaign, the Republikans distanced themselves from the more radical NPD -- although Republikan rhetoric displayed a clear link with National Socialist positions. Republikan propaganda called for a "national self-determination and spiritual-moral renewal." Similarly, the 1987 Republikan party program drew a negative picture of contemporary German culture, politics, social values, as well as reunification. Encapsulated in "Ja zu Deutschland" and "Recht und Ordnung," the Republikans demonstrated their commitment to a Germany for Germans and rejected German collective guilt for the crimes of National Socialism as well as the *Auschwitz-Lie*. Officially, Republikans soft-peddled their policy on foreigners. Nevertheless, Republikans and their supporters held to a clearly anti-foreigner and anti-democratic sentiments -- a point of irritation for the Republikans' more traditionally minded rank and file.[24]

The Republikans and their supporters were characteristically men (roughly two-thirds). However, younger men were modestly over-represented while their elder counterparts were under-represented. Although younger Republikans and supporters held stronger anti-democratic dispositions than their older counterparts, both were extremely dissatisfied with the political system. German pollsters and researchers interpreted the move to the right as a protest against the policies of the major parties. Republikans and their supporters also shared a propensity for identification with the middle or working class, a modest or vocational level of education, a relatively low level of income among both groups, and originate in the lower social stratum. These groups feared an evolving social system which undermined traditional conceptions of morality, as Europe and the world changed its economic and political complexion, and the influx of foreigners, immigrants, and refugees, appeared as a direct threat to their immediate welfare. Responses to these changes varied between those with more formal education, who tended towards more nationalistic positions, and those with less formal education and lower incomes, who were motivated by economic self-interest. Consequently, the Republikan Party became a loosely defined populist movement on the radical-right and a protest movement against the growing uncertainty of the times.[25]

A Turning Point: Unification, 1989-90

Anticipating Honecker's 1987 trip to Bonn, a top Kohl advisor informed journalists that "Reunification is completely beyond reality." Beyond reality, however, was the effect unification had on Germany and the Germans. The opening of the Berlin Wall in November 1989, Kohl's 10-point plan outlining a phased process of German unification, the March 1990 elections which endorsed unification, and the July currency union, were all historical mile-markers. However, as the *revolution* of 1989/90 unfolded, East Germans reformers lost control of the unification process to western bureaucrats, the East German economy crumbled, right-wing extremists hoped to recover ground lost since 1989 began, and right-wing radicals extended their campaign of violence into East Germany. As an uncertain future stared post-unification Germans in the face, Germany's traditional link with its difficult past broke and 1989 emerged as a second *Stunde Null*. As Joyce Mushaben saw it, "the root causes of [post-unification] extremism" were revealed in the "disruptive process of reunification itself."[26]

The Republikaner Recovery and Fall, 1989-1994

State elections in 1987-1988 signaled declining support for the Republikans (averaging roughly 1% of the vote in Bremen, Baden-Wuerttemberg, and Schleswig-Holstein). As party moral plummeted, it became equally clear that the rank-and-file lacked a developed sense of ideological cohesion. Party leaders responded during the June 1988 Hambach party convention by defining their movement as a "collective movement of the democratic and humane patriotism." Results came quickly. Republikan membership rose from 8600 in 1988 to 13,000 in 1989. In Berlin, Republikan electoral support reached 7.5% and eleven seats in the Berlin Senate -- replacing the more moderate FDP which failed the 5% minimum. (The Christian Democratic camp, however, refused any consideration of a coalition with the Republikans, a party on the radical right manipulating social and economic protests into a proto-Nazi, anti-democratic, anti-West, and authoritarian nationalism.) According to the *Mannheimer Forschungsgruppe*, Republikan supporters were especially concerned about their security of their jobs given increasing numbers of foreigners (63%), Berlin's housing shortage (64%), and the potential reduction in health benefits (72%). These statistics varied only slightly outside Berlin through the course of 1989.[27]

Republikan fortunes rose and fell between 1989 and 1990. European-wide election returns in June 1989 gave the Republikans 7.1% and six seats in the European Parliament. However, Bavarians provided

746,886 of the 2,005,555 Republikan votes were cast (37.2%) and 14.6% of the overall vote. Republikan votes were often drawn from Bavaria's smaller Catholic towns. After the summer of 1989, the Republikans lost steam. The events of November 1989 and German unification gave the center-right Christian Democrats a greater influence among the more nationalistically minded. The Republikans responded in 1990 by further radicalizing the party program. Nevertheless, in state election returns in Niedersachsen and Nordrhein-Westfalen, Republikans failed to break the 2% mark and the party began disintegrating. Outmaneuvered by extremists, Schoenhuber, resigned as party chairman in May 1990 and then retook his position in July. But the damage had been done. By 1994, right-wing radical violence and Republikan extremists had undermined "any chance" of entering the Bundestag.[28]

Violence Against Foreigners

Synonymous with the cities of Solingen, Hoyerswerda, Rostock, Moelln, and Luebeck, unification brought in its wake increased violence against foreigners -- and occasions of revived anti-Semitism. The right-wing extremists attempted to capitalize on these attitudes. There were roughly 300 attacks against asylum seekers in 1991 by right-wing radicals -- the first scene of extensive violence was Hoyarswerda in September 1991. German television (ARD) attempted to encourage a sense of civic duty by appealing to German pride in the constitution (noting especially Art. 1, regarding the protection of human dignity) versus the violence done to helpless victims. ARD campaigned against xenophobia and violence against foreigners in special series of broadcasts in 1991, with an estimated audience of 3.4 million, entitled *Auslaenderhass -- nicht mit uns*. Throughout Germany, on November 9, 1991, 100,000 individuals (25,00 in Berlin alone) demonstrated against *Auslaenderhass*, violence, xenophobia, right-wing radicalism, and right-wing extremism. In December 1991 German authorities responded to right-wing radicalism by raiding the homes of alleged right-wing extremists. After searching a 114 homes in 32 cities, German authorities confiscated ammunition, weapons, as well as neo-Nazi publications.[29]

But the violence continued. In 1992, German citizens looked on as police units responded to right-wing radicals attacks against foreigners in more than 100 German cities. The former Sachsenhausen and Ravensbrueck concentration camps were damaged during arson attacks. Right-wing radicals attacked refugee centers throughout eastern

Germany. Rostock and Eisenhuettenstadt, were hit hard. Quedlinburg was engulfed in violence for five consecutive days in September. In November, three Turks (a woman and two children) died in Moelln as a result of an arson attack. In May 1993, four men set fire to the house of a Turkish family in Solingen. Five Turkish women and girls died in the fire and several persons were injured. (In 1995, Duesseldorf Upper Regional Court found the four suspects involved in the arson attack guilty. The court's final report labeled the arson attack as one of Germany's worst anti-foreigner crimes since 1945 sentenced all four to 10-15 years in prison.) Speaking before the Bundestag on June 16, Chancellor Kohl condemned the attack as an "unfassbares Mass an sittlicher Verrohrung" and pledged that his government would fight right-wing violence with the same diligence used to eliminate violence perpetuated by the radical left.[30]

In March 1994 and again in 1995, Luebeck's synagogue suffered from repeated arson attacks. In April 1994, six right-wing suspects were arrested for arson in Bielefeld when they attempted to burn down a house occupied by fifteen Turks. In 1994, there were an estimated 42,400 right-wing radicals in Germany, while roughly 5600 were considered dangerous. Fortunately, right-wing violence against foreigners has decreased. The Office for the Protection of the Constitution (*Bundesamt fuer Verfassungsschutz*) registered 270 cases of right-wing violence in 1990, 1483 in 1991, 2285 in 1992 (2033 were directed against foreigners), and 1,814 in 1993. In 1992, these attacks results in 17 deaths and 708 cases of arson, and in 1993, 8 deaths and 302 cases of arson. By the first half of 1995, however, registered attacks descended to 921. Additionally, violence against foreigners undermined a wider acceptance of right-wing extremist groups and electoral support quickly dried up. Furthermore, the *Institut fuer Demoskopie* (Allensbach) reported in 1990 and 1992 that most Germans (77%) found right-wing extremists intolerable while Hans-Gerd Jaschke concluded that "the majority culture in Germany needs and uses the right-wing subculture to dissociate and liberate itself from its NS past" -- and not return to it.[31]

Explaining the Extreme Political Right

Sociological and psychological analyses of political orientations among radical right-wing elements of the early 1990's indicated no historically rooted political orientations and that not all violence is politically motivated. However, contemporary right-wing radicals were drawn largely from the ranks of disgruntled German youth (primarily males) who focused their anger and violence on foreigners. Similar to historical Nazism's *folkish* nationalism, right-wing extremists' disappointed expectations also reflected an identity crisis not satisfied by the pursuit of material goods. The Bielefeld study, directed by Wilhelm Heitmeyer, criticized economic explanations for presuming that those with jobs opposed right-wing radicalism and ignored additional social factors. These factors included the atomization of the individual in modern society, a disintegrating family structure, one's vocation, and declining sense of purpose and political orientation -- which apparently is compensated for by anti-foreigner sentiment in both the East and West (an observation which does not generally apply to German university students). Complimenting Heitmeyer's study, Ulrich Wagner (Ruhr University in Bochum) and Andreas Zick (Wuppertal University) found Germans harboring stronger feelings against foreigners than their western neighbors. Specifically, less educated Germans displayed a higher propensity for xenophobic dispositions, considered themselves politically conservative, and were drawn from Germany's lower classes.[32]

So Just What is the Prognosis for the Future?
A Few Concluding Observations

President Roman Herzog called upon all Germans to preserve the memory of Nazi crimes which will "serve again and again as the basis for a living future." German responses to attacks against foreigners in Luebeck and elsewhere suggest that those lessons have not been forgotten. However, Gains Post, Jr., reminds historians that "German unification has humbled whatever faith historians had in their predictive powers." Furthermore, in November-December 1994, the Emnid research institute survey revealed an increasingly egocentric German society resistant to calls for *solidarity*. As for foreigners, 44% feared (over 36% in 1992) the continued influx of foreigners would lead to increased domestic unrest. Additionally, 51% (over 46% in 1992) no longer believed calls for greater tolerance would eventually resolve the problem -- a consequence of the failed strategies of the political left? As Detlev J.K. Peukert feared, the government's chosen responses to right-wing elements have yet to accomplish their objective. Thus, it appears that Hannover's *Chaos-Tage* of August 1995 indicate a problem that is not going away but is growing. As Elie Wiesel stated, today's

German youth are Germany's future leaders and these "junge Deutschen koennten die Besten sein oder die Schlimmsten. Das ist ihre Wahl."[33]

In conclusion, there are clear ideological links between traditional Nazism and contemporary right-wing extremism. These links, however, do not easily extend to right-wing radicals. Second, although right-wing extremist groups have occasionally generated modest electoral victories, these groups have never successfully sustained that support. Internally, these groups lack ideological cohesion, regularly divide, sub-divide, and reemerge under a modified name and party platform. Consequently, Diethelm Prowe's "optimistic assessment of the prospects for the democratization and integration" in Germany appear realistic -- while not *feeling* very reassuring. Nevertheless, Bundestag President Dr. Rita Suessmuth asserted in June 1995 that there remained a deficit of democratic thinking in extreme right-wing German political circles which all Germans will be forced to confront until existing socio-economic conditions are improved.[34]

Notes

1. Ralf Dahrendorf, *Society and Democracy in Germany* (New York: Norton, 1979). Hans-Gerd Jaschke, "Sub-Cultural Aspects of Right-Wing Extremism," in Dirk Berg-Schlosser and Ralf Rytlewski's (editors) *Political Culture in Germany* (New York: St. Martin's Press, 1993), pp. 126-134. For an insight into right-wing extremism in the former German Democratic Republic, see Walter Suess's "Wahrnehmung und Interpretation des Rechtsextremismus in der DDR durch das MfS," *Deutschland Archiv*, April 1993. Werner Weidenfeld and Karl-Rudolf Korte (Hrsg.), *Handbuch zur deutschen Einheit* (Bonn: Bundeszentrale fuer politische Bildung, 1993), pp. 277-289. As for the differences between right-wing radicalism and right-wing extremism, Thomas Lillig defined *right-wing extremism* as expressed particular personality traits influenced by social and economic factors often resulting in a particular political orientation. *Right-wing radicalism*, on the other hand, is expressed in the actions and ideologies of various groups on the political right. Werner Weidenfeld and Karl-Rudolf Korte (Hrsg.), *Handbuch zur deutschen Einheit* (Bonn: Bundeszentrale fuer politische Bildung, 1994), pp. 277-289. See also Thomas Lillig's *Rechtsextremismus in den neuen Bundeslaendern. Erklaerungsansaetze, Einstellungspotentiale und organisatorische Strukturen* (Mainz: Universitaet Mainz, 1994).

2. Text: "Abkoppelung von weltpolitischen Entwicklungen," Moeller concludes, is "heute ebensowenig moeglich wie 1945 und 1989, gibt es doch noch andere Probleme als ihre eigenen -- und diese gesamteuropaeischen sind vermutlich gravierender." Diethelm Prowe, "The New Germany: 1945-1960, 1989-1991," *The Historian*, Volume 54/Autumn 1991, pp. 19-34. Horst Moeller, "Die Relativitaet historischen Epochen: Das Jahr 1945 in der Perspective des Jahres 1989," *Aus Zeit und Politik*, April 28, 1995, pp. 3-9.

3. Referred to in German as *Parteiverdrossenheit*. Manfred Rowold/Stefan Poguntke, "Im Schatten der Macht. Nicht-etablierte Kleinparteien," in Alf Mintzel and Heinrich Oberreuter's (Hrsg.) *Parteien in der Bundesrepublik Deutschland* (Bonn: Bundeszentrale fuer politische Bildung, 1992), pp. 368-69. Eckhard Jesse, "Rechtsextreme Gewalt" *Der Buerger im Staat* June 1993, pp. 123-127. See the various articles in *Aus Zeit und Politik*, February 2, 1996. Thomas Lillig outlined the seven basic trends emerging from eastern Germany in his work *Rechtextremismus in den neuen Bundeslaender* (Mainz: Universitaet Mainz, 1994), namely, (1) *Volk, Vaterland und Heimat*, (2) *Ethnocentrismus und Rassismus*, (3) *"Law and Order" und Militarismus*, (4) a rejection of the *Staats- und Gesellschaftsordnung Nachkriegsdeutschlands*, (5) a clearer identification with a National Socialist *Geschichtsbild*, (6) *Krisenwahrnehmung: Materialismus und sittliche Dekadenz*, and (7) an *Oekologische Sehnsuechte* (pp. 17-18).

4. Maria Mitchell, "Materialism and Secularism: CDU Politicians and National Socialism, 1945-1949," *The Journal of Modern History*, Volume 67, Number 2, June 1995. Daniel E. Rogers, *Politics after Hitler: The Western Allies and the German Party System* (New York: New York University Press, 1995). Office of the Military Government, United States, Office of the Political Advisor, "Report No. 131. 4 August 1948. Opinion Surveys Branch," POLAD 820/6 (Bundesarchiv, Koblenz), and the Elisabeth Noelle and Erich Peter Neumann, *The Germans: Public Opinion Polls, 1947-1966* (Bonn: Allensbach, 1967).

5. German text: "einheitlichen grossen Rechtspartei, in der alle konservativ, christlich und national eingestellten Deutschen ihre Heimat finden." Office of Military Government, United States (OMGUS), Files of the Director of Intelligence (ODI) 7/20-3/70, "Report on Nazi Underground Organizations," dated February 1947 (Bundesarchiv, Koblenz). These groups included the *Danube* (composed for former German intelligence personnel), the *Armee der Rache*, *Odessa*, *Dach*, *Sturmgruppe Nordwest*, and *Vierundvierzig* (appealing to former Schutzstaffel and Wehrmacht members), one composed of former members of the Stuerm Abteilungen (SA), two for former Luftwaffe personnel (*Skylark* and the *Green Devils*), as well as others composed of the disgruntled and the young, for example, the *Proppen Club*, *Schwarze Adler*, *Sonnenrad*

Division, and *SOMA*. Manfred Rowold/Stefan Poguntke, "Im Schatten der Macht. Konrad Adenauer, *Teegespraeche 1950-1954* (Berlin: Siedler Verlag, 1984), p. 652. Nicht-etablierte Kleinparteien," in Alf Mintzel and Heinrich Oberreuter's (Hrsg.) *Parteien in der Bundesrepublik Deutschland* (Bonn: Bundeszentrale fuer politische Bildung, 1992), p. 369-70. Uwe Backes/Eckhard Jesse, *Politscher Extremismus in der Bundesrepublik Deutschland* (Bonn: Bundeszentrale fuer politische Bildung, 1993), pp. 299-300.

6. German text: "Misserfolg des Nationalsozialismus war so eklatant, und seine ganzen Verbrechen dazu waren fuer das deutsche Volk eine so heilsame Lehre, dass [heute] eine Diktatur etwas voellig Falsches und Unmoeglich sei." Konrad Adenauer, *Teegespraeche 1961-1963* (Berlin: Siedler Verlag, 1992), pp. 404 & 621-622. Maria Mitchell, "Materialism and Secularism: CDU Politicians and National Socialism, 1945-1949," *The Journal of Modern History*, Volume 67, Number 2, June 1995. Konrad Adenauer, *Teegespraeche 1950-1954* (Berlin: Siedler Verlag, 1984), pp. 64-65, 163-164, 471, & 722.

7. German text: "nirgendwo die Empoerung ueber die Freveltaten so intensiv und allgemein ist wie in der Bundesrepublik." Konrad Adenauer, *Teegespraeche 1950-1954* (Berlin: Siedler Verlag, 1984), pp. 722-723. Henning Koehler, *Adenauer: eine politische Biographie* (Berlin: Propylaeen, 1994), pp. 1050-1052. Hans-Peter Schwarz, *Adenauer: Der Staatsmann: 1952-1967* (Stuttgart: Deutsche Verlags-Anstalt, 1991), pp. 529-530. Neither Koehler or Schwarz address Adenauer's concerns about extreme right-wing elements. Rather, Adenauer was confronted with public criticism of former Nazis within his government -- a fact which he did not hide. However, Adenauer was also convinced that these same individuals had no reservations about the democratic state and society they were creating. Konrad Adenauer, *Teegespraeche 1959-1961* (Berlin: Siedler Verlag, 1988), pp. 650-651.

8. Charles Maier, *The Unmasterable Past* (Cambridge: Harvard, 1988), and *Forever in the Shadow of Hitler? Original Documents of the Historikerstreit, the Controversy Concerning the Singularity of the Holocaust* (New Jersey: Humanities Press, 1993).

9. Eckhard Jesse, "Rechtsextreme Gewalt" *Der Buerger im Staat* June 1993, pp. 123-127.

10. Manfred Rowold/Stefan Poguntke, "Im Schatten der Macht. Nicht-etablierte Kleinparteien," in Alf Mintzel and Heinrich Oberreuter's (Hrsg.) *Parteien in der Bundesrepublik Deutschland* (Bonn: Bundeszentrale fuer politische Bildung, 1992), pp. 370-71. Donald P. Kommers, *The Constitutional Jurisprudence of the Federal Republic of Germany* (London: Duke University

Press, 1989), pp. 223-227. Thomas Schwartz, *America's Germany* (Cambridge: Harvard, 1991), pp. 145, 173 and 216.

11. German text: "Heidenangst vor Leute wie Remer und aehnlichen." Manfred Rowold/Stefan Poguntke, "Im Schatten der Macht. Nicht-etablierte Kleinparteien," in Alf Mintzel and Heinrich Oberreuter's (Hrsg.) *Parteien in der Bundesrepublik Deutschland* (Bonn: Bundeszentrale fuer politische Bildung, 1992),ue), pp. 144-145.

12. Donald P. Kommers, *The Constitutional Jurisprudence of the Federal Republic of Germany* (London: Duke University Press, 1989), pp. 223-227.

13. Manfred Rowold/Stefan Poguntke, "Im Schatten der Macht. Nicht-etablierte Kleinparteien," in Alf Mintzel and Heinrich Oberreuter's (Hrsg.) *Parteien in der Bundesrepublik Deutschland* (Bonn: Bundeszentrale fuer politische Bildung, 1992), p. 370-72. Robert Hofmann, *Geschichte der deutschen Parteien*, (Muenchen: Piper, 1993), pp. 276-280. Thomas Assheuer and Hans Sarkowicz, *Rechtsradikale in Deutschland* (Muenchen: Verlag C.H. Beck, 1992), pp. 14-16. Herbert Lilge, *Deutschland, 1945-1963* (Hannover: Verlag fuer Literatur und Zeitgeschehen, 1967), p. 247.

14. Manfred Rowold/Stefan Poguntke, "Im Schatten der Macht. Nicht-etablierte Kleinparteien," in Alf Mintzel and Heinrich Oberreuter's (Hrsg.) *Parteien in der Bundesrepublik Deutschland* (Bonn: Bundeszentrale fuer politische Bildung, 1992), p. 370-72.

15. *Ibid.,* pp. 372-373.

16. Uwe Backes and Eckhard Jesse, *Politischer Extremismus in der Bundesrepublik Deutschland* (Bonn: Bundeszentrale fuer politische Bildung, 1993), pp. 76-92. Donald P. Kommers, *The Constitutional Jurisprudence of the Federal Republic of Germany* (London: Duke University Press, 1989), p. 231.

17. Uwe Backes and Eckhard Jesse, *Politischer Extremismus in der Bundesrepublik Deutschland* (Bonn: Bundeszentrale fuer politische Bildung, 1993), pp. 254-257, and Eckhard Jesse, "Rechtsextreme Gewalt" *Der Buerger im Staat* June 1993, pp. 123-127. Francine S. Keifer, "Germans Take Steps to Curb Violence Against Foreigners," *Christian Science Monitor*, December 7, 1992. "Germany's Half-Step," *Christian Science Monitor*, December 10, 1992. Hans-Georg Betz, *Postmodern Politics in Germany* (New York: St. Martin's Press, 1991), pp. 110-132. See Charles Maier's *The Unmasterable Past* (Harvard: Harvard University Press, 1988) and Werner Weidenfeld's (Hrsg.) *Deutschland. Eine Nation -- doppelte Geschichte* (Koeln: Verlag Wissenschaft und Politik, 1993).

18. Girard C. Steichen, "German Reburial Prompts Debate Over Military Past," *Christian Science Monitor*, August 14, 1991. Tyler Marshall, "The Dark Winter of Helmut Kohl," *Los Angeles Times*, January 2, 1994. Ilya Levkov, editor, *Bitburg and Beyond* (New York: Shapolsky Publishers, 1987), pp. 42-44. Hans-Georg Betz, *Postmodern Politics in Germany* (New York: St. Martin's Press, 1991), p. 120. Kurt H. Biedenkopf, *Zeitsignale. Parteienlandschaft im Umbruch* (Muenchen: C. Bertelsmann, 1989), p. 235.

19. *German News* Sun, 9 Apr 1995, (de-news@vm.gmd.de). For example, "Ein Volk ausloeschen," by Elie Wiesel, *Die Zeit*, 21 April 1995). *German News - English Edition*, Sun, 7 May 1995, (de-news@vm.gmd.de). John Marks, "The Growing Pains of the New Germany," *U.S. News & World Report*, May 16, 1994.

20. Uwe Backes and Eckhard Jesse, *Politischer Extremismus in der Bundesrepublik Deutschland* (Bonn: Bundeszentrale fuer politische Bildung, 1993), pp. 93-95 and 295-98, and Eckhard Jesse, "Rechtsextreme Gewalt" *Der Buerger im Staat* June 1993, pp. 123-127. Wilhelm Heitmeyer, *Rechtsextremismus: "Warum handeln Menschen gegen ihre eigenen Interessen,"* (Koeln: Bund-Verlag, 1991), p. 28. Rone Tempest, "Europe Turns to the Right," *Los Angeles Times*, November 27, 1991, p.1. Manfred Rowold and Stefan Immerfall, "Im Schatten der Macht: Nicht-etablierte Kleinparteien," in Alf Mintzel and Heinrich Oberreuter's (Hrsg.) *Parteien in der Bundesrepublik Deutschland* (Bonn: Bundeszentrale fuer politische Bildung, 1992), pp. 362-420. Ute Erdsiek-Rave (Hrsg.), *Nationalsozialistische Gewaltverbrechen und der neue Rechtsextremismus von DVU und andere Organisationen. Debatte des Schleswig-Holsteinischen Landtages vom 30. Oktober 1992* (Kiel: Schmidt & Klaunig, 12/1992). German text: Die DVU reiht sich damit ein in das Bestreben rechtsextremer Kraefte, die Legitimation und das Ansehen der demokratischen Institutionen zu beschaedigen, geistige Grundlagen fuer antidemokratisches Denken und gewalttaetiges Verhalten zu legen und die Erinnerungsstaetten an die Opfer des Nationalsozialismus zu entwuerdigen.

21. Manfred Rowold/Stefan Poguntke, "Im Schatten der Macht. Nicht-etablierte Kleinparteien," in Alf Mintzel and Heinrich Oberreuter's (Hrsg.) *Parteien in der Bundesrepublik Deutschland* (Bonn: Bundeszentrale fuer politische Bildung, 1992), pp. 328-329. Nationalistische Front, *Grundsatz Programm*, 1980s, undated, originated in Bielefeld. Uwe Backes and Eckhard Jesse, *Politischer Extremismus in der Bundesrepublik Deutschland* (Bonn: Bundeszentrale fuer politische Bildung, 1993), pp. 92-93.

22. Uwe Backes and Eckhard Jesse, *Politischer Extremismus in der Bundesrepublik Deutschland* (Bonn: Bundeszentrale fuer politische Bildung, 1993), p. 329.

23. *Ibid.,* pp. 329-331.

24. *The Week in Germany*, January 21, 1994. See also *Das Parlament*, 1/8 July 1994, for additional information on right-wing views of the Holocaust. Uwe Backes and Eckhard Jesse, *Politischer Extremismus in der Bundesrepublik Deutschland* (Bonn: Bundeszentrale fuer politische Bildung, 1993), pp. 331-332. Wolfgang Rudzio, *Das politische System der Bundesrepublik Deutschland. 3. Auflage* (Opladen: Leske + Budrich, 1991), pp. 143-144.

25. Reiner-Olaf Schultze, et al., *Wahlverhalten* (Berlin: Kohlhammer, 1991), pp. 242-251. Hans-Joachim Veen, Norbert Lepszy, and Peter Mnich, *The Republikaner Party in Germany: Right-Wing Menace or Protest Catchall?* (London: Praeger, 1993). Hans-Joachim Veen and Norbert Lepszy, "Rechtsradikale in der parlamentarischen Praxis: Die 'Republikaner' in Kommunalen und Landsparlamenten sowie im Europaparlament," *Parlamentsfragen*, May 1994, pp. 203-216. Thomas Lillig, "REPS und DVU nicht politikfaehig," *Das Parlament*, January 14, 1994.

26. Clay Clemens, *Reluctant Realists. The Christian Democrats and West German Ostpolitik* (London: Duke University Press, 1989), p. 277-281. Konrad Jarausch, *The Rush to German Unity* (New York: Oxford University Press, 1994). Dirk Philipsen, *We Were The People* (London: Duke University Press, 1993). Elizabeth Pond, *Beyond the Wall* (Washington, D.C.: Twentieth Century Fund, 1993), pp. 202-203. See also Manfred Goertemaker's *Unifying Germany, 1989-1990* (New York: St. Martin's Press, 1994, through The Institute for East-West Studies), Stephen F. Szabo's *The Diplomacy of German Unification* (New York: St. Martin's Press, 1994), Mike Dennis's "Civil Society, Opposition, and the End of the GDR," in *Studies in GDR Culture and Society 11/12: The End of the GDR and the Problems of Integration* (Lanham, MD, 1993), Gert-Joachim Glaessner's *Der schwierige Weg zur Demokratie: Vom Ende der DDR zur deutschen Einheit* (Opladen, 1991), and Karin Lau and Karlheinz's (Hrsg.) *Deutschland auf dem Weg zur Einheit: Dokumente einer Revolution* (Braunschweig, 1990). Joyce M. Mushaben, "Behind The German Neo-Nazi Phenomenon," *Christian Science Monitor*, November 18, 1991. See also Marc Fisher, "East and West Grow Apart as They Come Together. The New Germany: "The Wall in the Mind," *Washington Post*, June 27-28, 1993.

27. Manfred Rowold/Stefan Poguntke, "Im Schatten der Macht. Nichtetablierte Kleinparteien," in Alf Mintzel and Heinrich Oberreuter's (Hrsg.) *Parteien in der Bundesrepublik Deutschland* (Bonn: Bundeszentrale fuer politische Bildung, 1992), pp. 332-334. Popular support for the Republikans came primarily from two districts within Berlin: Neukoeln (9.6%) and Wedding (9.9%). Both districts were overwhelmingly composed of working class elements. Amos Perlmutter, "Shades of Germany's 'Unmasterable Past,'" *Los Angeles Times*, February 12, 1989.

28. Uwe Backes and Eckhard Jesse, *Politischer Extremismus in der Bundesrepublik Deutschland* (Bonn: Bundeszentrale fuer politische Bildung, 1993), pp. 334-335. As seen in Tyler Marshall's "Asylum-Seekers Flood Munich, Stir Crisis," (*Los Angeles Times*, February 18, 1992), like their counterparts in Berlin, voters in southern Bavaria were also influenced by the growing presence of foreigners. Timothy Aeppel, "Pocketbook Issues Propel Far Right In West Germany: Will The Center Hold?," *Christian Science Monitor*, March 3, 1989. Christoph Butterwegge and Horst Isola (Hrsg.), *Rechtsextremismus im vereinten Deutschland* (Berlin: Ch.Links, 1991), pp. 80-92. Dieter Roth, "Is an Era of Stable Voting Behavior in Germany Coming to an End?," German Studies Association Conference, Dallas, September 30 - October 2, 1994.

29. Wolfgang Gehrmann, "Die Neonazis nebenan," *Die Zeit*, April 29, 1994. Wolfgang Gehrmann suggested that German society around Hamburg had been caught off-guard. Skinheads, *Freiheitliche Arbeiterpartei* (FAP) members and groupies, and sympathizers gathered during the summer of 1992 at train stations, pubs, and in the streets. Violence against Turks and other foreigners seemed a spontaneous outbreak of rage. *The Week in Germany*, October 2, 1992. From an interesting article on events in Hoyerswerda see Tyler Marshall's "A Dream Dies in Germany's Racist Hotbed" published in the *Los Angeles Times* on October 5, 1991, p. 1. Ursula Persak, "Television goes in to bat for foreigners," *Nuernberger Nachrichten*, November 23, 1991, taken from *The German Tribune*, No. 1496, December 15, 1991. See also the *Frankfurter Allgemeine Zeitung*, May 27, 1992. Tyler Marshall, "100,000 Germans Decry Attacks on Foreigners Ethnic bias: Urban rallies fall on anniversary of night of anti-Semitic terror in 1938 Nazi Germany," *Los Angeles Times*, November 10, 1991, p. 1. Klaus Walbaum, "Weapons seized, warrants issued, after raids on homes of right-wing extremists," *Hannoverische Allgemeine*, December 5, 1991, taken from *The German Tribune*, No. 1496, December 15, 1991.

30. *The Week in Germany*, October 30, 1992. *German News* (de-news@vm.gmd.de), October 14, 1995. *The Week in Germany*, November

27, 1992. *The Week in Germany*, December 11, 1992. *The Week in Germany*, June 4, 1993. *Das Parlament*, 25 June/2 July, 1993.

31. Michael Siedenhans, "Luebeck haelt den Atem an," *Die Zeit*, April 8, 1994. *The Week in Germany*, April 1, 1994. Mary Williams Walsh, "Rightist's Anti-Semitic Remarks Probed," *Los Angeles Times*, March 31, 1994. *The Week in Germany*, May 12, 1995. *The Week in Germany*, February 9, 1996. John Marks, "The Growing Pains of the New Germany," *U.S. News & World Report*, May 16, 1994, and Robert Leicht, "Die Lehre von Luebeck," *Die Zeit*, February 2, 1996. Eckhard Jesse, "Rechtsextreme Gewalt" *Der Buerger im Staat* June 1993, pp. 123-127. Jesse also illustrates that left-wing groups were also responsible for numerous acts of violence in the early 1990s. *The Week in Germany*, January 21, 1994. Hans-Gerd Jaschke, "Sub-Cultural Aspects of Right-Wing Extremism," in Dirk Berg-Schlosser and Falr Rytlewski's (editors) *Political Culture in Germany* (New York: St. Martin's Press, 1993), pp. 126-134. Hans-Gerd Jaschke, "Gefahr fuer die Demokratie?" *Das Parlament*, April 15, 1994. Francine S. Kiefer, "German Officials Count Fewer Racist Attacks," *Christian Science Monitor*, January 20, 1993. *The Week in Germany*, September 24, 1993. Hans-Georg Betz's "Radikal rechtspopulistische Parteien in Westeuropa" (*Aus Zeit und Politik*, October 25, 1991) indicates that right-wing radicalism and extremism appeared in comparable forms throughout western Europe, for example, in the violence against foreigners and the various motivating factors.

32. Torsten Baensch, *Jugendlichen Raum Lassen?* (Sachsen-Anhalt: Landeszentrale fuer politische Bildung, 1992). "Wrong tactics used against neo-Nazis" from the *Kieler Nachrichten*, 3 December 3, 1991, taken from *The German Tribune*, No. 1496, December 15, 1991. Eckhard Jesse, "Rechtsextreme Gewalt" *Der Buerger im Staat* June 1993, pp. 123-127. Felix Philipp Lutz, "Verantwortungsbewusstsein und Wohlstandschauvinismus: Die Bedeutung historisch-politischer Einstellungen der Deutschen nach der Einheit," in Werner Weidenfeld's (Hrsg.) *Deutschland. Eine Nation -- doppelte Geschichte* (Koeln: Verlag Wissenschaft und Politik, 1993), pp. 157-173. Bartholomaeus Grill, "Study into causes of right-wing extremism rejects oft-quoted truisms," *Die Zeit*, Hamburg, May 29, 1992, taken from *The German Tribune*, No. 1519, June 12, 1992. Renate Kingma, "Right-wing extremism: psychology in the east graduates into the real world" *Frankfurter Rundschau*, November 6, 1991, taken from *The German Tribune*, No. 1494, November 24, 1991. Francine S. Kiefer, "Young Extremists See No Future in New German State," *Christian Science Monitor*, September 27, 1991. Wilhelm Heitmeyer, u.a., *Die Bielefelder Rechtsextremismus-Studie* (Muenchen: Juventa, 1993), Holger Wuchold "Ursachenforschung. Rechtsextremismus aus Orientierungslosigkeit?," in *Das Parlament*, Nr. 2-3, 8./15. Januar 1993, p. 12, and Joachim Fritz-Vannahme's "Die optimistische Generation," *Die Zeit*,

October 27, 1995. Steffen Harbordt, "Erfolgreiche demokratische Sozialisation," *Aus Zeit und Politik*, November 17, 1995, and Hans-Uwe Otto and Roland Merten (Hrsg.) *Rechtsradikale Gewalt im vereinigten Deutschland* (Bonn: Bundeszentrale fuer politische Bildung, 1993). "Study Shows Common Social Pattern Among Xenophobes in Four Countries," *The Week in Germany*, December 13, 1991. Links between right-wing radicalism and violence can also be detected through a common music. Vito Antario, Holk Engelbrecht, Wulf-Dieter Lugert, Frauke Stolz, and Sibylle Wiekbold, "Schlachtrufe," subtitled "Rockmusik, Gewalt und Rechtsradikalismus," *Der Buerger im Staat*, June 1993, pp. 149-153. See also Francis Hueser's "Fremdenfeindlichkeit in Deutschland," (*Aus Zeit und Politik*, November 24, 1995); violence against foreigners resulted as a consequence a lack of contact with what ever group was designated as *foreign* as well as a consequence of socio-economic conditions. *The Week in Germany*, December 10, 1993. In addition, according to the Goettingen Administrative Center of the Metal Workers' Union, right-wing extremism lacked definitive gender-specific characteristics.

33. *Das Parlament*, January 26, 1996. *Der Spiegel*, January 8, 1996, and *Der Spiegel*, August 21, 1995. *Der Spiegel*, January 15, 1996. *The Week in Germany*, January 26, 1996. *Der Spiegel*, December 11, 1995. Robert Leicht, "Die Lehre von Luebeck," *Die Zeit*, February 2, 1996. Gains Post, Jr., "German Unification and Historical Memory," *The Historian*, Volume 58/Winter 1996, pp. 473-486. *Der Spiegel*, November 27, 1995, pp. 219-220. Wolfgang Kowalsky, *Rechtsaussen... und die verfehlten Strategien der deutschen Linken* (Berlin: Ullstein, 1992). Detlev J.K. Peukert and Frank Bajohr, *Rechtsradikalismus in Deutschland. Zwei historische Beitraege* (Hamburg: Ergebnisse, 1990). "Ein Volk auf dem Ego-Trip," *Focus*, July 3, 1995, pp. 52-60. "Stumpfes Schwert," *Der Spiegel*, February 5, 1996, pp. 36-38. One might also recall more recent efforts in Germany to eliminate Neo-Nazis from the world wide web and Internet as well. *The Week in Germany*, February 2, 1996. Elie Wiesel, "Ein Volk ausloesen," *Die Zeit*, April 21, 1995.

34. Diethelm Prowe, "The New Germany: 1945-1960, 1989-1991," *The Historian*, Volume 54/Autumn 1991, pp. 19-34. Interview with Bundestag President Dr. Rita Suessmuth, Bundeshaus, June 23, 1995, in conjunction with the Fulbright German Summer Seminar. Eckhard Jesse reached the same basic conclusion in his "Rechtsextreme Gewalt" *Der Buerger im Staat*, June 1993, pp. 123-127.

Chapter 18

PROTECTION AGAINST GENOCIDE: TOWARD A GLOBAL HUMAN RIGHTS REGIME

Neal Riemer

I. Introduction

Can an effective Global Human Rights Regime be put into place both to prevent and to stop genocide?[1] This is the terribly neglected, and excruciatingly difficult, problem that calls for a creative breakthrough in the future of international politics. Genocide must not only be outlawed (as in the rhetoric of U.N. pronouncements) but be made subject to effective international actions to prevent and stop it. "Thou shalt not commit genocide" must join the prophetic commandment, "Thou shalt not make nuclear war." In my affirmative answer, outlined in the futuristic scenario that follows, I shall argue that the creative breakthrough supporting such an affirmative answer calls for (l) strengthened institutions in a Global Human Rights Regime, guided by (2) a cogent theory of prudent prevention, (3) an operative theory of effective staged implementation, and (4) a wise theory of just humanitarian intercession.

The problem to be explored here is underscored by the tragic failure of the international community to develop an effective response to the evil of genocide in a post-World War II world traumatized by the Holocaust, a world that saw the passage of the U.N.'s convention against genocide, but a world still characterized by genocide.

The UN Convention on the Prevention and Punishment of the Crime of Genocide (adopted 1948; in force 1951) defines genocide as "any of the following acts committed with the intent to destroy, in whole or in part, a national, ethnic, racial, or religious group" by — for example — "Killing members of the group;" "Causing either bodily or mental harm to members of the group;" "Deliberately inflicting on the group conditions of life calculated to bring about its physical extermination in whole or in part."[2] Moreover, by interpretation or amendment, the anti-genocide convention should also clearly protect political groups or economic classes from genocidal killing.[3]

I take for granted that the problem of genocide is a real problem. First, genocide persists. Despite the global revulsion against the Nazi extermination of six million Jews and other target groups in the Holocaust — a revulsion that contributed to the UN's Convention on the Prevention and Punishment of Genocide — genocide has continued in the post-World War II world. It continued in Cambodia, in East Pakistan (now Bangladesh), in Bosnia, in Iraq, Rwanda, and in other areas of the world.[4]

Second, the problem of genocide remains a problem because of the continuing dominance of a short-sighted conventional wisdom. This conventional wisdom too often "realistically" notes the seeming inevitability of egregious violations of human rights, the principle of non-interference in the internal affairs of nation-states, the absence of a national self-interest in humanitarian intercession, the weaknesses of the United Nations, and the costs and dangers of intervention. Adverse critics thus conclude that a breakthrough to protection against genocide is wildly unrealistic, foolishly utopian, and unacceptably costly.

The persistence of the problem of genocide prompts us to address four neglected needs and thus to outline the key features of a creative breakthrough required to attend to these needs.

II. Key Features of a Creative Breakthrough Strengthened Institutions

The first need is the need to strengthen the institutions of the Global Human Rights Regime. By a Global Human Rights Regime I understand all those actors — e.g., the United Nations, key nations, certain regional organizations, committed non-governmental organizations — dedicated to the protection of human rights. These actors in the Global Human Rights Regime are committed to those norms, principles, institutions, policies, and practices concerned with the protection of human rights.[5] The norms, for example, are articulated in the U.N. Declaration of Human Rights, in the U.N. Convention

Against Genocide, and in other key U.N. documents. Here I will concentrate on institutions and the will to make them work. Key principles, policies, and practices will become clearer as I subsequently address theories of prudent prevention, staged implementation, and just humanitarian intercession.

Currently, we have a number of diverse political actors who respect and try to abide by these norms. These actors include certain nation-states committed to the protection of human rights; certain regional actors (e.g., Western European Union) equally respectful of human rights; most organs of the United Nations; a number of non-governmental organizations — e.g., Amnesty International — highly dedicated to human rights. Focusing only on the most promising of global human rights organizations — the United Nations — we find, however, that key institutions of the United Nations are weak and often untested. Thus the UN Security Council is potentially strong but actually weak in its ability either to prevent or intercede against genocide. The UN Commission on Human Rights lacks stronger powers to be effective.[6] The recently created UN High Commissioner on Human Rights is untested. UN policies and practices are theoretically promising, but weak. Clearly, there is a need — especially in the most promising global organization, the United Nations — to develop stronger institutions, policies, and practices that could make prudent prevention, effective staged implementation, and just humanitarian intercession genuinely meaningful.

The breakthrough I envisage requires a UN Security Council with the will to act; and this, in turn, means a will to act on the part of the permanent members of the Security Council. If the Security Council has power but often lacks will, other key UN institutions lack both power and will. The creative breakthrough proposed here envisages a strengthening of the UN High Commissioner for Human Rights and the UN Commission on Human Rights. The UN High Commissioner, in particular, working closely with an empowered UN Commission on Human Rights, has a particularly important role to play in monitoring the status of human rights and in utilizing the power of publicity. Strategy here would be to increase the powers of these organs to investigate and publicize genocidal threats or acts. The UN High Commissioner for Human Rights, working with the UN Commission on Human Rights, would then be required to recommend to the UN Security Council more stringent actions to prevent or stop genocide.

Several new UN institutions also need to be put into place. For example, to make monitoring more effective, a UN Human Rights Monitor needs to be established for every region of the world in order to cover every country of the world. For example, a UN Human Rights Protection Force needs to be established to be ready to move in the event that protection against genocide requires its use. Similarly, a UN Protectorate Agency needs to be established to ensure temporary guardianship of a country after a genocidal regime is removed and until a human-rights respecting regime is put into place in such a country.[7]

As key institutions of the Global Human Rights Regime are strengthened or developed, it will be helpful to address more clearly the broader operative political theory — the key principles, policies, and practices — that will guide those institutions. Again, neglected needs highlight the imperative of appropriate responses.

Prudent Prevention

The second neglected need is the need to articulate a cogent theory of prudent prevention of genocide.[8] My argument here is simple and compelling: It is far better to prevent genocide than to have to cope with it after it has occurred!

A theory of prudent prevention rests on three cardinal principles. First, there is a need to encourage the development of mature constitutional democracies. This is the best preventive principle because mature constitutional democracies do not practice genocide against their own citizens. Thus with the growth of mature constitutional democracies the danger of genocide would decline. Moreover, a world of mature constitutional democracies would contribute to a peaceful world because such democracies do not wage war on each other; and war is unquestionably the condition that makes possible the worst violations of human rights, including genocide.[9]

The world's existent mature constitutional democracies, regional organizations sensitive to the protection of human rights, the United Nations, and committed human rights NGOs — key members of a Global Human Rights Regime — have an ethical and prudential reason to foster constitutional democracies in a host of ways. The protection of human life is an ethical imperative. Prudentially, such actors recognize that such protection enlarges the global climate safer for each nation's vital interests, and safer too for the vital interests of regional organizations and the United Nations. These vital interests are clearly served when humanitarian intercession is not needed, and when the costs and dangers of legitimate intercession are either eliminated or minimized.

The Global Human Rights Regime would have the important, yet delicate, task of monitoring the evolution of constitutional democracies around the globe, and of supporting national, regional, and UN policies to assist in the maturation of constitutional democracies. The monitoring would look to the existential status of nations around the globe, with particular emphasis on genocide. Monitoring would also look to the empirical investigation of the necessary and sufficient conditions — social, cultural, political, economic — for the development and maturation of constitutional democracies. National, regional, and global policies to achieve these conditions would then logically flow from such monitoring. At a minimum such policies would stress the development of democratic civil societies, healthy economic and social systems, and functioning democratic constitutions and political institutions.

Second, there is a need to develop the philosophy and practice of deterrence of genocide. Deterrence is the next best preventive medicine. Deterrence is based on the premise that mature constitutional democracies will not come into existence immediately, or all over the globe. Authoritarian and despotic regimes will continue to operate for many years ahead. Consequently, a strategy of prevention must also contemplate additional ways of stopping egregious human rights violations — specifically acts of genocide — before they occur. A policy of deterrence is one such way. A policy of deterrence would warn potential genocidal violators of human rights that they will pay a high price for such violations. Deterrence would be premised on reliable monitoring to identify potentially genocidal violations. Publicity, in turn, would serve to signal violators, as well as the global community, that the Global Human Rights Regime is aware of dangerous conditions, and that egregious violations are unacceptable. The high price of egregious violations would include an escalating series of actions — political, economic, judicial, military. The credible threat of such actions would be designed to forestall genocidal violations.

Third, there is a need to develop the philosophy and practice of preemptive action in the event that deterrence doesn't work. Preemptive action is a fall-back preventive strategy. All three principles of a theory of prudent prevention rest on the irrefutable proposition that it is unquestionably better to prevent genocide than to stop it once it has occurred.

Preemptive action could include political, economic, judicial sanctions, with military intercession being the ultimate sanction. Military intercession would be based on overwhelmingly credible evidence of a clear and present danger of genocide.

The fuller conditions under which deterrence and preemptive action can occur, and policies and practices of implementation, will be spelled out as I speak to the following needs and thus speak to the issue of effective staged implementation and the issue of just humanitarian intercession.

Effectively Staged Implementation

The third need is the need to work out an operative theory of wisely staged implementation. Such an operative theory of implementation would guide the Global Human Rights Regime, and particularly the relevant UN organs of that regime. Seven key points in such a theory can be identified.

First, there is a crucial need to develop effective and respected machinery for monitoring/investigating/reporting. Ideally, the U.N. High Commissioner on Human Rights, working with an empowered U.N. Commission on Human Rights, would coordinate the diverse national, non-governmental, and United Nations monitoring that is currently going on in the arena of human rights. Reliable information about potential or actual genocide is the primary basis for a sensible response.

Second, the power of publicity must be employed to deter potential genocidal violations — where there is a clear and present danger of the eruption of genocide — and to solidify global support for just humanitarian intercession to stop genocide in progress. Such publicity would also be employed in cases of actual egregious violations—actual acts of genocide. Key UN organs (the UN High Commissioner on Human Rights; the UN Commission on Human Rights; the UN Security Council), effective regional organizations, key nations, and NGOs would function to publicize egregious violations.

Third, effective remedies — political, judicial, economic, military — must be on hand, to be prudently chosen and employed to prevent or stop genocide. Such remedies — to have any chance of success — must have the support of U.N. members willing and able to implement decisions of the U.N. Security Council. These decisions, for example, may involve such political actions as withdrawal of diplomatic recognition; such judicial remedies as trial and punishment of those guilty of genocide; such economic sanctions as a trade embargo, freezing of a countries assets; and such military sanctions as the use of force to stop genocidal actions.

Fourth, there is a crucial need to work out the problem of what might be called "human rights consolidation," namely, what it takes to ensure that human rights will continue to be respected after initial efforts of prevention or intercession have been successful. Consolidation might involve (1) temporary maintenance of a UN Human Rights Protection Force in the country involved; (2) placing the country involved temporarily in the status of a UN Protectorate; or (3) other prudent measures.

Just Humanitarian Intercession

The fourth tragically neglected need is the need to articulate a cogent theory of just humanitarian intercession.[10] Such a theory would include the following eight principles. First, an appropriate authority is required to bring the doctrine of just humanitarian intercession into action. The U.N. Security Council, for example, would be such an appropriate authority. Second, just humanitarian intercession could only be invoked in support of a just cause, for example, intercession to prevent or stop genocide. Third, military intercession would normally function as a last resort, after other pacific means — political, economic, judicial — have been tried and found wanting. Fourth, normally the consent of parties at risk — for example, targeted victims and their supporters — would be required for just humanitarian intercession. Fifth, the appropriate authority interceding would be required to make a prudent appraisal of the benefits and costs of intercession. Sixth, just humanitarian intercession must be based upon the expectation of a reasonable chance of success — immediate success in preventing or stopping egregious violations. Seventh, the interceding authority must employ humane and proportionate means to prevent or stop egregious violations, in the interest of minimizing harm, especially to the innocents involved in the conflict. Eighth, just humanitarian intercession must also calculate the long-run reasonable chance of success, success — for example — in putting into place a human rights-respecting regime to ensure the ongoing protection of human rights.

These eight principles of just humanitarian intercession are, of course, easier to state than to implement. Yet it is important to set forth the larger philosophy that guides both the deterrent and preemptive aspects of prudent prevention, and the conditions for actual intercession when preventive measures fail.

III. Conclusion

Clearly, the development of a responsible and effective Global Human Rights Regime, one capable of protecting against genocide, is long over-due. The difficulties attendant upon the very endeavor to achieve such a Global Human Rights Regime are, however, daunting. Devotees of the "realistic" conventional wisdom are very skeptical about the possibility of the breakthrough outlined in my argument. They argue that very little can be done; that the world lacks adequate policy, machinery, and will; that the costs of protection are too high; that nations (realistically concerned with protecting their own vital national interests) are not going to stick their humanitarian necks out for foreigners; that the United Nations is ill-equipped to handle such problems; that it is unwise, dangerous, unlawful to meddle in the internal, domestic affairs of sovereign nation-states; etc.

Yet, despite this skepticism, and despite the cogency of some of the arguments above, it is imperative that we confront the problem candidly and explore whether a creative breakthrough is really possible. A great deal is at stake here. If we cannot break through on the protection against genocide, then the effective global protection of other human rights is placed in jeopardy. On the other hand, if we can break through to protection against genocide, we may have worked out the policy and machinery that can then be employed to protect a wider range of human rights.

My prophetic scenario is designed to call attention to the imperative of seeking a creative breakthrough in politics — here a breakthrough to protection against genocide. Those seeking such prophetic breakthroughs must appreciate that it is important to do more than merely articulate prophetic values and to criticize the ugly reality of persisting genocide. It is also crucially important to propose constitutional courses of action that can practically and sensibly bring an end to genocide. Such courses of action, of course, are motivated by prophetic values (here, pointedly, respect for life and the end of genocidal oppression); and they rest on an empirical understanding of the reality of the Holocaust and the scandalous persistence of genocide. But the empirical study of genocide must also seek to understand the reasons for the persistence of genocide and both the current strengths and weaknesses of a Global Human Rights Regime capable of protecting against genocide. Moreover, an empirical critique of genocide must also lead, boldly, to sensible and effective constitutional efforts to overcome genocide. Such efforts must wisely take into account the realities that militate against a creative breakthrough to protect against genocide; but those pursuing such efforts must, nonetheless, persist in the achievement of that creative breakthrough.

The task of achieving a creative breakthrough to protection against genocide is, clearly, a difficult one. Those who pursue the task can, however, be encouraged by the reality, if rarity, of other significant creative breakthroughs in history. In the past, too, the conventional wisdom has "realistically" held that creative breakthroughs are impossible. Yet those with prophetic vision and wise constitutional commitment have demonstrated that in key areas of the world we have, for example, been able to move toward religious liberty, separation of church and state, and democratic governance despite the political "realists" who could only see the persistence of imposed religious conformity, religious war and persecution, and authoritarian government.[11] American Democracy, itself, is a tribute to those who, like James Madison, refused to accept the "realistic" conventional wisdom that held that it was impossible to reconcile liberty and large size. Our American "extensive republic" — our federal republic — illustrates persuasively that creative breakthroughs in politics are possible.[12]

Similarly, European Union today is yet another illustration of a creative breakthrough that "realists" adhering to the conventional wisdom doubted could ever occur. European Union, like other historical breakthroughs, is not perfect, and clearly it is an evolving phenomenon. Yet the movement toward economic and, then, political integration in Western Europe has clearly facilitated peace between historically warring neighbors in Western Europe, and has significantly strengthened the economies and constitutional democracies of all members of the Union.[13]

I mention these historical examples of creative breakthroughs in politics to underscore again the importance of a prophetic imagination willing to go beyond a short-sighted conventional wisdom; willing, too, to go beyond the mere endorsement of prophetic values, and beyond the easy criticism of political, economic, and social evils. If we are genuinely to "Confronting the Holocaust," it is crucial that we move beyond a skeptical, short-sighted "political realism" to articulate the constitutional principles and programs of action that can prudently and effectively protect against genocide. A Global Human Rights Regime — characterized by strengthened institutions, and guided by the principles and policies of prudent prevention, effectively staged implementation, and just humanitarian intercession - is the key to a most momentous breakthrough: the breakthrough to protection against genocide. Working toward such a breakthrough is the most significant way to confront the Holocaust.

Notes

1. See Leo Kuper, *Genocide: Its Political Use in the Twentieth Century* (New Haven, Conn.: Yale University Press, 1981); Leo Kuper, *The Prevention of Genocide* (New Haven, Conn.: Yale University Press, 1985); Herbert Hirsch, *Genocide and the Politics of Memory* (Chapel Hill, N.C.: University of North Carolina Press, 1995); Lucy S. Davidowicz, *The War Against the Jews* (New York: Bantam, 1975); Helen Fein, *Accounting for Genocide* (New York: Free Press, 1979), and *Genocide Watch* (New Haven, Conn.: Yale University Press, 1992). My argument in this paper draws from my chapter, "The Prophetic Mode and Challenge, Creative Breakthroughs, and the Future of Constitutional Democracy," in Neal Riemer, editor, *Let Justice Roll: The Prophetic Challenge in Religion, Politics, and Society* (Lanham, Md.: Rowman and Littlefield, forthcoming 1996).

2. The full text of the Convention on the Prevention of the Crime of Genocide may be found in Leo Kuper, *The Prevention of Genocide* (New Haven: Yale University Press, 1985), Appendix 1, pp. 241-246.

3. On this point I follow Leo Kuper, *Genocide: Its Political Use in the Twentieth Century* (New Haven: Yale University Press, 1981), especially pp. 9-10, and Chapter 8, "Related Atrocities," pp. 138-160.

4. See U.S. Department of State, *Country Reports on Human Rights Practices*, (Wash., D.C.: U.S. Government Printing Office, yearly).

5. On the concept of an international regime, see Stephen Krasner, ed., *International Regimes* (Ithaca, N.Y.P Cornell University Press).

6. For the weaknesses of the UN Commission on Human Rights, see Jack Donnelly, *International Human Rights* (Boulder, Col.: Westview Press, 1993).

7. Although in my scenario I concentrate on the UN, I do not exclude attention to protection against genocide at the level of effective regional organizations. The strengthening of comparable institutions at the regional level is quite in harmony with my argument.

8. Although my focus is on genocide (as the most egregious violation of a basic human right — the right to life), the ethical vision that animates a Global Human Rights Regime is also captured in such other UN documents as the International Covenant on the Elimination of All Forms of Racial Discrimination (adopted 1965, in force 1969); the International Covenant on Civil and Political Rights (1976); the International Covenant on Economic, Social, and Cultural rights (in force 1976); the UN Convention against Torture and Other Cruel, Inhuman or Degrading Treatment or Punishment (signed 1984, in force 1987).

9. See David Forsythe, *Human Rights and Peace: International and National Dimensions* (Lincoln, Neb.: University of Nebraska Press, 1993). To anticipate one criticism, let me note that mature constitutional democracies do engage in war, not with other mature constitutional democracies, but with other countries. Moreover, historically, the track record of *maturing* constitutional democracies (such as the United States) in dealing with American Indians, blacks, or women has by no means been exemplary! And, of course, a similar point could be made, historically, of other *maturing* constitutional democracies — the United Kingdom, France, Belgium, Holland.

10. See Fernando R. Teson, *Humanitarian Intervention: An Inquiry Into Law and Morality* (Dobbs Ferry, N.Y.: Transnational Publishers, 1988; Richard B. Lillich, ed., *Humanitarian Intervention and the United Nations* (Charlottesville, Va.: University Press of America, 1973); R.J. Vincent, *Human Rights and International Relations* (Cambridge: Cambridge University Press, 1984); Herbert Hirsh, *Genocide and the Politics of Memory* (Chapel Hill, N.C.: University of North Carolina Press, 1995). Clearly, this view of just humanitarian intercession owes a great deal to just war theory; and all the difficulties that confront just war theory also confront just humanitarian intercession.

11. See my article, "Religious Liberty and Creative Breakthroughs: the Contributions of Roger Williams and James Madison," in *Religion in American Politics*, Charles W. Dunn, editor (Wash., D.C.: Congressional Quarterly Press, 1989).

12. See Neal Riemer, *James Madison: Creating the American Constitution* (Wash., D.C.: Congressional Quarterly Press, 1986).

13. On European Union, see Desmond Dinan, *Ever Closer Union? An Introduction to the European Community* (Boulder, Col.: Lynne Rienner, 1994). On one of key architects of the European Community, see Francois Duchene, *Jean Monnet: The First Statesman of Interdependence* (New York: Norton, 1994).

Contributors

James Bernauer, S.J., is Professor of Philosophy at Boston College. He is the author of *Michel Foucault's Force of Flight: Toward an Ethics for Thought* (Humanities Press, 1990), and editor of *The Final Foucault* (MIT Press, 1988) and *Amor Mundi: Explorations in the Faith and Thought of Hannah Arendt* (Nijhoff, 1987). His current writing project is a book on the implications of Christian moral formation for ethical life in the Nazi period.

Franklin Bialystock is completing a doctoral dissertation in history at York University in Toronto on the impact of the Holocaust on the post-war Canadian Jewish community. He has been course director for Holocaust Studies at York, chairperson of the Holocaust Education Committee of Toronto Jewish Congress and of the Polish-Jewish Heritage Foundation of Canada. He has written curricula and education guides on the Holocaust for the Toronto Board of Education, Canadian Jewish Congress and the Departments of Education in Ontario and Nova Scotia.

Harry James Cargas is Professor Emeritus of Literature and Language at Webster University. Among his 32 books are *Conversations With Elie Wiesel* and *Reflections of a Post Auschwitz Christian.* Harry James Cargas has over 2500 Publications to his credit. He is the Vice-President of the Annual Scholars Conference on the Holocaust and the Churches and he serves on the Advisory Board of the National Catholic Center for Holocaust Education.

W. Royce Clark is Professor of Religion at Pepperdine University. He holds a Ph.D. from the School of Religion of the University of Iowa, and a J.D. from Pepperdine University School of Law. His publications focus on a variety of aspects of religion and culture.

Donald Dietrich is Professor of Church History at Boston College. He has written *God and Humanity in Auschwitz: Jewish-Christian Relations and Sanctioned Murder* (New Brunswick, NJ: Transaction Press/Rutgers University, 1995) and *Catholic Citizens in the Third Reich: Psycho-Social Principles and Moral Reasoning* (New Brunswick, NJ: Transaction Press/Rutgers University, 1988).

Stephen C. Feinstein is Professor of History at the University of Wisconsin-River Falls and has been Chairman of the department since 1990. He is the Acting Director of the Center for Holocaust and Genocide Studies at the University of Minnesota. His research interests focus on Russian avant garde art, art of the Holocaust, and the recent history of the Jews in the Soviet Union. He is currently writing a book entitled *Indelible Images: Artistic Responses to the Holocaust.*

Zev Garber is professor of Jewish Studies at Los Angeles Valley College. He is the editor of *Studies in Shoah.* His work includes *Shoah: The Paradigmatic Genocide, Methodology in the Academic Teaching of Judaism, Methodology in the Academic Teaching of the Holocaust, Teaching Hebrew Language and Literature at the College Level, Perspectives on Zionism* and consultant editor *to What Kind of God? Essays in Honor of Richard L. Rubenstein.*

Nurit Govrin is Professor of Hebrew Literature at Tel Aviv University. She served in the Israel Defense Forces and was a member of a kibbutz (1956-1958). Dr. Govrin was recently Visiting Professor at the University of Beijing, China. She has published 13 books and edited 12 books on Hebrew literature.

Gerda Schild-Haas was born in Ansbach, Germany, in 1922. She was a nurse at the Jewish Hospital in Berlin from 1941 to 1943, when she was deported to Theresienstadt. Released 1945, she came to the United States a year later, married Dr. Rudolph Haas of Lewiston, Maine, and raised four children. She is author of 2 books on the Holocaust and founder of the Holocaust Human Rights Center of Maine.

Marcia S. Littell is the Director of the National Academy for Holocaust and Genocide Teacher Training at The Richard Stockton College of New Jersey and Director of the Annual Scholars' Conference on the Holocaust and the Churches. Her edited and co-edited publications include *Confronting the Holocaust: A Mandate for the 21st*

Century, Part One (1997), *The Uses and Abuses of Knowledge* (1997) *The Holocaust: Lessons For the Third Generation* (1997), *Liturgies on the Holocaust: An Interfaith Anthology* (1996), *Remembrance and Recollection* (1996).

David Meier is Assistant Professor of History at Dickinson State University, North Dakota. His dissertation was titled, "Managing the West Germans," and since that time he has focused on German political history since 1945. His forthcoming publication will be published by Garland (New York), *Europe Since 1945: An Encyclopedia* (1997). David Meier taught the first regular course on the Holocaust in North Dakota, and created the first Holocaust resource center in North Dakota.

Susan E. Nowak is Assistant Professor of Religious Studies at Nazareth College of Rochester. She lectures and writes on Jewish-Christian relations, women and the Holocaust, and the impact of feminist theory upon interfaith dialogue. Dr. Nowak served on the writing committee for the Agreement signed between the Jewish Community Federation, the Board of Rabbis, and the Rochester Roman Catholic Diocese in Rochester, N.Y.

David Patterson is Dean of the University Honors Program at the University of Memphis in Tennessee. He is the author of *When Learned Men Murder: Essays on the Essence of Higher Education*, *Exile: The Sense of Alienation in Modern Russian Letters*, *Pilgrimage of a Proselyte: From Auschwitz to Jerusalem*, *The Shriek of Silence: A Phenomenology of the Holocaust Novel*, *In Dialogue and Dilemma with Elie Wiesel*, *Literature and Spirit: Essays on Bakhtin* (1988), and numerous other books and articles.

Neal Riemer is the Andrew V. Stout Professor of Political Philosophy, Emeritus in the Department of Political Science at Drew University. His books include *The Revival of Democratic Theory; James Madison; The Democratic Experiment; The Future of the Democratic Revolution: Toward a More Prophetic Politics; Karl Marx and Prophetic Politics; The New World of Politics*. He is also author/editor of *Let Justice Roll: The Prophetic Challenge in Religion, Politics, and Society*.

Robert W. Ross is Emeritus Professor of Religion at the University of Minnesota. He is presently Adjunct Professor at Fuller Theological Seminary. He is the author of numerous articles and books including *So It Was True: The American Protestant Press and the Nazi Persecution of the Jews.*

Leora Saposnik is the Holocaust Education Consultant to the Madison Metropolitan School District. She trains teachers, develops curriculum and works closely with local Holocaust survivors. She has produced a video of one survivor's account of his experiences during the Holocaust. Ms. Saposnik is also works with Steven Spielberg's Survivors of the Shoah Visual History Foundation.

Frederick M. Schweitzer is Professor of History at Manhattan College. He has written *A History of the Jews since the First Century A.D.* (1971), with Marvin Perry co-edited *Jewish-Christian Encounters over the Centuries* (1995), authored several essays on topics as diverse as the Dead Sea Scrolls, medieval perceptions of Jews and Judaism, Arnold J. Toynbee's misinterpretation of Jewish history, historiography, and numerous book reviews especially on the Shoah.

Karen Schierman was the Conference Coordinator for the Host Committee for the 1996 Conference. She is the Program Director for the Jay Phillips Center for Jewish-Christian Learning at the University of Saint Thomas in Saint Paul, Minnesota.

Kevin Spicer is a doctoral candidate in Modern European History at Boston College. Currently, he is completing a dissertation on the "Selective Resistance" of the Catholic Church to the National Socialist regime. His most recent article on this subject was published in the New Theology Review (November 1994). Spicer holds an M.Div. from St. Michael's College, Toronto and his B.A. in history from Stonehill College. He is an ordained member of the Congregation of Holy Cross.

Barry Trachtenberg is an adjunct Professor of History at the University of Vermont, teaching Modern United States History as well as Modern Eastern European Jewish History. He also teaches Humanities at the Community College of Vermont.

Gary Weissman is a doctoral student in the Modern Studies Program at the University of Wisconsin-Milwaukee. He is currently writing his dissertation on representations of the Holocaust in American popular culture and the academic field of Holocaust studies. His essay "A Fantasy of Witnessing," on the blurring of film and history in and around *Schindler's List*, appeared in *Media Culture and Society* 17.2 (April 1995).